Advanced Deep Learning with TensorFlow 2 and Keras

Second Edition

Apply DL, GANs, VAEs, deep RL, unsupervised learning, object detection and segmentation, and more

Rowel Atienza

BIRMINGHAM - MUMBAI

Advanced Deep Learning with TensorFlow 2 and Keras
Second Edition

Producer: Andrew Waldron
Project Editor: Janice Gonsalves
Content Development Editor: Dr. Ian Hough
Technical Editor: Karan Sonawane
Copy Editor: Safis Editing
Proofreader: Safis Editing
Indexer: Pratik Shirodkar
Production Designer: Sandip Tadge

First published: October 2018

Second edition: February 2020

Production reference: 1260220

Published by Packt Publishing Ltd.
Livery Place
35 Livery Street
Birmingham B3 2PB, UK.

ISBN 978-1-83882-165-4

www.packt.com

`packt.com`

Subscribe to our online digital library for full access to over 7,000 books and videos, as well as industry leading tools to help you plan your personal development and advance your career. For more information, please visit our website.

Why subscribe?

- Spend less time learning and more time coding with practical eBooks and Videos from over 4,000 industry professionals
- Learn better with Skill Plans built especially for you
- Get a free eBook or video every month
- Fully searchable for easy access to vital information
- Copy and paste, print, and bookmark content

Did you know that Packt offers eBook versions of every book published, with PDF and ePub files available? You can upgrade to the eBook version at `www.Packt.com` and as a print book customer, you are entitled to a discount on the eBook copy. Get in touch with us at `customercare@packtpub.com` for more details.

At `www.Packt.com`, you can also read a collection of free technical articles, sign up for a range of free newsletters, and receive exclusive discounts and offers on Packt books and eBooks.

Contributors

About the authors

Rowel Atienza is an Associate Professor at the Electrical and Electronics Engineering Institute of the University of the Philippines, Diliman. He holds the Dado and Maria Banatao Institute Professorial Chair in Artificial Intelligence and received his MEng from the National University of Singapore for his work on an AI-enhanced four-legged robot. He gained his Ph.D. at The Australian National University for his contribution in the field of active gaze tracking for human-robot interaction. His current research work focuses on AI and computer vision.

I would like to thank my family, Cherry, Diwa, and Jacob. They never cease to support my work.

I would like to thank my mother, who instilled into me the value of education.

I would like to express my gratitude to the people of Packt and this book's technical reviewer, Janice, Ian, Karan, and Valerio. They are inspiring and easy to work with.

I would like to thank the institutions who always support my teaching and research agenda, University of the Philippines, DOST, Samsung Research PH, and CHED-PCARI.

I would like to acknowledge my students. They have been patient as I develop my courses in AI.

About the reviewer

Valerio Maggio received his Ph.D in Computational Science by the Dept. of Mathematics of the University of Naples "Federico II", with a thesis in machine learning and software engineering entitled "Improving Software Maintenance using Unsupervised Machine Learning techniques." After some years as a postdoc researcher and lecturer at the University of Salerno and at the University of Basilicata, he joined the "Predictive Models for Biomedicine and Environment" lab at Fondazione Bruno Kessler (FBK), where he worked as a Research Associate. Valerio is currently a Senior Research Associate at the **Dynamic Genetics Lab** at University of Bristol (http://dynamicgenetics.org/). His research interests focus on methods and software for reproducible machine learning and deep learning for biomedicine. Valerio is also a **Cloud Research Software Engineer** as part of the Microsoft initiative for Higher Education and Research, and a very active member of the Python community. He is a lead member of the organising committee of many international conferences, such as EuroPython, PyCon/PyData Italy, and EuroScipy.

Table of Contents

Preface

In recent years, Deep Learning has made unprecedented success stories in difficult problems in vision, speech, natural language processing and understanding, and all other areas with abundance of data. The interest in this field from companies, universities, governments, and research organizations has accelerated the advances in the field. This book covers select important topics in Deep Learning with three new chapters, *Object Detection*, *Semantic Segmentation*, and *Unsupervised Learning using Mutual Information*. The advanced theories are explained by giving a background of the principles, digging into the intuition behind the concepts, implementing the equations and algorithms using Keras, and examining the results.

Artificial Intelligence (**AI**), as it stands today, is still far from being a well-understood field. **Deep Learning** (**DL**), as a sub field of AI, is in the same position. While it is far from being a mature field, many real-world applications such as vision-based detection and recognition, autonomous navigation, product recommendation, speech recognition and synthesis, energy conservation, drug discovery, finance, and marketing are already using DL algorithms. Many more applications will be discovered and built. The aim of this book is to explain advanced concepts, give sample implementations, and let the readers as experts in their field identify the target applications.

A field that is not completely mature is a double-edged sword. On one edge, it offers a lot of opportunities for discovery and exploitation. There are many unsolved problems in deep learning. This translates into opportunities to be the first to market – be that in product development, publication, or recognition. The other edge is it would be difficult to trust a not-fully-understood field in a mission-critical environment. We can safely say that if asked, very few machine learning engineers will ride an auto-pilot plane controlled by a deep learning system. There is a lot of work to be done to gain this level of trust. The advanced concepts that are discussed in this book have a high chance of playing a major role as the foundation in gaining this level of trust.

No DL book will be able to completely cover the whole field. This book is not an exception. Given time and space, we could have touched interesting areas like natural language processing and understanding, speech synthesis, automated machine learning (AutoML), graph neural networks (GNNs), Bayesian deep learning, and many others. However, this book believes in choosing and explaining select areas so that readers can take up other fields that are not covered.

As the reader who is about to embark upon reading this book, keep in mind that you chose an area that is exciting and can have a huge impact on society. We are fortunate to have a job that we look forward to working on as we wake up in the morning.

Who this book is for

The book is intended for machine learning engineers and students who would like to gain a better understanding of advanced topics in deep learning. Each discussion is supplemented with code implementation in Keras. In particular, the Keras API of TensorFlow 2 or simply `tf.keras` is what's used This book is for readers who would like to understand how to translate theory into working code implementation in Keras. Apart from understanding theories, code implementation is usually one of the difficult tasks in applying machine learning to real-world problems.

What this book covers

Chapter 1, Introducing Advanced Deep Learning with Keras, covers the key concepts of deep learning such as optimization, regularization, loss functions, fundamental layers, and networks and their implementation in `tf.keras`. This chapter serves as a review of both deep learning and `tf.keras` using the sequential API.

Chapter 2, Deep Neural Networks, discusses the functional API of `tf.keras`. Two widely used deep network architectures, ResNet and DenseNet, are examined and implemented in `tf.keras` using the functional API.

Chapter 3, Autoencoders, covers a common network structure called the autoencoder, which is used to discover the latent representation of input data. Two example applications of autoencoders, denoising and colorization, are discussed and implemented in `tf.keras`.

Chapter 4, Generative Adversarial Networks (GANs), discusses one of the recent significant advances in deep learning. GAN is used to generate new synthetic data that appear real. This chapter explains the principles of GAN. Two examples of GAN, DCGAN and CGAN, are examined and implemented in `tf.keras`.

Chapter 5, Improved GANs, covers algorithms that improve the basic GAN. The algorithms address the difficulty in training GANs and improve the perceptual quality of synthetic data. WGAN, LSGAN, and ACGAN are discussed and implemented in `tf.keras`.

Chapter 6, Disentangled Representation GANs, discusses how to control the attributes of the synthetic data generated by GANs. The attributes can be controlled if the latent representations are disentangled. Two techniques in disentangling representations, InfoGAN and StackedGAN, are covered and implemented in `tf.keras`.

Chapter 7, Cross-Domain GANs, covers a practical application of GAN, translating images from one domain to another, commonly known as cross-domain transfer. CycleGAN, a widely used cross-domain GAN, is discussed and implemented in `tf.keras`. This chapter demonstrates CycleGAN performing colorization and style transfer.

Chapter 8, Variational Autoencoders (VAEs), discusses another important topic in DL. Similar to GAN, VAE is a generative model that is used to produce synthetic data. Unlike GAN, VAE focuses on decodable continuous latent space that is suitable for variational inference. VAE and its variations, CVAE and β-VAE, are covered and implemented in `tf.keras`.

Chapter 9, Deep Reinforcement Learning, explains the principles of reinforcement learning and Q-learning. Two techniques in implementing Q-learning for discrete action space are presented, Q-table update and **Deep Q-Networks (DQNs)**. Implementation of Q-learning using Python and DQN in `tf.keras` are demonstrated in OpenAI Gym environments.

Chapter 10, Policy Gradient Methods, explains how to use neural networks to learn the policy for decision making in reinforcement learning. Four methods are covered and implemented in `tf.keras` and OpenAI Gym environments, REINFORCE, REINFORCE with Baseline, Actor-Critic, and Advantage Actor-Critic. The example presented in this chapter demonstrates policy gradient methods on a continuous action space.

Chapter 11, Object Detection, discusses one of the most common applications of computer vision, object detection or identifying and localizing objects in an image. Key concepts of a multi-scale object detection algorithm called SSD are covered and an implementation is built step by step using `tf.keras`. An example technique for dataset collection and labeling is presented. Afterward, the `tf.keras` implementation of SSD is trained and evaluated using the dataset.

Chapter 12, Semantic Segmentation, discusses another common application of computer vision, semantic segmentation or identifying the object class of each pixel in an image. Principles of segmentation are discussed. Then, semantic segmentation is covered in more detail. An example implementation of a semantic segmentation algorithm called FCN is built and evaluated using `tf.keras`. The same dataset collected in the previous chapter is used but relabeled for semantic segmentation.

Chapter 13, Unsupervised Learning Using Mutual Information, looks at how DL is not going to advance if it heavily depends on human labels. Unsupervised learning focuses on algorithms that do not require human labels. One effective technique to achieve unsupervised learning is to take advantage of the concept of **Mutual Information (MI)**. By maximizing MI, unsupervised clustering/classification is implemented and evaluated using `tf.keras`.

To get the most out of this book

- **Deep learning and Python**: The reader should have a fundamental knowledge of deep learning and its implementation in Python. While previous experience in using Keras to implement deep learning algorithms is important, it is not required. *Chapter 1, Introducing Advanced Deep Learning with Keras*, offers a review of deep learning concepts and their implementation in `tf.keras`.

- **Math**: The discussions in this book assume that the reader is familiar with calculus, linear algebra, statistics, and probability at college level.

- **GPU**: The majority of the `tf.keras` implementations in this book require a GPU. Without a GPU, it is not practical to execute many of the code examples because of the time involved (many hours to days). The examples in this book use reasonable amounts of data as much as possible in order to minimize the use of high-performance computers. The reader is expected to have access to at least NVIDIA GTX 1060.

- **Editor**: The example code in this book was edited using vim in Ubuntu Linux 18.04 LTS and MacOS Catalina. Any Python-aware text editor is acceptable.

- **TensorFlow 2**: The code examples in this book are written using the Keras API of TensorFlow 2 or `tf2`. Please ensure that the NVIDIA GPU driver and `tf2` are both properly installed.

- **GitHub**: We learn by example and experimentation. Please git pull or fork the code bundle for the book from its GitHub repository. After getting the code, examine it. Run it. Change it. Run it again. Do creative experiments by tweaking the code. It is the only way to appreciate all the theory explained in the chapters. Giving a star on the book's GitHub repository `https://github.com/PacktPublishing/Advanced-Deep-Learning-with-Keras` is also highly appreciated.

Download the example code files

The code bundle for the book is hosted on GitHub at:

https://github.com/PacktPublishing/Advanced-Deep-Learning-with-Keras

We also have other code bundles from our rich catalog of books and videos available at https://github.com/PacktPublishing/. Check them out!

Download the color images

We also provide color images of figures used in this book. You can download it here: https://static.packt-cdn.com/downloads/9781838821654_ColorImages.pdf.

Conventions used

The code in this book is in Python. More specifically, Python 3. For example:

A block of code is set as follows:

```
def build_generator(inputs, image_size):
    """Build a Generator Model

    Stack of BN-ReLU-Conv2DTranpose to generate fake images
    Output activation is sigmoid instead of tanh in [1].
    Sigmoid converges easily.

    Arguments:
        inputs (Layer): Input layer of the generator
            the z-vector)
        image_size (tensor): Target size of one side
            (assuming square image)

    Returns:
        generator (Model): Generator Model
    """

    image_resize = image_size // 4
    # network parameters
    kernel_size = 5
    layer_filters = [128, 64, 32, 1]

    x = Dense(image_resize * image_resize * layer_filters[0])(inputs)
    x = Reshape((image_resize, image_resize, layer_filters[0]))(x)
```

```
for filters in layer_filters:
    # first two convolution layers use strides = 2
    # the last two use strides = 1
    if filters > layer_filters[-2]:
        strides = 2
    else:
        strides = 1
    x = BatchNormalization()(x)
    x = Activation('relu')(x)
    x = Conv2DTranspose(filters=filters,
                        kernel_size=kernel_size,
                        strides=strides,
                        padding='same')(x)

x = Activation('sigmoid')(x)
generator = Model(inputs, x, name='generator')
return generator
```

When we wish to draw your attention to a particular part of a code block, the relevant lines or items are set in bold:

```
# generate fake images
fake_images = generator.predict([noise, fake_labels])
# real + fake images = 1 batch of train data
x = np.concatenate((real_images, fake_images))
# real + fake labels = 1 batch of train data labels
labels = np.concatenate((real_labels, fake_labels))
```

Whenever possible, docstrings are is included. At the very least, text comments are used to minimize space usage.

Any command-line code execution is written as follows:

```
python3 dcgan-mnist-4.2.1.py
```

The above example has the following layout: `algorithm-dataset-chapter.section.number.py`. The command-line example is DCGAN on the MNIST dataset in *Chapter 4*, *Generative Adversarial Networks (GANs)* second section and first listing. In some cases, the explicit command line to execute is not written but it is assumed to be:

```
python3 name-of-the-file-in-listing
```

The file name of the code example is included in the *Listing* caption. This book uses *Listing* to identify code examples in the text.

Bold: Indicates a new term, an important word, or words that you see on the screen, for example, in menus or dialog boxes, also appear in the text like this. For example: StackedGAN has two additional loss functions, **Conditional** and **Entropy**.

 Warnings or important notes appear like this.

Get in touch

Feedback from our readers is always welcome.

General feedback: Email feedback@packtpub.com, and mention the book's title in the subject of your message. If you have questions about any aspect of this book, please email us at questions@packtpub.com.

Errata: Although we have taken every care to ensure the accuracy of our content, mistakes do happen. If you have found a mistake in this book we would be grateful if you would report this to us. Please visit, http://www.packtpub.com/submit-errata, selecting your book, clicking on the Errata Submission Form link, and entering the details.

Piracy: If you come across any illegal copies of our works in any form on the Internet, we would be grateful if you would provide us with the location address or website name. Please contact us at copyright@packtpub.com with a link to the material.

If you are interested in becoming an author: If there is a topic that you have expertise in and you are interested in either writing or contributing to a book, please visit http://authors.packtpub.com.

Reviews

Please leave a review. Once you have read and used this book, why not leave a review on the site that you purchased it from? Potential readers can then see and use your unbiased opinion to make purchase decisions, we at Packt can understand what you think about our products, and our authors can see your feedback on their book. Thank you!

For more information about Packt, please visit packtpub.com.

1

Introducing Advanced Deep Learning with Keras

In this first chapter, we will introduce three deep learning artificial neural networks that we will be using throughout the book. These networks are MLP, CNN, and RNN (defined and described in Section 2), which are the building blocks of selected advanced deep learning topics covered in this book, such as autoregressive networks (autoencoder, GAN, and VAE), deep reinforcement learning, object detection and segmentation, and unsupervised learning using mutual information.

Together, we'll discuss how to implement MLP, CNN, and RNN based models using the Keras library in this chapter. More specifically, we will use the TensorFlow Keras library called `tf.keras`. We'll start by looking at why `tf.keras` is an excellent choice as a tool for us. Next, we'll dig into the implementation details within the three deep learning networks.

This chapter will:

- Establish why the `tf.keras` library is a great choice to use for advanced deep learning

- Introduce MLP, CNN, and RNN – the core building blocks of advanced deep learning models, which we'll be using throughout this book

- Provide examples of how to implement MLP, CNN, and RNN based models using `tf.keras`

- Along the way, start to introduce important deep learning concepts, including optimization, regularization, and loss function

By the end of this chapter, we'll have the fundamental deep learning networks implemented using `tf.keras`. In the next chapter, we'll get into the advanced deep learning topics that build on these foundations. Let's begin this chapter by discussing Keras and its capabilities as a deep learning library.

1. Why is Keras the perfect deep learning library?

Keras [1] is a popular deep learning library with over 370,000 developers using it at the time of writing – a number that is increasing by about 35% every year. Over 800 contributors actively maintain it. Some of the examples we'll use in this book have been contributed to the official Keras GitHub repository.

Google's TensorFlow, a popular open source deep learning library, uses Keras as a high-level API for its library. It is commonly called `tf.keras`. In this book, we will use the word Keras and `tf.keras` interchangeably.

`tf.keras` is a popular choice as a deep learning library since it is highly integrated into TensorFlow, which is known in production deployments for its reliability. TensorFlow also offers various tools for production deployment and maintenance, debugging and visualization, and running models on embedded devices and browsers. In the technology industry, Keras is used by Google, Netflix, Uber, and NVIDIA.

We have chosen `tf.keras` as our tool of choice to work with in this book because it is a library dedicated to accelerating the implementation of deep learning models. This makes Keras ideal for when we want to be practical and hands-on, such as when we're exploring the advanced deep learning concepts in this book. Because Keras is designed to accelerate the development, training, and validation of deep learning models, it is essential to learn the key concepts in this field before someone can maximize the use of the library.

 All of the examples in this book can be found on GitHub at the following link: `https://github.com/PacktPublishing/ Advanced-Deep-Learning-with-Keras`.

In the `tf.keras` library, layers are connected to one another like pieces of Lego, resulting in a model that is clean and easy to understand. Model training is straightforward, requiring only data, a number of epochs of training, and metrics to monitor.

The end result is that most deep learning models can be implemented with significantly fewer lines of code compared to other deep learning libraries such as PyTorch. By using Keras, we'll boost productivity by saving time in code implementation, which can instead be spent on more critical tasks such as formulating better deep learning algorithms.

Likewise, Keras is ideal for the rapid implementation of deep learning models, like the ones that we will be using in this book. Typical models can be built in just a few lines of code using the **Sequential model API**. However, do not be misled by its simplicity.

Keras can also build more advanced and complex models using its functional API and `Model` and `Layer` classes for dynamic graphs, which can be customized to satisfy unique requirements. The functional API supports building graph-like models, layer reuse, and creating models that behave like Python functions. Meanwhile, the `Model` and `Layer` classes provide a framework for implementing uncommon or experimental deep learning models and layers.

Installing Keras and TensorFlow

Keras is not an independent deep learning library. As you can see in *Figure 1.1.1*, it is built on top of another deep learning library or backend. This could be Google's TensorFlow, MILA's Theano, Microsoft's CNTK, or Apache MXNet. However, unlike the previous edition of this book, we will use Keras as provided by TensorFlow 2.0 (`tf2` or simply `tf`), which is better known as `tf.keras`, to take advantage of the useful tools offered by tf2. `tf.keras` is also considered the de facto frontend of TensorFlow, which has exhibited its proven reliability in the production environment. Furthermore, Keras' support for backends other than TensorFlow will no longer be available in the near future.

Migration from Keras to `tf.keras` is generally as straightforward as changing:

```
from keras... import ...
```

to

```
from tensorflow.keras... import ...
```

In this book, the code examples are all written in **Python 3** as support for **Python 2** ends in the year 2020.

On hardware, Keras runs on a CPU, GPU, and Google's TPU. In this book, we'll test on a CPU and NVIDIA GPUs (specifically, the GTX 1060, GTX 1080Ti, RTX 2080Ti, V100, and Quadro RTX 8000 models):

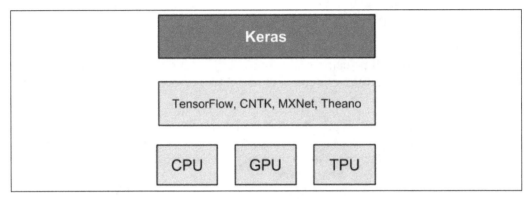

Figure 1.1.1: Keras is a high-level library that sits on top of other
deep learning frameworks. Keras is supported on CPU, GPU, and TPU.

Before proceeding with the rest of the book, we need to ensure that tf2 is correctly installed. There are multiple ways to perform the installation; one example is by installing tf2 using pip3:

```
$ sudo pip3 install tensorflow
```

If we have a supported NVIDIA GPU, with properly installed drivers, and both NVIDIA CUDA toolkit and the cuDNN Deep Neural Network library, it is highly recommended that you install the GPU-enabled version since it can accelerate both training and predictions:

```
$ sudo pip3 install tensorflow-gpu
```

There is no need to install Keras as it is already a package in tf2. If you are uncomfortable installing libraries system-wide, it is highly recommended to use an environment such as Anaconda (https://www.anaconda.com/distribution/). Other than having an isolated environment, the Anaconda distribution installs commonly used third-party packages for data sciences that are indispensable for deep learning.

The examples presented in this book will require additional packages, such as pydot, pydot_ng, vizgraph, python3-tk, and matplotlib. We'll need to install these packages before proceeding beyond this chapter.

The following should not generate any errors if tf2 is installed along with its dependencies:

```
$ python3
>>> import tensorflow as tf
>>> print(tf.__version__)
2.0.0
>>> from tensorflow.keras import backend as K
>>> print(K.epsilon())
1e-07
```

This book does not cover the complete Keras API. We'll only be covering the materials needed to explain selected advanced deep learning topics in this book. For further information, we can consult the official Keras documentation, which can be found at `https://keras.io` or `https://www.tensorflow.org/guide/keras/overview`.

In the succeeding sections, the details of MLP, CNN, and RNN will be discussed. These networks will be used to build a simple classifier using `tf.keras`.

2. MLP, CNN, and RNN

We've already mentioned that we'll be using three deep learning networks, they are:

- **MLP**: Multilayer Perceptron
- **CNN**: Convolutional Neural Network
- **RNN**: Recurrent Neural Network

These are the three networks that we will be using throughout this book. Later on, you'll find that they are often combined together in order to take advantage of the strength of each network.

In this chapter, we'll discuss these building blocks one by one in more detail. In the following sections, MLP is covered alongside other important topics such as loss functions, optimizers, and regularizers. Following this, we'll cover both CNNs and RNNs.

The differences between MLP, CNN, and RNN

An MLP is a **fully connected** (**FC**) network. You'll often find it referred to as either deep feed-forward network or feed-forward neural network in some literature. In this book, we will use the term MLP. Understanding this network in terms of known target applications will help us to get insights about the underlying reasons for the design of the advanced deep learning models.

MLPs are common in simple logistic and linear regression problems. However, MLPs are not optimal for processing sequential and multi-dimensional data patterns. By design, an MLP struggles to remember patterns in sequential data and requires a substantial number of parameters to process multi-dimensional data.

For sequential data input, RNNs are popular because the internal design allows the network to discover dependency in the history of the data, which is useful for prediction. For multi-dimensional data like images and videos, CNNs excel in extracting feature maps for classification, segmentation, generation, and other downstream tasks. In some cases, a CNN in the form of a 1D convolution is also used for networks with sequential input data. However, in most deep learning models, MLP and CNN or RNN are combined to make the most out of each network.

MLP, CNN, and RNN do not complete the whole picture of deep networks. There is a need to identify an **objective** or **loss function**, an **optimizer,** and a **regularizer**. The goal is to reduce the loss function value during training, since such a reduction is a good indicator that a model is learning.

To minimize this value, the model employs an optimizer. This is an algorithm that determines how weights and biases should be adjusted at each training step. A trained model must work not only on the training data but also on data outside of the training environment. The role of the regularizer is to ensure that the trained model generalizes to new data.

Now, let's get into the three networks – we'll begin by talking about the MLP network.

3. Multilayer Perceptron (MLP)

The first of the three networks we will be looking at is the MLP network. Let's suppose that the objective is to create a neural network for identifying numbers based on handwritten digits. For example, when the input to the network is an image of a handwritten number 8, the corresponding prediction must also be the digit 8. This is a classic job of classifier networks that can be trained using logistic regression. To both train and validate a classifier network, there must be a sufficiently large dataset of handwritten digits. The *Modified National Institute of Standards and Technology* dataset, or MNIST [2] for short, is often considered as the **Hello World!** of deep learning datasets. It is a suitable dataset for handwritten digit classification.

Before we discuss the MLP classifier model, it's essential that we understand the MNIST dataset. A large number of examples in this book use the MNIST dataset. MNIST is used to explain and validate many deep learning theories because the 70,000 samples it contains are small, yet sufficiently rich in information:

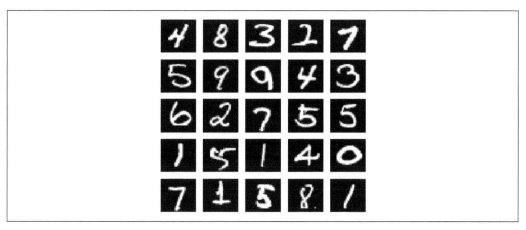

Figure 1.3.1: Example images from the MNIST dataset. Each grayscale image is 28 × 28-pixels.

In the following section, we'll briefly introduce MNIST.

The MNIST dataset

MNIST is a collection of handwritten digits ranging from 0 to 9. It has a training set of 60,000 images, and 10,000 test images that are classified into corresponding categories or labels. In some literature, the term **target** or **ground truth** is also used to refer to the **label**.

In the preceding figure, sample images of the MNIST digits, each being sized at 28 x 28 - pixel, in grayscale, can be seen. To use the MNIST dataset in Keras, an API is provided to download and extract images and labels automatically. *Listing 1.3.1* demonstrates how to load the MNIST dataset in just one line, allowing us to both count the train and test labels and then plot 25 random digit images.

Listing 1.3.1: `mnist-sampler-1.3.1.py`

```
import numpy as np
from tensorflow.keras.datasets import mnist
import matplotlib.pyplot as plt

# load dataset
(x_train, y_train), (x_test, y_test) = mnist.load_data()

# count the number of unique train labels
unique, counts = np.unique(y_train, return_counts=True)
print("Train labels: ", dict(zip(unique, counts)))

# count the number of unique test labels
```

```
unique, counts = np.unique(y_test, return_counts=True)
print("Test labels: ", dict(zip(unique, counts)))

# sample 25 mnist digits from train dataset
indexes = np.random.randint(0, x_train.shape[0], size=25)
images = x_train[indexes]
labels = y_train[indexes]

# plot the 25 mnist digits
plt.figure(figsize=(5,5))
for i in range(len(indexes)):
    plt.subplot(5, 5, i + 1)
    image = images[i]
    plt.imshow(image, cmap='gray')
    plt.axis('off')

plt.savefig("mnist-samples.png")
plt.show()
plt.close('all')
```

The `mnist.load_data()` method is convenient since there is no need to load all 70,000 images and labels individually and store them in arrays. Execute the following:

```
python3 mnist-sampler-1.3.1.py
```

On the command line, the code example prints the distribution of labels in the train and test datasets:

```
Train labels:{0: 5923, 1: 6742, 2: 5958, 3: 6131, 4: 5842, 5: 5421, 6: 5918, 7: 6265, 8: 5851, 9: 5949}
```

```
Test labels:{0: 980, 1: 1135, 2: 1032, 3: 1010, 4: 982, 5: 892, 6: 958, 7: 1028, 8: 974, 9: 1009}
```

Afterward, the code will plot 25 random digits, as shown in previously in *Figure 1.3.1.*

Before discussing the MLP classifier model, it is essential to keep in mind that while the MNIST data consists of two dimensional tensors, it should be reshaped depending on the type of input layer. The following *Figure 1.3.2* shows how a 3 × 3 grayscale image is reshaped for MLP, CNN, and RNN input layers:

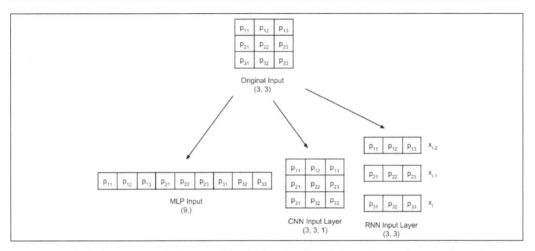

Figure 1.3.2: An input image similar to the MNIST data is reshaped depending on the type of input layer. For simplicity, the reshaping of a 3 × 3 grayscale image is shown.

In the following sections, an MLP classifier model for MNIST will be introduced. We will demonstrate how to efficiently build, train, and validate the model using `tf.keras`.

The MNIST digit classifier model

The proposed MLP model shown in *Figure 1.3.3* can be used for MNIST digit classification. When the units or perceptrons are exposed, the MLP model is a fully connected network, as shown in *Figure 1.3.4*. We will also show how the output of the perceptron is computed from inputs as a function of weights, wi, and bias, bn, for the n-th unit. The corresponding `tf.keras` implementation is illustrated in *Listing 1.3.2*:

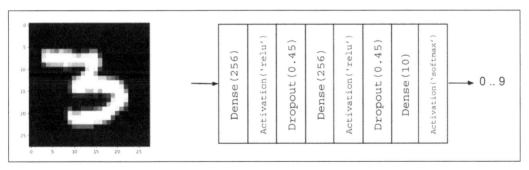

Figure 1.3.3: The MLP MNIST digit classifier model

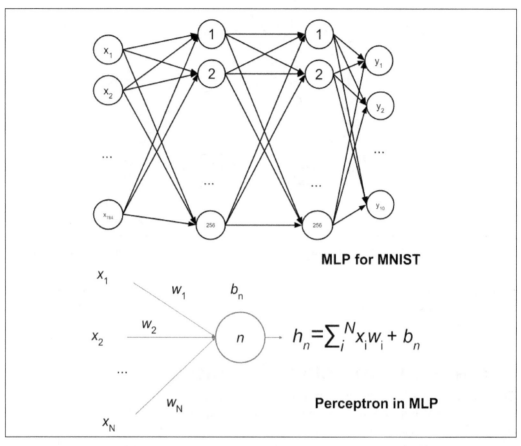

Figure 1.3.4: The MLP MNIST digit classifier in Figure 1.3.3 is made of fully connected layers. For simplicity, the activation and dropout layers are not shown. One unit or perceptron is also shown in detail.

Listing 1.3.2: `mlp-mnist-1.3.2.py`

```
import numpy as np
from tensorflow.keras.models import Sequential
from tensorflow.keras.layers import Dense, Activation, Dropout
from tensorflow.keras.utils import to_categorical, plot_model
from tensorflow.keras.datasets import mnist

# load mnist dataset
(x_train, y_train), (x_test, y_test) = mnist.load_data()

# compute the number of labels
num_labels = len(np.unique(y_train))

# convert to one-hot vector
```

```
y_train = to_categorical(y_train)
y_test = to_categorical(y_test)

# image dimensions (assumed square)
image_size = x_train.shape[1]
input_size = image_size * image_size

# resize and normalize
x_train = np.reshape(x_train, [-1, input_size])
x_train = x_train.astype('float32') / 255
x_test = np.reshape(x_test, [-1, input_size])
x_test = x_test.astype('float32') / 255

# network parameters
batch_size = 128
hidden_units = 256
dropout = 0.45

# model is a 3-layer MLP with ReLU and dropout after each layer
model = Sequential()
model.add(Dense(hidden_units, input_dim=input_size))
model.add(Activation('relu'))
model.add(Dropout(dropout))
model.add(Dense(hidden_units))
model.add(Activation('relu'))
model.add(Dropout(dropout))
model.add(Dense(num_labels))
# this is the output for one-hot vector
model.add(Activation('softmax'))
model.summary()
plot_model(model, to_file='mlp-mnist.png', show_shapes=True)

# loss function for one-hot vector
# use of adam optimizer
# accuracy is good metric for classification tasks
model.compile(loss='categorical_crossentropy',
              optimizer='adam',
              metrics=['accuracy'])
# train the network
model.fit(x_train, y_train, epochs=20, batch_size=batch_size)

# validate the model on test dataset to determine generalization
_, acc = model.evaluate(x_test,
                        y_test,
                        batch_size=batch_size,
```

```
                              verbose=0)
    print("\nTest accuracy: %.1f%%" % (100.0 * acc))
```

Before discussing the model implementation, the data must be in the correct shape and format. After loading the MNIST dataset, the number of labels is computed as:

```
# compute the number of labels
num_labels = len(np.unique(y_train))
```

Hardcoding `num_labels = 10` is also an option. But, it's always a good practice to let the computer do its job. The code assumes that `y_train` has labels 0 to 9.

At this point, the labels are in digit format, that is, from 0 to 9. This sparse scalar representation of labels is not suitable for the neural network prediction layer that outputs probabilities per class. A more suitable format is called a `one-hot vector`, a 10-dimensional vector with all elements 0, except for the index of the digit class. For example, if the label is 2, the equivalent `one-hot vector` is [0,0,1,0,0,0,0,0,0,0]. The first label has index 0.

The following lines convert each label into a `one-hot vector`:

```
# convert to one-hot vector
y_train = to_categorical(y_train)
y_test = to_categorical(y_test)
```

In deep learning, data are stored in tensors. The term tensor applies to a scalar (0D tensor), vector (1D tensor), matrix (two dimensional tensor), and multi-dimensional tensor.

From this point, the term tensor is used unless scalar, vector, or matrix makes the explanation clearer.

The rest of the code as shown below computes the image dimensions, the `input_size` value of the first dense layer, and scales each pixel value from 0 to 255 to range from 0.0 to 1.0. Although raw pixel values can be used directly, it is better to normalize the input data so as to avoid large gradient values that could make training difficult. The output of the network is also normalized. After training, there is an option to put everything back to the integer pixel values by multiplying the output tensor by 255.

The proposed model is based on MLP layers. Therefore, the input is expected to be a 1D tensor. As such, `x_train` and `x_test` are reshaped to [60,000, 28 * 28] and [10,000, 28 * 28], respectively. In NumPy, a size of -1 means to let the library compute the correct dimension. In the case of `x_train`, this is 60,000.

```
# image dimensions (assumed square) 400
image_size = x_train.shape[1]
input_size = image_size * image_size

# resize and normalize
x_train = np.reshape(x_train, [-1, input_size])
x_train = x_train.astype('float32') / 255
x_test = np.reshape(x_test, [-1, input_size])
x_test = x_test.astype('float32') / 255
```

After preparing the dataset, the following focuses on building the MLP classifier model using the Sequential API of Keras.

Building a model using MLP and Keras

After the data preparation, building the model is next. The proposed model is made of three MLP layers. In Keras, an MLP layer is referred to as **dense**, which stands for the densely connected layer. Both the first and second MLP layers are identical in nature with 256 units each, followed by the **Rectified Linear Unit (ReLU)** activation and dropout. 256 units are chosen since 128, 512, and 1,024 units have lower performance metrics. At 128 units, the network converges quickly but has a lower test accuracy. The additional number of units for 512 or 1,024 does not significantly increase the test accuracy.

The number of units is a hyperparameter. It controls the **capacity** of the network. The capacity is a measure of the complexity of the function that the network can approximate. For example, for polynomials, the degree is the hyperparameter. As the degree increases, the capacity of the function also increases.

As shown in the following lines of code, the classifier model is implemented using the Sequential API of Keras. This is sufficient if the model requires one input and one output as processed by a sequence of layers. For simplicity, we'll use this for now; however, in *Chapter 2*, *Deep Neural Networks*, the Functional API of Keras will be introduced to implement advanced deep learning models that require more complex structures such as multiple inputs and outputs.

```
# model is a 3-layer MLP with ReLU and dropout after each layer
model = Sequential()
model.add(Dense(hidden_units, input_dim=input_size))
model.add(Activation('relu'))
model.add(Dropout(dropout))
model.add(Dense(hidden_units))
model.add(Activation('relu'))
model.add(Dropout(dropout))
model.add(Dense(num_labels))
# this is the output for one-hot vector model.
add(Activation('softmax'))
```

Since a `Dense` layer is a linear operation, a sequence of `Dense` layers can only approximate a linear function. The problem is that the MNIST digit classification is inherently a non-linear process. Inserting a `relu` activation between the `Dense` layers will enable an MLP network to model non-linear mappings. `relu` or ReLU is a simple non-linear function. It's very much like a filter that allows positive inputs to pass through unchanged while clamping everything else to zero. Mathematically, `relu` is expressed in the following equation and is plotted in *Figure 1.3.5*:

$$ReLU(x) = max(0, x)$$

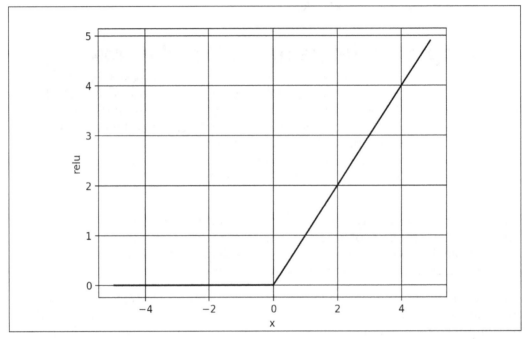

Figure 1.3.5: Plot of the ReLU function. The ReLU function introduces non-linearity in neural networks.

There are other non-linear functions that can be used, such as `elu`, `selu`, `softplus`, `sigmoid`, and `tanh`. However, `relu` is the most commonly used function and is computationally efficient due to its simplicity. The sigmoid and tanh functions are used as activation functions in the output layer and will be described later. *Table 1.3.1* shows the equation for each of these activation functions:

relu	$relu(x) = \max(0, x)$	1.3.1
softplus	$softplus(x) = \log(1 + e^x)$	1.3.2
elu	$$elu(x, a) = \begin{cases} x & if\ x \geq 0 \\ a(e^x - 1) & otherwise \end{cases}$$ where $a \geq 0$ and is a tunable hyperparameter	1.3.3
selu	$selu(x) = k \times elu(x,\ a)$ where $k = 1.0507009873554804934193349852946$ and $a = 1.6732632423543772848170429916717$	1.3.4
sigmoid	$$sigmoid(x) = \frac{1}{1 + e^{-x}}$$	1.3.5
tanh	$$\tanh(x) = \frac{e^x - e^{-x}}{e^x + e^{-x}}$$	1.3.6

Table 1.3.1: Definition of common non-linear activation functions

Although we have completed the key layers of the MLP classifier model, we have not addressed the issue of generalization or the ability of the model to perform beyond the train dataset. To address this issue, we will introduce regularization in the next section.

Regularization

A neural network has the tendency to memorize its training data, especially if it contains more than enough capacity. In such cases, the network fails catastrophically when subjected to the test data. This is the classic case of the network failing to generalize. To avoid this tendency, the model uses a regularizing layer or function. A common regularizing layer is Dropout.

The idea of dropout is simple. Given a dropout rate (here, it is set to dropout = 0.45), the Dropout layer randomly removes that fraction of units from participating in the next layer. For example, if the first layer has 256 units, after dropout = 0.45 is applied, only (1 - 0.45) * 256 units = 140 units from layer 1 participate in layer 2.

The Dropout layer makes neural networks robust to unforeseen input data because the network is trained to predict correctly, even if some units are missing. It's worth noting that dropout is not used in the output layer and it is only active during training. Moreover, dropout is not present during predictions.

There are regularizers that can be used other than dropouts such as l1 or l2. In Keras, the bias, weight, and activation outputs can be regularized per layer. l1 and l2 favor smaller parameter values by adding a penalty function. Both l1 and l2 enforce the penalty using a fraction of the sum of the absolute (l1) or square (l2) of parameter values. In other words, the penalty function forces the optimizer to find parameter values that are small. Neural networks with small parameter values are more insensitive to the presence of noise from within the input data.

As an example, an l2-weight regularizer with `fraction=0.001` can be implemented as:

```
from tensorflow.keras.regularizers import l2
model.add(Dense(hidden_units,
                kernel_regularizer=l2(0.001),
                input_dim=input_size))
```

No additional layer is added if an l1 or l2 regularization is used. The regularization is imposed in the `Dense` layer internally. For the proposed model, dropout still has a better performance than l2.

We are almost complete with our model. The next section focuses on the output layer and loss function.

Output activation and loss function

The output layer has 10 units followed by a `softmax` activation layer. The 10 units correspond to the 10 possible labels, classes, or categories. The `softmax` activation can be expressed mathematically, as shown in the following equation:

$$softmax(x_i) = \frac{e^{x_i}}{\sum_{j=0}^{N-1} e^{x_j}} \quad \text{(Equation 1.3.7)}$$

The equation is applied on all $N = 10$ outputs, x_i for $i = 0, 1 \ldots 9$ for the final prediction. The idea of `softmax` is surprisingly simple. It squashes the outputs into probabilities by normalizing the prediction. Here, each predicted output is a probability that the index is the correct label of the given input image. The sum of all the probabilities for all outputs is 1.0. For example, when the `softmax` layer generates a prediction, it will be a 10-dim 1D tensor that may look like the following output:

```
[3.57351579e-11    7.08998016e-08    2.30154569e-07    6.35787558e-07

5.57471187e-11    4.15353840e-09    3.55973775e-16    9.99995947e-01

1.29531730e-09    3.06023480e-06]
```

The prediction output tensor suggests that the input image is going to be 7 given that its index has the highest probability. The `numpy.argmax()` method can be used to determine the index of the element with the highest value.

There are other choices of output activation layer, such as `linear`, `sigmoid`, or `tanh`. The `linear` activation is an identity function. It copies its input to its output. The `sigmoid` function is more specifically known as a **logistic sigmoid**. This will be used if the elements of the prediction tensor will be independently mapped between 0.0 and 1.0. The summation of all the elements of the predicted tensor is not constrained to 1.0 unlike in `softmax`. For example, `sigmoid` is used as the last layer in sentiment prediction (from 0.0 to 1.0, 0.0 being bad, and 1.0 being good) or in image generation (0.0 is mapped to pixel level 0 and 1.0 is mapped to pixel 255).

The `tanh` function maps its input in the range -1.0 to 1.0. This is important if the output can swing in both positive and negative values. The `tanh` function is more popularly used in the internal layer of recurrent neural networks but has also been used as an output layer activation. If tanh is used to replace `sigmoid` in the output activation, the data used must be scaled appropriately. For example, instead of scaling each grayscale pixel in the range [0.0 1.0] using $x = \dfrac{x}{255}$, it is assigned in the range [-1.0 to 1.0] using $x = \dfrac{x - 127.5}{127.5}$.

The following graph in *Figure 1.3.6* shows the `sigmoid` and `tanh` functions. Mathematically, sigmoid can be expressed in the following equation:

$$sigmoid(x) = \sigma(x) = \frac{1}{1 + e^{-x}} \quad \text{(Equation 1.3.5)}$$

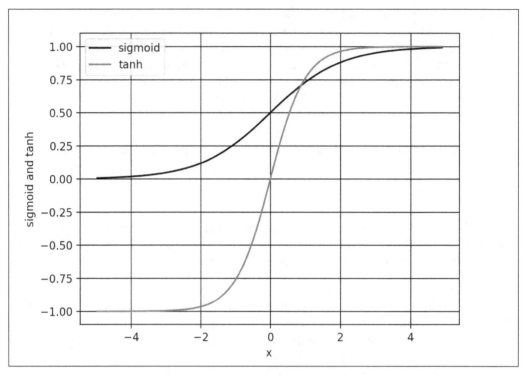

Figure 1.3.6: Plots of sigmoid and tanh

How far the predicted tensor is from the one-hot ground truth vector is called loss. One type of loss function is `mean_squared_error` (**MSE**), or the average of the squares of the differences between the target or label and the prediction. In the current example, we are using `categorical_crossentropy`. It's the negative of the sum of the product of the target or label and the logarithm of the prediction per category. There are other loss functions that are available in Keras, such as `mean_absolute_error` and `binary_crossentropy`. *Table 1.3.2* summarizes the common loss functions.

Loss Function	Equation
`mean_squared_error`	$$\frac{1}{categories} \sum_{i=1}^{categories} \left(y_i^{label} - y_i^{prediction} \right)^2$$
`mean_absolute_error`	$$\frac{1}{categories} \sum_{i=1}^{categories} \left| y_i^{label} - y_i^{prediction} \right|$$

categorical_crossentropy	$-\sum\limits_{i=1}^{categories} y_i^{label} \log y_i^{prediction}$
binary_crossentropy	$-y_1^{label} \log y_1^{prediction} -$ $\left(1 - y_1^{label}\right) \log\left(1 - y_1^{prediction}\right)$

Table 1.3.2: Summary of common loss functions. Categories refers to the number of classes (for example: 10 for MNIST) in both the label and the prediction. Loss equations shown are for one output only. The mean loss value is the average for the entire batch.

The choice of the loss function is not arbitrary but should be a criterion that the model is learning. For classification by category, either categorical_crossentropy or mean_squared_error is a good choice after the softmax activation layer. The binary_crossentropy loss function is normally used after the sigmoid activation layer, while mean_squared_error is an option for the tanh output.

In the next section, we will discuss optimization algorithms to minimize the loss functions that we discussed here.

Optimization

With optimization, the objective is to minimize the loss function. The idea is that if the loss is reduced to an acceptable level, the model has indirectly learned the function that maps inputs to outputs. Performance metrics are used to determine if a model has learned the underlying data distribution. The default metric in Keras is **loss**. During training, validation, and testing, other metrics such as **accuracy** can also be included. Accuracy is the percentage, or fraction, of correct predictions based on ground truth. In deep learning, there are many other performance metrics. However, it depends on the target application of the model. In literature, the performance metrics of the trained model on the **test dataset** is reported for comparison with other deep learning models.

In Keras, there are several choices for optimizers. The most commonly used optimizers are **stochastic gradient descent (SGD)**, **Adaptive Moments (Adam)**, and **Root Mean Squared Propagation (RMSprop)**. Each optimizer features tunable parameters like learning rate, momentum, and decay. Adam and RMSprop are variations of SGD with adaptive learning rates. In the proposed classifier network, Adam is used since it has the highest test accuracy.

SGD is considered the most fundamental optimizer. It's a simpler version of the gradient descent in calculus. In **gradient descent (GD)**, tracing the curve of a function downhill finds the minimum value, much like walking downhill in a valley until the bottom is reached.

The GD algorithm is illustrated in Figure 1.3.7. Let's suppose x is the parameter (for example, weight) being tuned to find the minimum value of y (for example, the loss function). Starting at an arbitrary point of x= -0.5. the gradient $\frac{dy}{dx} = -2.0$. The GD algorithm imposes that x is then updated to $x = -0.5 - \epsilon(-2.0)$. The new value of x is equal to the old value, plus the opposite of the gradient scaled by ϵ. The small number ϵ refers to the learning rate. If ϵ=0.01 then the new value of x = -0.48. GD is performed iteratively. At each step, y will get closer to its minimum value. At x = 0.5, $\frac{dy}{dx} = 0.0$. GD has found the absolute minimum value of y = -1.25. The gradient recommends no further change in x.

The choice of learning rate is crucial. A large value of ϵ may not find the minimum value since the search will just swing back and forth around the minimum value. On one hand, a large value of ϵ may take a significant number of iterations before the minimum is found. In the case of multiple minima, the search might get stuck in a local minimum.

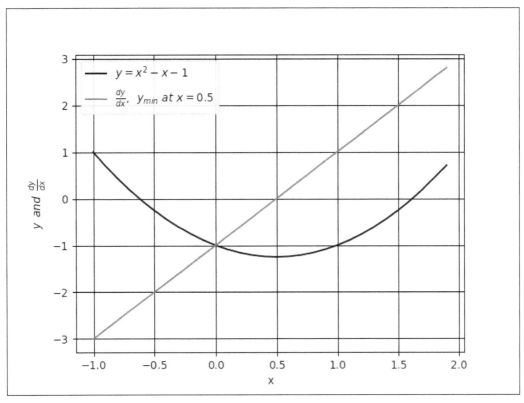

Figure 1.3.7: GD is similar to walking downhill on the function curve until the lowest point is reached. In this plot, the global minimum is at x = 0.5.

An example of multiple minima can be seen in *Figure 1.3.8*. If for some reason the search started at the left side of the plot and the learning rate is very small, there is a high probability that GD will find $x = -1.51$ as the minimum value of y. GD will not find the global minimum at $x = 1.66$. A sufficiently valued learning rate will enable the GD to overcome the hill at $x = 0.0$.

In deep learning practices, it is normally recommended to start with a bigger learning rate (for example, 0.1 to 0.001) and gradually decrease this as the loss gets closer to the minimum.

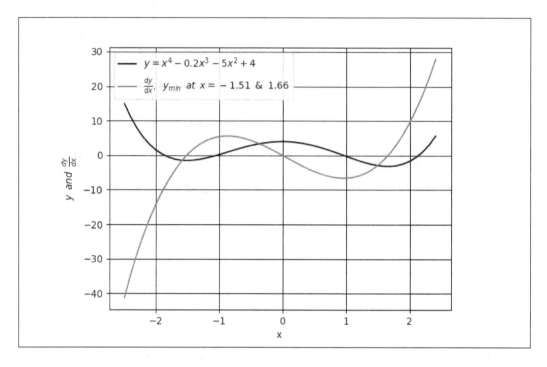

Figure 1.3.8: Plot of a function with 2 minima, x = -1.51 and x = 1.66. Also shown is the derivative of the function.

GD is not typically used in deep neural networks since it is common to encounter millions of parameters to train. It is computationally inefficient to perform a full GD. Instead, SGD is used. In SGD, a mini batch of samples is chosen to compute an approximate value of the descent. The parameters (for example, weights and biases) are adjusted by the following equation:

$$\boldsymbol{\theta} \leftarrow \boldsymbol{\theta} - \epsilon \mathbf{g}$$

In this equation, $\boldsymbol{\theta}$ and $\mathbf{g} = \dfrac{1}{m} \nabla_{\boldsymbol{\theta}} \sum L$ are the parameters and gradient tensor of the loss function, respectively. The $\mathbf{g}$ is computed from partial derivatives of the loss function. The mini-batch size is recommended to be a power of 2 for GPU optimization purposes. In the proposed network, `batch_size = 128`.

Equation 1.3.8 computes the last layer parameter updates. So, how do we adjust the parameters of the preceding layers? In this case, the chain rule of differentiation is applied to propagate the derivatives to the lower layers and compute the gradients accordingly. This algorithm is known as **backpropagation** in deep learning. The details of backpropagation are beyond the scope of this book. However, a good online reference can be found at http://neuralnetworksanddeeplearning.com.

Since optimization is based on differentiation, it follows that an important criterion of the loss function is that it must be smooth or differentiable. This is an important constraint to keep in mind when introducing a new loss function.

Given the training dataset, the choice of the loss function, the optimizer, and the regularizer, the model can now be trained by calling the fit() function:

```
# loss function for one-hot vector
# use of adam optimizer
# accuracy is a good metric for classification tasks model.
compile(loss='categorical_crossentropy',
optimizer='adam', metrics=['accuracy'])

# train the network
model.fit(x_train, y_train, epochs=20, batch_size=batch_size)
```

This is another helpful feature of Keras. By just supplying both the x and y data, the number of epochs to train, and the batch size, fit() does the rest. In other deep learning frameworks, this translates to multiple tasks such as preparing the input and output data in the proper format, loading, monitoring, and so on. While all of these must be done inside a for loop, in Keras, everything is done in just one line.

In the fit() function, an epoch is the complete sampling of the entire training data. The batch_size parameter is the sample size of the number of inputs to process at each training step. To complete one epoch, fit() will process the number of steps equal to the size of the train dataset divided by the batch size plus 1 to compensate for any fractional part.

After training the model, we can now evaluate its performance.

Performance evaluation

At this point, the model for the MNIST digit classifier is now complete. Performance evaluation will be the next crucial step to determine if the proposed trained model has come up with a satisfactory solution. Training the model for 20 epochs will be sufficient to obtain comparable performance metrics.

The following table, *Table 1.3.3*, shows the different network configurations and corresponding performance measures. Under Layers, the number of units is shown for layers 1 to 3. For each optimizer, the default parameters in `tf.keras` are used. The effects of varying the regularizer, optimizer, and the number of units per layer can be observed. Another important observation in *Table 1.3.3* is that bigger networks do not necessarily translate to better performance.

Increasing the depth of this network shows no added benefits in terms of accuracy for both the training and testing datasets. On the other hand, a smaller number of units, like 128, could also lower both the test and train accuracy. The best train accuracy at `99.93%` is obtained when the regularizer is removed, and 256 units per layer are used. The test accuracy, however, is much lower, at `98.0%`, as a result of the network overfitting.

The highest test accuracy is with the Adam optimizer and `Dropout(0.45)` at `98.5%`. Technically, there is still some degree of overfitting given that its training accuracy is `99.39%`. Both the train and test accuracy are the same at `98.2%` for `256-512-256`, `Dropout(0.45)`, and SGD. Removing both the Regularizer and ReLU layers results in it having the worst performance. Generally, we'll find that the `Dropout` layer has a better performance than `l2`.

The following table demonstrates a typical deep neural network performance during tuning:

Layers	Regularizer	Optimizer	ReLU	Train Accuracy (%)	Test Accuracy (%)
256-256-256	None	SGD	None	93.65	92.5
256-256-256	L2(0.001)	SGD	Yes	99.35	98.0
256-256-256	L2(0.01)	SGD	Yes	96.90	96.7
256-256-256	None	SGD	Yes	99.93	98.0
256-256-256	Dropout(0.4)	SGD	Yes	98.23	98.1
256-256-256	Dropout(0.45)	SGD	Yes	98.07	98.1
256-256-256	Dropout(0.5)	SGD	Yes	97.68	98.1
256-256-256	Dropout(0.6)	SGD	Yes	97.11	97.9

256-512-256	Dropout(0.45)	SGD	Yes	98.21	98.2
512-512-512	Dropout(0.2)	SGD	Yes	99.45	98.3
512-512-512	Dropout(0.4)	SGD	Yes	98.95	98.3
512-1024-512	Dropout(0.45)	SGD	Yes	98.90	98.2
1024-1024-1024	Dropout(0.4)	SGD	Yes	99.37	98.3
256-256-256	Dropout(0.6)	Adam	Yes	98.64	98.2
256-256-256	Dropout(0.55)	Adam	Yes	99.02	98.3
256-256-256	Dropout(0.45)	Adam	Yes	99.39	98.5
256-256-256	Dropout(0.45)	RMSprop	Yes	98.75	98.1
128-128-128	Dropout(0.45)	Adam	Yes	98.70	97.7

Table 1.3.3 Different MLP network configurations and performance measures

The example indicates that there is a need to improve the network architecture. After discussing the MLP classifier model summary in the next section, we will present another MNIST classifier. The next model is based on CNN and demonstrates a significant improvement in test accuracy.

Model summary

Using the Keras library provides us with a quick mechanism to double-check the model description by calling:

```
model.summary()
```

Listing 1.3.3 below shows the model summary of the proposed network. It requires a total of 269,322 parameters. This is substantial considering that we have a simple task of classifying MNIST digits. MLPs are not parameter efficient. The number of parameters can be computed from *Figure 1.3.4* by focusing on how the output of the perceptron is computed. From the input to the Dense layer: `784 × 256 + 256 = 200,960`. From the first Dense layer to the second Dense layer: `256 × 256 + 256 = 65,792`. From the second Dense layer to the output layer: `10 × 256 + 10 = 2,570`. The total is `269,322`.

Listing 1.3.3: Summary of an MLP MNIST digit classifier model:

Layer (type)	Output Shape	Param #
dense_1 (Dense)	(None, 256)	200960
activation_1 (Activation)	(None, 256)	0
dropout_1 (Dropout)	(None, 256)	0
dense_2 (Dense)	(None, 256)	65792
activation_2 (Activation)	(None, 256)	0
dropout_2 (Dropout)	(None, 256)	0
dense_3 (Dense)	(None, 10)	2570
activation_3 (Activation)	(None, 10)	0

```
Total params: 269,322
Trainable params: 269,322
Non-trainable params: 0
```

Another way of verifying the network is by calling:

```
plot_model(model, to_file='mlp-mnist.png', show_shapes=True)
```

Figure 1.3.9 shows the plot. You'll find that this is similar to the results of summary() but graphically shows the interconnection and I/O of each layer.

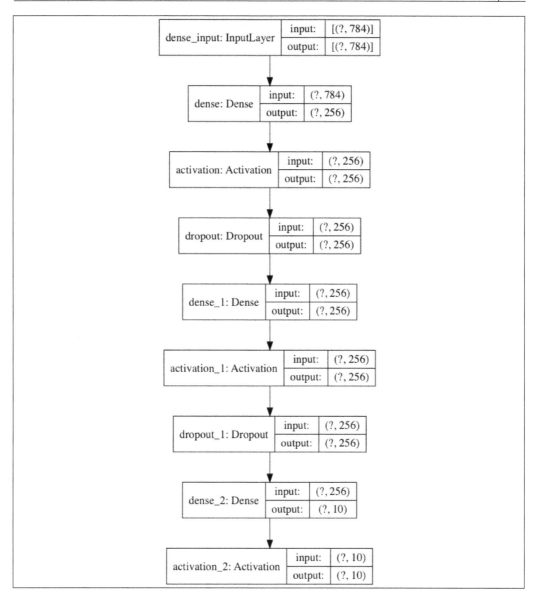

Figure 1.3.9: The graphical description of the MLP MNIST digit classifier

Having summarized our model, this concludes our discussion of MLPs. In the next section, we will build a MNIST digit classifier model based on CNN.

4. Convolutional Neural Network (CNN)

We are now going to move onto the second artificial neural network, CNN. In this section, we're going to solve the same MNIST digit classification problem, but this time using a CNN.

Figure 1.4.1 shows the CNN model that we'll use for the MNIST digit classification, while its implementation is illustrated in *Listing 1.4.1*. Some changes in the previous model will be needed to implement the CNN model. Instead of having an input vector, the input tensor now has new dimensions (height, width, channels) or (image_size, image_size, 1) = (28, 28, 1) for the grayscale MNIST images. Resizing the train and test images will be needed to conform to this input shape requirement.

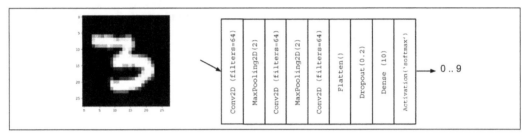

Figure 1.4.1: The CNN model for MNIST digit classification

Implement the preceding figure:

Listing 1.4.1: cnn-mnist-1.4.1.py

```
import numpy as np
from tensorflow.keras.models import Sequential
from tensorflow.keras.layers import Activation, Dense, Dropout
from tensorflow.keras.layers import Conv2D, MaxPooling2D, Flatten
from tensorflow.keras.utils import to_categorical, plot_model
from tensorflow.keras.datasets import mnist

# load mnist dataset
(x_train, y_train), (x_test, y_test) = mnist.load_data()

# compute the number of labels
num_labels = len(np.unique(y_train))

# convert to one-hot vector
y_train = to_categorical(y_train)
y_test = to_categorical(y_test)

# input image dimensions
image_size = x_train.shape[1]
# resize and normalize
x_train = np.reshape(x_train, [-1, image_size, image_size, 1])
```

```
x_test = np.reshape(x_test,[-1, image_size, image_size, 1])
x_train = x_train.astype('float32') / 255
x_test = x_test.astype('float32') / 255

# network parameters
# image is processed as is (square grayscale)
input_shape = (image_size, image_size, 1)
batch_size = 128
kernel_size = 3
pool_size = 2
filters = 64
dropout = 0.2

# model is a stack of CNN-ReLU-MaxPooling
model = Sequential()
model.add(Conv2D(filters=filters,
                 kernel_size=kernel_size,
                 activation='relu',
                 input_shape=input_shape))
model.add(MaxPooling2D(pool_size))
model.add(Conv2D(filters=filters,
                 kernel_size=kernel_size,
                 activation='relu'))
model.add(MaxPooling2D(pool_size))
model.add(Conv2D(filters=filters,
                 kernel_size=kernel_size,
                 activation='relu'))
model.add(Flatten())
# dropout added as regularizer
model.add(Dropout(dropout))
# output layer is 10-dim one-hot vector
model.add(Dense(num_labels))
model.add(Activation('softmax'))
model.summary()
plot_model(model, to_file='cnn-mnist.png', show_shapes=True)

# loss function for one-hot vector
# use of adam optimizer
# accuracy is good metric for classification tasks
model.compile(loss='categorical_crossentropy',
              optimizer='adam',
              metrics=['accuracy'])
# train the network
model.fit(x_train, y_train, epochs=10, batch_size=batch_size)

_, acc = model.evaluate(x_test,
                        y_test,
                        batch_size=batch_size,
                    verbose=0)
print("\nTest accuracy: %.1f%%" % (100.0 * acc))
```

The major change here is the use of the `Conv2D` layers. The `ReLU` activation function is already an argument of `Conv2D`. The `ReLU` function can be brought out as an `Activation` layer when the `batch normalization` layer is included in the model. `Batch normalization` is used in deep CNNs so that large learning rates can be utilized without causing instability during training.

Convolution

If, in the MLP model, the number of units characterizes the Dense layers, the kernel characterizes the CNN operations. As shown in *Figure 1.4.2*, the kernel can be visualized as a rectangular patch or window that slides through the whole image from left to right, and from top to bottom. This operation is called convolution. It transforms the input image into a feature map, which is a representation of what the kernel has learned from the input image. The feature map is then transformed into another feature map in the succeeding layer and so on. The number of feature maps generated per `Conv2D` is controlled by the `filters` argument.

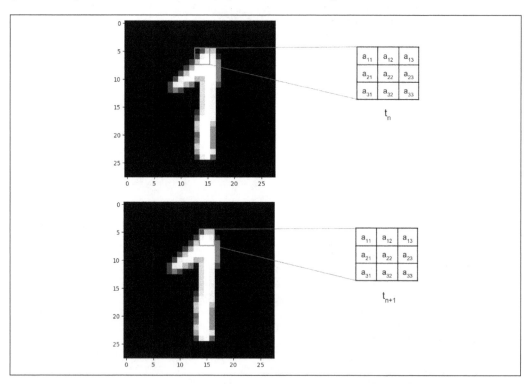

Figure 1.4.2: A 3 × 3 kernel is convolved with an MNIST digit image.

The convolution is shown in steps t_n and t_{n+1} where the kernel moved by a stride of 1 pixel to the right.

The computation involved in the convolution is shown in *Figure 1.4.3*:

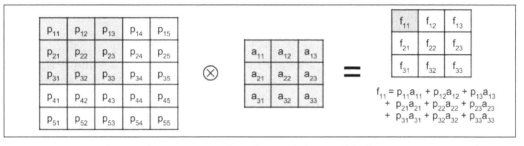

Figure 1.4.3: The convolution operation shows how one element of the feature map is computed

For simplicity, a 5 × 5 input image (or input feature map) where a 3 × 3 kernel is applied is illustrated. The resulting feature map is shown after the convolution. The value of one element of the feature map is shaded. You'll notice that the resulting feature map is smaller than the original input image, this is because the convolution is only performed on valid elements. The kernel cannot go beyond the borders of the image. If the dimensions of the input should be the same as the output feature maps, Conv2D accepts the option padding='same'. The input is padded with zeros around its borders to keep the dimensions unchanged after the convolution.

Pooling operations

The last change is the addition of a MaxPooling2D layer with the argument pool_size=2. MaxPooling2D compresses each feature map. Every patch of size pool_size × pool_size is reduced to 1 feature map point. The value is equal to the maximum feature point value within the patch. MaxPooling2D is shown in the following figure for two patches:

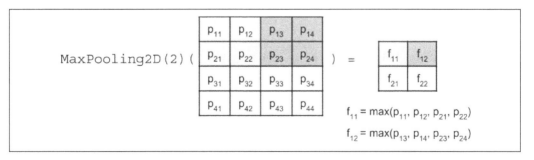

Figure 1.4.4: MaxPooling2D operation.
For simplicity, the input feature map is 4 × 4, resulting in a 2 × 2 feature map.

The significance of `MaxPooling2D` is the reduction in feature map size, which translates to an increase in receptive field size. For example, after `MaxPooling2D(2)`, the 2 × 2 kernel is now approximately convolving with a 4 × 4 patch. The CNN has learned a new set of feature maps for a different receptive field size.

There are other means of pooling and compression. For example, to achieve a 50% size reduction as `MaxPooling2D(2)`, `AveragePooling2D(2)` takes the average of a patch instead of finding the maximum. Strided convolution, `Conv2D(strides=2,…)`, will skip every two pixels during convolution and will still have the same 50% size reduction effect. There are subtle differences in the effectiveness of each reduction technique.

In `Conv2D` and `MaxPooling2D`, both `pool_size` and `kernel` can be non-square. In these cases, both the row and column sizes must be indicated. For example, `pool_size = (1, 2)` and `kernel = (3, 5)`.

The output of the last `MaxPooling2D` operation is a stack of feature maps. The role of `Flatten` is to convert the stack of feature maps into a vector format that is suitable for either Dropout or Dense layers, similar to the MLP model output layer.

In the next section, we will evaluate the performance of the trained MNIST CNN classifier model.

Performance evaluation and model summary

As shown in *Listing 1.4.2*, the CNN model in *Listing 1.4.1* requires a smaller number of parameters at 80,226 compared to 269,322 when MLP layers are used. The `conv2d_1` layer has 640 parameters because each kernel has 3 × 3 = 9 parameters, and each of the 64 feature maps has one kernel and one bias parameter. The number of parameters for other convolution layers can be computed in a similar way.

Listing 1.4.2: Summary of a CNN MNIST digit classifier

Layer (type)	Output Shape	Param #
conv2d_1 (Conv2D)	(None, 26, 26, 64)	640
max_pooling2d_1 (MaxPooling2)	(None, 13, 13, 64)	0
conv2d_2 (Conv2D)	(None, 11, 11, 64)	36928
max_pooling2d_2 (MaxPooling2)	(None, 5.5, 5, 64)	0
conv2d_3 (Conv2D)	(None, 3.3, 3, 64)	36928
flatten_1 (Flatten)	(None, 576)	0
dropout_1 (Dropout)	(None, 576)	0
dense_1 (Dense)	(None, 10)	5770
activation_1 (Activation)	(None, 10)	0

===

Total params: 80,266

Trainable params: 80,266

Non-trainable params: 0

Figure 1.4.5: shows a graphical representation of the CNN MNIST digit classifier.

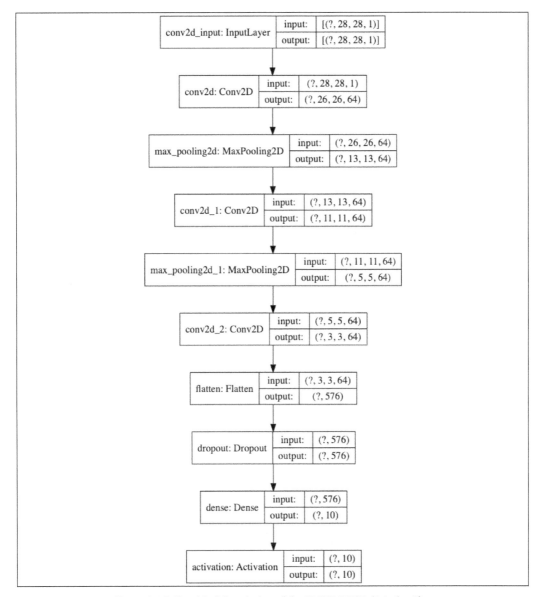

Figure 1.4.5: Graphical description of the CNN MNIST digit classifier

Table 1.4.1 shows a maximum test accuracy of 99.4%, which can be achieved for a 3-layer network with 64 feature maps per layer using the Adam optimizer with `dropout=0.2`. CNNs are more parameter efficient and have a higher accuracy than MLPs. Likewise, CNNs are also suitable for learning representations from sequential data, images, and videos.

Layers	Optimizer	Regularizer	Train Accuracy (%)	Test Accuracy (%)
64-64-64	SGD	Dropout(0.2)	97.76	98.50
64-64-64	RMSprop	Dropout(0.2)	99.11	99.00
64-64-64	Adam	Dropout(0.2)	99.75	99.40
64-64-64	Adam	Dropout(0.4)	99.64	99.30

Table 1.4.1: Different CNN network configurations and performance measures for the CNN MNIST digit classifier.

Having looked at CNNs and evaluated the trained model, let's look at the final core network that we will discuss in this chapter: RNN.

5. Recurrent Neural Network (RNN)

We're now going to look at the last of our three artificial neural networks, RNN.

RNNs are a family of networks that are suitable for learning representations of sequential data like text in **natural language processing** (NLP) or a stream of sensor data in instrumentation. While each MNIST data sample is not sequential in nature, it is not hard to imagine that every image can be interpreted as a sequence of rows or columns of pixels. Thus, a model based on RNNs can process each MNIST image as a sequence of 28-element input vectors with timesteps equal to 28. The following listing shows the code for the RNN model in *Figure 1.5.1*:

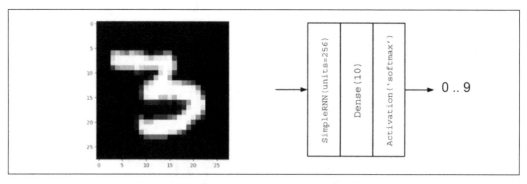

Figure 1.5.1: RNN model for MNIST digit classification

Listing 1.5.1: rnn-mnist-1.5.1.py

```python
import numpy as np
from tensorflow.keras.models import Sequential
from tensorflow.keras.layers import Dense, Activation, SimpleRNN
from tensorflow.keras.utils import to_categorical, plot_model
from tensorflow.keras.datasets import mnist

# load mnist dataset
(x_train, y_train), (x_test, y_test) = mnist.load_data()

# compute the number of labels
num_labels = len(np.unique(y_train))

# convert to one-hot vector
y_train = to_categorical(y_train)
y_test = to_categorical(y_test)

# resize and normalize
image_size = x_train.shape[1]
x_train = np.reshape(x_train,[-1, image_size, image_size])
x_test = np.reshape(x_test,[-1, image_size, image_size])
x_train = x_train.astype('float32') / 255
x_test = x_test.astype('float32') / 255

# network parameters
input_shape = (image_size, image_size)
batch_size = 128
units = 256
dropout = 0.2

# model is RNN with 256 units, input is 28-dim vector 28 timesteps
model = Sequential()
model.add(SimpleRNN(units=units,
                    dropout=dropout,
                    input_shape=input_shape))
model.add(Dense(num_labels))
model.add(Activation('softmax'))
model.summary()
plot_model(model, to_file='rnn-mnist.png', show_shapes=True)

# loss function for one-hot vector
# use of sgd optimizer
# accuracy is good metric for classification tasks
```

```
model.compile(loss='categorical_crossentropy',
              optimizer='sgd',
              metrics=['accuracy'])
# train the network
model.fit(x_train, y_train, epochs=20, batch_size=batch_size)

_, acc = model.evaluate(x_test,
                        y_test,
                        batch_size=batch_size,
                        verbose=0)
print("\nTest accuracy: %.1f%%" % (100.0 * acc))
```

There are two main differences between the RNN classifier and the two previous models. First is the `input_shape = (image_size, image_size)`, which is actually `input_ shape = (timesteps, input_dim)` or a sequence of `input_dim`-dimension vectors of timesteps length. Second is the use of a SimpleRNN layer to represent an RNN cell with `units=256`. The units variable represents the number of output units. If the CNN is characterized by the convolution of kernels across the input feature map, the RNN output is a function not only of the present input but also of the previous output or hidden state. Since the previous output is also a function of the previous input, the current output is also a function of the previous output and input and so on. The SimpleRNN layer in Keras is a simplified version of the true RNN. The following equation describes the output of SimpleRNN:

$$\mathbf{h}_t = \tanh(\mathbf{b} + \mathbf{W}\mathbf{h}_{t-1} + \mathbf{U}\mathbf{x}_t)....\text{(Equation 1.5.1)}$$

In this equation, **b** is the bias, while **W** and **U** are called recurrent kernel (weights for the previous output) and kernel (weights for the current input), respectively. Subscript t is used to indicate the position in the sequence. For a `SimpleRNN` layer with `units=256`, the total number of parameters is $256 + 256 \times 256 + 256 \times 28 = 72,960$, corresponding to **b**, **W**, and **U** contributions.

The following figure shows the diagrams of both SimpleRNN and RNN when used for classification tasks. What makes SimpleRNN simpler than an RNN is the absence of the output values $\mathbf{o}_t = \mathbf{V}\mathbf{h}_t + \mathbf{c}$ before the `softmax` function is computed:

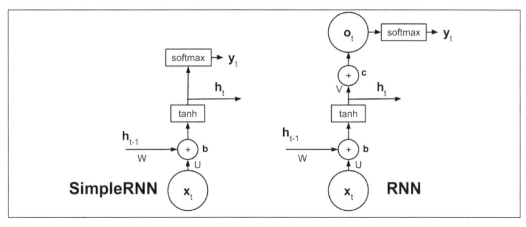

Figure 1.5.2: Diagram of SimpleRNN and RNN

RNNs might be initially harder to understand when compared to MLPs or CNNs. In an MLP, the perceptron is the fundamental unit. Once the concept of the perceptron is understood, an MLP is just a network of perceptrons. In a CNN, the kernel is a patch or window that slides through the feature map to generate another feature map. In an RNN, the most important is the concept of self-loop. There is in fact just one cell.

The illusion of multiple cells appears because a cell exists per timestep, but in fact it is just the same cell reused repeatedly unless the network is unrolled. The underlying neural networks of RNNs are shared across cells.

The summary in *Listing 1.5.2* indicates that using a SimpleRNN requires a fewer number of parameters.

Listing 1.5.2: Summary of an RNN MNIST digit classifier

```
Layer (type)                 Output Shape         Param #
=================================================================

    simple_rnn_1 (SimpleRNN)    (None, 256)           72960

    dense_1 (Dense)             (None, 10)            2570

    activation_1 (Activation)   (None, 10)            0
```

===

```
Total params: 75,530

Trainable params: 75,530

Non-trainable params: 0
```

Figure 1.5.3 shows the graphical description of the RNN MNIST digit classifier. The model is very concise:

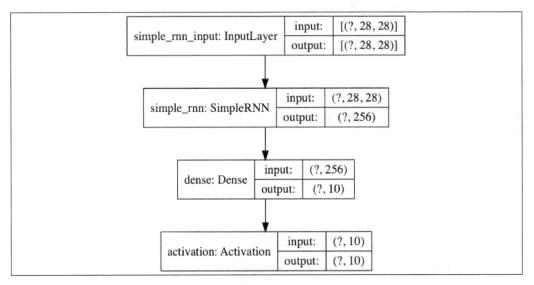

Figure 1.5.3: The RNN MNIST digit classifier graphical description

Table 1.5.1 shows that the SimpleRNN has the lowest accuracy among the networks presented:

Layers	Optimizer	Regularizer	Train Accuracy (%)	Test Accuracy (%)
256	SGD	Dropout(0.2)	97.26	98.00
256	RMSprop	Dropout(0.2)	96.72	97.60
256	Adam	Dropout(0.2)	96.79	97.40
512	SGD	Dropout(0.2)	97.88	98.30

Table 1.5.1: The different SimpleRNN network configurations and performance measures

In many deep neural networks, other members of the RNN family are more commonly used. For example, **Long Short-Term Memory (LSTM)** has been used in both machine translation and question answering problems. LSTM addresses the problem of long-term dependency or remembering relevant past information to the present output.

Unlike an RNN or a SimpleRNN, the internal structure of the LSTM cell is more complex. *Figure 1.5.4* shows a diagram of LSTM. LSTM uses not only the present input and past outputs or hidden states, but it introduces a cell state, s_t, that carries information from one cell to the other. The information flow between cell states is controlled by three gates, f_t, i_t, and q_t. The three gates have the effect of determining which information should be retained or replaced and the amount of information in the past and current input that should contribute to the current cell state or output. We will not discuss the details of the internal structure of the LSTM cell in this book. However, an intuitive guide to LSTMs can be found at `http://colah.github.io/posts/2015-08-Understanding-LSTMs`.

The `LSTM()` layer can be used as a drop-in replacement for `SimpleRNN()`. If LSTM is overkill for the task at hand, a simpler version called a **Gated Recurrent Unit (GRU)** can be used. A GRU simplifies LSTM by combining the cell state and hidden state together. A GRU also reduces the number of gates by one. The `GRU()` function can also be used as a drop-in replacement for `SimpleRNN()`.

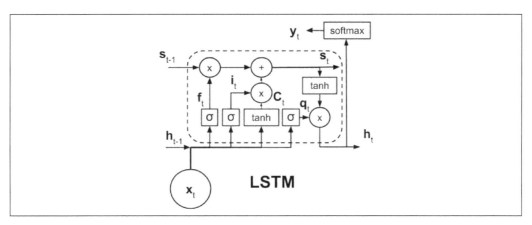

Figure 1.5.4: Diagram of LSTM. The parameters are not shown for clarity.

There are many other ways to configure RNNs. One way is making an RNN model that is bidirectional. By default, RNNs are unidirectional in the sense that the current output is only influenced by the past states and the current input.

In bidirectional RNNs, future states can also influence the present and past states by allowing information to flow backward. Past outputs are updated as needed depending on the new information received. RNNs can be made bidirectional by calling a wrapper function. For example, the implementation of bidirectional LSTM is `Bidirectional(LSTM())`.

For all types of RNNs, increasing the number of units will also increase the capacity. However, another way of increasing the capacity is by stacking the RNN layers. It should be noted though that as a general rule of thumb, the capacity of the model should only be increased if needed. Excess capacity may contribute to overfitting, and, as a result, may lead to both a longer training time and a slower performance during prediction.

6. Conclusion

This chapter provided an overview of the three deep learning models – MLP, RNN, CNN – and also introduced TensorFlow 2 `tf.keras`, a library for rapid development, training, and testing deep learning models that is suitable for a production environment. The Sequential API of Keras was also discussed. In the next chapter, the Functional API will be presented, which will enable us to build more complex models specifically for advanced deep neural networks.

This chapter also reviewed the important concepts of deep learning such as optimization, regularization, and loss functions. For ease of understanding, these concepts were presented in the context of MNIST digit classification.

Different solutions to MNIST digit classification using artificial neural networks, specifically MLP, CNN, and RNN, which are important building blocks of deep neural networks, were also discussed together with their performance measures.

With an understanding of deep learning concepts and how Keras can be used as a tool with them, we are now equipped to analyze advanced deep learning models. After discussing the Functional API in the next chapter, we'll move on to the implementation of popular deep learning models. Subsequent chapters will discuss selected advanced topics such as autoregressive models (autoencoder, GAN, VAE), deep reinforcement learning, object detection and segmentation, and unsupervised learning using mutual information. The accompanying Keras code implementations will play an important role in understanding these topics.

7. References

1. Chollet, François. Keras (2015). `https://github.com/keras-team/keras`.

2. LeCun, Yann, Corinna Cortes, and C. J. Burges. *MNIST handwritten digit database*. AT&T Labs [Online]. Available: `http://yann.lecun.com/exdb/mnist2` (2010).

2
Deep Neural Networks

In this chapter, we'll be examining deep neural networks. These networks have shown excellent performance in terms of the accuracy of their classification on more challenging datasets like ImageNet, CIFAR10 (https://www.cs.toronto.edu/~kriz/learning-features-2009-TR.pdf), and CIFAR100. For conciseness, we'll only be focusing on two networks: **ResNet** [2][4] and **DenseNet** [5]. While we will go into much more detail, it's important to take a minute to introduce these networks.

ResNet introduced the concept of residual learning, which enabled it to build very deep networks by addressing the vanishing gradient problem (discussed in section 2) in deep convolutional networks.

DenseNet improved ResNet further by allowing every convolution to have direct access to inputs, and lower layer feature maps. It's also managed to keep the number of parameters low in deep networks by utilizing both the **Bottleneck** and **Transition layers**.

But why these two models, and not others? Well, since their introduction, there have been countless models such as **ResNeXt** [6] and **WideResNet** [7] which have been inspired by the technique used by these two networks. Likewise, with an understanding of both ResNet and DenseNet, we'll be able to use their design guidelines to build our own models. By using transfer learning, this will also allow us to take advantage of pretrained ResNet and DenseNet models for our own purposes such as for object detection and segmentation. These reasons alone, along with their compatibility with Keras, make the two models ideal for exploring and complimenting the advanced deep learning scope of this book.

While this chapter's focus is on deep neural networks; we'll begin this chapter by discussing an important feature of Keras called the **Functional API**. This API acts as an alternative method for building networks in `tf.keras` and enables us to build more complex networks that cannot be accomplished by the Sequential model API. The reason why we're focusing so much on this API is that it will become a very useful tool for building deep networks such as the two we're focusing on in this chapter. It's recommended that you've completed *Chapter 1, Introducing Advanced Deep Learning with Keras*, before moving onto this chapter as we'll refer to introductory level code and concepts explored in that chapter as we take them to an advanced level in this chapter.

The goals of this chapter are to introduce:

- The Functional API in Keras, as well as exploring examples of networks running it
- Deep Residual Networks (ResNet versions 1 and 2) implementation in `tf.keras`
- The implementation of Densely Connected Convolutional Networks (DenseNet) in `tf.keras`
- Explore the two popular deep learning models, **ResNet** and **DenseNet**

Let's begin by discussing the Functional API.

1. Functional API

In the Sequential model API that we first introduced in *Chapter 1, Introducing Advanced Deep Learning with Keras*, a layer is stacked on top of another layer. Generally, the model will be accessed through its input and output layers. We also learned that there is no simple mechanism if we find ourselves wanting to add an auxiliary input at the middle of the network, or even to extract an auxiliary output before the last layer.

That model also had its downsides; for example, it doesn't support graph-like models or models that behave like Python functions. In addition, it's also difficult to share layers between the two models. Such limitations are addressed by the Functional API and are the reason why it's a vital tool for anyone wanting to work with deep learning models.

The Functional API is guided by the following two concepts:

- A layer is an instance that accepts a tensor as an argument. The output of a layer is another tensor. To build a model, the layer instances are objects that are chained to one another through both input and output tensors. This will have a similar end-result to stacking multiple layers in the Sequential model. However, using layer instances makes it easier for models to have either auxiliary or multiple inputs and outputs since the input/output of each layer will be readily accessible.

- A model is a function between one or more input tensors and output tensors. In between the model input and output, tensors are the layer instances that are chained to one another by layer input and output tensors. A model is, therefore, a function of one or more input layers and one or more output layers. The model instance formalizes the computational graph on how the data flows from input(s) to output(s).

After you've completed building the Functional API model, the training and evaluation are then performed by the same functions used in the Sequential model. To illustrate, in a Functional API, a two dimensional convolutional layer, Conv2D, with 32 filters and with x as the layer input tensor and y as the layer output tensor can be written as:

```
y = Conv2D(32)(x)
```

We're also able to stack multiple layers to build our models. For example, we can rewrite the **Convolutional Neural Network** (**CNN**) on MNIST cnn-mnist-1.4.1.py using the Functional API as shown in the following listing:

Listing 2.1.1: cnn-functional-2.1.1.py

```
import numpy as np
from tensorflow.keras.layers import Dense, Dropout, Input
from tensorflow.keras.layers import Conv2D, MaxPooling2D, Flatten
from tensorflow.keras.models import Model
from tensorflow.keras.datasets import mnist
from tensorflow.keras.utils import to_categorical


# load MNIST dataset
(x_train, y_train), (x_test, y_test) = mnist.load_data()

# from sparse label to categorical
num_labels = len(np.unique(y_train))
y_train = to_categorical(y_train)
y_test = to_categorical(y_test)
```

```
# reshape and normalize input images
image_size = x_train.shape[1]
x_train = np.reshape(x_train,[-1, image_size, image_size, 1])
x_test = np.reshape(x_test,[-1, image_size, image_size, 1])
x_train = x_train.astype('float32') / 255
x_test = x_test.astype('float32') / 255

# network parameters
input_shape = (image_size, image_size, 1)
batch_size = 128
kernel_size = 3
filters = 64
dropout = 0.3

# use functional API to build cnn layers
inputs = Input(shape=input_shape)
y = Conv2D(filters=filters,
           kernel_size=kernel_size,
           activation='relu')(inputs)
y = MaxPooling2D()(y)
y = Conv2D(filters=filters,
           kernel_size=kernel_size,
           activation='relu')(y)
y = MaxPooling2D()(y)
y = Conv2D(filters=filters,
           kernel_size=kernel_size,
           activation='relu')(y)
# image to vector before connecting to dense layer
y = Flatten()(y)
# dropout regularization
y = Dropout(dropout)(y)
outputs = Dense(num_labels, activation='softmax')(y)

# build the model by supplying inputs/outputs
model = Model(inputs=inputs, outputs=outputs)
# network model in text
model.summary()

# classifier loss, Adam optimizer, classifier accuracy
model.compile(loss='categorical_crossentropy',
              optimizer='adam',
              metrics=['accuracy'])
```

```
# train the model with input images and labels
model.fit(x_train,
          y_train,
          validation_data=(x_test, y_test),
          epochs=20,
          batch_size=batch_size)

# model accuracy on test dataset
score = model.evaluate(x_test,
                       y_test,
                       batch_size=batch_size,
                       verbose=0)
print("\nTest accuracy: %.1f%%" % (100.0 * score[1]))
```

By default, `MaxPooling2D` uses `pool_size=2`, so the argument has been removed.

In the preceding listing, every layer is a function of a tensor. Each layer generates a tensor as an output which becomes the input to the next layer. To create this model, we can call `Model()` and supply both the `inputs` and `outputs` tensors, or alternatively the lists of tensors. Everything else remains the same.

The same listing can also be trained and evaluated using the `fit()` and `evaluate()` functions, similar to the Sequential model. The `Sequential` class is, in fact, a subclass of the `Model` class. We need to remember that we inserted the `validation_data` argument in the `fit()` function to see the progress of validation accuracy during training. The accuracy ranges from 99.3% to 99.4% in 20 epochs.

Creating a two-input and one-output model

We're now going to do something really exciting, creating an advanced model with two inputs and one output. Before we start, it's important to know that the Sequential model API is designed for building 1-input and 1-output models only.

Let's suppose a new model for the MNIST digit classification is invented, and it's called the Y-Network, as shown in *Figure 2.1.1*. The Y-Network uses the same input twice, both on the left and right CNN branches. The network combines the results using a `concatenate` layer. The merge operation `concatenate` is similar to stacking two tensors of the same shape along the concatenation axis to form one tensor. For example, concatenating two tensors of shape (3, 3, 16) along the last axis will result in a tensor of shape (3, 3, 32).

Everything else after the `concatenate` layer will remain the same as the previous chapter's CNN MNIST classifier model: `Flatten`, then `Dropout`, and then `Dense`:

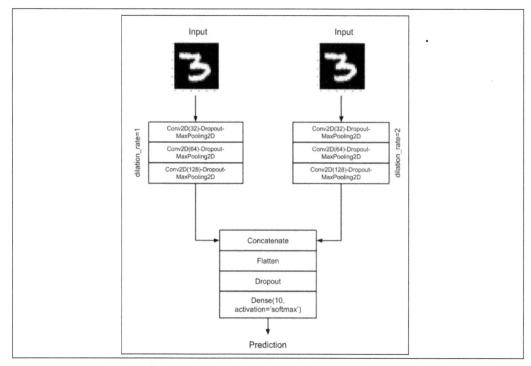

Figure 2.1.1: The Y-Network accepts the same input twice but processes the input in two branches of convolutional networks. The outputs of the branches are combined using the concatenate layer. The last layer prediction is going to be similar to the previous chapter's CNN MNIST classifier model.

To improve the performance of the model in *Listing 2.1.1*, we can propose several changes. Firstly, the branches of the Y-Network are doubling the number of filters to compensate for the halving of the feature maps size after `MaxPooling2D()`. For example, if the output of the first convolution is (28, 28, 32), after max pooling the new shape is (14, 14, 32). The next convolution will have a filter size of 64 and output dimensions of (14, 14, 64).

Second, although both branches have the same kernel size of 3, the right branch uses a dilation rate of 2. *Figure 2.1.2* shows the effect of different dilation rates on a kernel with size 3. The idea is that by increasing the effective receptive field size of the kernel using dilation rate, the CNN will enable the right branch to learn different feature maps. Using a dilation rate greater than 1 is a computationally efficient approximate method to increase receptive field size. It is approximate since the kernel is not actually a full-blown kernel. It is efficient since we use the same number of operations as with a dilation rate equal to 1.

To appreciate the concept of the receptive field, notice that when the kernel computes each point of a feature map, its input is a patch in the previous layer feature map which is also dependent on its previous layer feature map. If we continue tracking this dependency down to the input image, the kernel depends on an image patch called the receptive field.

We'll use the option `padding='same'` to ensure that we will not have negative tensor dimensions when the dilated CNN is used. By using `padding='same'`, we'll keep the dimensions of the input the same as the output feature maps. This is accomplished by padding the input with zeros to make sure that the output has the **same** size.

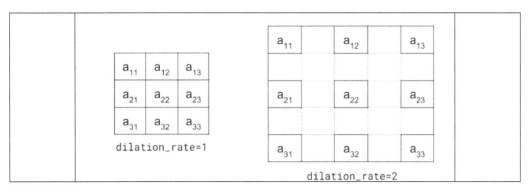

Figure 2.1.2: By increasing the dilation rate from 1, the effective kernel receptive field size also increases

Listing 2.1.2 for `cnn-y-network-2.1.2.py` shows the implementation of the Y-Network using the Functional API. The two branches are created by the two `for` loops. Both branches expect the same input shape. The two `for` loops will create two 3-layer stacks of `Conv2D-Dropout-MaxPooling2D`. While we used the `concatenate` layer to combine the outputs of the left and right branches, we could also utilize the other merge functions of `tf.keras`, such as `add`, `dot`, and `multiply`. The choice of the merge function is not purely arbitrary but must be based on a sound model design decision.

In the Y-Network, `concatenate` will not discard any portion of the feature maps. Instead, we'll let the `Dense` layer figure out what to do with the concatenated feature maps.

Listing 2.1.2: `cnn-y-network-2.1.2.py`

```
import numpy as np

from tensorflow.keras.layers import Dense, Dropout, Input
from tensorflow.keras.layers import Conv2D, MaxPooling2D
from tensorflow.keras.layers import Flatten, concatenate
from tensorflow.keras.models import Model
from tensorflow.keras.datasets import mnist
```

```
from tensorflow.keras.utils import to_categorical
from tensorflow.keras.utils import plot_model

# load MNIST dataset
(x_train, y_train), (x_test, y_test) = mnist.load_data()

# from sparse label to categorical
num_labels = len(np.unique(y_train))
y_train = to_categorical(y_train)
y_test = to_categorical(y_test)

# reshape and normalize input images
image_size = x_train.shape[1]
x_train = np.reshape(x_train,[-1, image_size, image_size, 1])
x_test = np.reshape(x_test,[-1, image_size, image_size, 1])
x_train = x_train.astype('float32') / 255
x_test = x_test.astype('float32') / 255

# network parameters
input_shape = (image_size, image_size, 1)
batch_size = 32
kernel_size = 3
dropout = 0.4
n_filters = 32

# left branch of Y network
left_inputs = Input(shape=input_shape)
x = left_inputs
filters = n_filters
# 3 layers of Conv2D-Dropout-MaxPooling2D
# number of filters doubles after each layer (32-64-128)
for i in range(3):
    x = Conv2D(filters=filters,
               kernel_size=kernel_size,
               padding='same',
               activation='relu')(x)
    x = Dropout(dropout)(x)
    x = MaxPooling2D()(x)
    filters *= 2

# right branch of Y network
right_inputs = Input(shape=input_shape)
y = right_inputs
filters = n_filters
# 3 layers of Conv2D-Dropout-MaxPooling2Do
# number of filters doubles after each layer (32-64-128)
for i in range(3):
    y = Conv2D(filters=filters,
               kernel_size=kernel_size,
               padding='same',
```

```
                    activation='relu',
                    dilation_rate=2)(y)
        y = Dropout(dropout)(y)
        y = MaxPooling2D()(y)
        filters *= 2

    # merge left and right branches outputs
    y = concatenate([x, y])
    # feature maps to vector before connecting to Dense
    y = Flatten()(y)
    y = Dropout(dropout)(y)
    outputs = Dense(num_labels, activation='softmax')(y)

    # build the model in functional API
    model = Model([left_inputs, right_inputs], outputs)
    # verify the model using graph
    plot_model(model, to_file='cnn-y-network.png', show_shapes=True)
    # verify the model using layer text description
    model.summary()

    # classifier loss, Adam optimizer, classifier accuracy
    model.compile(loss='categorical_crossentropy',
                  optimizer='adam',
                  metrics=['accuracy'])

    # train the model with input images and labels
    model.fit([x_train, x_train],
              y_train,
              validation_data=([x_test, x_test], y_test),
              epochs=20,
              batch_size=batch_size)

    # model accuracy on test dataset
    score = model.evaluate([x_test, x_test],
                           y_test,
                           batch_size=batch_size,
                           verbose=0)
    print("\nTest accuracy: %.1f%%" % (100.0 * score[1]))
```

Taking a step back, we can note that the Y-Network is expecting two inputs for training and validation. The inputs are identical, so [x_train, x_train] is supplied.

Over the course of the 20 epochs, the accuracy of the Y-Network ranges from 99.4% to 99.5%. This is a slight improvement over the 3-stack CNN which achieved a range between 99.3% and 99.4% accuracy. However, this was at the cost of both higher complexity and more than double the number of parameters.

The following figure, *Figure 2.1.3*, shows the architecture of the Y-Network as understood by Keras and generated by the `plot_model()` function:

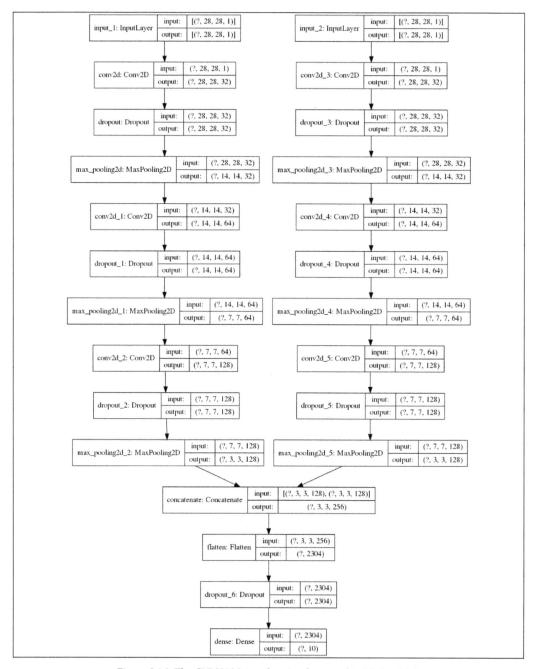

Figure 2.1.3: The CNN Y-Network as implemented in Listing 2.1.2

This concludes our look at the Functional API. We should take this time to remember that the focus of this chapter is building deep neural networks, specifically ResNet and DenseNet. Therefore, we're only covering the Functional API materials needed to build them, as covering the entire API would be beyond the scope of this book. With that said, let's move on to discussing ResNet.

 The reader is referred to `https://keras.io/` for additional information on the Functional API.

2. Deep Residual Network (ResNet)

One key advantage of deep networks is that they have a great ability to learn different levels of representation from both inputs and feature maps. In classification, segmentation, detection, and a number of other computer vision problems, learning different feature maps generally leads to a better performance.

However, you'll find that it's not easy to train deep networks because the gradient may vanish (or explode) with depth in the shallow layers during backpropagation. *Figure 2.2.1* illustrates the problem of vanishing gradient. The network parameters are updated by backpropagation from the output layer to all previous layers. Since backpropagation is based on the chain rule, there is a tendency for the gradient to diminish as it reaches the shallow layers. This is due to the multiplication of small numbers, especially for small loss functions and parameter values.

The number of multiplication operations will be proportional to the depth of the network. It's also worth noting that if the gradient degrades, the parameters will not be updated appropriately.

Hence, the network will fail to improve its performance.

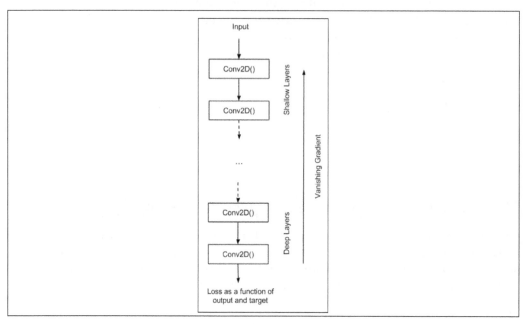

Figure 2.2.1: A common problem in deep networks is that the gradient vanishes as it reaches the shallow layers during backpropagation.

To alleviate the degradation of the gradient in deep networks, ResNet introduced the concept of a deep residual learning framework. Let's analyze a block: a small segment of our deep network.

Figure 2.2.2 shows a comparison between a typical CNN block and a ResNet residual block. The idea of ResNet is that in order to prevent the gradient from degrading, we'll let the information flow through the shortcut connections to reach the shallow layers.

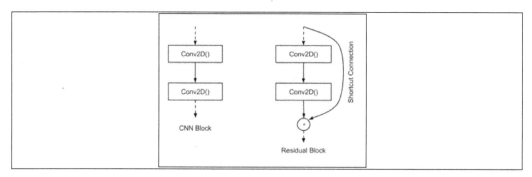

Figure 2.2.2: A comparison between a block in a typical CNN and a block in ResNet. To prevent the degradation of the gradient during backpropagation, a shortcut connection is introduced.

Next, we're going to look at more details within the discussion of the differences between the two blocks. *Figure 2.2.3* shows more details of the CNN block of another commonly used deep network, **VGG** [3], and ResNet. We'll represent the layer feature maps as x. The feature maps at layer *l* are x_l. The operations in the CNN layer are **Conv2D-Batch Normalization(BN)-ReLU**.

Let's suppose we represent this set of operations in the form of `H() = Conv2D-Batch Normalization(BN)-ReLU`; then:

$$x_{l-1} = H(x_{l-2}) \quad \text{(Equation 2.2.1)}$$

$$x_l = H(x_{l-1}) \quad \text{(Equation 2.2.2)}$$

In other words, the feature maps at layer *l* - 2 are transformed to x_{l-1} by `H()` `=Conv2D-Batch Normalization(BN)-ReLU`. The same set of operations is applied to transform x_{l-1} to x_l. To put this another way, if we have an 18-layer VGG, then there are 18 *H()* operations before the input image is transformed to the 18th layer feature map.

Generally speaking, we can observe that the layer *l* output feature maps are directly affected by the previous feature maps only. Meanwhile, for ResNet:

$$x_{l-1} = H(x_{l-2}) \quad \text{(Equation 2.2.3)}$$

$$x_l = ReLU(F(x_{l-1}) + x_{l-2}) \quad \text{(Equation 2.2.4)}$$

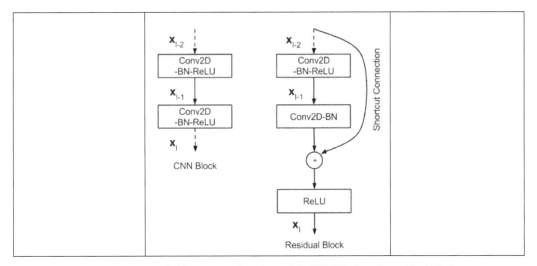

Figure 2.2.3: Detailed layer operations for a plain CNN block and a residual block

$F(\mathbf{x}_{l-1})$ is made of `Conv2D-BN`, which is also known as the residual mapping. The + sign is a tensor element-wise addition between the shortcut connection and the output of $F(\mathbf{x}_{l-1})$. The shortcut connection doesn't add extra parameters nor extra computational complexity.

The add operation can be implemented in `tf.keras` by the `add()` merge function. However, both $F(\mathbf{x}_{l-1})$ and $\mathbf{x}_{l-2}$ should have the same dimensions.

If the dimensions are different, for example, when changing the feature maps size, we should perform a linear projection on $\mathbf{x}_{l-2}$ as to match the size of $F(\mathbf{x}_{l-1})$. In the original paper, the linear projection for the case, when the feature maps size is halved, is done by a `Conv2D` with a 1 × 1 kernel and `strides=2`.

Back in *Chapter 1, Introducing Advanced Deep Learning with Keras*, we discussed that `stride > 1` is equivalent to skipping pixels during convolution. For example, if `strides=2`, we could skip every other pixel when we slide the kernel during the convolution process.

The preceding *Equation 2.2.3* and *Equation 2.2.4* both model ResNet residual block operations. They imply that if the deeper layers can be trained to have fewer errors, then there is no reason why the shallower layers should have higher errors.

Knowing the basic building blocks of ResNet, we're able to design a deep residual network for image classification. This time, however, we're going to tackle a more challenging dataset.

In our examples, we're going to consider CIFAR10, which was one of the datasets the original paper was validated on. In this example, `tf.keras` provides an API to conveniently access the CIFAR10 dataset, as shown:

```
from tensorflow.keras.datasets import cifar10
(x_train, y_train), (x_test, y_test) = cifar10.load_data()
```

Like MNIST, the CIFAR10 dataset has 10 categories. The dataset is a collection of small (32 × 32) RGB real-world images of an airplane, an automobile, a bird, a cat, a deer, a dog, a frog, a horse, a ship, and a truck corresponding to each of the 10 categories. *Figure 2.2.4* shows sample images from CIFAR10.

In the dataset, there are 50,000 labeled train images and 10,000 labeled test images for validation:

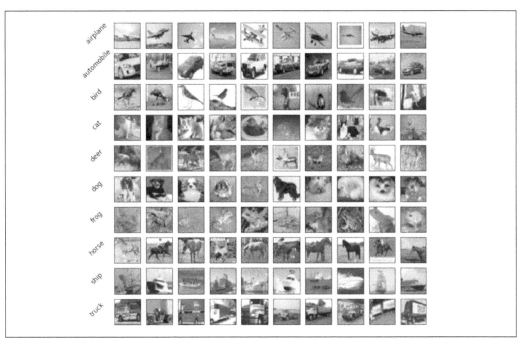

Figure 2.2.4: Sample images from the CIFAR10 dataset. The full dataset has 50,000 labeled train images and 10,000 labeled test images for validation.

For the CIFAR10 data, ResNet can be built using different network architectures as shown in *Table 2.2.1. Table 2.2.1* means we have three sets of residual blocks. Each set has *2n* layers corresponding to *n* residual blocks. The extra layer in 32 × 32 is the first layer for the input image.

Layers	Output Size	Filter Size	Operations
Convolution	32 × 32	16	3 x 3 *Conv2D*
Residual Block (1)	32 × 32		$\begin{Bmatrix} 3 \times 3 & Conv2D \\ 3 \times 3 & Conv2D \end{Bmatrix} \times n$
Transition Layer (1)	32 × 32 16 × 16		{1 x 1 *Conv2D, strides* = 2}

Residual Block (2)	16 × 16	32	$\left\{\begin{array}{ll} 3 \times 3 & Conv2D, strides = 2\ if\ 1st\ Conv2D \\ 3 \times 3 & Conv2D \end{array}\right\} \times n$
Transition Layer (2)	16 × 16 8 × 8		{1 × 1 *Conv2D, strides = 2*}
Residual Block (3)	8 × 8	64	$\left\{\begin{array}{ll} 3 \times 3 & Conv2D, strides = 2\ if\ 1st\ Conv2D \\ 3 \times 3 & Conv2D \end{array}\right\} \times n$
Average Pooling	1 × 1		8 × 8 *AveragePooling2D*

Table 2.2.1: ResNet network architecture configuration

The kernel size is 3, except for the transition between two feature maps with different sizes, which implements a linear mapping. For example, a `Conv2D` with a kernel size of 1 and `strides=2`. For the sake of consistency with DenseNet, we'll use the term `Transition` layer when we join two residual blocks of different sizes.

ResNet uses `kernel_initializer='he_normal'` in order to aid the convergence when backpropagation is taking place [1]. The last layer is made of `AveragePooling2D-Flatten-Dense`. It's worth noting at this point that ResNet does not use dropout. It also appears that the `add` merge operation and the 1 × 1 convolution have a self-regularizing effect. *Figure 2.2.5* shows the ResNet model architecture for the CIFAR10 dataset as described in *Table 2.2.1*.

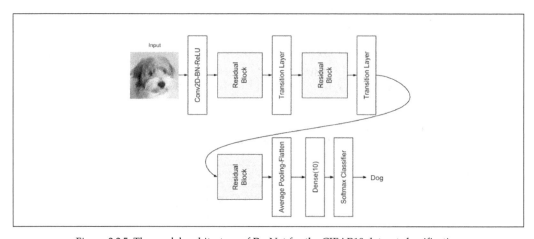

Figure 2.2.5: The model architecture of ResNet for the CIFAR10 dataset classification

The following code snippet shows the partial ResNet implementation in `tf.keras`. The code has been contributed to the Keras GitHub repository. From *Table 2.2.2* (to be shown shortly) we can also see that by modifying the value of *n*, we're able to increase the depth of the networks.

For example, for *n = 18*, we already have ResNet110, a deep network with 110 layers. To build ResNet20, we use *n = 3*:

```
n = 3

# model version
# orig paper: version = 1 (ResNet v1),
# improved ResNet: version = 2 (ResNet v2)
version = 1

# computed depth from supplied model parameter n
if version == 1:
    depth = n * 6 + 2
elif version == 2:
    depth = n * 9 + 2


if version == 2:
    model = resnet_v2(input_shape=input_shape, depth=depth)
else:
    model = resnet_v1(input_shape=input_shape, depth=depth)
```

The `resnet_v1()` method is a model builder for ResNet. It uses a utility function, `resnet_layer()`, to help build the stack of `Conv2D-BN-ReLU`.

It's referred to as version 1, as we will see in the next section, an improved ResNet was proposed, and that has been called ResNet version 2, or v2. Over ResNet, ResNet v2 has an improved residual block design resulting to a better performance.

The following listing shows the partial code of `resnet-cifar10-2.2.1.py`, which is the `tf.keras` model implementation of ResNet v1.

Listing 2.2.1: `resnet-cifar10-2.2.1.py`

```
def resnet_v1(input_shape, depth, num_classes=10):
    """ResNet Version 1 Model builder [a]

    Stacks of 2 x (3 x 3) Conv2D-BN-ReLU
    Last ReLU is after the shortcut connection.
    At the beginning of each stage, the feature map size is halved
    (downsampled) by a convolutional layer with strides=2, while
    the number of filters is doubled. Within each stage,
    the layers have the same number filters and the
    same number of filters.
    Features maps sizes:
    stage 0: 32x32, 16
```

```
stage 1: 16x16, 32
stage 2:  8x8,  64
The Number of parameters is approx the same as Table 6 of [a]:
ResNet20 0.27M
ResNet32 0.46M
ResNet44 0.66M
ResNet56 0.85M
ResNet110 1.7M

Arguments:
    input_shape (tensor): shape of input image tensor
    depth (int): number of core convolutional layers
    num_classes (int): number of classes (CIFAR10 has 10)

Returns:
    model (Model): Keras model instance
"""
if (depth - 2) % 6 != 0:
    raise ValueError('depth should be 6n+2 (eg 20, 32, in [a])')
# Start model definition.
num_filters = 16
num_res_blocks = int((depth - 2) / 6)

inputs = Input(shape=input_shape)
x = resnet_layer(inputs=inputs)
# instantiate the stack of residual units
for stack in range(3):
    for res_block in range(num_res_blocks):
        strides = 1
        # first layer but not first stack
        if stack > 0 and res_block == 0:
            strides = 2  # downsample
        y = resnet_layer(inputs=x,
                         num_filters=num_filters,
                         strides=strides)
        y = resnet_layer(inputs=y,
                         num_filters=num_filters,
                         activation=None)
        # first layer but not first stack
        if stack > 0 and res_block == 0:
            # linear projection residual shortcut
            # connection to match changed dims
            x = resnet_layer(inputs=x,
                             num_filters=num_filters,
```

```
                                    kernel_size=1,
                                    strides=strides,
                                    activation=None,
                                    batch_normalization=False)
            x = add([x, y])
            x = Activation('relu')(x)
        num_filters *= 2


    # add classifier on top.
    # v1 does not use BN after last shortcut connection-ReLU
    x = AveragePooling2D(pool_size=8)(x)
    y = Flatten()(x)
    outputs = Dense(num_classes,
                    activation='softmax',
                    kernel_initializer='he_normal')(y)


    # instantiate model.
    model = Model(inputs=inputs, outputs=outputs)
    return model
```

The performance of ResNet on various values of *n* are shown in *Table 2.2.2.*

# Layers	n	% Accuracy on CIFAR10 (Original paper)	% Accuracy on CIFAR10 (This book)
ResNet20	3	91.25	92.16
ResNet32	5	92.49	92.46
ResNet44	7	92.83	92.50
ResNet56	9	93.03	92.71
ResNet110	18	93.57	92.65

Table 2.2.2: ResNet architecture validated with CIFAR10 for different values of n

There are some minor differences from the original implementation of ResNet. In particular, we don't use SGD, and instead, we'll use Adam. This is because ResNet is easier to converge with Adam. We'll also use a learning rate (lr) scheduler, lr_schedule(), in order to schedule the decrease in lr at 80, 120, 160, and 180 epochs from the default 1e-3. The lr_schedule() function will be called after every epoch during training as part of the callbacks variable.

The other callback saves the checkpoint every time there is progress made in the validation accuracy. When training deep networks, it is a good practice to save the model or weight checkpoint. This is because it takes a substantial amount of time to train deep networks.

When you want to use your network, all you need to do is simply reload the checkpoint, and the trained model is restored. This can be accomplished by calling `tf.keras load_model()`. The `lr_reducer()` function is included. In case the metric has plateaued before the scheduled reduction, this callback will reduce the learning rate by a certain factor supplied in the argument if the validation loss has not improved after `patience = 5` epochs.

The **callbacks** variable is supplied when the `model.fit()` method is called. Similar to the original paper, the `tf.keras` implementation uses data augmentation, `ImageDataGenerator()`, in order to provide additional training data as part of the regularization schemes. As the number of training data increases, generalization will improve.

For example, a simple data augmentation is flipping a photo of a dog, as shown in *Figure 2.2.6* (`horizontal_flip = True`). If it is an image of a dog, then the flipped image is still an image of a dog. You can also perform other transformation, such as scaling, rotation, whitening, and so on, and the label will still remain the same:

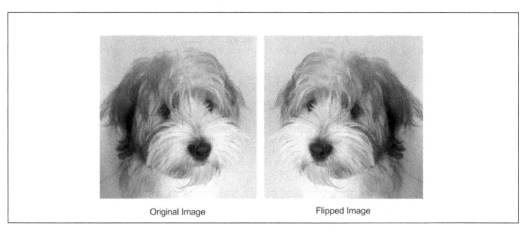

Original Image   Flipped Image

Figure 2.2.6: A simple data augmentation is flipping the original image

The complete code is available on GitHub: `https://github.com/ PacktPublishing/Advanced-Deep-Learning-with-Keras`.

It's often difficult to exactly duplicate the implementation of the original paper. In this book, we used a different optimizer and data augmentation. This may result in slight differences in the performance of the `tf.keras` ResNet as implemented in this book and the model in the original paper.

After the release of the second paper on **ResNet** [4], the original model presented in this section is known as ResNet v1. The improved ResNet is commonly called ResNet v2, which we will discuss in the next section.

3. ResNet v2

The improvements for ResNet v2 are mainly found in the arrangement of layers in the residual block as shown in *Figure 2.3.1*.

The prominent changes in ResNet v2 are:

- The use of a stack of 1 x 1 – 3 x 3 – 1 × 1 `BN-ReLU-Conv2D`

- Batch normalization and ReLU activation come before two dimensional convolution

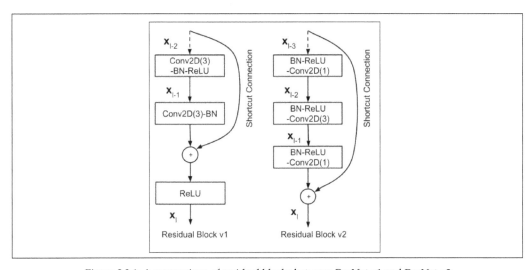

Figure 2.3.1: A comparison of residual blocks between ResNet v1 and ResNet v2

ResNet v2 is also implemented in the same code as `resnet-cifar10-2.2.1.py`, as can be seen in *Listing 2.2.1*:

Listing 2.2.1: `resnet-cifar10-2.2.1.py`

```
def resnet_v2(input_shape, depth, num_classes=10):
    """ResNet Version 2 Model builder [b]

    Stacks of (1 x 1)-(3 x 3)-(1 x 1) BN-ReLU-Conv2D or
    also known as bottleneck layer.
    First shortcut connection per layer is 1 x 1 Conv2D.
    Second and onwards shortcut connection is identity.
    At the beginning of each stage,
    the feature map size is halved (downsampled)
    by a convolutional layer with strides=2,
    while the number of filter maps is
    doubled. Within each stage, the layers have
```

```
the same number filters and the same filter map sizes.
Features maps sizes:
conv1  : 32x32,  16
stage 0: 32x32,  64
stage 1: 16x16, 128
stage 2:  8x8,  256

Arguments:
    input_shape (tensor): shape of input image tensor
    depth (int): number of core convolutional layers
    num_classes (int): number of classes (CIFAR10 has 10)

Returns:
    model (Model): Keras model instance
"""
if (depth - 2) % 9 != 0:
    raise ValueError('depth should be 9n+2 (eg 110 in [b])')
# start model definition.
num_filters_in = 16
num_res_blocks = int((depth - 2) / 9)

inputs = Input(shape=input_shape)
# v2 performs Conv2D with BN-ReLU
# on input before splitting into 2 paths
x = resnet_layer(inputs=inputs,
                 num_filters=num_filters_in,
                 conv_first=True)

# instantiate the stack of residual units
for stage in range(3):
    for res_block in range(num_res_blocks):
        activation = 'relu'
        batch_normalization = True
        strides = 1
        if stage == 0:
            num_filters_out = num_filters_in * 4
            # first layer and first stage
            if res_block == 0:
                activation = None
                batch_normalization = False
        else:
            num_filters_out = num_filters_in * 2
            # first layer but not first stage
            if res_block == 0:
```

```
                    # downsample
                    strides = 2

            # bottleneck residual unit
            y = resnet_layer(inputs=x,
                             num_filters=num_filters_in,
                             kernel_size=1,
                             strides=strides,
                             activation=activation,
                             batch_normalization=batch_normalization,
                             conv_first=False)
            y = resnet_layer(inputs=y,
                             num_filters=num_filters_in,
                             conv_first=False)
            y = resnet_layer(inputs=y,
                             num_filters=num_filters_out,
                             kernel_size=1,
                             conv_first=False)
            if res_block == 0:
                # linear projection residual shortcut connection
                # to match changed dims
                x = resnet_layer(inputs=x,
                                 num_filters=num_filters_out,
                                 kernel_size=1,
                                 strides=strides,
                                 activation=None,
                                 batch_normalization=False)
            x = add([x, y])

        num_filters_in = num_filters_out

    # add classifier on top.
    # v2 has BN-ReLU before Pooling
    x = BatchNormalization()(x)
    x = Activation('relu')(x)
    x = AveragePooling2D(pool_size=8)(x)
    y = Flatten()(x)
    outputs = Dense(num_classes,
                    activation='softmax',
                    kernel_initializer='he_normal')(y)

    # instantiate model.
    model = Model(inputs=inputs, outputs=outputs)
    return model
```

ResNet v2's model builder is shown in the following code. For example, to build ResNet110 v2, we'll use n = 12 and version = 2:

n = 12

```
# model version
# orig paper: version = 1 (ResNet v1),
# improved ResNet: version = 2 (ResNet v2)
version = 2

# computed depth from supplied model parameter n
if version == 1:
    depth = n * 6 + 2
elif version == 2:
    depth = n * 9 + 2


if version == 2:
    model = resnet_v2(input_shape=input_shape, depth=depth)
else:
    model = resnet_v1(input_shape=input_shape, depth=depth)
```

The accuracy of ResNet v2 is shown in *Table 2.3.1* below:

# Layers	n	% Accuracy on CIFAR10 (Original paper)	% Accuracy on CIFAR10 (This book)
ResNet56	9	NA	93.01
ResNet110	18	93.63	93.15

Table 2.3.1: The ResNet v2 architectures validated on the CIFAR10 dataset

In the Keras applications package, certain ResNet v1 and v2 models (for example: 50, 101, 152) have been implemented. These are alternative implementations with pre-trained weights unclear and can be easily reused for transfer learning. The models used in this book provide flexibility in terms of number of layers.

We have completed the discussion on one of the most commonly used deep neural networks, ResNet v1 and v2. In the following section, DenseNet, another popular deep neural network architecture, is covered.

4. Densely Connected Convolutional Network (DenseNet)

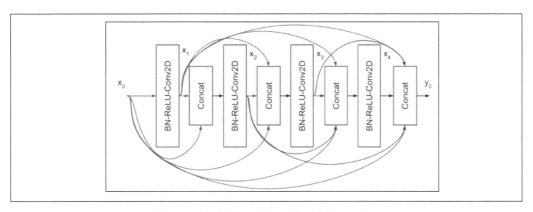

Figure 2.4.1: A 4-layer Dense block in DenseNet.
The input to each layer is made of all the previous feature maps.

DenseNet attacks the problem of vanishing gradient using a different approach. Instead of using shortcut connections, all the previous feature maps will become the input of the next layer. The preceding figure shows an example of a Dense interconnection in one Dense block.

For simplicity, in this figure, we'll only show four layers. Notice that the input to layer l is the concatenation of all previous feature maps. If we let BN-ReLU-Conv2D be represented by the operation $H(x)$, then the output of layer l is:

$$x_l = H (x_0, x_1, x_2, \ldots, x_{l-1}) \quad \text{(Equation 2.4.1)}$$

Conv2D uses a kernel of size 3. The number of feature maps generated per layer is called the growth rate, k. Normally, $k = 12$, but $k = 24$ is also used in the paper *Densely Connected Convolutional Networks* by Huang et al. (2017) [5]. Therefore, if the number of feature maps x_0 is k_0, then the total number of feature maps at the end of the 4-layer Dense block in *Figure 2.4.1* will be $4 \times k + k_0$.

DenseNet recommends that the Dense block is preceded by BN-ReLU-Conv2D, along with a number of feature maps that is twice the growth rate, $k_0 = 2 \times k$. At the end of the Dense block, the total number of feature maps will be $4 \times 12 + 2 \times 12 = 72$.

At the output layer, DenseNet suggests that we perform an average pooling before the Dense() with a softmax layer. If the data augmentation is not used, a dropout layer must follow the Dense block Conv2D.

As the network gets deeper, two new problems will occur. Firstly, since every layer contributes k feature maps, the number of inputs at layer l is $(l - 1) \times k + k_0$. The feature maps can grow rapidly within deep layers, slowing down the computation. For example, for a 101-layer network this will be $1200 + 24 = 1224$ for $k = 12$.

Secondly, similar to ResNet, as the network gets deeper the feature maps size will be reduced to increase the receptive field size of the kernel. If DenseNet uses concatenation in the merge operation, it must reconcile the differences in size.

To prevent the number of feature maps from increasing to the point of being computationally inefficient, DenseNet introduced the Bottleneck layer as shown in *Figure 2.4.2*. The idea is that after every concatenation, a 1 x 1 convolution with a filter size equal to $4k$ is now applied. This dimensionality reduction technique prevents the number of feature maps to be processed by Conv2D(3) from rapidly increasing.

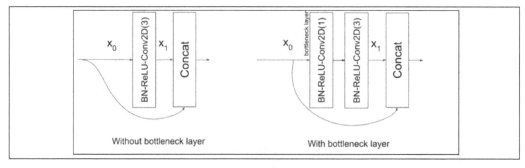

Figure 2.4.2: A layer in a Dense block of DenseNet, with and without the bottleneck layer BN-ReLU-Conv2D(1). We'll include the kernel size as an argument of Conv2D for clarity.

The Bottleneck layer then modifies the DenseNet layer as BN-ReLU-Conv2D(1) - BN- ReLU-Conv2D(3), instead of just BN-ReLU-Conv2D(3). We've included the kernel size as an argument of Conv2D for clarity. With the Bottleneck layer, every Conv2D(3) is processing just the $4k$ feature maps instead of $(l - 1) \times k + k_0$ for layer l. For example, for the 101-layer network, the input of the last Conv2D(3) is still 48 feature maps for $k = 12$ instead of 1224 as previously computed.

To solve the problem in feature maps size mismatch, DenseNet divides a deep network into multiple Dense blocks that are joined together by transition layers as shown in *Figure 2.4.3*. Within each Dense block, the feature map size (that is, width and height) will remain constant.

The role of the transition layer is to transition from one feature map size to a smaller feature map size between two `Dense` blocks. The reduction in size is usually half. This is accomplished by the average pooling layer. For example, an `AveragePooling2D` with default `pool_size=2` reduces the size from (64, 64, 256) to (32, 32, 256). The input to the transition layer is the output of the last concatenation layer in the previous Dense block.

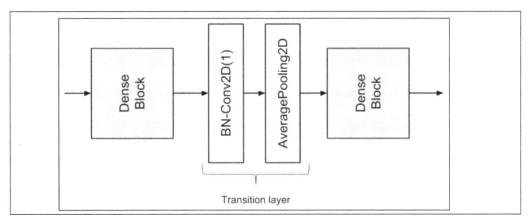

Figure 2.4.3: The transition layer in between two Dense blocks

However, before the feature maps are passed to average pooling, their number will be reduced by a certain compression factor, $0 < \theta < 1$, using `Conv2D(1)`. DenseNet uses $\theta = 0.5$ in their experiment. For example, if the output of the last concatenation of the previous `Dense` block is (64, 64, 512), then after `Conv2D(1)` the new dimensions of the feature maps will be (64, 64, 256). When compression and dimensionality reduction are put together, the transition layer is made of `BN-Conv2D(1)-AveragePooling2D` layers. In practice, batch normalization precedes the convolutional layer.

We have now covered the important concepts of DenseNet. Next, we'll build and validate a DenseNet-BC for the CIFAR10 dataset in `tf.keras`.

Building a 100-layer DenseNet-BC for CIFAR10

We're now going to build a **DenseNet-BC (Bottleneck-Compression)** with 100 layers for the CIFAR10 dataset, using the design principles that we discussed above.

Table 2.4.1 shows the model configuration, while *Figure 2.4.4* shows the model architecture. The listing shows us the partial Keras implementation of DenseNet-BC with 100 layers. We need to take note that we use `RMSprop` since it converges better than SGD or Adam when using DenseNet.

Layers	Output Size	DenseNet-100 BC
Convolution	32 x 32	$3 \times 3 \quad Conv2D$
Dense Block (1)	32 x 32	$\begin{Bmatrix} 1 \times 1 & Conv2D \\ 3 \times 3 & Conv2D \end{Bmatrix} \times 16$
Transition Layer (1)	32 x 32 16 x 16	$\begin{Bmatrix} 1 \times 1 & Conv2D \\ 2 \times 2 & AveragePooling2D \end{Bmatrix}$
Dense Block (2)	16 x 16	$\begin{Bmatrix} 1 \times 1 & Conv2D \\ 3 \times 3 & Conv2D \end{Bmatrix} \times 16$
Transition Layer (2)	16 x 16 8 x 8	$\begin{Bmatrix} 1 \times 1 & Conv2D \\ 2 \times 2 & AveragePooling2D \end{Bmatrix}$
Dense Block (3)	8 x 8	$\begin{Bmatrix} 1 \times 1 & Conv2D \\ 3 \times 3 & Conv2D \end{Bmatrix} \times 16$
Average Pooling	1 x 1	$8 \times 8 \quad AveragePooling2D$
Classification Layer		`Flatten-Dense(10)-softmax`

Table 2.4.1: DenseNet-BC with 100 layers for CIFAR10 classification

Moving from configuration to architecture:

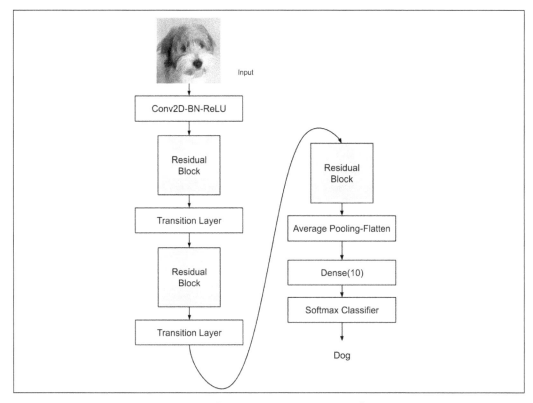

Figure 2.4.4: Model architecture of DenseNet-BC with 100 layers for CIFAR10 classification

Below in *Listing 2.4.1* is the partial Keras implementation of DenseNet-BC with 100 layers as shown in *Table 2.4.1*.

Listing 2.4.1: `densenet-cifar10-2.4.1.py`

```
# start model definition
# densenet CNNs (composite function) are made of BN-ReLU-Conv2D
inputs = Input(shape=input_shape)
x = BatchNormalization()(inputs)
x = Activation('relu')(x)
x = Conv2D(num_filters_bef_dense_block,
           kernel_size=3,
           padding='same',
           kernel_initializer='he_normal')(x)
x = concatenate([inputs, x])

# stack of dense blocks bridged by transition layers
for i in range(num_dense_blocks):
    # a dense block is a stack of bottleneck layers
    for j in range(num_bottleneck_layers):
        y = BatchNormalization()(x)
        y = Activation('relu')(y)
        y = Conv2D(4 * growth_rate,
                   kernel_size=1,
                   padding='same',
                   kernel_initializer='he_normal')(y)
        if not data_augmentation:
            y = Dropout(0.2)(y)
        y = BatchNormalization()(y)
        y = Activation('relu')(y)
        y = Conv2D(growth_rate,
                   kernel_size=3,
                   padding='same',
                   kernel_initializer='he_normal')(y)
        if not data_augmentation:
            y = Dropout(0.2)(y)
        x = concatenate([x, y])

    # no transition layer after the last dense block
    if i == num_dense_blocks - 1:
        continue
```

```
    # transition layer compresses num of feature maps and # reduces
the size by 2
    num_filters_bef_dense_block += num_bottleneck_layers * growth_rate
    num_filters_bef_dense_block = int(num_filters_bef_dense_block *
compression_factor)
    y = BatchNormalization()(x)
    y = Conv2D(num_filters_bef_dense_block,
               kernel_size=1,
               padding='same',
               kernel_initializer='he_normal')(y)
    if not data_augmentation:
        y = Dropout(0.2)(y)
    x = AveragePooling2D()(y)


# add classifier on top
# after average pooling, size of feature map is 1 x 1
x = AveragePooling2D(pool_size=8)(x)
y = Flatten()(x)
outputs = Dense(num_classes,
               kernel_initializer='he_normal',
               activation='softmax')(y)
# instantiate and compile model
# orig paper uses SGD but RMSprop works better for DenseNet
model = Model(inputs=inputs, outputs=outputs)
model.compile(loss='categorical_crossentropy',
             optimizer=RMSprop(1e-3),
             metrics=['accuracy'])
model.summary()
```

Training the `tf.keras` implementation of DenseNet for 200 epochs achieves a 93.74% accuracy vs. the 95.49% reported in the paper. Data augmentation is used. We used the same callback functions in ResNet v1/v2 for DenseNet.

For the deeper layers, the `growth_rate` and `depth` variables must be changed using the table on the Python code. However, it will take a substantial amount of time to train the network at a depth of 190 or 250 as done in the paper. To give us an idea of training time, each epoch runs for about an hour on a 1060Ti GPU. Similar to ResNet, Keras applications package has pre-trained models for DenseNet 121 and higher.

DenseNet completes our discussion on deep neural networks. Together with ResNet, the two networks have been indispensable as is or as feature extractor networks in many downstream tasks.

5. Conclusion

In this chapter, we've presented the Functional API as an advanced method for building complex deep neural network models using `tf.keras`. We also demonstrated how the Functional API could be used to build the multi-input-single-output Y-Network. This network, when compared to a single branch CNN network, achieves better accuracy. For the rest of the book, we'll find the Functional API indispensable in building more complex and advanced models. For example, in the next chapter, the Functional API will enable us to build a modular encoder, decoder, and autoencoder.

We also spent a significant amount of time exploring two important deep networks, ResNet and DenseNet. Both of these networks have been used not only in classification but also in other areas, such as segmentation, detection, tracking, generation, and visual semantic understanding. In *Chapter 11*, *Object Detection*, and *Chapter 12*, *Semantic Segmentation*, we will use ResNet for object detection and segmentation. We need to remember that it's more important that we understand the model design decisions in ResNet and DenseNet more closely than just following the original implementation. In that manner, we'll be able to use the key concepts of ResNet and DenseNet for our purposes.

6. References

1. Kaiming He et al. *Delving Deep into Rectifiers: Surpassing Human-Level Performance on ImageNet Classification*. Proceedings of the IEEE international conference on computer vision, 2015 (`https://www.cv-foundation.org/openaccess/content_iccv_2015/papers/He_Delving_Deep_into_ICCV_2015_paper.pdf?spm=5176.100239.blogcont55892.28.pm8zm1&file=He_Delving_Deep_into_ICCV_2015_paper.pdf`).

2. Kaiming He et al. *Deep Residual Learning for Image Recognition*. Proceedings of the IEEE conference on computer vision and pattern recognition, 2016a (`http://openaccess.thecvf.com/content_cvpr_2016/papers/He_Deep_Residual_Learning_CVPR_2016_paper.pdf`).

3. Karen Simonyan and Andrew Zisserman. *Very Deep Convolutional Networks for Large-Scale Image Recognition*. ICLR, 2015 (`https://arxiv.org/pdf/1409.1556/`).

4. Kaiming He et al. *Identity Mappings in Deep Residual Networks*. European Conference on Computer Vision. Springer International Publishing, 2016b (`https://arxiv.org/pdf/1603.05027.pdf`).

5. Gao Huang et al. *Densely Connected Convolutional Networks*. Proceedings of the IEEE conference on computer vision and pattern recognition, 2017 (`http://openaccess.thecvf.com/content_cvpr_2017/papers/Huang_Densely_Connected_Convolutional_CVPR_2017_paper.pdf`).

6. Saining Xie et al. *Aggregated Residual Transformations for Deep Neural Networks*. Computer Vision and Pattern Recognition (CVPR), 2017 IEEE Conference on. IEEE, 2017 (`http://openaccess.thecvf.com/content_cvpr_2017/papers/Xie_Aggregated_Residual_Transformations_CVPR_2017_paper.pdf`).

7. Zagoruyko, Sergey, and Nikos Komodakis. *"Wide residual networks."* arXiv preprint arXiv:1605.07146 (2016).

3

Autoencoders

In the previous chapter, *Chapter 2, Deep Neural Networks*, we introduced the concept of deep neural networks. We're now going to move on to look at autoencoders, which are a neural network architecture that attempts to find a compressed representation of the given input data.

Similar to the previous chapters, the input data may be in multiple forms, including speech, text, image, or video. An autoencoder will attempt to find a representation or piece of code in order to perform useful transformations on the input data. As an example, when denoising autoencoders, a neural network will attempt to find a code that can be used to transform noisy data into clean data. Noisy data could be in the form of an audio recording with static noise that is then converted into clear sound. Autoencoders will learn the code automatically from the data alone without human labeling. As such, autoencoders can be classified under **unsupervised** learning algorithms.

In later chapters of this book, we will look at **Generative Adversarial Networks (GANs)** and **Variational Autoencoders (VAEs)**, which are also representative forms of unsupervised learning algorithms. This is in contrast to the supervised learning algorithms that we discussed in the previous chapters, where human annotations were required.

In summary, this chapter presents:

- The principles of autoencoders
- How to implement autoencoders using `tf.keras`
- The practical applications of denoising and colorization autoencoders

Let's begin by getting into what an autoencoder is, and the principles of autoencoders.

1. Principles of autoencoders

In its simplest form, an autoencoder will learn the representation or code by trying to copy the input to output. However, using an autoencoder is not as simple as copying the input to output. Otherwise, the neural network would not be able to uncover the hidden structure in the input distribution.

An autoencoder will encode the input distribution into a low-dimensional tensor, which usually takes the form of a vector. This will approximate the hidden structure that is commonly referred to as the latent representation, code, or vector. This process constitutes the encoding part. The latent vector will then be decoded by the decoder part to recover the original input.

As a result of the latent vector being a low-dimensional compressed representation of the input distribution, it should be expected that the output recovered by the decoder can only approximate the input. The dissimilarity between the input and the output can be measured by a loss function.

But why would we use autoencoders? Simply put, autoencoders have practical applications both in their original form or as part of more complex neural networks.

They're a key tool in understanding the advanced topics of deep learning as they give us a low-dimensional representation of data that is suitable for density estimation. Furthermore, it can be efficiently processed to perform structural operations on the input data. Common operations include denoising, colorization, feature-level arithmetic, detection, tracking, and segmentation, to name just a few.

In this section, we're going to go over the principles of autoencoders. We're going to look at autoencoders with the MNIST dataset, which was introduced in the previous chapters.

Firstly, we need to be made aware that an autoencoder has two operators, these being:

- **Encoder**: This transforms the input, x, into a low-dimensional latent vector, $z = f(x)$. Since the latent vector is of low dimension, the encoder is forced to learn only the most important features of the input data. For example, in the case of MNIST digits, the important features to learn may include writing style, tilt angle, roundness of stroke, thickness, and so on. Essentially, these are the most important bits of information needed to represent the digits zero to nine.

- **Decoder**: This tries to recover the input from the latent vector, $g(z) = \tilde{x}$.

Although the latent vector has a low dimension, it has a sufficient size to allow the decoder to recover the input data.

The goal of the decoder is to make $\tilde{x}$ as close as possible to x. Generally, both the encoder and decoder are non-linear functions. The dimension of z is a measure of the number of salient features it can represent. The dimension is usually much smaller than the input dimensions for efficiency and in order to constrain the latent code to learn only the most salient properties of the input distribution [1].

An autoencoder has the tendency to memorize the input when the dimension of the latent code is significantly bigger than x.

A suitable loss function, $\mathcal{L}(x,\tilde{x})$, is a measure of how dissimilar the input, x, is from the output, which is the recovered input, $\tilde{x}$. As shown in the following equation, the mean squared error (MSE) is an example of such a loss function:

$$\mathcal{L}(x,\tilde{x}) = MSE = \frac{1}{m}\sum_{i=1}^{i=m}\left(x_i - \tilde{x}_i\right)^2 \qquad \text{(Equation 3.1.1)}$$

In this example, m is the output dimension (for example, in MNIST $m = width \times height \times channels = 28 \times 28 \times 1 = 784$). x_i and $\tilde{x}_i$ are the elements of x and $\tilde{x}$, respectively. Since the loss function is a measure of dissimilarity between the input and output, we're able to use alternative reconstruction loss functions such as binary cross entropy or the structural similarity index (SSIM).

Similar to other neural networks, an autoencoder tries to make this error or loss function as small as possible during training. *Figure 3.1.1* shows an autoencoder. The encoder is a function that compresses the input, x, into a low-dimensional latent vector, z. This latent vector represents the important features of the input distribution. The decoder then tries to recover the original input from the latent vector in the form of $\tilde{x}$.

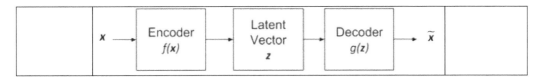

Figure 3.1.1: Block diagram of an autoencoder

To put the autoencoder into context, x can be an MNIST digit that has a dimension of $28 \times 28 \times 1 = 784$. The encoder transforms the input into a low-dimensional z that can be a 16-dimension latent vector. The decoder will attempt to recover the input in the form of $\tilde{x}$ from z.

Visually, every MNIST digit **x** appears similar to $\tilde{x}$. *Figure 3.1.2* demonstrates this autoencoding process to us.

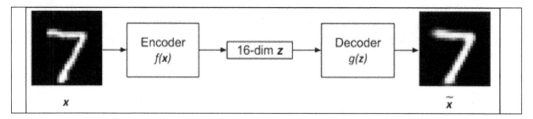

Figure 3.1.2: An autoencoder with MNIST digit input and output. The latent vector is 16-dim

We can observe that the decoded digit 7, while not exactly the same, remains close enough.

Since both the encoder and decoder are non-linear functions, we can use neural networks to implement both. For example, in the MNIST dataset, the autoencoder can be implemented by MLP or CNN. The autoencoder can be trained by minimizing the loss function through backpropagation. Similar to other neural networks, a requirement of backpropagation is that the loss function must be differentiable.

If we treat the input as a distribution, we can interpret the encoder as an encoder of distribution, $p(z \mid x)$, and the decoder as the decoder of distribution, $p(x \mid z)$. The loss function of the autoencoder is expressed as follows:

$$\mathcal{L} = -\log p(x|z) \quad \text{(Equation 3.1.2)}$$

The loss function simply means that we would like to maximize the chances of recovering the input distribution given the latent vector distribution. If the decoder output distribution is assumed to be Gaussian, then the loss function boils down to MSE since:

$$\mathcal{L} = -\log p(x|z) = -\log \prod_{i=1}^{m} \mathcal{N}(x_i; \tilde{x}_i, \sigma^2) = -\sum_{i=1}^{m} \log \mathcal{N}(x_i; \tilde{x}_i, \sigma^2) \propto \sum_{i=1}^{m} (x_i - \tilde{x}_i)^2$$

(Equation 3.1.3)

In this example, $\mathcal{N}(x_i; \tilde{x}_i, \sigma^2)$ represents a Gaussian distribution with a mean of $\tilde{x}_i$ and a variance of σ^2. A constant variance is assumed. The decoder output, $\tilde{x}_i$, is assumed to be independent. m is the output dimension.

Understanding the principles behind autoencoders will help us in the code implementation. In the next section, we will take a look at how to use the `tf.keras` functional API to build the encoder, decoder, and autoencoder.

2. Building an autoencoder using Keras

We're now going to move onto something really exciting, building an autoencoder using the `tf.keras` library. For simplicity, we'll be using the MNIST dataset for the first set of examples. The autoencoder will then generate a latent vector from the input data and recover the input using the decoder. The latent vector in this first example is 16-dim.

Firstly, we're going to implement the autoencoder by building the encoder.

Listing 3.2.1 shows the encoder that compresses the MNIST digit into a 16-dim latent vector. The encoder is a stack of two `Conv2D`. The final stage is a `Dense` layer with 16 units to generate the latent vector.

Listing 3.2.1: `autoencoder-mnist-3.2.1.py`

```
from tensorflow.keras.layers import Dense, Input
from tensorflow.keras.layers import Conv2D, Flatten
from tensorflow.keras.layers import Reshape, Conv2DTranspose
from tensorflow.keras.models import Model
from tensorflow.keras.datasets import mnist
from tensorflow.keras.utils import plot_model
from tensorflow.keras import backend as K

import numpy as np
import matplotlib.pyplot as plt

# load MNIST dataset
(x_train, _), (x_test, _) = mnist.load_data()

# reshape to (28, 28, 1) and normalize input images
image_size = x_train.shape[1]
x_train = np.reshape(x_train, [-1, image_size, image_size, 1])
x_test = np.reshape(x_test, [-1, image_size, image_size, 1])
x_train = x_train.astype('float32') / 255
x_test = x_test.astype('float32') / 255

# network parameters
input_shape = (image_size, image_size, 1)
batch_size = 32
kernel_size = 3
latent_dim = 16
# encoder/decoder number of CNN layers and filters per layer
layer_filters = [32, 64]
```

```
# build the autoencoder model
# first build the encoder model
inputs = Input(shape=input_shape, name='encoder_input')
x = inputs
# stack of Conv2D(32)-Conv2D(64)
for filters in layer_filters:
    x = Conv2D(filters=filters,
               kernel_size=kernel_size,
               activation='relu',
               strides=2,
               padding='same')(x)

# shape info needed to build decoder model
# so we don't do hand computation
# the input to the decoder's first
# Conv2DTranspose will have this shape
# shape is (7, 7, 64) which is processed by
# the decoder back to (28, 28, 1)
shape = K.int_shape(x)

# generate latent vector
x = Flatten()(x)
latent = Dense(latent_dim, name='latent_vector')(x)

# instantiate encoder model
encoder = Model(inputs,
                latent,
                name='encoder')
encoder.summary()
plot_model(encoder,
           to_file='encoder.png',
           show_shapes=True)

# build the decoder model
latent_inputs = Input(shape=(latent_dim,), name='decoder_input')
# use the shape (7, 7, 64) that was earlier saved
x = Dense(shape[1] * shape[2] * shape[3])(latent_inputs)
# from vector to suitable shape for transposed conv
x = Reshape((shape[1], shape[2], shape[3]))(x)

# stack of Conv2DTranspose(64)-Conv2DTranspose(32)
for filters in layer_filters[::-1]:
    x = Conv2DTranspose(filters=filters,
                        kernel_size=kernel_size,
```

```
                         activation='relu',
                         strides=2,
                         padding='same')(x)


# reconstruct the input
outputs = Conv2DTranspose(filters=1,
                          kernel_size=kernel_size,
                          activation='sigmoid',
                          padding='same',
                          name='decoder_output')(x)


# instantiate decoder model
decoder = Model(latent_inputs, outputs, name='decoder')
decoder.summary()
plot_model(decoder, to_file='decoder.png', show_shapes=True)


# autoencoder = encoder + decoder
# instantiate autoencoder model
autoencoder = Model(inputs,
                    decoder(encoder(inputs)),
                    name='autoencoder')
autoencoder.summary()
plot_model(autoencoder,
           to_file='autoencoder.png',
           show_shapes=True)


# Mean Square Error (MSE) loss function, Adam optimizer
autoencoder.compile(loss='mse', optimizer='adam')


# train the autoencoder
autoencoder.fit(x_train,
                x_train,
                validation_data=(x_test, x_test),
                epochs=1,
                batch_size=batch_size)


# predict the autoencoder output from test data
x_decoded = autoencoder.predict(x_test)


# display the 1st 8 test input and decoded images
imgs = np.concatenate([x_test[:8], x_decoded[:8]])
imgs = imgs.reshape((4, 4, image_size, image_size))
imgs = np.vstack([np.hstack(i) for i in imgs])
plt.figure()
```

```
plt.axis('off')
plt.title('Input: 1st 2 rows, Decoded: last 2 rows')
plt.imshow(imgs, interpolation='none', cmap='gray')
plt.savefig('input_and_decoded.png')
plt.show()
```

Figure 3.2.1 shows the architecture model diagram generated by `plot_model()`, which is the same as the text version produced by `encoder.summary()`. The shape of the output of the last `Conv2D` is saved to compute the dimensions of the decoder input layer for easy reconstruction of the MNIST image: `shape = K.int_shape(x)`.

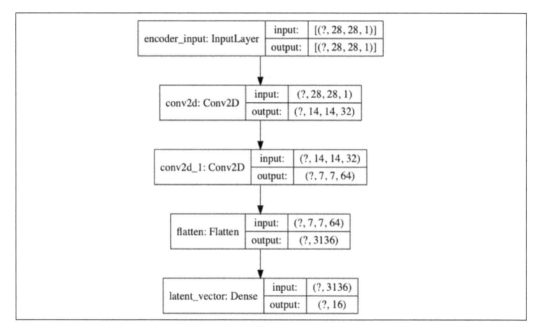

Figure 3.2.1: The encoder model is made up of Conv2D(32)-Conv2D(64)-Dense(16) in order to generate the low-dimensional latent vector

The decoder in *Listing 3.2.1* decompresses the latent vector in order to recover the MNIST digit. The decoder input stage is a `Dense` layer that will accept the latent vector. The number of units is equal to the product of the saved `Conv2D` output dimensions from the encoder. This is done so that we can easily resize the output of the `Dense` layer for `Conv2DTranspose` to finally recover the original MNIST image dimensions.

The decoder is made of a stack of three `Conv2DTranspose`. In our case, we're going to use a **Transposed CNN** (sometimes called **deconvolution**), which is more commonly used in decoders. We can imagine transposed CNN (`Conv2DTranspose`) as the reversed process of CNN.

In a simple example, if the CNN converts an image into feature maps, the transposed CNN will produce an image given feature maps. *Figure 3.2.2* shows the decoder model:

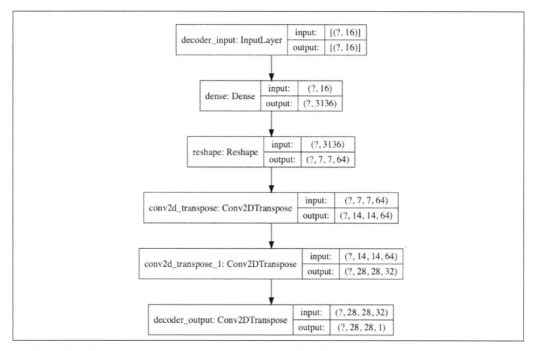

Figure 3.2.2: The decoder model is made up of Dense(16)-Conv2DTranspose(64)-Conv2DTranspose(32)-Conv2DTranspose(1). The input is the latent vector decoded to recover the original input

By joining the encoder and decoder together, we're able to build the autoencoder. *Figure 3.2.3* illustrates the model diagram of the autoencoder:

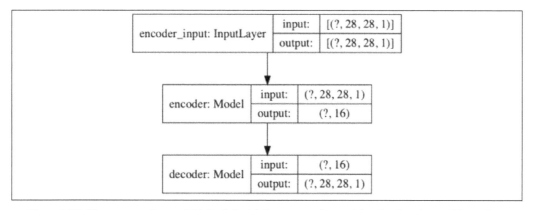

Figure 3.2.3: The autoencoder model is built by joining an encoder model and a decoder model together. There are 178 k parameters for this autoencoder

The tensor output of the encoder is also the input to a decoder that generates the output of the autoencoder. In this example, we'll be using the MSE loss function and Adam optimizer. During training, the input is the same as the output, x_train. We should note that in our example, there are only a few layers that are sufficient to drive the validation loss to 0.01 in one epoch. For more complex datasets, we may need a deeper encoder and decoder, as well as more epochs of training.

After training the autoencoder for one epoch with a validation loss of 0.01, we're able to verify if it can encode and decode the MNIST data that it has not seen before. *Figure 3.2.4* shows us eight samples from the test data and the corresponding decoded images:

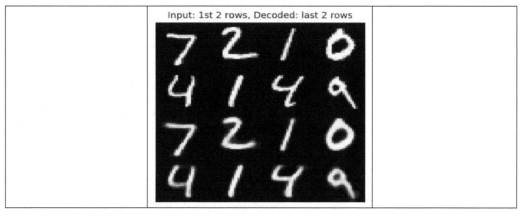

Figure 3.2.4: Prediction of the autoencoder from the test data. The first two rows are the original input test data. The last two rows are the predicted data

Except for minor blurring in the images, we're able to easily recognize that the autoencoder is able to recover the input with good quality. The results will improve as we train for a larger number of epochs.

At this point, we may be wondering: how can we visualize the latent vector in space? A simple method for visualization is to force the autoencoder to learn the MNIST digits features using a 2-dim latent vector. From there, we're able to project this latent vector on a two dimensional space in order to see how the MNIST latent vectors are distributed. *Figure 3.2.5* and *Figure 3.2.6* show the distribution of MNIST digits as a function of latent code dimensions.

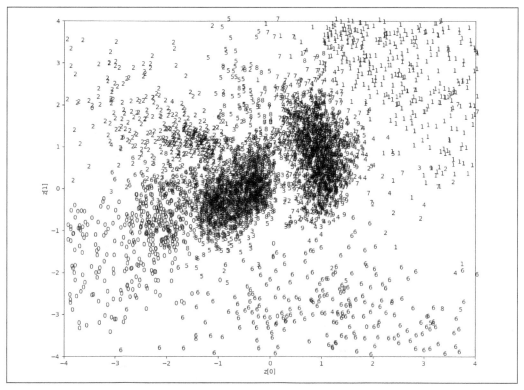

Figure 3.2.5: A MNIST digit distribution as a function of latent code dimensions, z[0] and z[1].
The original photo can be found in this book's GitHub repository at, https://github.com/PacktPublishing/
Advanced-Deep-Learning-with-Keras/blob/master/chapter3-autoencoders/README.md

In *Figure 3.2.5*, we can see that the latent vectors for a specific digit are clustering on a region in space. For example, digit 0 is in the lower left quadrant, while digit 1 is in the upper right quadrant. Such clustering is mirrored in the figure. In fact, the same figure shows the result of navigating or generating new digits from the latent space, as shown in *Figure 3.2.5*.

For example, starting from the center and varying the value of a 2-dim latent vector toward the upper right quadrant, this shows us that the digit changes from 9 to 1. This is expected since, from *Figure 3.2.5*, we're able to see that the latent code values for the digit 9 clusters are near the center, and digit 1 code values cluster in the upper right quadrant.

For *Figure 3.2.5* and *Figure 3.2.6*, we've only explored the regions between -4.0 and +4.0 for each latent vector dimension:

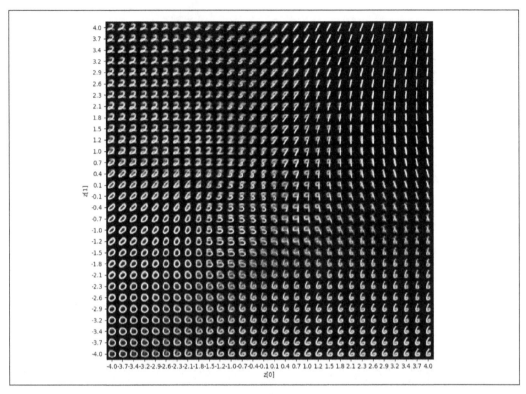

Figure 3.2.6: Digits generated as the 2-dim latent vector space is navigated

As can be seen in *Figure 3.2.5*, the latent code distribution is not continuous. Ideally, it should look like a circle where there are valid values everywhere. Because of this discontinuity, there are regions where, if we decode the latent vector, hardly any recognizable digits will be produced.

Figure 3.2.5 and *Figure 3.2.6* were generated after 20 epochs of training. The `autoencoder-mnist-3.2.1.py` code was modified by setting `latent_dim = 2`. The `plot_ results()` function plots the MNIST digit as a function of the 2-dim latent vector. For convenience, the program is saved as `autoencoder-2dim-mnist-3.2.2.py` with the partial code shown in *Listing 3.2.2*. The rest of the code is practically similar to *Listing 3.2.1* and no longer shown here.

Listing 3.2.2: `autoencoder-2dim-mnist-3.2.2.py`

```
def plot_results(models,
                 data,
                 batch_size=32,
```

```
                    model_name="autoencoder_2dim"):
    """Plots 2-dim latent values as scatter plot of digits
        then, plot MNIST digits as function of 2-dim latent vector

    Arguments:
        models (list): encoder and decoder models
        data (list): test data and label
        batch_size (int): prediction batch size
        model_name (string): which model is using this function
    """

    encoder, decoder = models
    x_test, y_test = data
    xmin = ymin = -4
    xmax = ymax = +4
    os.makedirs(model_name, exist_ok=True)

    filename = os.path.join(model_name, "latent_2dim.png")
    # display a 2D plot of the digit classes in the latent space
    z = encoder.predict(x_test,
                        batch_size=batch_size)
    plt.figure(figsize=(12, 10))

    # axes x and y ranges
    axes = plt.gca()
    axes.set_xlim([xmin,xmax])
    axes.set_ylim([ymin,ymax])

    # subsample to reduce density of points on the plot
    z = z[0::2]
    y_test = y_test[0::2]
    plt.scatter(z[:, 0], z[:, 1], marker="")
    for i, digit in enumerate(y_test):
        axes.annotate(digit, (z[i, 0], z[i, 1]))
    plt.xlabel("z[0]")
    plt.ylabel("z[1]")
    plt.savefig(filename)
    plt.show()

    filename = os.path.join(model_name, "digits_over_latent.png")
    # display a 30x30 2D manifold of the digits
    n = 30
    digit_size = 28
    figure = np.zeros((digit_size * n, digit_size * n))
```

```
# linearly spaced coordinates corresponding to the 2D plot
# of digit classes in the latent space
grid_x = np.linspace(xmin, xmax, n)
grid_y = np.linspace(ymin, ymax, n)[::-1]

for i, yi in enumerate(grid_y):
    for j, xi in enumerate(grid_x):
        z = np.array([[xi, yi]])
        x_decoded = decoder.predict(z)
        digit = x_decoded[0].reshape(digit_size, digit_size)
        figure[i * digit_size: (i + 1) * digit_size,
               j * digit_size: (j + 1) * digit_size] = digit

plt.figure(figsize=(10, 10))
start_range = digit_size // 2
end_range = n * digit_size + start_range + 1
pixel_range = np.arange(start_range, end_range, digit_size)
sample_range_x = np.round(grid_x, 1)
sample_range_y = np.round(grid_y, 1)
plt.xticks(pixel_range, sample_range_x)
plt.yticks(pixel_range, sample_range_y)
plt.xlabel("z[0]")
plt.ylabel("z[1]")
plt.imshow(figure, cmap='Greys_r')
plt.savefig(filename)
plt.show()
```

This completes the implementation and examination of autoencoders. The upcoming chapters focus on their practical applications. We will start with denoising autoencoders.

3. Denoising autoencoders (DAEs)

We're now going to build an autoencoder with a practical application. Firstly, let's paint a picture and imagine that the MNIST digit images were corrupted by noise, thus making it harder for humans to read. We're able to build a denoising autoencoder (DAE) to remove the noise from these images. *Figure 3.3.1* shows us three sets of MNIST digits. The top rows of each set (for example, MNIST digits 7, 2, 1, 9, 0, 6, 3, 4, and 9) are the original images. The middle rows show the inputs to the DAE, which are the original images corrupted by noise. As humans, we can find that it is difficult to read the corrupted MNIST digits. The last rows show the outputs of the DAE.

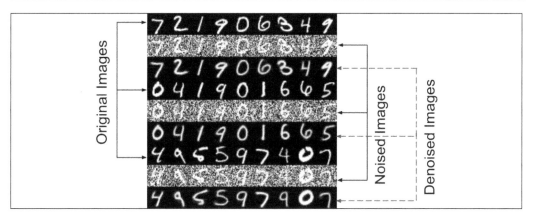

Figure 3.3.1: Original MNIST digits (top rows), corrupted original images (middle rows),
and denoised images (last rows)

As shown in *Figure 3.3.2*, the denoising autoencoder has practically the same
structure as the autoencoder for MNIST that we presented in the previous section.

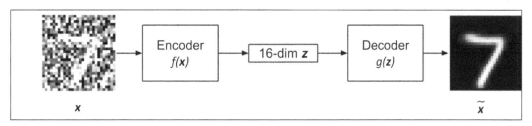

Figure 3.3.2: The input to the denoising autoencoder is the corrupted image.
The output is the clean or denoised image. The latent vector is assumed to be 16-dim

The input in *Figure 3.3.2* is defined as:

$$\mathbf{x} = \mathbf{x}_{orig} + noise \quad \text{(Equation 3.3.1)}$$

In this formula, $\mathbf{x}_{orig}$ represents the original MNIST image corrupted by *noise*. The
objective of the encoder is to discover how to produce the latent vector, $\mathbf{z}$, which will
enable the decoder to recover such as MSE, as shown through: $\mathbf{x}_{orig}$ by minimizing the
dissimilarity loss function:

$$\mathcal{L}\left(\boldsymbol{x}_{orig}, \widetilde{\boldsymbol{x}}\right) = MSE = \frac{1}{m}\sum_{i=1}^{i=m}\left(x_{orig_i} - \widetilde{x}_i\right)^2 \quad \text{(Equation 3.3.2)}$$

In this example, m is the output dimension (for example, in MNIST, m = *width* ×
height × *channels* = 28 × 28 × 1 = 784). x_{orig_i} and $\widetilde{x}_i$ are the elements of $\mathbf{x}_{orig}$ and $\widetilde{\boldsymbol{x}}$,
respectively.

To implement theDAE, we're going to need to make a few changes to the autoencoder presented in the previous section. Firstly, the training input data should be corrupted MNIST digits. The training output data is the same original clean MNIST digits. This is like telling the autoencoder what the corrected images should be or asking it to figure out how to remove noise given a corrupted image. Lastly, we must validate the autoencoder on the corrupted MNIST test data.

The MNIST digit 7 shown on the left of *Figure 3.3.2* is an actual corrupted image input. The one on the right is the clean image output of a trained denoising autoencoder.

Listing 3.3.1: `denoising-autoencoder-mnist-3.3.1.py`

```
from tensorflow.keras.layers import Dense, Input
from tensorflow.keras.layers import Conv2D, Flatten
from tensorflow.keras.layers import Reshape, Conv2DTranspose
from tensorflow.keras.models import Model
from tensorflow.keras import backend as K
from tensorflow.keras.datasets import mnist
import numpy as np
import matplotlib.pyplot as plt
from PIL import Image


np.random.seed(1337)

# load MNIST dataset
(x_train, _), (x_test, _) = mnist.load_data()

# reshape to (28, 28, 1) and normalize input images
image_size = x_train.shape[1]
x_train = np.reshape(x_train, [-1, image_size, image_size, 1])
x_test = np.reshape(x_test, [-1, image_size, image_size, 1])
x_train = x_train.astype('float32') / 255
x_test = x_test.astype('float32') / 255

# generate corrupted MNIST images by adding noise with normal dist
# centered at 0.5 and std=0.5
noise = np.random.normal(loc=0.5, scale=0.5, size=x_train.shape)
x_train_noisy = x_train + noise
noise = np.random.normal(loc=0.5, scale=0.5, size=x_test.shape)
x_test_noisy = x_test + noise

# adding noise may exceed normalized pixel values>1.0 or <0.0
# clip pixel values >1.0 to 1.0 and <0.0 to 0.0
x_train_noisy = np.clip(x_train_noisy, 0., 1.)
x_test_noisy = np.clip(x_test_noisy, 0., 1.)
```

```
# network parameters
input_shape = (image_size, image_size, 1)
batch_size = 32
kernel_size = 3
latent_dim = 16
# encoder/decoder number of CNN layers and filters per layer
layer_filters = [32, 64]

# build the autoencoder model
# first build the encoder model
inputs = Input(shape=input_shape, name='encoder_input')
x = inputs

# stack of Conv2D(32)-Conv2D(64)
for filters in layer_filters:
    x = Conv2D(filters=filters,
               kernel_size=kernel_size,
               strides=2,
               activation='relu',
               padding='same')(x)

# shape info needed to build decoder model so we don't do hand
computation
# the input to the decoder's first Conv2DTranspose will have this
shape
# shape is (7, 7, 64) which can be processed by the decoder back to
(28, 28, 1)
shape = K.int_shape(x)

# generate the latent vector
x = Flatten()(x)
latent = Dense(latent_dim, name='latent_vector')(x)

# instantiate encoder model
encoder = Model(inputs, latent, name='encoder')
encoder.summary()

# build the decoder model
latent_inputs = Input(shape=(latent_dim,), name='decoder_input')
# use the shape (7, 7, 64) that was earlier saved
x = Dense(shape[1] * shape[2] * shape[3])(latent_inputs)
# from vector to suitable shape for transposed conv
x = Reshape((shape[1], shape[2], shape[3]))(x)

# stack of Conv2DTranspose(64)-Conv2DTranspose(32)
for filters in layer_filters[::-1]:
    x = Conv2DTranspose(filters=filters,
```

```
                          kernel_size=kernel_size,
                          strides=2,
                          activation='relu',
                          padding='same')(x)

# reconstruct the denoised input
outputs = Conv2DTranspose(filters=1,
                          kernel_size=kernel_size,
                          padding='same',
                          activation='sigmoid',
                          name='decoder_output')(x)

# instantiate decoder model
decoder = Model(latent_inputs, outputs, name='decoder')
decoder.summary()

# autoencoder = encoder + decoder
# instantiate autoencoder model
autoencoder = Model(inputs, decoder(encoder(inputs)),
name='autoencoder')
autoencoder.summary()

# Mean Square Error (MSE) loss function, Adam optimizer
autoencoder.compile(loss='mse', optimizer='adam')

# train the autoencoder
autoencoder.fit(x_train_noisy,
                x_train,
                validation_data=(x_test_noisy, x_test),
                epochs=10,
                batch_size=batch_size)

# predict the autoencoder output from corrupted test images
x_decoded = autoencoder.predict(x_test_noisy)

# 3 sets of images with 9 MNIST digits
# 1st rows - original images
# 2nd rows - images corrupted by noise
# 3rd rows - denoised images
rows, cols = 3, 9
num = rows * cols
imgs = np.concatenate([x_test[:num], x_test_noisy[:num], x_
decoded[:num]])
imgs = imgs.reshape((rows * 3, cols, image_size, image_size))
imgs = np.vstack(np.split(imgs, rows, axis=1))
imgs = imgs.reshape((rows * 3, -1, image_size, image_size))
imgs = np.vstack([np.hstack(i) for i in imgs])
```

```
imgs = (imgs * 255).astype(np.uint8)
plt.figure()
plt.axis('off')
plt.title('Original images: top rows, '
          'Corrupted Input: middle rows, '
          'Denoised Input:  third rows')
plt.imshow(imgs, interpolation='none', cmap='gray')
Image.fromarray(imgs).save('corrupted_and_denoised.png')
plt.show()
```

Listing 3.3.1 shows the denoising autoencoder, which has been contributed to the official Keras GitHub repository. Using the same MNIST dataset, we're able to simulate corrupted images by adding random noise. The noise added is a Gaussian distribution with a mean of $\mu = 0.5$ and a standard deviation of $\sigma = 0.5$. Since adding random noise may push the pixel data into invalid values of less than 0 or greater than 1, the pixel values are clipped to the [0.1, 1.0] range.

Everything else will remain practically the same as the autoencoder from the previous section. We'll use the same MSE loss function and Adam optimizer. However, the number of epochs for training has increased to 10. This is to allow sufficient parameter optimization.

Figure 3.3.3 shows a certain level of robustness of the DAE as the level of noise is increased from $\sigma = 0.5$ to $\sigma = 0.75$ and $\sigma = 1.0$. At $\sigma = 0.75$, the DAE is still able to recover the original images. However, at $\sigma = 1.0$, a few digits, such as 4 and 5 in the second and third sets, can no longer be recovered correctly.

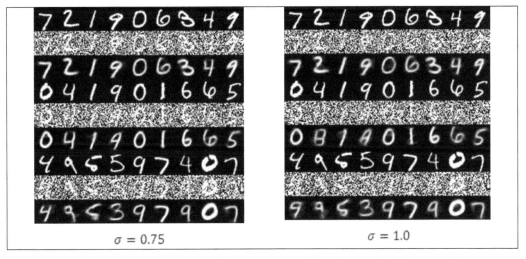

Figure 3.3.3: Performance of the denoising autoencoder as the noise level is increased

We have completed the discussion and implementation of denoising autoencoders. Although the concept was demonstrated on MNIST digits, the idea is applicable to other signals as well. In the next section, we will cover another practical application of autoencoders called the colorization autoencoder.

4. Automatic colorization autoencoder

We're now going to work on another practical application of autoencoders. In this case, we're going to imagine that we have a grayscale photo and that we want to build a tool that will automatically add color to it. We would like to replicate the human abilities in identifying that the sea and sky are blue, the grass field and trees are green, while the clouds are white, and so on.

As shown in *Figure 3.4.1*, if we are given a grayscale photo (left) of a rice field in the foreground, a volcano in the background, and sky on the top, we're able to add the appropriate colors (right).

Figure 3.4.1: Adding color to a grayscale photo of the Mayon Volcano. A colorization network should replicate human abilities by adding color to a grayscale photo. The left photo is grayscale. The right photo is color. The original color photo can be found in this book's GitHub repository at, https://github.com/PacktPublishing/Advanced-Deep-Learning-with-Keras/blob/master/chapter3-autoencoders/README.md

A simple automatic colorization algorithm seems like a suitable problem for autoencoders. If we can train the autoencoder with a sufficient number of grayscale photos as input and the corresponding colored photos as output, it could possibly discover the hidden structure on properly applying colors. Roughly, it is the reverse process of denoising. The question is, can an autoencoder add color (good noise) to the original grayscale image?

Listing 3.4.1 shows the colorization autoencoder network. The colorization autoencoder network is a modified version of the denoising autoencoder that we used for the MNIST dataset. Firstly, we need a dataset of grayscale to colored photos. The CIFAR10 database, which we have used before, has 50,000 training and 10,000 testing 32 × 32 RGB photos that can be converted to grayscale. As shown in the following listing, we're able to use the `rgb2gray()` function to apply weights on R, G, and B components to convert from color to grayscale:

Listing 3.4.1: `colorization-autoencoder-cifar10-3.4.1.py`

```
from tensorflow.keras.layers import Dense, Input
from tensorflow.keras.layers import Conv2D, Flatten
from tensorflow.keras.layers import Reshape, Conv2DTranspose
from tensorflow.keras.models import Model
from tensorflow.keras.callbacks import ReduceLROnPlateau
from tensorflow.keras.callbacks import ModelCheckpoint
from tensorflow.keras.datasets import cifar10
from tensorflow.keras.utils import plot_model
from tensorflow.keras import backend as K

import numpy as np
import matplotlib.pyplot as plt
import os

def rgb2gray(rgb):
    """Convert from color image (RGB) to grayscale.
       Source: opencv.org
       grayscale = 0.299*red + 0.587*green + 0.114*blue
    Argument:
        rgb (tensor): rgb image
    Return:
        (tensor): grayscale image
    """
    return np.dot(rgb[...,:3], [0.299, 0.587, 0.114])


# load the CIFAR10 data
(x_train, _), (x_test, _) = cifar10.load_data()

# input image dimensions
# we assume data format "channels_last"
img_rows = x_train.shape[1]
img_cols = x_train.shape[2]
channels = x_train.shape[3]
```

```
# create saved_images folder
imgs_dir = 'saved_images'
save_dir = os.path.join(os.getcwd(), imgs_dir)
if not os.path.isdir(save_dir):
        os.makedirs(save_dir)

# display the 1st 100 input images (color and gray)
imgs = x_test[:100]
imgs = imgs.reshape((10, 10, img_rows, img_cols, channels))
imgs = np.vstack([np.hstack(i) for i in imgs])
plt.figure()
plt.axis('off')
plt.title('Test color images (Ground  Truth)')
plt.imshow(imgs, interpolation='none')
plt.savefig('%s/test_color.png' % imgs_dir)
plt.show()

# convert color train and test images to gray
x_train_gray = rgb2gray(x_train)
x_test_gray = rgb2gray(x_test)

# display grayscale version of test images
imgs = x_test_gray[:100]
imgs = imgs.reshape((10, 10, img_rows, img_cols))
imgs = np.vstack([np.hstack(i) for i in imgs])
plt.figure()
plt.axis('off')
plt.title('Test gray images (Input)')
plt.imshow(imgs, interpolation='none', cmap='gray')
plt.savefig('%s/test_gray.png' % imgs_dir)
plt.show()


# normalize output train and test color images
x_train = x_train.astype('float32') / 255
x_test = x_test.astype('float32') / 255

# normalize input train and test grayscale images
x_train_gray = x_train_gray.astype('float32') / 255
x_test_gray = x_test_gray.astype('float32') / 255

# reshape images to row x col x channel for CNN output/validation
x_train = x_train.reshape(x_train.shape[0], img_rows, img_cols,
```

```
channels)
x_test = x_test.reshape(x_test.shape[0], img_rows, img_cols, channels)

# reshape images to row x col x channel for CNN input
x_train_gray = x_train_gray.reshape(x_train_gray.shape[0], img_rows,
img_cols, 1)
x_test_gray = x_test_gray.reshape(x_test_gray.shape[0], img_rows, img_
cols, 1)

# network parameters
input_shape = (img_rows, img_cols, 1)
batch_size = 32
kernel_size = 3
latent_dim = 256
# encoder/decoder number of CNN layers and filters per layer
layer_filters = [64, 128, 256]

# build the autoencoder model
# first build the encoder model
inputs = Input(shape=input_shape, name='encoder_input')
x = inputs
# stack of Conv2D(64)-Conv2D(128)-Conv2D(256)
for filters in layer_filters:
    x = Conv2D(filters=filters,
               kernel_size=kernel_size,
               strides=2,
               activation='relu',
               padding='same')(x)

# shape info needed to build decoder model so we don't do hand
computation
# the input to the decoder's first Conv2DTranspose will have this
shape
# shape is (4, 4, 256) which is processed by the decoder back to (32,
32, 3)
shape = K.int_shape(x)

# generate a latent vector
x = Flatten()(x)
latent = Dense(latent_dim, name='latent_vector')(x)

# instantiate encoder model
encoder = Model(inputs, latent, name='encoder')
encoder.summary()
```

```
# build the decoder model
latent_inputs = Input(shape=(latent_dim,), name='decoder_input')
x = Dense(shape[1]*shape[2]*shape[3])(latent_inputs)
x = Reshape((shape[1], shape[2], shape[3]))(x)

# stack of Conv2DTranspose(256)-Conv2DTranspose(128)-
Conv2DTranspose(64)
for filters in layer_filters[::-1]:
    x = Conv2DTranspose(filters=filters,
                        kernel_size=kernel_size,
                        strides=2,
                        activation='relu',
                        padding='same')(x)

outputs = Conv2DTranspose(filters=channels,
                          kernel_size=kernel_size,
                          activation='sigmoid',
                          padding='same',
                          name='decoder_output')(x)

# instantiate decoder model
decoder = Model(latent_inputs, outputs, name='decoder')
decoder.summary()

# autoencoder = encoder + decoder
# instantiate autoencoder model
autoencoder = Model(inputs, decoder(encoder(inputs)),
name='autoencoder')
autoencoder.summary()

# prepare model saving directory.
save_dir = os.path.join(os.getcwd(), 'saved_models')
model_name = 'colorized_ae_model.{epoch:03d}.h5'
if not os.path.isdir(save_dir):
        os.makedirs(save_dir)
filepath = os.path.join(save_dir, model_name)

# reduce learning rate by sqrt(0.1) if the loss does not improve in 5
epochs
lr_reducer = ReduceLROnPlateau(factor=np.sqrt(0.1),
                               cooldown=0,
                               patience=5,
                               verbose=1,
                               min_lr=0.5e-6)
```

```
# save weights for future use (e.g. reload parameters w/o training)
checkpoint = ModelCheckpoint(filepath=filepath,
                             monitor='val_loss',
                             verbose=1,
                             save_best_only=True)

# Mean Square Error (MSE) loss function, Adam optimizer
autoencoder.compile(loss='mse', optimizer='adam')

# called every epoch
callbacks = [lr_reducer, checkpoint]

# train the autoencoder
autoencoder.fit(x_train_gray,
                x_train,
                validation_data=(x_test_gray, x_test),
                epochs=30,
                batch_size=batch_size,
                callbacks=callbacks)

# predict the autoencoder output from test data
x_decoded = autoencoder.predict(x_test_gray)

# display the 1st 100 colorized images
imgs = x_decoded[:100]
imgs = imgs.reshape((10, 10, img_rows, img_cols, channels))
imgs = np.vstack([np.hstack(i) for i in imgs])
plt.figure()
plt.axis('off')
plt.title('Colorized test images (Predicted)')
plt.imshow(imgs, interpolation='none')
plt.savefig('%s/colorized.png' % imgs_dir)
plt.show()
```

We've increased the capacity of the autoencoder by adding one more block of convolution and transposed convolution. We've also doubled the number of filters at each CNN block. The latent vector is now 256-dim in order to increase the number of salient properties it can represent, as discussed in the autoencoder section. Finally, the output filter size has increased to three, or is equal to the number of channels in RGB of the expected colored output.

The colorization autoencoder is now trained with the grayscale as inputs and original RGB images as outputs. The training will take more epochs and uses the learning rate reducer to scale down the learning rate when the validation loss is not improving. This can be easily done by telling the callbacks argument in the `tf.keras fit()` function to call the `lr_reducer()` function.

Figure 3.4.2 demonstrates the colorization of grayscale images from the test dataset of CIFAR10.

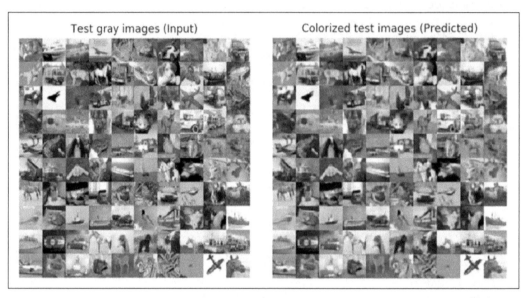

Figure 3.4.2: Automatic grayscale to color image conversion using the autoencoder. CIFAR10 test grayscale input images (left) and predicted color images (right). The original color photo can be found in this Book's GitHub repository at, https://github.com/PacktPublishing/Advanced-Deep-Learning-with-Keras/blob/master/chapter3-autoencoders/README.md

Figure 3.4.3 compares the ground truth with the colorization autoencoder prediction:

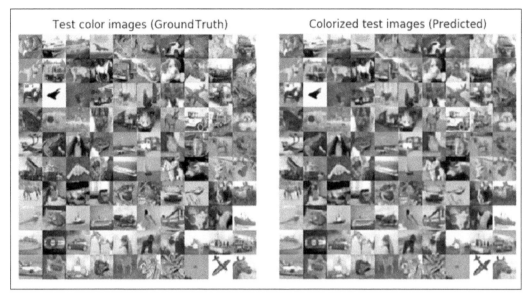

Figure 3.4.3: A side-by-side comparison of ground truth color images and predicted colorized images. The original color photos can be found in this book's GitHub repository at, https://github.com/PacktPublishing/ Advanced-Deep-Learning-with-Keras/blob/master/chapter3-autoencoders/README.md

The autoencoder performs an acceptable colorization job. The sea or sky is predicted to be blue, animals have varying shades of brown, the cloud is white, and so on.

There are some noticeable incorrect predictions, such as red vehicles have become blue or blue vehicles have become red, and the occasional green field has been mistaken as blue skies, and dark or golden skies are converted into blue skies.

This is the last section on autoencoders. In the following chapters, we will revisit the concept of encoding and decoding in one form or another. The concept of representation learning is very fundamental in deep learning.

5. Conclusion

In this chapter, we've been introduced to autoencoders, which are neural networks that compress input data into low-dimensional representations in order to efficiently perform structural transformations, such as denoising and colorization. We've laid the foundations to the more advanced topics of GANs and VAEs, which we will introduce in later chapters. We've demonstrated how to implement an autoencoder from two building block models, both encoders and decoders. We've also learned how the extraction of a hidden structure of input distribution is one of the common tasks in AI.

Once the latent code has been learned, there are many structural operations that can be performed on the original input distribution. In order to gain a better understanding of the input distribution, the hidden structure in the form of the latent vector can be visualized using low-level embedding, similar to what we did in this chapter, or through more sophisticated dimensionality reduction techniques such as t-SNE or PCA.

Apart from denoising and colorization, autoencoders are used in converting input distribution into low-dimensional latent vectors that can be further processed for other tasks such as segmentation, detection, tracking, reconstruction, and visual understanding. In *Chapter 8, Variational Autoencoders (VAEs)*, we will discuss VAEs, which are structurally the same as autoencoders but differ by having interpretable latent code that can produce a continuous latent vector projection.

In the next chapter, we will embark on one of the most important recent breakthroughs in AI, the introduction of GANs. In the next chapter, we will learn about the core strength of GANs, which is their ability to synthesize data that looks real.

6. References

1. Ian Goodfellow et al.: *Deep Learning*. Vol. 1. Cambridge: MIT press, 2016 (http://www.deeplearningbook.org/).

4

Generative Adversarial Networks (GANs)

In this chapter, we'll be investigating **generative adversarial networks (GANs)** [1]. GANs belong to the family of generative models. However, unlike autoencoders, generative models are able to create new and meaningful outputs given arbitrary encodings.

In this chapter, the working principles of GANs will be discussed. We'll also review the implementations of several early GANs using `tf.keras`, while, later on in the chapter, we'll demonstrate the techniques needed to achieve stable training. The scope of this chapter covers two popular examples of GAN implementations, **Deep Convolutional GAN (DCGAN)** [2] and **Conditional GAN (CGAN)** [3].

In summary, the goals of this chapter are:

- To introduce the principles of GAN
- To present one of the early working implementations of GAN, called DCGAN
- An improved DCGAN called CGAN, which uses a condition
- To implement DCGAN and CGAN in `tf.keras`

Let's begin with an overview of GANs.

1. An Overview of GANs

Before we move into the more advanced concepts of GANs, let's start by going over GANs and introducing the underlying concepts behind them. GANs are very powerful; this simple statement is proven by the fact that they can generate new human faces that are not of real people by performing latent space interpolations.

The advanced features of GANs can be seen in these YouTube videos:

- Progressive GAN [4]: `https://youtu.be/G06dEcZ-QTg`
- StyleGAN v1 [5]: `https://youtu.be/kSLJriaOumA`
- StyleGAN v2 [6]: `https://youtu.be/c-NJtV9Jvp0`

The videos that show how GANs can be utilized to produce realistic faces demonstrate how powerful they can be. This topic is much more advanced than anything we've looked at before in this book. For example, the above videos demonstrate things that can't be accomplished easily by autoencoders, which we covered in *Chapter 3*, *Autoencoders*.

GANs are able to learn how to model the input distribution by training two competing (and cooperating) networks referred to as **generator** and **discriminator** (sometimes known as **critic**). The role of the generator is to keep on figuring out how to generate fake data or signals (this includes audio and images) that can fool the discriminator. Meanwhile, the discriminator is trained to distinguish between fake and real signals. As the training progresses, the discriminator will no longer be able to see the difference between the synthetically generated data and the real data. From there, the discriminator can be discarded, and the generator can then be used to create new realistic data that have never been observed before.

The underlying concept of GANs is straightforward. However, one thing we'll find is that the most challenging question is how do we achieve stable training of the generator-discriminator network? There must be a healthy competition between the generator and discriminator in order for both networks to be able to learn simultaneously. Since the loss function is computed from the output of the discriminator, its parameters update quickly. When the discriminator converges faster, the generator no longer receives sufficient gradient updates for its parameters and fails to converge. Other than being hard to train, GANs can also suffer from either a partial or total modal collapse, a situation wherein the generator is producing almost similar outputs for different latent encodings.

Principles of GANs

As shown in *Figure 4.1.1*, a GAN is analogous to a counterfeiter (generator)–police (discriminator) scenario. At the academy, the police are taught how to determine whether a dollar bill is either genuine or fake. Samples of real dollar bills from the bank and fake money from the counterfeiter are used to train the police. However, from time to time, the counterfeiter will attempt to pretend that he printed real dollar bills. Initially, the police will not be fooled and will tell the counterfeiter why the money is fake. Taking into consideration this feedback, the counterfeiter hones his skills again and attempts to produce new fake dollar bills. As expected, the police will be able to both spot the money as fake and justify why the dollar bills are fake:

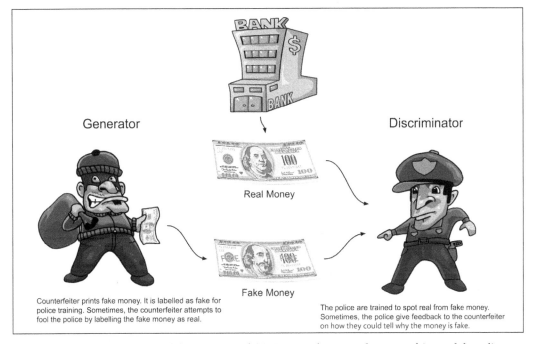

Figure 4.1.1: The generator and discriminator of GANs are analogous to the counterfeiter and the police. The goal of the counterfeiter is to fool the police into believing that the dollar bill is real

This process continues indefinitely, but it will come to a point where the counterfeiter has mastered the creation of fake money to the extent that the fakes are indistinguishable from real money – even to the most highly practiced of police. The counterfeiter can then infinitely print dollar bills without getting caught by the police as they are no longer identifiable as counterfeit.

As shown in *Figure 4.1.2*, a GAN is made up of two networks, a generator and a discriminator:

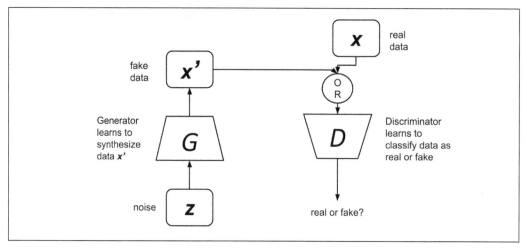

Figure 4.1.2: A GAN is made up of two networks, a generator and a discriminator.
The discriminator is trained to distinguish between real and fake signals or data.
The generator's job is to generate fake signals or data that can eventually fool the discriminator

The input to the generator is noise, and the output is synthesized data. Meanwhile, the discriminator's input will either be real or synthesized data. Genuine data comes from the true sampled data, while the fake data comes from the generator. All of the valid data is labeled 1.0 (that is, a 100 % probability of being real), while all the synthesized data is labeled 0.0 (that is, a 0 % probability of being real). Since the labeling process is automated, GANs are still considered part of the unsupervised learning approach in deep learning.

The objective of the discriminator is to learn from this supplied dataset on how to distinguish real data from fake data. During this part of GAN training, only the discriminator parameters will be updated. Like a typical binary classifier, the discriminator is trained to predict on a range of 0.0 to 1.0 in confidence values on how close the given input data is to the real data. However, this is only half of the story.

At regular intervals, the generator will pretend that its output is genuine data and will ask the GAN to label it as 1.0. When the fake data is then presented to the discriminator, naturally it will be classified as fake with a label close to 0.0.

The optimizer computes the generator parameter updates based on the presented label (that is, 1.0). It also takes its own prediction into account when training on this new data. In other words, the discriminator has some doubts regarding its prediction, and so, the GAN takes that into consideration. This time, the GAN will let the gradients backpropagate from the last layer of the discriminator down to the first layer of the generator. However, in most practices, during this phase of training, the discriminator parameters are temporarily frozen. The generator will use the gradients to update its parameters and improve its ability to synthesize fake data.

Overall, the whole process is akin to two networks competing with one another while still cooperating at the same time. When the GAN training converges, the end result is a generator that can synthesize data that appears genuine. The discriminator thinks this synthesized data is real or with a label near 1.0, which means the discriminator can then be discarded. The generator part will be useful in producing meaningful outputs from arbitrary noise inputs.

The process is outlined in *Figure 4.1.3* below:

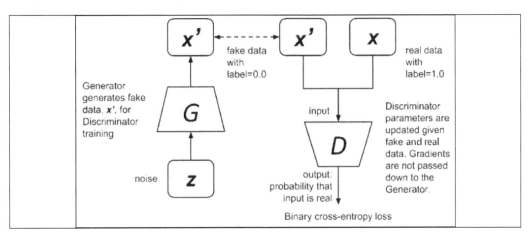

Figure 4.1.3: Training the discriminator is similar to training a binary classifier network using binary cross-entropy loss. The fake data is supplied by the generator, while the real data is from true samples

As shown in the preceding figure, the discriminator can be trained by minimizing the loss function in the following equation:

$$\mathcal{L}^{(D)}\big(\theta^{(G)}, \theta^{(D)}\big) = -\mathbb{E}_{x \sim p_{data}} \log \mathcal{D}(x) - \mathbb{E}_z \log\big(1 - \mathcal{D}(\mathcal{G}(z))\big) \qquad \text{(Equation 4.1.1)}$$

The equation is just the standard binary cross-entropy cost function. The loss is the negative sum of the expectation of correctly identifying real data, $\mathcal{D}(x)$, and the expectation of 1.0 minus correctly identifying synthetic data, $1 - \mathcal{D}(\mathcal{G}(z))$. The log does not change the location of the local minima.

Two mini-batches of data are supplied to the discriminator during training:

1. $\mathbf{x}$, real data from the sampled data (in other words, $\mathbf{x} \sim p_{data}$) with a label 1.0
2. $\mathbf{x}' = \mathcal{G}(\mathbf{z})$, fake data from the generator with a label 0.0

In order to minimize the loss function, the discriminator parameters, $\boldsymbol{\theta}^{(D)}$, will be updated through backpropagation by correctly identifying the genuine data, $\mathcal{D}(\mathbf{x})$, and synthetic data, $1 - \mathcal{D}(\mathcal{G}(\mathbf{z}))$. Correctly identifying real data is equivalent to $\mathcal{D}(\mathbf{x}) \rightarrow 1.0$, while correctly classifying fake data is the same as $\mathcal{D}(\mathcal{G}(\mathbf{z})) \rightarrow 0.0$ or $(1 - \mathcal{D}(\mathcal{G}(\mathbf{z}))) \rightarrow 1.0$. In this equation, $\mathbf{z}$ is the arbitrary encoding or noise vector that is used by the generator to synthesize new signals. Both contribute to minimizing the loss function.

To train the generator, GAN considers the total of the discriminator and generator losses as a zero-sum game. The generator loss function is simply the negative of the discriminator loss function:

$$\mathcal{L}^{(G)}\left(\boldsymbol{\theta}^{(G)}, \boldsymbol{\theta}^{(D)}\right) = -\mathcal{L}^{(D)}\left(\boldsymbol{\theta}^{(G)}, \boldsymbol{\theta}^{(D)}\right) \quad \text{(Equation 4.1.2)}$$

This can then be rewritten more aptly as a value function:

$$\mathcal{V}^{(G)}\left(\boldsymbol{\theta}^{(G)}, \boldsymbol{\theta}^{(D)}\right) = -\mathcal{L}^{(D)}\left(\boldsymbol{\theta}^{(G)}, \boldsymbol{\theta}^{(D)}\right) \quad \text{(Equation 4.1.3)}$$

From the perspective of the generator, *Equation 4.1.3* should be minimized. From the point of view of the discriminator, the value function should be maximized. Therefore, the generator training criterion can be written as a minimax problem:

$$\boldsymbol{\theta}^{(G)*} = arg \min_{\boldsymbol{\theta}^{(G)}} \max_{\boldsymbol{\theta}^{(D)}} \mathcal{V}^{(G)}\left(\boldsymbol{\theta}^{(G)}, \boldsymbol{\theta}^{(D)}\right) \quad \text{(Equation 4.1.4)}$$

Occasionally, we'll try to fool the discriminator by pretending that the synthetic data is real with a label 1.0. By maximizing with respect to $\boldsymbol{\theta}^{(D)}$, the optimizer sends gradient updates to the discriminator parameters to consider this synthetic data as real. At the same time, by minimizing with respect to $\boldsymbol{\theta}^{(G)}$, the optimizer will train the generator's parameters on how to trick the discriminator. However, in practice, the discriminator is confident in its prediction in classifying the synthetic data as fake and will not update the GAN parameters. Furthermore, the gradient updates are small and have diminished significantly as they propagate to the generator layers. As a result, the generator fails to converge.

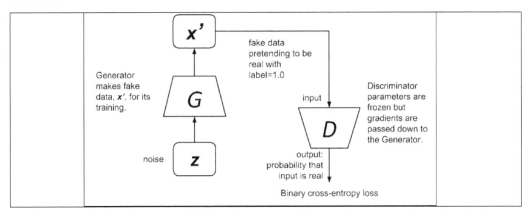

Figure 4.1.4: Training the generator is like training a network using a binary cross-entropy loss function. The fake data from the generator is presented as genuine

The solution is to reformulate the loss function of the generator in the following form:

$$\mathcal{L}^{(G)}\left(\boldsymbol{\theta}^{(G)}, \boldsymbol{\theta}^{(D)}\right) = -\mathbb{E}_z \log \mathcal{D}(\mathcal{G}(\boldsymbol{z})) \quad \text{(Equation 4.1.5)}$$

The loss function simply maximizes the chance of the discriminator believing that the synthetic data is real by training the generator. The new formulation is no longer zero-sum and is purely heuristics-driven. *Figure 4.1.4* shows the generator during training. In this figure, the generator parameters are only updated when the whole adversarial network is trained. This is because the gradients are passed down from the discriminator to the generator. However, in practice, the discriminator weights are only temporarily frozen during adversarial training.

In deep learning, both the generator and discriminator can be implemented using a suitable neural network architecture. If the data or signal is an image, both the generator and discriminator networks will use a CNN. For single-dimensional sequences such as audio, both networks are usually recurrent (RNN, LSTM, or GRU).

In this section, we learned that the principles behind GANs are straightforward. We also learned how GANs can be implemented by familiar network layers. What differentiates GANs from other networks is they are notoriously difficult to train. Something as simple as a minor change in the layers can drive the network to training instability. In the following section, we'll examine one of the early successful implementations of GANs using deep CNNs. It is called DCGAN [3].

2. Implementing DCGAN in Keras

Figure 4.2.1 shows DCGAN that is used to generate fake MNIST images:

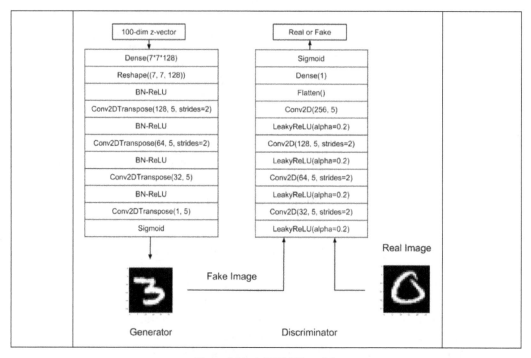

Figure 4.2.1: A DCGAN model

DCGAN implements the following design principles:

- Use *strides > 1*, and a convolution instead of `MaxPooling2D` or `UpSampling2D`. With *strides > 1*, the CNN learns how to resize the feature maps.

- Avoid using `Dense` layers. Use CNN in all layers. The `Dense` layer is utilized only as the first layer of the generator to accept the z-vector. The output of the `Dense` layer is resized and becomes the input of the succeeding CNN layers.

- Use **Batch Normalization (BN)** to stabilize learning by normalizing the input to each layer to have zero mean and unit variance. There is no BN in the generator output layer and discriminator input layer. In the implementation example to be presented here, no batch normalization is used in the discriminator.

- **Rectified Linear Unit (ReLU)** is used in all layers of the generator except in the output layer, where the `tanh` activation is utilized. In the implementation example to be presented here, `sigmoid` is used instead of `tanh` in the output of the generator since it generally results in more stable training for MNIST digits.
- Use **Leaky ReLU** in all layers of the discriminator. Unlike ReLU, instead of zeroing out all outputs when the input is less than zero, Leaky ReLU generates a small gradient equal to *alpha x input*. In the following example, *alpha* = 0.2.

The generator learns to generate fake images from 100-dim input vectors ([-1.0, 1.0] range 100-dim random noise with uniform distribution). The discriminator classifies real from fake images, but inadvertently coaches the generator in terms of how to generate real images when the adversarial network is trained. The kernel size used in our DCGAN implementation is 5. This is to allow it to increase the receptive field size and expressive power of the convolution.

The generator accepts the 100-dim *z*-vector generated by a uniform distribution with a range of -1.0 to 1.0. The first layer of the generator is a 7 x 7 x 128 = 6,272-unit Dense layer. The number of units is computed based on the intended ultimate dimensions of the output image (28 x 28 x 1, 28 being a multiple of 7) and the number of filters of the first `Conv2DTranspose`, which is equal to 128.

We can imagine transposed CNNs (`Conv2DTranspose`) as the reversed process of CNN. In a simple example, if a CNN converts an image to feature maps, a transposed CNN will produce an image given feature maps. Hence, transposed CNNs were used in the decoder in the previous chapter and on generators in this chapter.

After undergoing two `Conv2DTranspose` with `strides = 2`, the feature maps will have a size of 28 x 28 x *number of filters*. Each `Conv2DTranspose` is preceded by batch normalization and ReLU. The final layer has *sigmoid* activation, which generates the 28 x 28 x 1 fake MNIST images. Each pixel is normalized to [0.0, 1.0] corresponding to [0, 255] grayscale levels. *Listing 4.2.1* below shows the implementation of the generator network in `tf.keras`. A function is defined to build the generator model. Due to the length of the entire code, we will limit the listing to the particular lines being discussed.

The complete code is available on GitHub: `https://github.com/PacktPublishing/Advanced-Deep-Learning-with-Keras`

Listing 4.2.1: `dcgan-mnist-4.2.1.py`

```python
def build_generator(inputs, image_size):
    """Build a Generator Model

    Stack of BN-ReLU-Conv2DTranpose to generate fake images
    Output activation is sigmoid instead of tanh in [1].
    Sigmoid converges easily.

    Arguments:
        inputs (Layer): Input layer of the generator
            the z-vector)
        image_size (tensor): Target size of one side
            (assuming square image)

    Returns:
        generator (Model): Generator Model
    """

    image_resize = image_size // 4
    # network parameters
    kernel_size = 5
    layer_filters = [128, 64, 32, 1]

    x = Dense(image_resize * image_resize * layer_filters[0])(inputs)
    x = Reshape((image_resize, image_resize, layer_filters[0]))(x)

    for filters in layer_filters:
        # first two convolution layers use strides = 2
        # the last two use strides = 1
        if filters > layer_filters[-2]:
            strides = 2
        else:
            strides = 1
        x = BatchNormalization()(x)
        x = Activation('relu')(x)
        x = Conv2DTranspose(filters=filters,
                            kernel_size=kernel_size,
                            strides=strides,
                            padding='same')(x)

    x = Activation('sigmoid')(x)
    generator = Model(inputs, x, name='generator')
    return generator
```

The discriminator is similar to many CNN-based classifiers. The input is a 28 x 28 x 1 MNIST image that is classified as either real (1.0) or fake (0.0). There are four CNN layers. Except for the last convolution, each `Conv2D` uses `strides` = 2 to downsample the feature maps by two. Each `Conv2D` is then preceded by a Leaky ReLU layer. The final filter size is 256, while the initial filter size is 32 and doubles every convolution layer. The final filter size of 128 also works. However, we'll find that the generated images look better with 256. The final output layer is flattened, and a single unit `Dense` layer generates the prediction between 0.0 and 1.0 after scaling by the sigmoid activation layer. The output is modeled as a Bernoulli distribution. Hence, the binary cross-entropy loss function is used.

After building the generator and discriminator models, the adversarial model is made by concatenating the generator and discriminator networks. Both discriminator and adversarial networks use the RMSprop optimizer. The learning rate for the discriminator is 2e-4, while for the adversarial network, it is 1e-4. RMSprop decay rates of 6e-8 for the discriminator, and 3e-8 for the adversarial network, are applied.

Setting the learning rate of the adversarial equal to half of the discriminator will result in more stable training. You'll recall from *Figure 4.1.3* and *Figure 4.1.4* that the GAN training has two parts: discriminator training and generator training, which is adversarial training with discriminator weights frozen.

Listing 4.2.2 shows the implementation of the discriminator in `tf.keras`. A function is defined to build the discriminator model.

Listing 4.2.2: `dcgan-mnist-4.2.1.py`

```
def build_discriminator(inputs):
    """Build a Discriminator Model

    Stack of LeakyReLU-Conv2D to discriminate real from fake.
    The network does not converge with BN so it is not used here
    unlike in [1] or original paper.

    Arguments:
        inputs (Layer): Input layer of the discriminator (the image)

    Returns:
        discriminator (Model): Discriminator Model
    """
    kernel_size = 5
    layer_filters = [32, 64, 128, 256]

    x = inputs
    for filters in layer_filters:
```

```
        # first 3 convolution layers use strides = 2
        # last one uses strides = 1
        if filters == layer_filters[-1]:
            strides = 1
        else:
            strides = 2
        x = LeakyReLU(alpha=0.2)(x)
        x = Conv2D(filters=filters,
                   kernel_size=kernel_size,
                   strides=strides,
                   padding='same')(x)

    x = Flatten()(x)
    x = Dense(1)(x)
    x = Activation('sigmoid')(x)
    discriminator = Model(inputs, x, name='discriminator')
    return discriminator
```

In *Listing 4.2.3*, we'll illustrate how to build GAN models. Firstly, the discriminator model is built and, following on from that, the generator model is instantiated. The adversarial model is just the generator and the discriminator put together. Across many GANs, the batch size of 64 appears to be the most common. The network parameters are shown in *Listing 4.2.3*.

Listing 4.2.3: dcgan-mnist-4.2.1.py

Function to build DCGAN models and call the training routine:

```
def build_and_train_models():
    # load MNIST dataset
    (x_train, _), (_, _) = mnist.load_data()

    # reshape data for CNN as (28, 28, 1) and normalize
    image_size = x_train.shape[1]
    x_train = np.reshape(x_train, [-1, image_size, image_size, 1])
    x_train = x_train.astype('float32') / 255

    model_name = "dcgan_mnist"
    # network parameters
    # the latent or z vector is 100-dim
    latent_size = 100
    batch_size = 64
    train_steps = 40000
    lr = 2e-4
    decay = 6e-8
```

```
input_shape = (image_size, image_size, 1)

# build discriminator model
inputs = Input(shape=input_shape, name='discriminator_input')
discriminator = build_discriminator(inputs)
# [1] or original paper uses Adam,
# but discriminator converges easily with RMSprop
optimizer = RMSprop(lr=lr, decay=decay)
discriminator.compile(loss='binary_crossentropy',
                      optimizer=optimizer,
                      metrics=['accuracy'])
discriminator.summary()

# build generator model
input_shape = (latent_size, )
inputs = Input(shape=input_shape, name='z_input')
generator = build_generator(inputs, image_size)
generator.summary()

# build adversarial model
optimizer = RMSprop(lr=lr * 0.5, decay=decay * 0.5)
# freeze the weights of discriminator during adversarial training
discriminator.trainable = False
# adversarial = generator + discriminator
adversarial = Model(inputs,
                    discriminator(generator(inputs)),
                    name=model_name)
adversarial.compile(loss='binary_crossentropy',
                    optimizer=optimizer,
                    metrics=['accuracy'])
adversarial.summary()

# train discriminator and adversarial networks
models = (generator, discriminator, adversarial)
params = (batch_size, latent_size, train_steps, model_name)
train(models, x_train, params)
```

As can be seen in *Listing 4.2.1* and *Listing 4.2.2*, the DCGAN models are straightforward. What makes them difficult to build is the fact that small changes in the network design can easily break the training convergence. For example, if batch normalization is used in the discriminator, or if strides = 2 in the generator is transferred to the latter CNN layers, DCGAN will fail to converge.

Listing 4.2.4 shows the function dedicated to training the discriminator and adversarial networks. Due to custom training, the usual `fit()` function is not going to be used. Instead, `train_on_batch()` is called up to run a single gradient update for the given batch of data. The generator is then trained via an adversarial network. The training first randomly picks a batch of real images from the dataset. This is labeled as real (1.0). Then, a batch of fake images will be generated by the generator. This is labeled as fake (0.0). The two batches are concatenated and are used to train the discriminator.

After this is complete, a new batch of fake images will be generated by the generator and labeled as real (1.0). This batch will be used to train the adversarial network. The two networks are trained alternately for about 40,000 steps. At regular intervals, the generated MNIST digits based on a certain noise vector are saved on the filesystem. At the last training step, the network has converged. The generator model is also saved on a file so we can easily reuse the trained model for future MNIST digit generation. However, only the generator model is saved since that is the useful part of this DCGAN in the generation of new MNIST digits. For example, we can generate new and random MNIST digits by executing:

```
python3 dcgan-mnist-4.2.1.py --generator=dcgan_mnist.h5
```

Listing 4.2.4: `dcgan-mnist-4.2.1.py`

Function to train the discriminator and adversarial networks:

```
def train(models, x_train, params):
    """Train the Discriminator and Adversarial Networks

    Alternately train Discriminator and Adversarial networks by batch.
    Discriminator is trained first with properly real and fake images.
    Adversarial is trained next with fake images pretending to be real
    Generate sample images per save_interval.

    Arguments:
        models (list): Generator, Discriminator, Adversarial models
        x_train (tensor): Train images
        params (list) : Networks parameters

    """
    # the GAN component models
    generator, discriminator, adversarial = models
    # network parameters
    batch_size, latent_size, train_steps, model_name = params
    # the generator image is saved every 500 steps
    save_interval = 500
```

```
    # noise vector to see how the generator output evolves during
training
    noise_input = np.random.uniform(-1.0, 1.0, size=[16, latent_size])
    # number of elements in train dataset
    train_size = x_train.shape[0]
    for i in range(train_steps):
        # train the discriminator for 1 batch
        # 1 batch of real (label=1.0) and fake images (label=0.0)
        # randomly pick real images from dataset
        rand_indexes = np.random.randint(0, train_size, size=batch_
size)
        real_images = x_train[rand_indexes]
        # generate fake images from noise using generator
        # generate noise using uniform distribution
        noise = np.random.uniform(-1.0,
                                  1.0,
                                  size=[batch_size, latent_size])
        # generate fake images
        fake_images = generator.predict(noise)
        # real + fake images = 1 batch of train data
        x = np.concatenate((real_images, fake_images))
        # label real and fake images
        # real images label is 1.0
        y = np.ones([2 * batch_size, 1])
        # fake images label is 0.0
        y[batch_size:, :] = 0.0
        # train discriminator network, log the loss and accuracy
        loss, acc = discriminator.train_on_batch(x, y)
        log = "%d: [discriminator loss: %f, acc: %f]" % (i, loss, acc)

        # train the adversarial network for 1 batch
        # 1 batch of fake images with label=1.0
        # since the discriminator weights
        # are frozen in adversarial network
        # only the generator is trained
        # generate noise using uniform distribution
        noise = np.random.uniform(-1.0,
                                  1.0,
                                  size=[batch_size, latent_size])
        # label fake images as real or 1.0
        y = np.ones([batch_size, 1])
        # train the adversarial network
        # note that unlike in discriminator training,
        # we do not save the fake images in a variable
```

```
        # the fake images go to the discriminator input of the
adversarial
        # for classification
        # log the loss and accuracy
        loss, acc = adversarial.train_on_batch(noise, y)
        log = "%s [adversarial loss: %f, acc: %f]" % (log, loss, acc)
        print(log)
        if (i + 1) % save_interval == 0:
            # plot generator images on a periodic basis
            plot_images(generator,
                        noise_input=noise_input,
                        show=False,
                        step=(i + 1),
                        model_name=model_name)

    # save the model after training the generator
    # the trained generator can be reloaded for
    # future MNIST digit generation
    generator.save(model_name + ".h5")
```

Figure 4.2.2 shows the evolution of fake images from the generator as a function of training steps. At 5,000 steps, the generator is already producing recognizable images. It's very much like having an agent that knows how to draw digits. It's worth noting that some digits change from one recognizable form (for example, 8 in the second column of the last row) to another (for example, 0). When the training converges, the discriminator loss approaches 0.5, while the adversarial loss approaches 1.0 as follows:

```
39997: [discriminator loss: 0.423329, acc: 0.796875] [adversarial loss:
0.819355, acc: 0.484375]
39998: [discriminator loss: 0.471747, acc: 0.773438] [adversarial loss:
1.570030, acc: 0.203125]
39999: [discriminator loss: 0.532917, acc: 0.742188] [adversarial loss:
0.824350, acc: 0.453125]
```

We can see the outcome below:

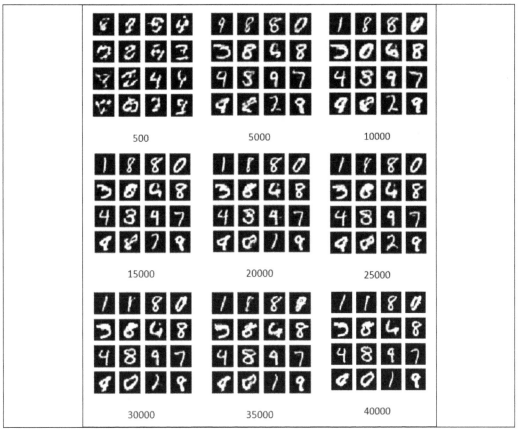

Figure 4.2.2: The fake images generated by the DCGAN generator at different training steps

In this section, the fake images generated by the DCGAN are random.

There is no control over which specific digits will be produced by the generator. There is no mechanism for how to request a particular digit from the generator. This problem can be addressed by a variation of GAN called CGAN [4], as we will discuss in the next section.

3. Conditional GAN

Using the same GAN as in the previous section, a condition is imposed on both the generator and discriminator inputs. The condition is in the form of a one-hot vector version of the digit. This is associated with the image to be produced (generator) or classified as real or fake (discriminator). The CGAN model is shown in *Figure 4.3.1*.

CGAN is similar to DCGAN except for the additional one-hot vector input. For the generator, the one-hot label is concatenated with the latent vector before the `Dense` layer. For the discriminator, a new `Dense` layer is added. The new layer is used to process the one-hot vector and reshape it so that it is suitable for concatenation to the other input of the succeeding CNN layer.

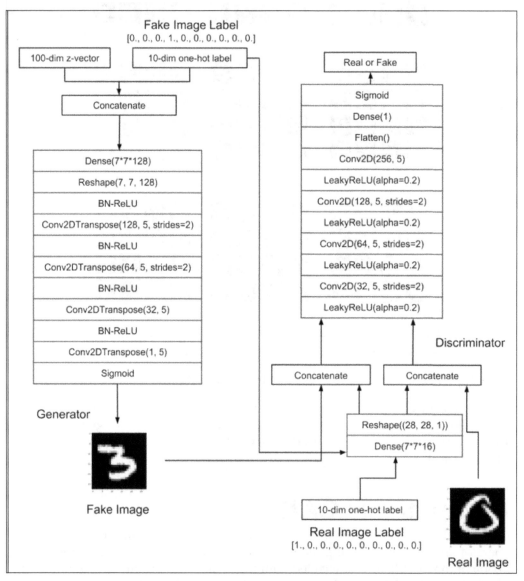

Figure 4.3.1: The CGAN model is similar to DCGAN except for the one-hot vector, which is used to condition the generator and discriminator outputs

The generator learns to generate fake images from a 100-dim input vector and a specified digit. The discriminator classifies real from fake images based on real and fake images and their corresponding labels.

The basis of a CGAN is still the same as the original GAN principle except that the discriminator and generator inputs are conditioned on one-hot labels, y.

By incorporating this condition in *Equation 4.1.1* and *Equation 4.1.5*, the loss functions for the discriminator and generator are shown in *Equation 4.3.1* and *Equation 4.3.2*, respectively:

$$\mathcal{L}^{(D)}\left(\boldsymbol{\theta}^{(G)}, \boldsymbol{\theta}^{(D)}\right) = -\mathbb{E}_{x \sim p_{data}} \log \mathcal{D}(x|y) - \mathbb{E}_z \log\left(1 - \mathcal{D}\left(\mathcal{G}(z|y')\right)\right) \quad \text{(Equation 4.3.1)}$$

$$\mathcal{L}^{(G)}\left(\boldsymbol{\theta}^{(G)}, \boldsymbol{\theta}^{(D)}\right) = -\mathbb{E}_z \log \mathcal{D}\left(\mathcal{G}(z|y')\right) \quad \text{(Equation 4.3.2)}$$

Given *Figure 4.3.2*, it may be more appropriate to write the loss functions as:

$$\mathcal{L}^{(D)}\left(\boldsymbol{\theta}^{(G)}, \boldsymbol{\theta}^{(D)}\right) = -\mathbb{E}_{x \sim p_{data}} \log \mathcal{D}(x|y) - \mathbb{E}_z \log\left(1 - \mathcal{D}(\mathcal{G}(z|y')|y')\right) \quad \text{(Equation 4.3.3)}$$

$$\mathcal{L}^{(G)}\left(\boldsymbol{\theta}^{(G)}, \boldsymbol{\theta}^{(D)}\right) = -\mathbb{E}_z \log \mathcal{D}(\mathcal{G}(z|y')|y') \quad \text{(Equation 4.3.4)}$$

The new loss function of the discriminator aims to minimize the error of predicting real images coming from the dataset and fake images coming from the generator given their one-hot labels. *Figure 4.3.2* shows how to train the discriminator.

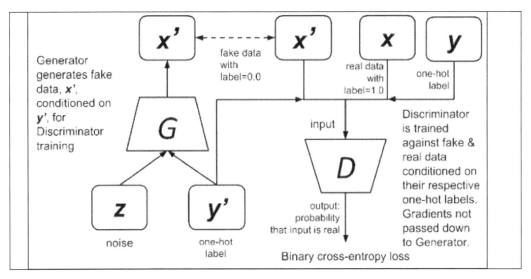

Figure 4.3.2: Training the CGAN discriminator is similar to training the GAN discriminator. The only difference is that both the generated fake and the dataset's real images are conditioned with their corresponding one-hot labels

The new loss function of the generator minimizes the correct prediction of the discriminator on fake images conditioned on the specified one-hot labels. The generator learns how to generate the specific MNIST digit given its one-hot vector, which can fool the discriminator. *Figure 4.3.3* shows how to train the generator.

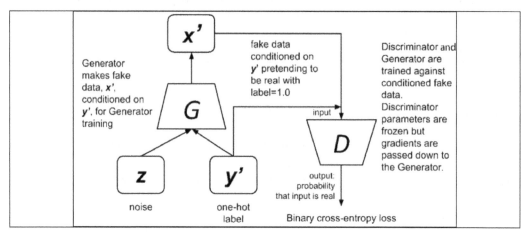

Figure 4.3.3: Training the CGAN generator through the adversarial network is similar to training the GAN generator. The only difference is that the generated fake images are conditioned with one-hot labels

Listing 4.3.1 highlights the minor changes needed in the discriminator model. The code processes the one-hot vector using a Dense layer and concatenates it with the input image. The Model instance is modified for the image and one-hot vector inputs.

Listing 4.3.1: cgan-mnist-4.3.1.py

Highlighted are the changes made in DCGAN:

```
def build_discriminator(inputs, labels, image_size):
    """Build a Discriminator Model

    Inputs are concatenated after Dense layer.
    Stack of LeakyReLU-Conv2D to discriminate real from fake.
    The network does not converge with BN so it is not used here
    unlike in DCGAN paper.

    Arguments:
        inputs (Layer): Input layer of the discriminator (the image)
        labels (Layer): Input layer for one-hot vector to
    condition
            the inputs
        image_size: Target size of one side (assuming square image)
```

```
    Returns:
        discriminator (Model): Discriminator Model
    """
    kernel_size = 5
    layer_filters = [32, 64, 128, 256]

    x = inputs

    y = Dense(image_size * image_size)(labels)
    y = Reshape((image_size, image_size, 1))(y)
    x = concatenate([x, y])

    for filters in layer_filters:
        # first 3 convolution layers use strides = 2
        # last one uses strides = 1
        if filters == layer_filters[-1]:
            strides = 1
        else:
            strides = 2
        x = LeakyReLU(alpha=0.2)(x)
        x = Conv2D(filters=filters,
                   kernel_size=kernel_size,
                   strides=strides,
                   padding='same')(x)

    x = Flatten()(x)
    x = Dense(1)(x)
    x = Activation('sigmoid')(x)
    # input is conditioned by labels
    discriminator = Model([inputs, labels], x,
name='discriminator')
    return discriminator
```

The following *Listing 4.3.2* highlights the code changes to incorporate the conditioning one-hot labels in the generator builder function. The Model instance is modified for the *z*-vector and one-hot vector inputs.

Listing 4.3.2: cgan-mnist-4.3.1.py

Highlighted are the changes made in DCGAN:

```
def build_generator(inputs, labels, image_size):
    """Build a Generator Model
```

```
    Inputs are concatenated before Dense layer.
    Stack of BN-ReLU-Conv2DTranpose to generate fake images.
    Output activation is sigmoid instead of tanh in orig DCGAN.
    Sigmoid converges easily.

    Arguments:
        inputs (Layer): Input layer of the generator (the z-vector)
        labels (Layer): Input layer for one-hot vector to
condition the inputs
        image_size: Target size of one side (assuming square image)

    Returns:
        generator (Model): Generator Model
    """
    image_resize = image_size // 4
    # network parameters
    kernel_size = 5
    layer_filters = [128, 64, 32, 1]

    x = concatenate([inputs, labels], axis=1)
    x = Dense(image_resize * image_resize * layer_filters[0])(x)
    x = Reshape((image_resize, image_resize, layer_filters[0]))(x)

    for filters in layer_filters:
        # first two convolution layers use strides = 2
        # the last two use strides = 1
        if filters > layer_filters[-2]:
            strides = 2
        else:
            strides = 1
        x = BatchNormalization()(x)
        x = Activation('relu')(x)
        x = Conv2DTranspose(filters=filters,
                            kernel_size=kernel_size,
                            strides=strides,
                            padding='same')(x)

    x = Activation('sigmoid')(x)
    # input is conditioned by labels
    generator = Model([inputs, labels], x, name='generator')
    return generator
```

Listing 4.3.3 highlights the changes made in the `train()` function to accommodate the conditioning one-hot vector for the discriminator and the generator. The CGAN discriminator is firstly trained with one batch of real and fake data conditioned on their respective one-hot labels. Then, the generator parameters are updated by training the adversarial network given one-hot label conditioned fake data pretending to be real. Similar to DCGAN, the discriminator weights are frozen during adversarial training.

Listing 4.3.3: cgan-mnist-4.3.1.py

Highlighted are the changes made in DCGAN:

```
def train(models, data, params):
    """Train the Discriminator and Adversarial Networks

    Alternately train Discriminator and Adversarial networks by batch.
    Discriminator is trained first with properly labelled real and
fake images.
    Adversarial is trained next with fake images pretending to be
real.
    Discriminator inputs are conditioned by train labels for real
images,
    and random labels for fake images.
    Adversarial inputs are conditioned by random labels.
    Generate sample images per save_interval.

    Arguments:
        models (list): Generator, Discriminator, Adversarial models
        data (list): x_train, y_train data
        params (list): Network parameters

    """
    # the GAN models
    generator, discriminator, adversarial = models
    # images and labels
    x_train, y_train = data
    # network parameters
    batch_size, latent_size, train_steps, num_labels, model_name =
params
    # the generator image is saved every 500 steps
    save_interval = 500
    # noise vector to see how the generator output evolves during
training
    noise_input = np.random.uniform(-1.0, 1.0, size=[16, latent_size])
    # one-hot label the noise will be conditioned to
```

```
        noise_class = np.eye(num_labels) [np.arange(0, 16) % num_
labels]
        # number of elements in train dataset
        train_size = x_train.shape[0]

        print(model_name,
              "Labels for generated images: ",
              np.argmax(noise_class, axis=1))

    for i in range(train_steps):
        # train the discriminator for 1 batch
        # 1 batch of real (label=1.0) and fake images (label=0.0)
        # randomly pick real images from dataset
        rand_indexes = np.random.randint(0, train_size, size=batch_
size)
        real_images = x_train[rand_indexes]
        # corresponding one-hot labels of real images
        real_labels = y_train[rand_indexes]
        # generate fake images from noise using generator
        noise = np.random.uniform(-1.0,
                                  1.0,
                                  size=[batch_size, latent_size])
        # assign random one-hot labels
        fake_labels = np.eye(num_labels) [np.random.choice(num_
labels,batch_size)]

        # generate fake images conditioned on fake labels
        fake_images = generator.predict([noise, fake_labels])
        # real + fake images = 1 batch of train data
        x = np.concatenate((real_images, fake_images))
        # real + fake one-hot labels = 1 batch of train one-hot
labels
        labels = np.concatenate((real_labels, fake_labels))

        # label real and fake images
        # real images label is 1.0
        y = np.ones([2 * batch_size, 1])
        # fake images label is 0.0
        y[batch_size:, :] = 0.0
        # train discriminator network, log the loss and accuracy
        loss, acc = discriminator.train_on_batch([x, labels], y)
        log = "%d: [discriminator loss: %f, acc: %f]" % (i, loss, acc)
```

```
# train the adversarial network for 1 batch
# 1 batch of fake images conditioned on fake 1-hot labels
# w/ label=1.0
# since the discriminator weights are frozen in
# adversarial network only the generator is trained
# generate noise using uniform distribution
noise = np.random.uniform(-1.0,
                          1.0,
                          size=[batch_size, latent_size])
# assign random one-hot labels
fake_labels = np.eye(num_labels)[np.random.choice(num_
labels,batch_size)]


# label fake images as real or 1.0
y = np.ones([batch_size, 1])
# train the adversarial network
# note that unlike in discriminator training,
# we do not save the fake images in a variable
# the fake images go to the discriminator input of the
adversarial
# for classification
# log the loss and accuracy
loss, acc = adversarial.train_on_batch([noise, fake_
labels], y)
log = "%s [adversarial loss: %f, acc: %f]" % (log, loss, acc)
print(log)
if (i + 1) % save_interval == 0:
    # plot generator images on a periodic basis
    plot_images(generator,
                noise_input=noise_input,
                noise_class=noise_class,
                show=False,
                step=(i + 1),
                model_name=model_name)


# save the model after training the generator
# the trained generator can be reloaded for
# future MNIST digit generation
generator.save(model_name + ".h5")
```

Figure 4.3.4 shows the evolution of MNIST digits generated when the generator is conditioned to produce digits with the following labels:

```
[0  1  2  3
4  5  6  7
8  9  0  1
2  3  4  5]
```

We can see the results below:

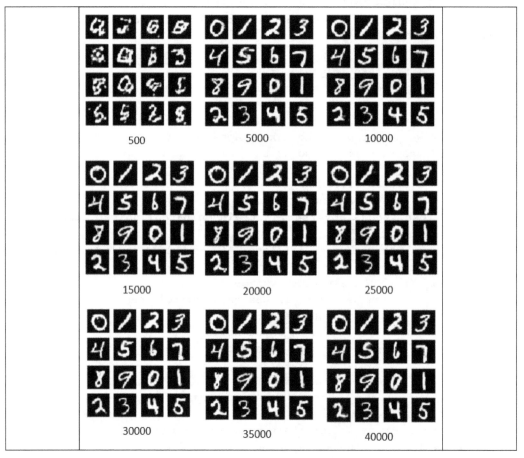

Figure 4.3.4: The fake images generated by CGAN at different training steps when conditioned with labels [0 1 2 3 4 5 6 7 8 9 0 1 2 3 4 5]

You're encouraged to run the trained generator model to see new synthesized MNIST digit images:

```
python3 cgan-mnist-4.3.1.py --generator=cgan_mnist.h5
```

Alternatively, a specific digit (for example, 8) to be generated can also be requested:

```
python3 cgan-mnist-4.3.1.py --generator=cgan_mnist.h5 --digit=8
```

With CGAN, it's like having an agent that we can ask to draw digits similar to how humans write digits. The key advantage of CGAN over DCGAN is that we can specify which digit we want the agent to draw.

4. Conclusion

This chapter discussed the general principles behind GANs so as to give you a foundation for the more advanced topics we'll now move on to, including improved GANs, disentangled representation GANs, and cross-domain GANs. We started this chapter by understanding how GANs are made up of two networks, called generator and discriminator. The role of the discriminator is to discriminate between real and fake signals. The aim of the generator is to fool the discriminator. The generator is normally combined with the discriminator to form an adversarial network. It is through training the adversarial network that the generator learns how to produce fake data that can trick the discriminator.

We also learned how GANs are easy to build but notoriously difficult to train. Two example implementations in `tf.keras` were presented. DCGAN demonstrated that it is possible to train GANs to generate fake images using deep CNNs. The fake images were MNIST digits. However, the DCGAN generator had no control over which specific digit it should draw. CGAN addressed this problem by conditioning the generator to draw a specific digit. The condition was in the form of a one-hot label. CGAN is useful if we want to build an agent that can generate data of a specific class.

In the next chapter, improvements on the DCGAN and CGAN will be introduced. In particular, the focus will be on how to stabilize the training of DCGAN and how to improve the perceptive quality of CGAN. This will be done by introducing new loss functions and slightly different model architectures.

5. References

1. Ian Goodfellow. *NIPS 2016 Tutorial: Generative Adversarial Networks*. arXiv preprint arXiv:1701.00160, 2016 (https://arxiv.org/pdf/1701.00160.pdf).

2. Alec Radford, Luke Metz, and Soumith Chintala. *Unsupervised Representation Learning with Deep Convolutional Generative Adversarial Networks*. arXiv preprint arXiv:1511.06434, 2015 (https://arxiv.org/pdf/1511.06434.pdf).

3. Mehdi Mirza and Simon Osindero. *Conditional Generative Adversarial Nets.* arXiv preprint arXiv:1411.1784, 2014 (`https://arxiv.org/pdf/1411.1784.pdf`).

4. Tero Karras et al. *Progressive Growing of GANs for Improved Quality, Stability, and Variation.* ICLR, 2018 (`https://arxiv.org/pdf/1710.10196.pdf`).

5. Tero Karras, , Samuli Laine, and Timo Aila. *A Style-Based Generator Architecture for Generative Adversarial Networks.* Proceedings of the IEEE Conference on Computer Vision and Pattern Recognition. 2019.

6. Tero Karras et al. *Analyzing and Improving the Image Quality of StyleGAN.* 2019 (`https://arxiv.org/abs/1912.04958`).

5
Improved GANs

Since the introduction of **Generative Adversarial Networks (GANs)** in 2014[1], their popularity has rapidly increased. GANs have proven to be a useful generative model that can synthesize new data that looks real. Many of the research papers in deep learning that followed proposed measures to address the difficulties and limitations of the original GAN.

As we discussed in previous chapters, GANs can be notoriously difficult to train, and are prone to mode collapse. Mode collapse is a situation where the generator is producing outputs that look the same even though the loss functions are already optimized. In the context of MNIST digits, with mode collapse, the generator may only be producing digits 4 and 9 since they look similar. The **Wasserstein GAN (WGAN)**[2] addressed these problems by arguing that stable training and mode collapse can be avoided by simply replacing the GAN loss function based on **Wasserstein 1**, also known as the **Earth Mover's Distance (EMD)**.

However, the issue of stability is not the only problem with GANs. There is also the increasing need to improve the perceptive quality of the generated images. The **Least Squares GAN (LSGAN)**[3] proposed addressing both these problems simultaneously. The basic premise is that sigmoid cross-entropy loss leads to a vanishing gradient during training. This results in poor image quality. Least squares loss does not induce vanishing gradients. The resulting generated images are of higher perceptive quality when compared to vanilla GAN-generated images.

In the previous chapter, CGAN introduced a method for conditioning the output of the generator. For example, if we wanted to get digit 8, we would include the conditioning label in the input to the generator. Inspired by CGAN, the **Auxiliary Classifier GAN (ACGAN)**[4] proposed a modified conditional algorithm that results in better perceptive quality and diversity of the outputs.

In summary, the goal of this chapter is to present:

- The theoretical formulation of WGAN
- An understanding of the principles of LSGAN
- An understanding of the principles of ACGAN
- The `tf.keras` implementation of improved GANs – WGAN, LSGAN, and ACGAN

Let's start off by discussing WGAN.

1. Wasserstein GAN

As we've mentioned before, GANs are notoriously hard to train. The opposing objectives of the two networks, the discriminator and the generator, can easily cause training instability. The discriminator attempts to correctly classify the fake data from the real data. Meanwhile, the generator tries its best to trick the discriminator. If the discriminator learns faster than the generator, the generator parameters will fail to optimize. On the other hand, if the discriminator learns more slowly, then the gradients may vanish before reaching the generator. In the worst case, if the discriminator is unable to converge, the generator is not going to be able to get any useful feedback.

WGAN argued that a GAN's inherent instability is due to its loss function, which is based on the **Jensen-Shannon** (**JS**) distance. In a GAN, the objective of the generator is to learn how to transform from one source distribution (for example, noise) to an estimated target distribution (for example, MNIST digits). Using the original formulation of a GAN, the loss function is actually minimizing the distance between the target distribution and its estimate. The problem is, for some pairs of distributions, there is no smooth path to minimize this JS distance. Hence, the training will fail to converge.

In the following section, we will investigate three distance functions and analyze what could be a good substitute for the JS distance function that is more suitable for GAN optimization.

Distance functions

The stability in training a GAN can be understood by examining its loss functions. To better understand GAN loss functions, we're going to review the common distance or divergence functions between two probability distributions.

Our concern is the distance between p_{data} for true data distribution, and p_g for generator data distribution. The goal of GANs is to make $p_g \rightarrow p_{data}$. *Table 5.1.1* shows the divergence functions.

In most maximum likelihood tasks, we'll use **Kullback-Leibler (KL)** divergence, or D_{KL}, in the loss function as a measure of how far our neural network model prediction is from the true distribution function. As shown in *Equation 5.1.1*, D_{KL} is not symmetric since $D_{KL}(p_{data}\|p_g) \neq D_{KL}(p_g\|p_{data})$.

JS, or D_{JS}, is a divergence that is based on D_{KL}. However, unlike D_{KL}, D_{JS} is symmetrical and is finite. In this section, we'll demonstrate that optimizing GAN loss functions is equivalent to optimizing D_{JS}:

Divergence	Expression
Kullback-Leibler (KL) Equation 5.1.1	$$D_{KL}(p_{data}\|p_g) = \mathbb{E}_{x \sim p_{data}} \log \frac{p_{data}(x)}{p_g(x)}$$ $$\neq D_{KL}(p_g\|p_{data}) = \mathbb{E}_{x \sim p_g} \log \frac{p_g(x)}{p_{data}(x)}$$
Jensen-Shannon (JS) Equation 5.1.2	$$D_{JS}(p_{data}\|p_g) = \frac{1}{2}\mathbb{E}_{x \sim p_{data}} \log \frac{p_{data}(x)}{\frac{p_{data}(x)+p_g(x)}{2}} + \frac{1}{2}\mathbb{E}_{x \sim p_g} \log \frac{p_g(x)}{\frac{p_{data}(x)+p_g(x)}{2}} = D_{JS}(p_g\|p_{data})$$
Earth Mover's Distance (EMD) or Wasserstein 1 Equation 5.1.3	$$W(p_{data}, p_g) = \inf_{\gamma \in \prod(p_{data}, p_g)} \mathbb{E}_{(x,y) \sim \gamma}[\|x - y\|]$$ where $\prod(p_{data}, p_g)$ is the set of all joint distributions $\gamma(x,y)$ whose marginals are p_{data} and p_g.

Table 5.1.1: The divergence functions between two probability distribution functions, p_{data} and p_g

The idea behind EMD is that it is a measure of how much mass $\gamma(x,y)$ should be transported by $d = \|x - y\|$ for the probability distribution p_{data} in order to match the probability distribution p_g. $\gamma(x,y)$ is a joint distribution in the space of all possible joint distributions $\prod(p_{data}, p_g)$. $\gamma(x,y)$ is also known as a transport plan, to reflect the strategy for transporting masses to match the two probability distributions. There are many possible transport plans given the two probability distributions. Roughly speaking, *inf* indicates a transport plan with the minimum cost.

For example, *Figure 5.1.1* shows us two simple discrete distributions x and y:

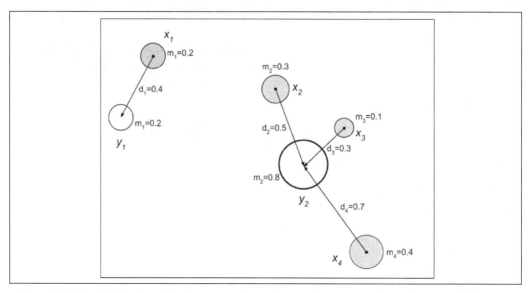

Figure 5.1.1: The EMD is the weighted amount of mass from x to be transported in order to match the target distribution, y

x has masses m_i for i = 1, 2, 3, and 4 at locations x_i for i = 1, 2, 3, and 4. Meanwhile, y has masses m_i for i = 1 and 2 at locations y_i for i = 1 and 2. To match the distribution y the arrows show the minimum transport plan to move each mass x_i by d_i. The EMD is computed as:

$$EMD = \sum_{i=1}^{4} x_i d_i = 0.2(0.4) + 0.3(0.5) + 0.1(0.3) + 0.4(0.7) = 0.54 \quad \text{(Equation 5.1.4)}$$

In *Figure 5.1.1*, the EMD can be interpreted as the least amount of work needed to move the pile of dirt x to fill the holes y. While in this example, the *inf* can also be deduced from the figure, in most cases, especially in continuous distributions, it is intractable to exhaust all possible transport plans. We will come back to this problem later on in this chapter. In the meantime, we'll show how the GAN loss functions are, in fact, minimizing the **JS** divergence.

Distance function in GANs

We're now going to compute the optimal discriminator given any generator from the loss function in the previous chapter. We'll recall the following equation from the previous chapter:

$$\mathcal{L}^{(D)} = -\mathbb{E}_{x \sim p_{data}} \log \mathcal{D}(x) - \mathbb{E}_z \log\big(1 - \mathcal{D}(\mathcal{G}(z))\big) \quad \text{(Equation 4.1.1)}$$

Instead of sampling from the noise distribution, the preceding equation can also be expressed as sampling from the generator distribution:

$$\mathcal{L}^{(D)} = -\mathbb{E}_{x \sim p_{data}} \log \mathcal{D}(x) - \mathbb{E}_{x \sim p_g} \log\big(1 - \mathcal{D}(x)\big) \quad \text{(Equation 5.1.5)}$$

To find the minimum $\mathcal{L}^{(D)}$:

$$\mathcal{L}^{(D)} = -\int_x p_{data}(x) \log \mathcal{D}(x) dx - \int_x p_g(x) \log\big(1 - \mathcal{D}(x)\big) dx \quad \text{(Equation 5.1.6)}$$

$$\mathcal{L}^{(D)} = -\int_x \big(p_{data}(x) \log \mathcal{D}(x) + p_g(x) \log\big(1 - \mathcal{D}(x)\big)\big) dx \quad \text{(Equation 5.1.7)}$$

The term inside the integral is in the form $y \to a \log y + b \log(1 - y)$, which has a known maximum value at $\dfrac{a}{a + b}$ for $y \in [0, 1]$ for any $a, b \in \mathbb{R}^2$ not including $\{0, 0\}$. Since the integral does not change the location of the maximum value (or the minimum value of $\mathcal{L}^{(D)}$) for this expression, the optimal discriminator is:

$$\mathcal{D}^*(x) = \frac{p_{data}}{p_{data} + p_g} \quad \text{(Equation 5.1.8)}$$

Consequently, the loss function given the optimal discriminator is:

$$\mathcal{L}^{(D^*)} = -\mathbb{E}_{x \sim p_{data}} \log \frac{p_{data}}{p_{data} + p_g} - \mathbb{E}_{x \sim p_g} \log\left(1 - \frac{p_{data}}{p_{data} + p_g}\right) \quad \text{(Equation 5.1.9)}$$

$$\mathcal{L}^{(D^*)} = -\mathbb{E}_{x \sim p_{data}} \log \frac{p_{data}}{p_{data} + p_g} - \mathbb{E}_{x \sim p_g} \log\left(\frac{p_g}{p_{data} + p_g}\right) \quad \text{(Equation 5.1.10)}$$

$$\mathcal{L}^{(D^*)} = 2\log 2 - D_{KL}\left(p_{data} \,\middle\|\, \frac{p_{data} + p_g}{2}\right) - D_{KL}\left(p_g \,\middle\|\, \frac{p_{data} + p_g}{2}\right) \quad \text{(Equation 5.1.11)}$$

$$\mathcal{L}^{(D^*)} = 2\log 2 - 2D_{JS}\big(p_{data} \,\|\, p_g\big) \quad \text{(Equation 5.1.12)}$$

We can observe from *Equation 5.1.12* that the loss function of the optimal discriminator is a constant minus twice the JS divergence between the true distribution, p_{data}, and any generator distribution, p_g. Minimizing $\mathcal{L}^{(D^*)}$ implies maximizing $D_{JS}(p_{data} \| p_g)$ or the discriminator must correctly classify fake from real data.

Meanwhile, we can safely argue that the optimal generator is when the generator distribution is equal to the true data distribution:

$$\mathcal{G}^*(x) \rightarrow p_g = p_{data} \quad \text{(Equation 5.1.13)}$$

This makes sense since the objective of the generator is to fool the discriminator by learning the true data distribution. Effectively, we can arrive at the optimal generator by minimizing D_{JS} or by making $p_g \rightarrow p_{data}$. Given an optimal generator, the optimal discriminator is $\mathcal{D}^*(x) = \frac{1}{2}$ with $\mathcal{L}^{(D^*)} = 2\log 2 = 0.60$.

The problem is that when the two distributions have no overlap, there's no smooth function that will help to close the gap between them. Training GANs will not converge by gradient descent. For example, let's suppose:

$$p_{data} = (x, y) \text{ where } x = 0, \qquad y \sim U(0,1) \quad \text{(Equation 5.1.14)}$$

$$p_g = (x, y) \text{ where } x = \theta, \qquad y \sim U(0,1) \quad \text{(Equation 5.1.15)}$$

These two distributions are shown in *Figure 5.1.2*:

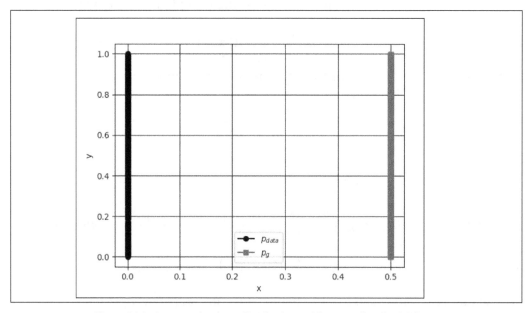

Figure 5.1.2: An example of two distributions with no overlap. $\theta = 0.5$ for p_g

$U(0, 1)$ is the uniform distribution. The divergence for each distance function is as follows:

- $D_{KL}\left(p_{data}\middle\|p_g\right) = \mathbb{E}_{x=0, y\sim U(0,1)} \log \dfrac{p_{data}(x, y)}{p_g(x, y)} = \sum 1 \log \dfrac{1}{0} = +\infty$

- $D_{KL}\left(p_g\middle\|p_{data}\right) = \mathbb{E}_{x=\theta, y\sim U(0,1)} \log \dfrac{p_g(x, y)}{p_{data}(x, y)} = \sum 1 \log \dfrac{1}{0} = +\infty$

- $$D_{JS}\left(p_{data}\middle\|p_g\right) = \frac{1}{2}\mathbb{E}_{x=0, y\sim U(0,1)} \log \frac{p_{data}(x, y)}{\frac{p_{data}(x, y) + p_g(x, y)}{2}} + \frac{1}{2}\mathbb{E}_{x=\theta, y\sim U(0,1)} \log \frac{p_g(x, y)}{\frac{p_{data}(x, y) + p_g(x, y)}{2}}$$
$$= \frac{1}{2}\sum 1 \log \frac{1}{\frac{1}{2}} + \frac{1}{2}\sum 1 \log \frac{1}{\frac{1}{2}} = \log 2$$

- $W\left(p_{data}, p_g\right) = |\theta|$

Since D_{JS} is a constant, the GAN will not have a sufficient gradient to drive $p_g \rightarrow p_{data}$. We'll also find that D_{KL}, or reverse D_{KL}, is not helpful either. However, with $W(p_{data}, p_g)$, we can have a smooth function in order to attain $p_g \rightarrow p_{data}$ by gradient descent. The EMD or Wasserstein 1 seems to be a more logical loss function in order to optimize GANs since D_{JS} fails in situations when two distributions have minimal to no overlap.

To aid understanding further, an excellent discussion on distance functions can be found at: `https://lilianweng.github.io/lil-log/2017/08/20/from-GAN-to-WGAN.html`.

In the next section, we will focus on using the EMD or the Wasserstein 1 distance function to develop an alternative loss function that will encourage stable training of GANs.

Use of Wasserstein loss

Before using EMD or Wasserstein 1, there is one more problem to overcome. It is intractable to exhaust the space of $\overset{inf}{\prod}(p_{data}, p_g)$ to find $\gamma \in \prod(p_{data}, p_g)$. The proposed solution is to use its Kantorovich-Rubinstein dual:

$$W\left(p_{data}, p_g\right) = \frac{1}{K} \sup_{\|f\|_L \leq K} \mathbb{E}_{x\sim p_{data}}[f(x)] - \mathbb{E}_{x\sim p_g}[f(x)] \quad \text{(Equation 5.1.16)}$$

Equivalently, EMD, $\sup\limits_{\|f\|_L \leq 1}$, is the supremum (roughly, maximum value) over all K-Lipschitz functions: $f: \mathcal{X} \rightarrow \mathbb{R}$. K-Lipschitz functions satisfy the constraint:

$$|f(x_1) - f(x_2)| \leq K|x_1 - x_2| \quad \text{(Equation 5.1.17)}$$

for all $x_1, x_2 \in \mathbb{R}$. K-Lipschitz functions have bounded derivatives and are almost always continuously differentiable (for example, $f(x) = |x|$ has bounded derivatives and is continuous but not differentiable at $x = 0$).

Equation 5.1.16 can be solved by finding a family of K-Lipschitz functions $\{f_w\}_{w \in \mathcal{W}}$:

$$W(p_{data}, p_g) = \max_{w \in \mathcal{W}} \mathbb{E}_{x \sim p_{data}}[f_w(x)] - \mathbb{E}_{x \sim p_g}[f_w(x)] \quad \text{(Equation 5.1.18)}$$

In the context of GANs, *Equation 5.1.18* can be rewritten by sampling from **z**-noise distribution and replacing f_w with the discriminator function, D_w:

$$W(p_{data}, p_g) = \max_{w \in \mathcal{W}} \mathbb{E}_{x \sim p_{data}}[D_w(x)] - \mathbb{E}_z[D_w(G(z))] \quad \text{(Equation 5.1.19)}$$

where we use bold letters to highlight the generality to multi-dimensional samples. The last problem is how to find the family of functions, $w \in \mathcal{W}$. The proposed solution is at every gradient update; the weights of the discriminator w are clipped between lower and upper bounds (for example, -0.01 and 0.01):

$$w \leftarrow clip(w, -0.01, 0.01) \quad \text{(Equation 5.1.20)}$$

The small values of w constrain the discriminator to a compact parameter space, thus ensuring Lipschitz continuity.

We can use *Equation 5.1.19* as the basis of our new GAN loss functions. EMD or Wasserstein 1 is the loss function that the generator aims to minimize and the cost function that the discriminator tries to maximize (or minimize $-W(p_{data}, p_g)$):

$$\mathcal{L}^{(D)} = -\mathbb{E}_{x \sim p_{data}} D_w(x) + \mathbb{E}_z D_w(G(z)) \quad \text{(Equation 5.1.21)}$$

$$\mathcal{L}^{(G)} = -\mathbb{E}_z D_w(G(z)) \quad \text{(Equation 5.1.22)}$$

In the generator loss function, the first term disappears since it is not directly optimizing with respect to the real data.

Table 5.1.2 shows the difference between the loss functions of a GAN and a WGAN. For conciseness, we simplified the notation for $\mathcal{L}^{(D)}$ and $\mathcal{L}^{(G)}$:

Network	Loss Functions	Equation
GAN	$\mathcal{L}^{(D)} = -\mathbb{E}_{x \sim p_{data}} \log \mathcal{D}(x) - \mathbb{E}_z \log\left(1 - \mathcal{D}(\mathcal{G}(z))\right)$	4.1.1
	$\mathcal{L}^{(G)} = -\mathbb{E}_z \log \mathcal{D}(\mathcal{G}(z))$	4.1.5
WGAN	$\mathcal{L}^{(D)} = -\mathbb{E}_{x \sim p_{data}} \mathcal{D}_w(x) + \mathbb{E}_z \mathcal{D}_w(\mathcal{G}(z))$	5.1.21
	$\mathcal{L}^{(G)} = -\mathbb{E}_z \mathcal{D}_w(\mathcal{G}(z))$	5.1.22
	$w \leftarrow clip(w, -0.01, 0.01)$	5.1.20

Table 5.1.2: A comparison between the loss functions of a GAN and a WGAN

These loss functions are used in training a WGAN, as shown in *Algorithm 5.1.1*.

Algorithm 5.1.1 WGAN. The values of the parameters are $\alpha = 0.00005, c = 0.01$, $m = 64$, and $n_{critic} = 5$.

Require: α, the learning rate. c, the clipping parameter. m, the batch size. n_{critic}, the number of the critic (discriminator) iterations per generator iteration.

Require: w_0, initial critic (discriminator) parameters. θ_0, initial generator parameters:

1.   while θ has not converged do
2.   for $t = 1, \dots, n_{critic}$ do
3.   Sample a batch $\{x^{(i)}\}_{i=1}^{m} \sim p_{data}$ from real data
4.   Sample a batch $\{z^{(i)}\}_{i=1}^{m} \sim p(z)$ from uniform noise distribution
5. $g_w \leftarrow \nabla_w \left[-\dfrac{1}{m} \sum_{i=1}^{m} \mathcal{D}_w(x^{(i)}) + \dfrac{1}{m} \sum_{i=1}^{m} \mathcal{D}_w\left(\mathcal{G}_\theta(z^{(i)})\right) \right]$, compute
         discriminator gradients
6. $w \leftarrow w - \alpha \times RMSProp(w, g_w)$, update discriminator parameters
7. $w \leftarrow clip(w, -c, c)$, clip discriminator weights
8.   end for

9. Sample a batch $\left\{z^{(i)}\right\}_{i=1}^{m} \sim p(z)$ from uniform noise distribution

10. $g_\theta \leftarrow -\nabla_\theta \frac{1}{m} \sum_{i=1}^{m} \mathcal{D}_w\left(\mathcal{G}_\theta(z^{(i)})\right)$, compute generator gradients

11. $\theta \leftarrow \theta - \alpha \times RMSProp(\theta, \mathcal{G}_\theta)$, update generator parameters

12. end while

Figure 5.1.3 illustrates that a WGAN model is practically the same as a DCGAN except for the fake/true data labels and loss functions:

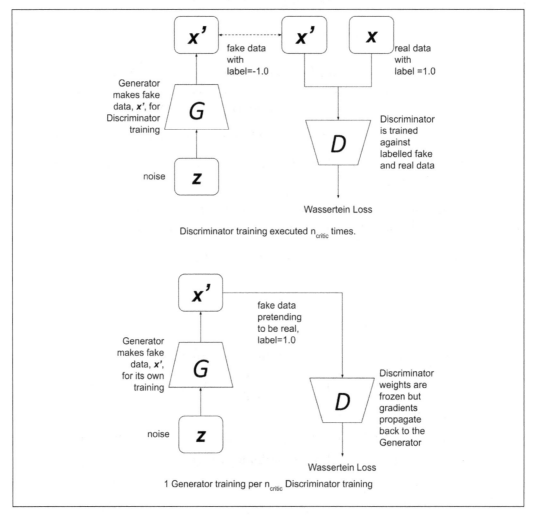

Figure 5.1.3: Top: Training the WGAN discriminator requires fake data from the generator and real data from the true distribution. Bottom: Training the WGAN generator requires fake data from the generator pretending to be real

Similar to GANs, WGAN alternately trains the discriminator and generator (through adversarial). However, in WGAN, the discriminator (also called the critic) trains n_{critic} iterations (lines 2 to 8) before training the generator for one iteration (lines 9 to 11). This is in contrast to GANs with an equal number of training iterations for both the discriminator and generator. In other words, in GANs, $n_{critic} = 1$.

Training the discriminator means learning the parameters (weights and biases) of the discriminator. This requires sampling a batch from the real data (line 3) and a batch from the fake data (line 4) and computing the gradient of discriminator parameters (line 5) after feeding the sampled data to the discriminator network. The discriminator parameters are optimized using RMSProp (line 6). Both lines 5 and 6 are the optimization of *Equation 5.1.21*.

Lastly, the Lipschitz constraint in the EM distance optimization is imposed by clipping the discriminator parameters (line 7). Line 7 is the implementation of *Equation 5.1.20*. After n_{critic} iterations of discriminator training, the discriminator parameters are frozen. The generator training starts by sampling a batch of fake data (line 9). The sampled data is labeled as real (1.0), endeavoring to fool the discriminator network. The generator gradients are computed in line 10 and optimized using the RMSProp in line 11. Lines 10 and 11 perform gradient updates to optimize *Equation 5.1.22*.

After training the generator, the discriminator parameters are unfrozen, and another n_{critic} discriminator training iteration starts. We should note that there is no need to freeze the generator parameters during discriminator training as the generator is only involved in the fabrication of data. Similar to GANs, the discriminator can be trained as a separate network. However, training the generator always requires the participation of the discriminator through the adversarial network since the loss is computed from the output of the generator network.

Unlike GANs, in a WGAN, real data is labeled 1.0, while fake data is labeled -1.0 as a workaround in computing the gradient in line 5. Lines 5-6 and 10-11 perform gradient updates to optimize *Equations 5.1.21* and *5.1.22*, respectively. Each term in lines 5 and 10 is modeled as:

$$\mathcal{L} = -y_{label}\frac{1}{m}\sum_{i=1}^{m} y_{pred} \quad \text{(Equation 5.1.23)}$$

Where $y_{label} = 1.0$ for the real data and $y_{label} = -1.0$ for the fake data. We removed the superscript (i) for simplicity of notation. For the discriminator, WGAN increases $y_{pred} = \mathcal{D}_w(x)$ to minimize the loss function when training using the real data.

When training using fake data, WGAN decreases $y_{pred} = \mathcal{D}_w(\mathcal{G}(z))$ to minimize the loss function. For the generator, WGAN increases $y_{pred} = \mathcal{D}_w(\mathcal{G}(z)))$ as to minimize the loss function when the fake data is labeled as real during training. Note that y_{label} has no direct contribution in the loss function other than its sign. In tf.keras, *Equation 5.1.23* is implemented as:

```
def wasserstein_loss(y_label, y_pred):
    return -K.mean(y_label * y_pred)
```

The most important part of this section is the new loss function for the stable training of GANs. It is based on the EMD or Wasserstein 1. *Algorithm 5.1.1* formalizes the complete training algorithm of WGAN, including the loss function. In the next section, the implementation of the training algorithm in tf.keras is presented.

WGAN implementation using Keras

To implement WGAN in tf.keras, we can reuse the DCGAN implementation of GANs, something we introduced in the previous chapter. The DCGAN builder and utility functions are implemented in gan.py in the lib folder as a module.

The functions include:

- generator(): A generator model builder
- discriminator(): A discriminator model builder
- train(): A DCGAN trainer
- plot_images(): A generic generator outputs plotter
- test_generator(): A generic generator test utility

As shown in *Listing 5.1.1*, we can build a discriminator by simply calling:

```
discriminator = gan.discriminator(inputs, activation='linear')
```

WGAN uses linear output activation. For the generator, we execute:

```
generator = gan.generator(inputs, image_size)
```

The overall network model in tf.keras is similar to the one seen in *Figure 4.2.1* for DCGAN.

Listing 5.1.1 highlights the use of the RMSprop optimizer and Wasserstein loss function. The hyperparameters in *Algorithm 5.1.1* are used during training.

The complete code is available on GitHub: `https://github.com/PacktPublishing/Advanced-Deep-Learning-with-Keras`

Listing 5.1.1: `wgan-mnist-5.1.2.py`

```
def build_and_train_models():
    """Load the dataset, build WGAN discriminator,
    generator, and adversarial models.
    Call the WGAN train routine.
    """
    # load MNIST dataset
    (x_train, _), (_, _) = mnist.load_data()

    # reshape data for CNN as (28, 28, 1) and normalize
    image_size = x_train.shape[1]
    x_train = np.reshape(x_train, [-1, image_size, image_size, 1])
    x_train = x_train.astype('float32') / 255

    model_name = "wgan_mnist"
    # network parameters
    # the latent or z vector is 100-dim
    latent_size = 100
    # hyper parameters from WGAN paper [2]
    n_critic = 5
    clip_value = 0.01
    batch_size = 64
    lr = 5e-5
    train_steps = 40000
    input_shape = (image_size, image_size, 1)

    # build discriminator model
    inputs = Input(shape=input_shape, name='discriminator_input')
    # WGAN uses linear activation in paper [2]
    discriminator = gan.discriminator(inputs, activation='linear')
    optimizer = RMSprop(lr=lr)
    # WGAN discriminator uses wassertein loss
    discriminator.compile(loss=wasserstein_loss,
                          optimizer=optimizer,
                          metrics=['accuracy'])
    discriminator.summary()
```

```
# build generator model
input_shape = (latent_size, )
inputs = Input(shape=input_shape, name='z_input')
generator = gan.generator(inputs, image_size)
generator.summary()

# build adversarial model = generator + discriminator
# freeze the weights of discriminator during adversarial training
discriminator.trainable = False
adversarial = Model(inputs,
                    discriminator(generator(inputs)),
                    name=model_name)
adversarial.compile(loss=wasserstein_loss,
                    optimizer=optimizer,
                    metrics=['accuracy'])
adversarial.summary()

# train discriminator and adversarial networks
models = (generator, discriminator, adversarial)
params = (batch_size,
          latent_size,
          n_critic,
          clip_value,
          train_steps,
          model_name)
train(models, x_train, params)
```

Listing 5.1.2 is the training function that closely follows *Algorithm 5.1.1*. However, there is a minor tweak in the training of the discriminator. Instead of training the weights in a single combined batch of both real and fake data, we'll train with one batch of real data first and then a batch of fake data. This tweak will prevent the gradient from vanishing because of the opposite sign in the label of real and fake data and the small magnitude of weights due to clipping.

Listing 5.1.2: wgan-mnist-5.1.2.py

Training algorithm for WGAN:

```
def train(models, x_train, params):
    """Train the Discriminator and Adversarial Networks
    Alternately train Discriminator and Adversarial
    networks by batch.
    Discriminator is trained first with properly labelled
    real and fake images for n_critic times.
    Discriminator weights are clipped as a requirement
    of Lipschitz constraint.
```

```
Generator is trained next (via Adversarial) with
fake images pretending to be real.
Generate sample images per save_interval
Arguments:
    models (list): Generator, Discriminator,
        Adversarial models
    x_train (tensor): Train images
    params (list) : Networks parameters
"""
# the GAN models
generator, discriminator, adversarial = models
# network parameters
(batch_size, latent_size, n_critic,
        clip_value, train_steps, model_name) = params
# the generator image is saved every 500 steps
save_interval = 500
# noise vector to see how the
# generator output evolves during training
noise_input = np.random.uniform(-1.0,
                                  1.0,
                                  size=[16, latent_size])
# number of elements in train dataset
train_size = x_train.shape[0]
# labels for real data
real_labels = np.ones((batch_size, 1))
for i in range(train_steps):
    # train discriminator n_critic times
    loss = 0
    acc = 0
    for _ in range(n_critic):
        # train the discriminator for 1 batch
        # 1 batch of real (label=1.0) and
        # fake images (label=-1.0)
        # randomly pick real images from dataset
        rand_indexes = np.random.randint(0,
                                           train_size,
                                           size=batch_size)
        real_images = x_train[rand_indexes]
        # generate fake images from noise using generator
        # generate noise using uniform distribution
        noise = np.random.uniform(-1.0,
                                   1.0,
                                   size=[batch_size, latent_size])
        fake_images = generator.predict(noise)

        # train the discriminator network
        # real data label=1, fake data label=-1
```

```
            # instead of 1 combined batch of real and fake images,
            # train with 1 batch of real data first, then 1 batch
            # of fake images.
            # this tweak prevents the gradient
            # from vanishing due to opposite
            # signs of real and fake data labels (i.e. +1 and -1) and
            # small magnitude of weights due to clipping.
            real_loss, real_acc = \
                discriminator.train_on_batch(real_images,
                                                  real_labels)
            fake_loss, fake_acc = \
                discriminator.train_on_batch(fake_images,
                                                  -real_labels)
            # accumulate average loss and accuracy
            loss += 0.5 * (real_loss + fake_loss)
            acc += 0.5 * (real_acc + fake_acc)

            # clip discriminator weights to satisfy Lipschitz
constraint
            for layer in discriminator.layers:
                weights = layer.get_weights()
                weights = [np.clip(weight,
                                    -clip_value,
                                    clip_value) for weight in weights]
                layer.set_weights(weights)

        # average loss and accuracy per n_critic training iterations
        loss /= n_critic
        acc /= n_critic
        log = "%d: [discriminator loss: %f, acc: %f]" % (i, loss, acc)

        # train the adversarial network for 1 batch
        # 1 batch of fake images with label=1.0
        # since the discriminator weights are frozen in
        # adversarial network only the generator is trained
        # generate noise using uniform distribution
        noise = np.random.uniform(-1.0,
                                    1.0,
                                    size=[batch_size, latent_size])
        # train the adversarial network
        # note that unlike in discriminator training,
        # we do not save the fake images in a variable
        # the fake images go to the discriminator
        # input of the adversarial for classification
        # fake images are labelled as real
        # log the loss and accuracy
        loss, acc = adversarial.train_on_batch(noise, real_labels)
```

```
log = "%s [adversarial loss: %f, acc: %f]" % (log, loss, acc)
print(log)
if (i + 1) % save_interval == 0:
    # plot generator images on a periodic basis
    gan.plot_images(generator,
                    noise_input=noise_input,
                    show=False,
                    step=(i + 1),
                    model_name=model_name)

# save the model after training the generator
# the trained generator can be reloaded
# for future MNIST digit generation
generator.save(model_name + ".h5")
```

Figure 5.1.4 shows the evolution of the WGAN outputs on the MNIST dataset:

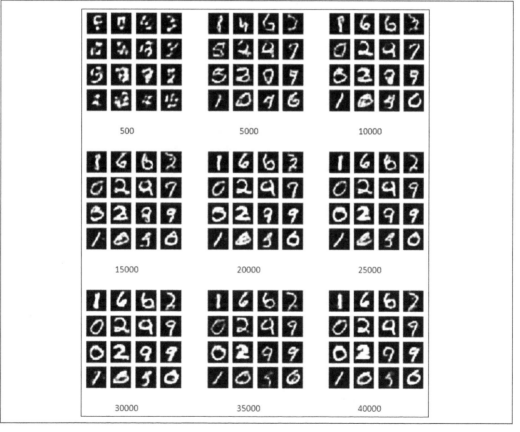

Figure 5.1.4: The sample outputs of WGAN versus training steps. WGAN does not suffer mode collapse in any of the outputs during training and testing

The WGAN is stable even under network configuration changes. For example, DCGAN is known to be unstable when batch normalization is inserted before the ReLU in the discriminator network. The same configuration is stable in WGAN.

The following *Figure 5.1.5* shows us the outputs of both DCGAN and WGAN with batch normalization on the discriminator network:

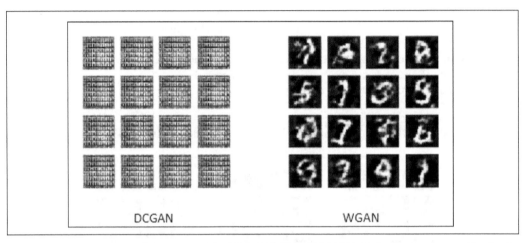

Figure 5.1.5: A comparison of the output of the DCGAN (left) and WGAN (right) when batch normalization is inserted before the ReLU activation in the discriminator network

Similar to the GAN training in the previous chapter, the trained model is saved on a file after 40,000 training steps. Using the trained generator model, new synthesized MNIST digit images are generated by running the following command:

```
python3 wgan-mnist-5.1.2.py --generator=wgan_mnist.h5
```

As we have discussed, the original GAN is difficult to train. The problem arises when the GAN optimizes its loss function; it's actually optimizing the *JS* divergence, D_{JS}. It is difficult to optimize D_{JS} when there is little to no overlap between two distribution functions.

WGAN proposed to address the problem by using the EMD or Wasserstein 1 loss function, which has a smooth differentiable function even when there is little or no overlap between the two distributions. However, WGAN is not concerned with the generated image quality. Apart from stability issues, there are still areas of improvement in terms of perceptive quality in the generated images of the original GAN. LSGAN theorizes that the twin problems can be solved simultaneously. We'll take a look at LSGAN in the following section.

2. Least-squares GAN (LSGAN)

LSGAN proposes the least squares loss. *Figure 5.2.1* demonstrates why the use of a sigmoid cross-entropy loss in GANs results in poorly generated data quality:

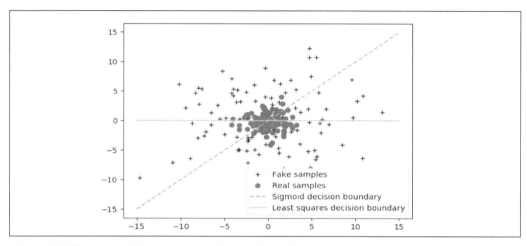

Figure 5.2.1: Both real and fake sample distributions divided by their respective decision boundaries: sigmoid and least squares

Ideally, the fake sample distribution should be as close as possible to the true samples' distribution. However, for GANs, once the fake samples are already on the correct side of the decision boundary, the gradients vanish.

This prevents the generator from having enough motivation to improve the quality of the generated fake data. Fake samples far from the decision boundary will no longer attempt to move closer to the true samples' distribution. Using the least squares loss function, the gradients do not vanish as long as the fake sample distribution is far from the real samples' distribution. The generator will strive to improve its estimate of real density distribution even if the fake samples are already on the correct side of the decision boundary.

Table 5.2.1 shows the comparison of the loss functions between GAN, WGAN, and LSGAN:

Network	Loss Functions	Equation
GAN	$\mathcal{L}^{(D)} = -\mathbb{E}_{x \sim p_{data}} \log \mathcal{D}(x) - \mathbb{E}_z \log\big(1 - \mathcal{D}(\mathcal{G}(z))\big)$	4.1.1
	$\mathcal{L}^{(G)} = -\mathbb{E}_z \log \mathcal{D}(\mathcal{G}(z))$	4.1.5

WGAN	$\mathcal{L}^{(D)} = -\mathbb{E}_{x \sim p_{data}} \mathcal{D}_w(x) + \mathbb{E}_z \mathcal{D}_w(\mathcal{G}(z))$	5.1.21
	$\mathcal{L}^{(G)} = -\mathbb{E}_z \mathcal{D}_w(\mathcal{G}(z))$	5.1.22
	$w \leftarrow clip(w, -0.01, 0.01)$	5.1.20
LSGAN	$\mathcal{L}^{(D)} = \mathbb{E}_{x \sim p_{data}} (\mathcal{D}(x) - 1)^2 + \mathbb{E}_z \mathcal{D}(\mathcal{G}(z))^2$	5.2.1
	$\mathcal{L}^{(G)} = \mathbb{E}_z (\mathcal{D}(\mathcal{G}(z)) - 1)^2$	5.2.2

Table 5.2.1: A comparison between the loss functions of GAN, WGAN, and LSGAN

Minimizing *Equation 5.2.1* or the discriminator loss function implies that the MSE between real data classification and the true label 1.0 should be close to zero. In addition, the MSE between the fake data classification and the true label 0.0 should be close to zero.

Similar to other GANs, the LSGAN discriminator is trained to classify real from fake data samples. Minimizing *Equation 5.2.2* means fooling the discriminator to think that the generated fake sample data is real with the help of label 1.0.

Implementing LSGAN using the DCGAN code in the previous chapter as the basis only requires a few changes. As shown in *Listing 5.2.1*, the discriminator sigmoid activation is removed. The discriminator is built by calling:

```
discriminator = gan.discriminator(inputs, activation=None)
```

The generator is similar to the original DCGAN:

```
generator = gan.generator(inputs, image_size)
```

Both the discriminator and adversarial loss functions are replaced by mse. All the network parameters are the same as in DCGAN. The network model of LSGAN in tf.keras is similar to *Figure 4.2.1* except that there is linear or no output activation. The training process is similar to that seen in DCGAN and is provided by the utility function:

```
gan.train(models, x_train, params)
```

Listing 5.2.1: lsgan-mnist-5.2.1.py

```
def build_and_train_models():
    """Load the dataset, build LSGAN discriminator,
    generator, and adversarial models.
    Call the LSGAN train routine.
    """
    # load MNIST dataset
    (x_train, _), (_, _) = mnist.load_data()
```

```
# reshape data for CNN as (28, 28, 1) and normalize
image_size = x_train.shape[1]
x_train = np.reshape(x_train,
                     [-1, image_size, image_size, 1])
x_train = x_train.astype('float32') / 255

model_name = "lsgan_mnist"
# network parameters
# the latent or z vector is 100-dim
latent_size = 100
input_shape = (image_size, image_size, 1)
batch_size = 64
lr = 2e-4
decay = 6e-8
train_steps = 40000


# build discriminator model
inputs = Input(shape=input_shape, name='discriminator_input')
discriminator = gan.discriminator(inputs, activation=None)
# [1] uses Adam, but discriminator easily
# converges with RMSprop
optimizer = RMSprop(lr=lr, decay=decay)
# LSGAN uses MSE loss [2]
discriminator.compile(loss='mse',
                      optimizer=optimizer,
                      metrics=['accuracy'])
discriminator.summary()

# build generator model
input_shape = (latent_size, )
inputs = Input(shape=input_shape, name='z_input')
generator = gan.generator(inputs, image_size)
generator.summary()

# build adversarial model = generator + discriminator
optimizer = RMSprop(lr=lr*0.5, decay=decay*0.5)
# freeze the weights of discriminator
# during adversarial training
discriminator.trainable = False
adversarial = Model(inputs,
                    discriminator(generator(inputs)),
                    name=model_name)
# LSGAN uses MSE loss [2]
adversarial.compile(loss='mse',
                    optimizer=optimizer,
                    metrics=['accuracy'])
adversarial.summary()

# train discriminator and adversarial networks
```

```
models = (generator, discriminator, adversarial)
params = (batch_size, latent_size, train_steps, model_name)
gan.train(models, x_train, params)
```

Figure 5.2.2 shows generated samples after training LSGAN using the MNIST dataset for 40,000 training steps:

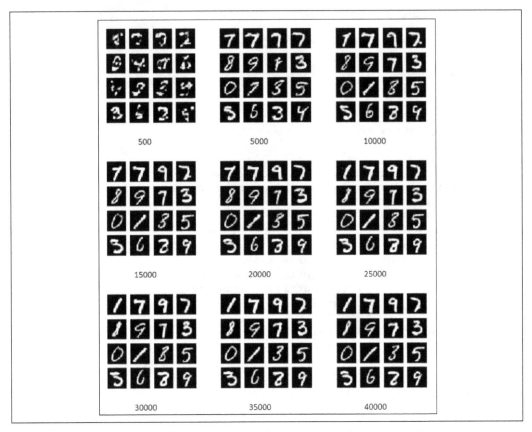

Figure 5.2.2: Sample outputs of LSGAN versus training steps

The output images have better perceptual quality compared to *Figure 4.2.1* in DCGAN seen in the previous chapter.

Using the trained generator model, new synthesized MNIST digit images are generated by running the following command:

```
python3 lsgan-mnist-5.2.1.py --generator=lsgan_mnist.h5
```

In this section, we discussed another improvement in the loss function. With the use of MSE or L2, we addressed the twin problems of training the stability and perceptive quality of the GANs. In the next section, another improvement is proposed, this time in relation to CGAN, which was discussed in the previous chapter.

3. Auxiliary Classifier GAN (ACGAN)

ACGAN is similar in principle to the **Conditional GAN (CGAN)** that we discussed in the previous chapter. We're going to compare both CGAN and ACGAN. For both CGAN and ACGAN, the generator inputs are noise and its label. The output is a fake image belonging to the input class label. For CGAN, the inputs to the discriminator are an image (fake or real) and its label. The output is the probability that the image is real. For ACGAN, the input to the discriminator is an image, whilst the output is the probability that the image is real and its class is a label.

Figure 5.3.1 highlights the difference between CGAN and ACGAN during generator training:

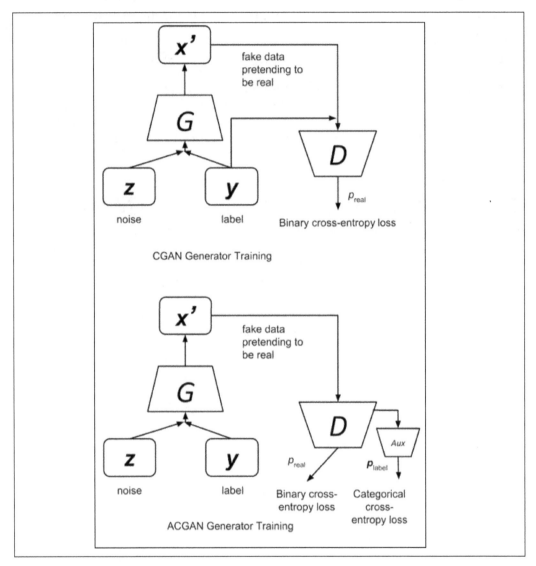

Figure 5.3.1: CGAN versus ACGAN generator training.
The main difference is the input and output of the discriminator

Essentially, in CGAN we feed the network with side information (label). In ACGAN, we try to reconstruct the side information using an auxiliary class decoder network. ACGAN theory argues that forcing the network to do additional tasks is known to improve the performance of the original task. In this case, the additional task is image classification. The original task is the generation of fake images.

Table 5.3.1 shows ACGAN loss functions as compared to CGAN loss functions:

Network	Loss Functions	Number
CGAN	$$\mathcal{L}^{(D)} = -\mathbb{E}_{x \sim p_{data}} \log \mathcal{D}(x|y) - \mathbb{E}_z \log\left(1 - \mathcal{D}(\mathcal{G}(z|y))\right)$$	4.3.1
	$$\mathcal{L}^{(G)} = -\mathbb{E}_z \log \mathcal{D}(\mathcal{G}(z|y))$$	4.3.2
ACGAN	$\mathcal{L}^{(D)} = -\mathbb{E}_{x \sim p_{data}} \log \mathcal{D}(x) - \mathbb{E}_z \log\left(1 - \mathcal{D}(\mathcal{G}(z|y))\right) - \mathbb{E}_{x \sim p_{data}} \log \mathcal{P}(c|x) - \mathbb{E}_z \log \mathcal{P}(c|\mathcal{G}(z|y))$	5.3.1
	$$\mathcal{L}^{(G)} = -\mathbb{E}_z \log \mathcal{D}(\mathcal{G}(z|y)) - \mathbb{E}_z \log \mathcal{P}(c|\mathcal{G}(z|y))$$	5.3.2

Table 5.3.1: A comparison between the loss functions of CGAN and ACGAN

ACGAN loss functions are the same as CGAN except for the additional classifier loss functions. Apart from the original task of identifying real from fake images $\left(-\mathbb{E}_{x \sim p_{data}} \log \mathcal{D}(x|y) - \mathbb{E}_z \log\left(1 - \mathcal{D}(\mathcal{G}(z|y))\right)\right)$, *Equation 5.3.1* of the discriminator has the additional task of correctly classifying real and fake images $\left(-\mathbb{E}_{x \sim p_{data}} \log \mathcal{P}(c|x) - \mathbb{E}_z \log \mathcal{P}(c|\mathcal{G}(z|y))\right)$. *Equation 5.3.2* of the generator means that apart from trying to fool the discriminator with fake images $(-\mathbb{E}_z \log \mathcal{D}(\mathcal{G}(z|y)))$, it is asking the discriminator to correctly classify those fake images $(-\mathbb{E}_z \log \mathcal{P}(c|\mathcal{G}(z|y)))$.

Starting with the CGAN code, only the discriminator and the training function are modified to implement an ACGAN. The discriminator and generator builder functions are also provided by gan.py. To see the changes made on the discriminator, *Listing 5.3.1* shows the builder function, where the auxiliary decoder network that performs image classification and the dual outputs are highlighted.

Listing 5.3.1: gan.py

```
def discriminator(inputs,
                  activation='sigmoid',
                  num_labels=None,
                  num_codes=None):
    """Build a Discriminator Model

    Stack of LeakyReLU-Conv2D to discriminate real from fake
    The network does not converge with BN so it is not used here
    unlike in [1]
```

```
            Arguments:
                inputs (Layer): Input layer of the discriminator (the image)
                activation (string): Name of output activation layer
                num_labels (int): Dimension of one-hot labels for ACGAN &
        InfoGAN
                num_codes (int): num_codes-dim Q network as output
                        if StackedGAN or 2 Q networks if InfoGAN


            Returns:
                Model: Discriminator Model
            """
            kernel_size = 5
            layer_filters = [32, 64, 128, 256]

            x = inputs
            for filters in layer_filters:
                # first 3 convolution layers use strides = 2
                # last one uses strides = 1
                if filters == layer_filters[-1]:
                    strides = 1
                else:
                    strides = 2
                x = LeakyReLU(alpha=0.2)(x)
                x = Conv2D(filters=filters,
                        kernel_size=kernel_size,
                        strides=strides,
                        padding='same')(x)

            x = Flatten()(x)
            # default output is probability that the image is real
            outputs = Dense(1)(x)
            if activation is not None:
                print(activation)
                outputs = Activation(activation)(outputs)

            if num_labels:
                # ACGAN and InfoGAN have 2nd output
                # 2nd output is 10-dim one-hot vector of label
                layer = Dense(layer_filters[-2])(x)
                labels = Dense(num_labels)(layer)
                labels = Activation('softmax', name='label')(labels)
                if num_codes is None:
                    outputs = [outputs, labels]
```

```
    else:
        # InfoGAN have 3rd and 4th outputs
        # 3rd output is 1-dim continous Q of 1st c given x
        code1 = Dense(1)(layer)
        code1 = Activation('sigmoid', name='code1')(code1)

        # 4th output is 1-dim continuous Q of 2nd c given x
        code2 = Dense(1)(layer)
        code2 = Activation('sigmoid', name='code2')(code2)

        outputs = [outputs, labels, code1, code2]
    elif num_codes is not None:
        # StackedGAN Q0 output
        # z0_recon is reconstruction of z0 normal distribution
        z0_recon =  Dense(num_codes)(x)
        z0_recon = Activation('tanh', name='z0')(z0_recon)
        outputs = [outputs, z0_recon]

    return Model(inputs, outputs, name='discriminator')
```

The discriminator is then built by calling:

```
discriminator = gan.discriminator(inputs, num_labels=num_labels)
```

The generator is the same as the one in WGAN and LSGAN. To recall, the generator builder is shown in the following *Listing 5.3.2*. We should note that both *Listings 5.3.1* and *5.3.2* are the same builder functions used by WGAN and LSGAN in the previous sections. Highlighted are the parts applicable to LSGAN.

Listing 5.3.2: gan.py

```
def generator(inputs,
              image_size,
              activation='sigmoid',
              labels=None,
              codes=None):
    """Build a Generator Model

    Stack of BN-ReLU-Conv2DTranpose to generate fake images.
    Output activation is sigmoid instead of tanh in [1].
    Sigmoid converges easily.

    Arguments:
        inputs (Layer): Input layer of the generator (the z-vector)
        image_size (int): Target size of one side
            (assuming square image)
```

```
        activation (string): Name of output activation layer
        labels (tensor): Input labels
        codes (list): 2-dim disentangled codes for InfoGAN

    Returns:
        Model: Generator Model
    """
    image_resize = image_size // 4
    # network parameters
    kernel_size = 5
    layer_filters = [128, 64, 32, 1]

    if labels is not None:
        if codes is None:
            # ACGAN labels
            # concatenate z noise vector and one-hot labels
            inputs = [inputs, labels]
        else:
            # infoGAN codes
            # concatenate z noise vector,
            # one-hot labels and codes 1 & 2
            inputs = [inputs, labels] + codes
        x = concatenate(inputs, axis=1)
    elif codes is not None:
        # generator 0 of StackedGAN
        inputs = [inputs, codes]
        x = concatenate(inputs, axis=1)
    else:
        # default input is just 100-dim noise (z-code)
        x = inputs

    x = Dense(image_resize * image_resize * layer_filters[0])(x)
    x = Reshape((image_resize, image_resize, layer_filters[0]))(x)

    for filters in layer_filters:
        # first two convolution layers use strides = 2
        # the last two use strides = 1
        if filters > layer_filters[-2]:
            strides = 2
        else:
            strides = 1
        x = BatchNormalization()(x)
        x = Activation('relu')(x)
        x = Conv2DTranspose(filters=filters,
```

```
                kernel_size=kernel_size,
                strides=strides,
                padding='same')(x)

    if activation is not None:
        x = Activation(activation)(x)

    # generator output is the synthesized image x
    return Model(inputs, x, name='generator')
```

In ACGAN, the generator is instantiated as:

```
generator = gan.generator(inputs, image_size, labels=labels)
```

Figure 5.3.2 shows the network model of ACGAN in `tf.keras`:

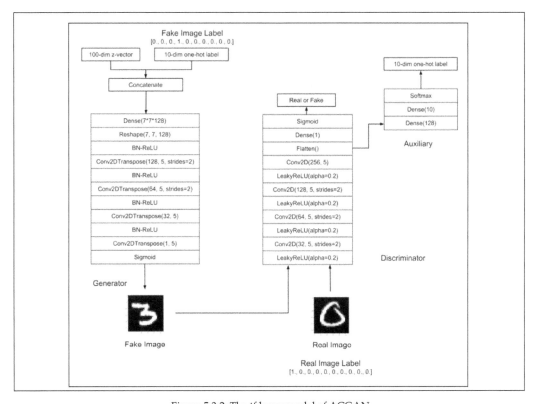

Figure 5.3.2: The tf.keras model of ACGAN

As shown in *Listing 5.3.3*, the discriminator and adversarial models are modified to accommodate the changes in the discriminator network. We now have two loss functions. The first is the original binary cross-entropy to train the discriminator in estimating the probability of the input image being real.

The second is the image classifier predicting the class label. The output is a one-hot vector of 10 dimensions.

Listing 5.3.3: `acgan-mnist-5.3.1.py`

Highlighted are the changes implemented in the discriminator and adversarial networks:

```
def build_and_train_models():
    """Load the dataset, build ACGAN discriminator,
    generator, and adversarial models.
    Call the ACGAN train routine.
    """
    # load MNIST dataset
    (x_train, y_train), (_, _) = mnist.load_data()

    # reshape data for CNN as (28, 28, 1) and normalize
    image_size = x_train.shape[1]
    x_train = np.reshape(x_train,
                         [-1, image_size, image_size, 1])
    x_train = x_train.astype('float32') / 255

    # train labels
    num_labels = len(np.unique(y_train))
    y_train = to_categorical(y_train)

    model_name = "acgan_mnist"
    # network parameters
    latent_size = 100
    batch_size = 64
    train_steps = 40000
    lr = 2e-4
    decay = 6e-8
    input_shape = (image_size, image_size, 1)
    label_shape = (num_labels, )

    # build discriminator Model
    inputs = Input(shape=input_shape,
                   name='discriminator_input')
    # call discriminator builder
    # with 2 outputs, pred source and labels
    discriminator = gan.discriminator(inputs,
                                      num_labels=num_labels)
    # [1] uses Adam, but discriminator
    # easily converges with RMSprop
```

```
optimizer = RMSprop(lr=lr, decay=decay)
# 2 loss fuctions: 1) probability image is real
# 2) class label of the image
loss = ['binary_crossentropy', 'categorical_crossentropy']
discriminator.compile(loss=loss,
                      optimizer=optimizer,
                      metrics=['accuracy'])
discriminator.summary()

# build generator model
input_shape = (latent_size, )
inputs = Input(shape=input_shape, name='z_input')
labels = Input(shape=label_shape, name='labels')
# call generator builder with input labels
generator = gan.generator(inputs,
                          image_size,
                          labels=labels)
generator.summary()

# build adversarial model = generator + discriminator
optimizer = RMSprop(lr=lr*0.5, decay=decay*0.5)
# freeze the weights of discriminator
# during adversarial training
discriminator.trainable = False
adversarial = Model([inputs, labels],
                    discriminator(generator([inputs, labels])),
                    name=model_name)
# same 2 loss fuctions: 1) probability image is real
# 2) class label of the image
adversarial.compile(loss=loss,
                    optimizer=optimizer,
                    metrics=['accuracy'])
adversarial.summary()

# train discriminator and adversarial networks
models = (generator, discriminator, adversarial)
data = (x_train, y_train)
params = (batch_size, latent_size, \
          train_steps, num_labels, model_name)
train(models, data, params)
```

In *Listing 5.3.4*, we highlight the changes implemented in the training routine. The main difference compared to CGAN code is that the output label must be supplied during discriminator and adversarial training.

Listing 5.3.4: acgan-mnist-5.3.1.py

```python
def train(models, data, params):
    """Train the discriminator and adversarial Networks
    Alternately train discriminator and adversarial
    networks by batch.
    Discriminator is trained first with real and fake
    images and corresponding one-hot labels.
    Adversarial is trained next with fake images pretending
    to be real and corresponding one-hot labels.
    Generate sample images per save_interval.
    # Arguments
        models (list): Generator, Discriminator,
            Adversarial models
        data (list): x_train, y_train data
        params (list): Network parameters
    """
    # the GAN models
    generator, discriminator, adversarial = models
    # images and their one-hot labels
    x_train, y_train = data
    # network parameters
    batch_size, latent_size, train_steps, num_labels, model_name \
        = params
    # the generator image is saved every 500 steps
    save_interval = 500
    # noise vector to see how the generator
    # output evolves during training
    noise_input = np.random.uniform(-1.0,
                                     1.0,
                                     size=[16, latent_size])
    # class labels are 0, 1, 2, 3, 4, 5,
    # 6, 7, 8, 9, 0, 1, 2, 3, 4, 5
    # the generator must produce these MNIST digits
    noise_label = np.eye(num_labels)[np.arange(0, 16) % num_labels]
    # number of elements in train dataset
    train_size = x_train.shape[0]
    print(model_name,
          "Labels for generated images: ",
          np.argmax(noise_label, axis=1))

    for i in range(train_steps):
        # train the discriminator for 1 batch
        # 1 batch of real (label=1.0) and fake images (label=0.0)
```

```
# randomly pick real images and
# corresponding labels from dataset
rand_indexes = np.random.randint(0,
                                  train_size,
                                  size=batch_size)
real_images = x_train[rand_indexes]
real_labels = y_train[rand_indexes]
# generate fake images from noise using generator
# generate noise using uniform distribution
noise = np.random.uniform(-1.0,
                          1.0,
                          size=[batch_size, latent_size])
# randomly pick one-hot labels
fake_labels = np.eye(num_labels)[np.random.choice(num_labels,
                                                  batch_size)]
# generate fake images
fake_images = generator.predict([noise, fake_labels])
# real + fake images = 1 batch of train data
x = np.concatenate((real_images, fake_images))
# real + fake labels = 1 batch of train data labels
labels = np.concatenate((real_labels, fake_labels))

# label real and fake images
# real images label is 1.0
y = np.ones([2 * batch_size, 1])
# fake images label is 0.0
y[batch_size:, :] = 0
# train discriminator network, log the loss and accuracy
# ['loss', 'activation_1_loss',
# 'label_loss', 'activation_1_acc', 'label_acc']
metrics  = discriminator.train_on_batch(x, [y, labels])
fmt = "%d: [disc loss: %f, srcloss: %f,"
fmt += "lblloss: %f, srcacc: %f, lblacc: %f]"
log = fmt % (i, metrics[0], metrics[1], \
        metrics[2], metrics[3], metrics[4])

# train the adversarial network for 1 batch
# 1 batch of fake images with label=1.0 and
# corresponding one-hot label or class
# since the discriminator weights are frozen
# in adversarial network only the generator is trained
# generate noise using uniform distribution
noise = np.random.uniform(-1.0,
                          1.0,
```

```
                                          size=[batch_size, latent_size])
              # randomly pick one-hot labels
              fake_labels = np.eye(num_labels)[np.random.choice(num_labels,
                                                                batch_size)]

              # label fake images as real
              y = np.ones([batch_size, 1])
              # train the adversarial network
              # note that unlike in discriminator training,
              # we do not save the fake images in a variable
              # the fake images go to the discriminator input
              # of the adversarial for classification
              # log the loss and accuracy
              metrics  = adversarial.train_on_batch([noise, fake_labels],
                                                    [y, fake_labels])
              fmt = "%s [advr loss: %f, srcloss: %f,"
              fmt += "lblloss: %f, srcacc: %f, lblacc: %f]"
              log = fmt % (log, metrics[0], metrics[1],\
                      metrics[2], metrics[3], metrics[4])
              print(log)
              if (i + 1) % save_interval == 0:
                  # plot generator images on a periodic basis
                  gan.plot_images(generator,
                              noise_input=noise_input,
                              noise_label=noise_label,
                              show=False,
                              step=(i + 1),
                              model_name=model_name)

          # save the model after training the generator
          # the trained generator can be reloaded
          # for future MNIST digit generation
          generator.save(model_name + ".h5")
```

It transpires that with the additional task, the performance improvement in ACGAN is significant compared to all GANs that we have discussed previously. ACGAN training is stable, as shown in *Figure 5.3.3* sample outputs of ACGAN for the following labels:

```
[0    1    2    3

 4    5    6    7

 8    9    0    1

 2    3    4    5]
```

Unlike in CGAN, the appearance of the sample outputs does not vary widely during training. The MNIST digit image perceptive quality is also better.

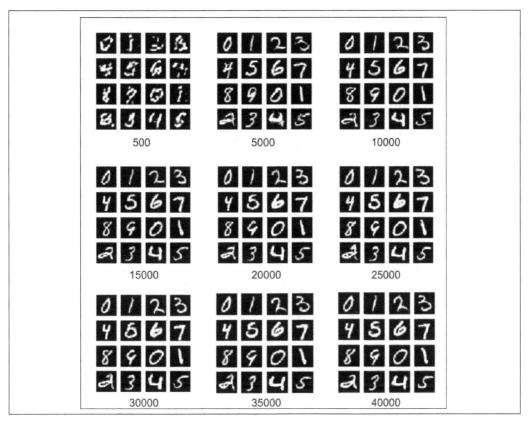

Figure 5.3.3: The sample outputs generated by the ACGAN as a function
of training steps for labels [0 1 2 3 4 5 6 7 8 9 0 1 2 3 4 5]

Using the trained generator model, new synthesized MNIST digit images are generated by running:

```
python3 acgan-mnist-5.3.1.py --generator=acgan_mnist.h5
```

Alternatively, the generation of a specific digit (for example, 3) to be generated can also be requested:

```
python3 acgan-mnist-5.3.1.py --generator=acgan_mnist.h5 --digit=3
```

Figure 5.3.4 shows a side-by-side comparison of every MNIST digit produced by both CGAN and ACGAN. Digits 2-6 are of better quality in ACGAN than in CGAN:

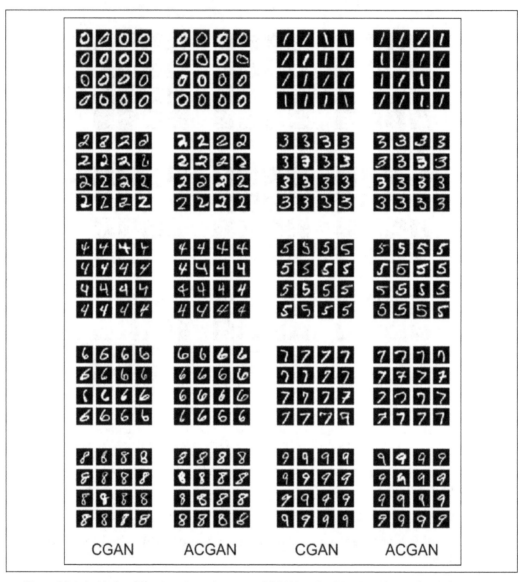

Figure 5.3.4: A side-by-side comparison of outputs of CGAN and ACGAN conditioned with digits 0 to 9

Similar to WGAN and LSGAN, ACGAN provided an improvement in an existing GAN, CGAN, by fine-tuning its loss function. In the chapters to come, we will discover new loss functions that will enable GANs to perform new useful tasks.

4. Conclusion

In this chapter, we've presented various improvements to the original GAN algorithm, first introduced in the previous chapter. WGAN proposed an algorithm to improve the stability of training by using the EMD or Wasserstein 1 loss. LSGAN argued that the original cross-entropy function of GANs is prone to vanishing gradients, unlike least squares loss. LSGAN proposed an algorithm to achieve stable training and quality outputs. ACGAN convincingly improved the quality of the conditional generation of MNIST digits by requiring the discriminator to perform a classification task on top of determining whether the input image was fake or real.

In the next chapter, we'll study how to control the attributes of generator outputs. Whilst CGAN and ACGAN are able to indicate the desired digits to produce, we have not analyzed GANs that can specify the attributes of outputs. For example, we may want to control the writing style of the MNIST digits, such as roundness, tilt angle, and thickness. Therefore, the goal will be to introduce GANs with disentangled representations to control the specific attributes of the generator outputs.

5. References

1. Ian Goodfellow et al.: *Generative Adversarial Nets*. Advances in neural information processing systems, 2014 (`http://papers.nips.cc/paper/5423-generative-adversarial-nets.pdf`).

2. Martin Arjovsky, Soumith Chintala, and Léon Bottou: *Wasserstein GAN*. arXiv preprint, 2017 (`https://arxiv.org/pdf/1701.07875.pdf`).

3. Xudong Mao et al.: *Least Squares Generative Adversarial Networks*. 2017 IEEE International Conference on Computer Vision (ICCV). IEEE 2017 (`http://openaccess.thecvf.com/content_ICCV_2017/papers/Mao_Least_Squares_Generative_ICCV_2017_paper.pdf`).

4. Augustus Odena, Christopher Olah, and Jonathon Shlens. *Conditional Image Synthesis with Auxiliary Classifier GANs*. ICML, 2017 (`http://proceedings.mlr.press/v70/odena17a/odena17a.pdf`).

6
Disentangled Representation GANs

As we've explored, GANs can generate meaningful outputs by learning the data distribution. However, there was no control over the attributes of the generated outputs. Some variations of GANs, like **conditional GAN (CGAN)** and **auxiliary classifier GAN (ACGAN)**, as discussed in the previous two chapters, are able to train a generator that is conditioned to synthesize specific outputs. For example, both CGAN and ACGAN can induce the generator to produce a specific MNIST digit. This is achieved by using both a 100-dim noise code and the corresponding one-hot label as inputs. However, other than the one-hot label, we have no other ways to control the properties of generated outputs.

 For a review of CGAN and ACGAN, please refer to *Chapter 4, Generative Adversarial Networks (GANs)*, and *Chapter 5, Improved GANs*.

In this chapter, we will be covering the variations of GANs that enable us to modify the generator outputs. In the context of the MNIST dataset, apart from which number to produce, we may find that we want to control the writing style. This could involve the tilt or the width of the desired digit. In other words, GANs can also learn disentangled latent codes or representations that we can use to vary the attributes of the generator outputs. A disentangled code or representation is a tensor that can change a specific feature or attribute of the output data while not affecting the other attributes.

In the first section of this chapter, we will be discussing *InfoGAN: Interpretable Representation Learning by Information Maximizing Generative Adversarial Nets* [1], an extension to GANs. InfoGAN learns the disentangled representations in an unsupervised manner by maximizing the mutual information between the input codes and the output observation. On the MNIST dataset, InfoGAN disentangles the writing styles from the digits dataset.

In the following part of the chapter, we'll also be discussing the *Stacked Generative Adversarial Networks or StackedGAN* [2], another extension to GANs.

StackedGAN uses a pretrained encoder or classifier in order to aid in disentangling the latent codes. StackedGAN can be viewed as a stack of models, with each being made of an encoder and a GAN. Each GAN is trained in an adversarial manner by using the input and output data of the corresponding encoder.

In summary, the goal of this chapter is to present:

- The concepts of disentangled representations
- The principles of both InfoGAN and StackedGAN
- Implementation of both InfoGAN and StackedGAN using `tf.keras`

Let's begin by discussing disentangled representations.

1. Disentangled representations

The original GAN was able to generate meaningful outputs, but the downside was that its attributes couldn't be controlled. For example, if we trained a GAN to learn a distribution of celebrity faces, the generator would produce new images of celebrity-looking people. However, there is no way to influence the generator regarding the specific attributes of the face that we want. For example, we're unable to ask the generator for a face of a female celebrity with long black hair, a fair complexion, brown eyes, and who is smiling. The fundamental reason for this is because the 100-dim noise code that we use entangles all of the salient attributes of the generator outputs. We can recall that in `tf.keras`, the `100-dim` code was generated by the random sampling of uniform noise distribution:

```
# generate fake images from noise using generator
# generate noise using uniform distribution
noise = np.random.uniform(-1.0,
                           1.0,
                           size=[batch_size, latent_size])
# generate fake images
fake_images = generator.predict(noise)
```

If we are able to modify the original GAN such that the representation is separated into entangled and disentangled interpretable latent code vectors, we would be able to tell the generator what to synthesize.

Figure 6.1.1 shows us a GAN with an entangled code and its variation with a mixture of entangled and disentangled representations. In the context of the hypothetical celebrity face generation, with the disentangled codes, we are able to indicate the gender, hairstyle, facial expression, skin complexion, and eye color of the face we wish to generate. The n-dim entangled code is still needed to represent all the other facial attributes that we have not disentangled, such as the face shape, facial hair, eye-glasses, as just three examples. The concatenation of entangled and disentangled code vectors serves as the new input to the generator. The total dimension of the concatenated code may not be necessarily 100:

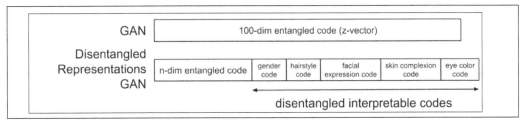

Figure 6.1.1: The GAN with the entangled code and its variation with both entangled and disentangled codes. This example is shown in the context of celebrity face generation

Looking at the preceding figure, it appears that GANs with disentangled representations can also be optimized in the same way as a vanilla GAN can be. This is because the generator output can be represented as:

$$\mathcal{G}(z, c) = \mathcal{G}(\mathbf{z}) \quad \text{(Equation 6.1.1)}$$

The code z = (z, c) comprises two elements:

- Incompressible entangled noise code similar to GANs z or noise vector.
- Latent codes, $c_1, c_2, ..., c_L$, which represent the interpretable disentangled codes of the data distribution. Collectively, all latent codes are represented by c.

For simplicity, all the latent codes are assumed to be independent:

$$p(c_1, c_2, ..., c_L) = \prod_{i=1}^{L} p(c_i) \quad \text{(Equation 6.1.2)}$$

The generator function $\boldsymbol{x} = \mathcal{G}(z, c) = \mathcal{G}(\mathbf{z})$ is provided with both the incompressible noise code and the latent codes. From the point of view of the generator, optimizing z = (z, c) is the same as optimizing z.

The generator network will simply ignore the constraint imposed by the disentangled codes when coming up with a solution.

The generator learns the distribution $p_g(x|c) = p_g(x)$. This will practically defeat the objective of disentangled representations.

The key idea of InfoGAN is to force the GAN not to ignore the latent code c. This is done by maximizing the mutual information between c and $G(z, c)$. In the next section, we will formulate the loss function of InfoGAN.

InfoGAN

To enforce the disentanglement of codes, InfoGAN proposed a regularizer to the original loss function that maximizes the mutual information between the latent codes c and $G(z, c)$:

$$I\big(c; G(z, c)\big) = I\big(c; G(\mathbf{z})\big) \quad \text{(Equation 6.1.3)}$$

The regularizer forces the generator to consider the latent codes when it formulates a function that synthesizes the fake images. In the field of information theory, the mutual information between latent codes c and $G(z, c)$ is defined as:

$$I\big(c; G(z, c)\big) = H(c) - H\big(c|G(z, c)\big) \quad \text{(Equation 6.1.4)}$$

Where $H(c)$ is the entropy of latent code, c, and $H\big(c|G(z, c)\big)$ is the conditional entropy of c after observing the output of the generator, $G(z, c)$. Entropy is a measure of uncertainty of a random variable or an event. For example, information such as **the sun rises in the east** has a low entropy, whereas **winning the jackpot in the lottery** has a high entropy. A more detailed discussion on mutual information can be found in *Chapter 13, Unsupervised Learning Using Mutual Information*.

In *Equation 6.1.4*, maximizing the mutual information means minimizing $H\big(c|G(z, c)\big)$ or decreasing the uncertainty in the latent code upon observing the generated output. This makes sense since, for example, in the MNIST dataset, the generator becomes more confident in synthesizing the digit 8 if the GAN sees that it observed the digit 8.

However, it is hard to estimate $H\big(c|G(z,c)\big)$ since it requires knowledge of the posterior $P\big(c|G(z,c)\big) = P(c|x)$, which is something that we don't have access to. For simplicity, we will use the regular letter x to represent the data distribution.

The workaround is to estimate the lower bound of mutual information by estimating the posterior with an auxiliary distribution $Q(c|x)$. InfoGAN estimates the lower bound of mutual information as:

$$I\big(c;G(z,c)\big) \geq L_I(G,Q) = E_{c\sim P(c),x\sim G(z,c)}[\log Q(c|x)] + H(c) \quad \text{(Equation 6.1.5)}$$

In InfoGAN, $H(c)$ is assumed to be a constant. Therefore, maximizing the mutual information is a matter of maximizing the expectation. The generator must be confident that it has generated an output with the specific attributes. We should note that the maximum value of this expectation is zero. Therefore, the maximum of the lower bound of the mutual information is $H(c)$. In InfoGAN, $Q(c|x)$ for discrete latent codes can be represented by `softmax` nonlinearity. The expectation is the negative `categorical_crossentropy` loss in `tf.keras`.

For continuous codes of a single dimension, the expectation is a double integral over c and x. This is due to the expectation that samples from both disentangled code distribution and generator distribution. One way of estimating the expectation is by assuming the samples as a good measure of continuous data. Therefore, the loss is estimated as $c \log Q(c|x)$. In *Chapter 13, Unsupervised Learning Using Mutual Information*, we will present a more precise estimation of mutual information.

To complete the network of an InfoGAN, we should have an implementation of $Q(c|x)$. For simplicity, the network Q is an auxiliary network attached to the second to last layer of the discriminator. Therefore, this has a minimal impact on the training of the original GAN.

Figure 6.1.2 shows the InfoGAN network diagram:

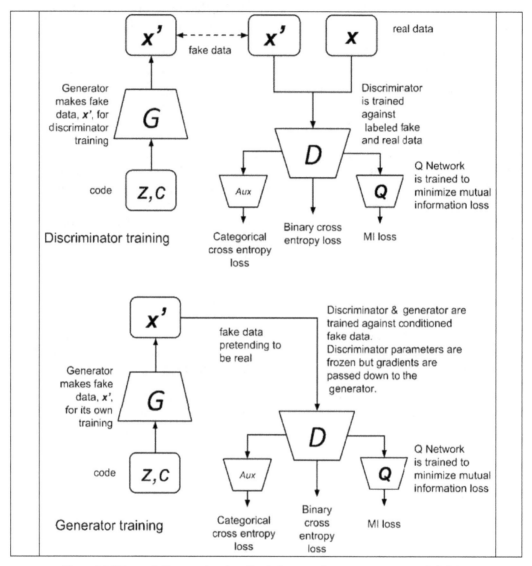

Figure 6.1.2 Network diagram showing discriminator and generator training in InfoGAN

Table 6.1.1 shows the loss functions of InfoGAN as compared to GAN:

Network	Loss Functions	Number
GAN	$\mathcal{L}^{(D)} = -\mathbb{E}_{x \sim p_{data}} \log \mathcal{D}(x) - \mathbb{E}_z \log\big(1 - \mathcal{D}(\mathcal{G}(z))\big)$	4.1.1
	$\mathcal{L}^{(G)} = -\mathbb{E}_z \log \mathcal{D}(\mathcal{G}(z))$	4.1.5
InfoGAN	$\mathcal{L}^{(D)} = -\mathbb{E}_{x \sim p_{data}} \log \mathcal{D}(x) - \mathbb{E}_{z,c} \log\Big(1 - \mathcal{D}\big(\mathcal{G}(z,c)\big)\Big) - \lambda I\big(c; \mathcal{G}(z,c)\big)$	6.1.1
	$\mathcal{L}^{(G)} = -\mathbb{E}_{z,c} \log \mathcal{D}(\mathcal{G}(z,c)) - \lambda I\big(c; \mathcal{G}(z,c)\big)$	6.1.2
	For continuous codes, InfoGAN recommends a value of $\lambda < 1$. In our example, we set $\lambda = 0.5$. For discrete codes, InfoGAN recommends $\lambda = 1$.	

Table 6.1.1: A comparison between the loss functions of GAN and InfoGAN

The loss functions of InfoGAN differ from GANs by an additional term, $-\lambda I\big(c; \mathcal{G}(z,c)\big)$, where λ is a small positive constant. Minimizing the loss function of an InfoGAN translates to minimizing the loss of the original GAN and maximizing the mutual information $I\big(c; \mathcal{G}(z,c)\big)$.

If applied to the MNIST dataset, InfoGAN can learn the disentangled discrete and continuous codes in order to modify the generator output attributes. For example, like CGAN and ACGAN, the discrete code in the form of a 10-dim one-hot label will be used to specify the digit to generate. However, we can add two continuous codes, one for controlling the angle of writing style and another for adjusting the stroke width. *Figure 6.1.3* shows the codes for the MNIST digit in InfoGAN. We retain the entangled code with a smaller dimensionality to represent all other attributes:

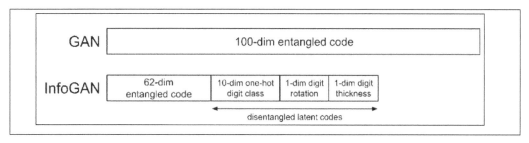

Figure 6.1.3: The codes for both GAN and InfoGAN in the context of the MNIST dataset

Having discussed some of the concepts behind InfoGAN, let's take a look at InfoGAN implementation in tf.keras.

Implementation of InfoGAN in Keras

To implement an InfoGAN on the MNIST dataset, there are some changes that need to be made in the base code of the ACGAN. As highlighted in *Listing 6.1.1*, the generator concatenates both entangled (*z* noise code) and disentangled codes (one-hot label and continuous codes) to serve as input:

```
inputs = [inputs, labels] + codes
```

The builder functions for the `generator` and `discriminator` are also implemented in `gan.py` in the `lib` folder.

> The complete code is available on GitHub: `https://github.com/PacktPublishing/Advanced-Deep-Learning-with-Keras`.

Listing 6.1.1: `infogan-mnist-6.1.1.py`

Highlighted are the lines that are specific to InfoGAN:

```
def generator(inputs,
              image_size,
              activation='sigmoid',
              labels=None,
              codes=None):
    """Build a Generator Model

    Stack of BN-ReLU-Conv2DTranpose to generate fake images.
    Output activation is sigmoid instead of tanh in [1].
    Sigmoid converges easily.

    Arguments:
        inputs (Layer): Input layer of the generator (the z-vector)
        image_size (int): Target size of one side
            (assuming square image)
        activation (string): Name of output activation layer
        labels (tensor): Input labels
        codes (list): 2-dim disentangled codes for InfoGAN

    Returns:
        Model: Generator Model
    """
    image_resize = image_size // 4
    # network parameters
```

```
kernel_size = 5
layer_filters = [128, 64, 32, 1]

if labels is not None:
    if codes is None:
        # ACGAN labels
        # concatenate z noise vector and one-hot labels
        inputs = [inputs, labels]
    else:
        # infoGAN codes
        # concatenate z noise vector,
        # one-hot labels and codes 1 & 2
        inputs = [inputs, labels] + codes
    x = concatenate(inputs, axis=1)
elif codes is not None:
    # generator 0 of StackedGAN
    inputs = [inputs, codes]
    x = concatenate(inputs, axis=1)
else:
    # default input is just 100-dim noise (z-code)
    x = inputs

x = Dense(image_resize * image_resize * layer_filters[0])(x)
x = Reshape((image_resize, image_resize, layer_filters[0]))(x)

for filters in layer_filters:
    # first two convolution layers use strides = 2
    # the last two use strides = 1
    if filters > layer_filters[-2]:
        strides = 2
    else:
        strides = 1
    x = BatchNormalization()(x)
    x = Activation('relu')(x)
    x = Conv2DTranspose(filters=filters,
                        kernel_size=kernel_size,
                        strides=strides,
                        padding='same')(x)

if activation is not None:
    x = Activation(activation)(x)

# generator output is the synthesized image x
return Model(inputs, x, name='generator')
```

Listing 6.1.2 shows the discriminator and Q network with the original default GAN output. The three auxiliary outputs corresponding to discrete code (for one-hot label) `softmax` prediction and the continuous code probabilities given the input MNIST digit image are highlighted.

Listing 6.1.2: `infogan-mnist-6.1.1.py`

Highlighted are the lines that are specific to InfoGAN:

```
def discriminator(inputs,
                  activation='sigmoid',
                  num_labels=None,
                  num_codes=None):
    """Build a Discriminator Model

    Stack of LeakyReLU-Conv2D to discriminate real from fake
    The network does not converge with BN so it is not used here
    unlike in [1]

    Arguments:
        inputs (Layer): Input layer of the discriminator (the image)
        activation (string): Name of output activation layer
        num_labels (int): Dimension of one-hot labels for ACGAN &
InfoGAN
        num_codes (int): num_codes-dim Q network as output
                    if StackedGAN or 2 Q networks if InfoGAN


    Returns:
        Model: Discriminator Model
    """
    kernel_size = 5
    layer_filters = [32, 64, 128, 256]

    x = inputs
    for filters in layer_filters:
        # first 3 convolution layers use strides = 2
        # last one uses strides = 1
        if filters == layer_filters[-1]:
            strides = 1
        else:
            strides = 2
        x = LeakyReLU(alpha=0.2)(x)
        x = Conv2D(filters=filters,
                   kernel_size=kernel_size,
```

```
                    strides=strides,
                    padding='same')(x)

x = Flatten()(x)
# default output is probability that the image is real
outputs = Dense(1)(x)
if activation is not None:
    print(activation)
    outputs = Activation(activation)(outputs)

if num_labels:
    # ACGAN and InfoGAN have 2nd output
    # 2nd output is 10-dim one-hot vector of label
    layer = Dense(layer_filters[-2])(x)
    labels = Dense(num_labels)(layer)
    labels = Activation('softmax', name='label')(labels)
    if num_codes is None:
        outputs = [outputs, labels]
    else:
        # InfoGAN have 3rd and 4th outputs
        # 3rd output is 1-dim continous Q of 1st c given x
        code1 = Dense(1)(layer)
        code1 = Activation('sigmoid', name='code1')(code1)

        # 4th output is 1-dim continuous Q of 2nd c given x
        code2 = Dense(1)(layer)
        code2 = Activation('sigmoid', name='code2')(code2)

        outputs = [outputs, labels, code1, code2]
elif num_codes is not None:
    # StackedGAN Q0 output
    # z0_recon is reconstruction of z0 normal distribution
    z0_recon =  Dense(num_codes)(x)
    z0_recon = Activation('tanh', name='z0')(z0_recon)
    outputs = [outputs, z0_recon]

return Model(inputs, outputs, name='discriminator')
```

Figure 6.1.4 shows the InfoGAN model in `tf.keras`:

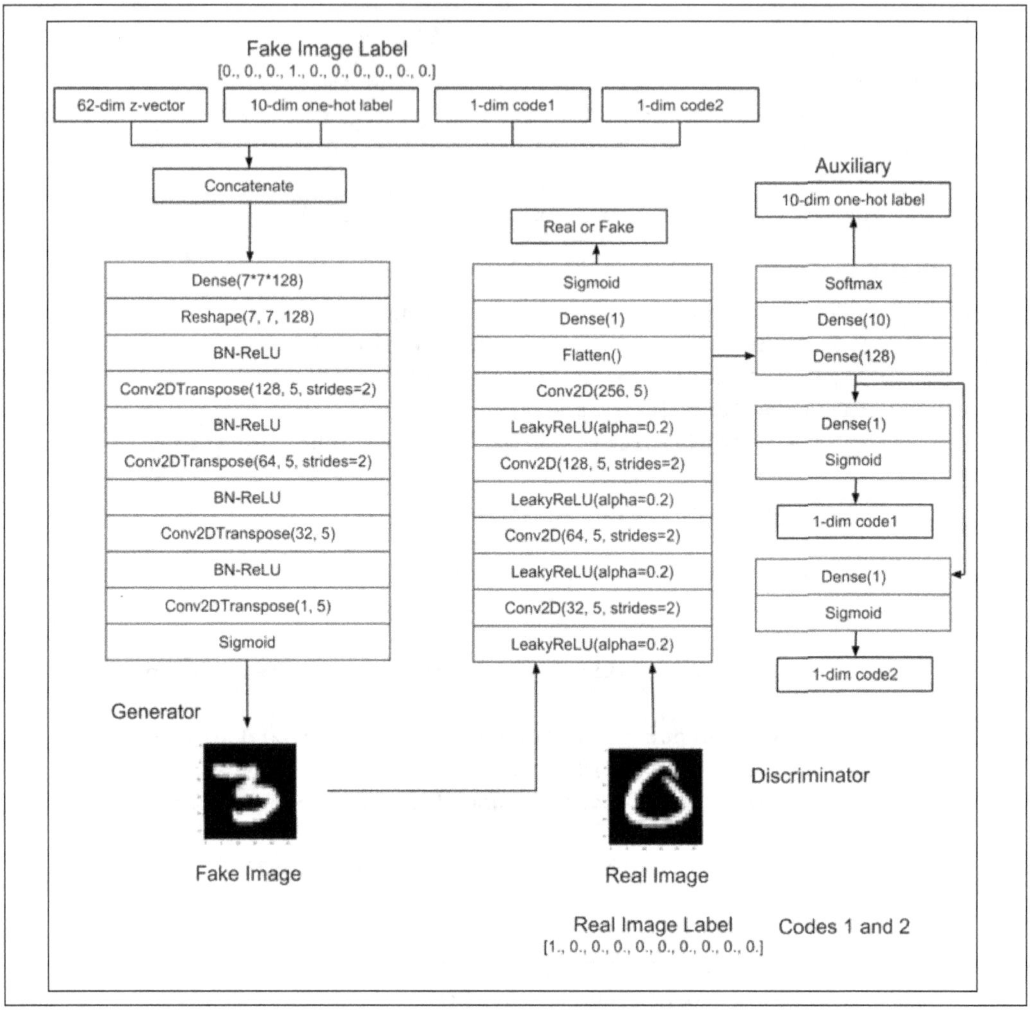

Figure 6.1.4: The InfoGAN Keras model

Building the discriminator and adversarial models also requires a number of changes. The changes are on the loss functions used. The original discriminator loss function, `binary_crossentropy`, the `categorical_crossentropy` for discrete code, and the `mi_loss` function for each continuous code comprise the overall loss function. Each loss function is given a weight of 1.0, except for the `mi_loss` function, which is given 0.5, corresponding to $\lambda = 0.5$ for the continuous code.

Listing 6.1.3 highlights the changes made. However, we should note that by using the builder function, the discriminator is instantiated as:

```
# call discriminator builder with 4 outputs:
# source, label, and 2 codes
discriminator = gan.discriminator(inputs,
                                  num_labels=num_labels,
                                  num_codes=2)
```

The generator is created by:

```
# call generator with inputs,
# labels and codes as total inputs to generator
generator = gan.generator(inputs,
                          image_size,
                          labels=labels,
                          codes=[code1, code2])
```

Listing 6.1.3: `infogan-mnist-6.1.1.py`

Mutual information loss function as well as building and training the InfoGAN discriminator and adversarial networks is demonstrated in the following code:

```
def mi_loss(c, q_of_c_given_x):
    """ Mutual information, Equation 5 in [2],
        assuming H(c) is constant
    """
    # mi_loss = -c * log(Q(c|x))
    return K.mean(-K.sum(K.log(q_of_c_given_x + K.epsilon()) * c,
                         axis=1))


def build_and_train_models(latent_size=100):
    """"Load the dataset, build InfoGAN discriminator,
    generator, and adversarial models.
    Call the InfoGAN train routine.
    """

    # load MNIST dataset
    (x_train, y_train), (_, _) = mnist.load_data()

    # reshape data for CNN as (28, 28, 1) and normalize
    image_size = x_train.shape[1]
    x_train = np.reshape(x_train, [-1, image_size, image_size, 1])
    x_train = x_train.astype('float32') / 255

    # train labels
    num_labels = len(np.unique(y_train))
```

```
y_train = to_categorical(y_train)

model_name = "infogan_mnist"
# network parameters
batch_size = 64
train_steps = 40000
lr = 2e-4
decay = 6e-8
input_shape = (image_size, image_size, 1)
label_shape = (num_labels, )
code_shape = (1, )

# build discriminator model
inputs = Input(shape=input_shape, name='discriminator_input')
# call discriminator builder with 4 outputs:
# source, label, and 2 codes
discriminator = gan.discriminator(inputs,
                                  num_labels=num_labels,
                                  num_codes=2)
# [1] uses Adam, but discriminator converges easily with RMSprop
optimizer = RMSprop(lr=lr, decay=decay)
# loss functions: 1) probability image is real
# (binary crossentropy)
# 2) categorical cross entropy image label,
# 3) and 4) mutual information loss
loss = ['binary_crossentropy',
        'categorical_crossentropy',
        mi_loss,
        mi_loss]
# lamda or mi_loss weight is 0.5
loss_weights = [1.0, 1.0, 0.5, 0.5]
discriminator.compile(loss=loss,
                      loss_weights=loss_weights,
                      optimizer=optimizer,
                      metrics=['accuracy'])
discriminator.summary()

# build generator model
input_shape = (latent_size, )
inputs = Input(shape=input_shape, name='z_input')
labels = Input(shape=label_shape, name='labels')
code1 = Input(shape=code_shape, name="code1")
code2 = Input(shape=code_shape, name="code2")
# call generator with inputs,
```

```
# labels and codes as total inputs to generator
generator = gan.generator(inputs,
                          image_size,
                          labels=labels,
                          codes=[code1, code2])
generator.summary()

# build adversarial model = generator + discriminator
optimizer = RMSprop(lr=lr*0.5, decay=decay*0.5)
discriminator.trainable = False
# total inputs = noise code, labels, and codes
inputs = [inputs, labels, code1, code2]
adversarial = Model(inputs,
                    discriminator(generator(inputs)),
                    name=model_name)
# same loss as discriminator
adversarial.compile(loss=loss,
                    loss_weights=loss_weights,
                    optimizer=optimizer,
                    metrics=['accuracy'])
adversarial.summary()

# train discriminator and adversarial networks
models = (generator, discriminator, adversarial)
data = (x_train, y_train)
params = (batch_size,
          latent_size,
          train_steps,
          num_labels,
          model_name)
train(models, data, params)
```

As far as the training is concerned, we can see that the InfoGAN is similar to ACGAN, except that we need to supply c for the continuous code. c is drawn from normal distribution with a standard deviation of 0.5 and a mean of 0.0. We'll use randomly sampled labels for the fake data and dataset class labels for the real data to represent discrete latent code.

Listing 6.1.4 highlights the changes made to the training function. Similar to all previous GANs, the discriminator and generator (through adversarial training) are alternately trained. During adversarial training, the discriminator weights are frozen.

Sample generator output images are saved every 500 interval steps by using the `gan.py plot_images()` function.

Listing 6.1.4: `infogan-mnist-6.1.1.py`

```python
def train(models, data, params):
    """Train the Discriminator and Adversarial networks

    Alternately train discriminator and adversarial networks by batch.
    Discriminator is trained first with real and fake images,
    corresponding one-hot labels and continuous codes.
    Adversarial is trained next with fake images pretending
    to be real, corresponding one-hot labels and continous codes.
    Generate sample images per save_interval.

    # Arguments
        models (Models): Generator, Discriminator, Adversarial models
        data (tuple): x_train, y_train data
        params (tuple): Network parameters
    """
    # the GAN models
    generator, discriminator, adversarial = models
    # images and their one-hot labels
    x_train, y_train = data
    # network parameters
    batch_size, latent_size, train_steps, num_labels, model_name = \
            params
    # the generator image is saved every 500 steps
    save_interval = 500
    # noise vector to see how the generator output
    # evolves during training
    noise_input = np.random.uniform(-1.0,
                                     1.0,
                                     size=[16, latent_size])
    # random class labels and codes
    noise_label = np.eye(num_labels)[np.arange(0, 16) % num_labels]
    noise_code1 = np.random.normal(scale=0.5, size=[16, 1])
    noise_code2 = np.random.normal(scale=0.5, size=[16, 1])
    # number of elements in train dataset
    train_size = x_train.shape[0]
    print(model_name,
            "Labels for generated images: ",
            np.argmax(noise_label, axis=1))

    for i in range(train_steps):
        # train the discriminator for 1 batch
        # 1 batch of real (label=1.0) and fake images (label=0.0)
```

```
# randomly pick real images and
# corresponding labels from dataset
rand_indexes = np.random.randint(0,
                                 train_size,
                                 size=batch_size)
real_images = x_train[rand_indexes]
real_labels = y_train[rand_indexes]
# random codes for real images
real_code1 = np.random.normal(scale=0.5,
                              size=[batch_size, 1])
real_code2 = np.random.normal(scale=0.5,
                              size=[batch_size, 1])
# generate fake images, labels and codes
noise = np.random.uniform(-1.0,
                          1.0,
                          size=[batch_size, latent_size])
fake_labels = np.eye(num_labels)[np.random.choice(num_labels,
                                                  batch_size)]
fake_code1 = np.random.normal(scale=0.5,
                              size=[batch_size, 1])
fake_code2 = np.random.normal(scale=0.5,
                              size=[batch_size, 1])
inputs = [noise, fake_labels, fake_code1, fake_code2]
fake_images = generator.predict(inputs)

# real + fake images = 1 batch of train data
x = np.concatenate((real_images, fake_images))
labels = np.concatenate((real_labels, fake_labels))
codes1 = np.concatenate((real_code1, fake_code1))
codes2 = np.concatenate((real_code2, fake_code2))

# label real and fake images
# real images label is 1.0
y = np.ones([2 * batch_size, 1])
# fake images label is 0.0
y[batch_size:, :] = 0

# train discriminator network,
# log the loss and label accuracy
outputs = [y, labels, codes1, codes2]
# metrics = ['loss', 'activation_1_loss', 'label_loss',
# 'code1_loss', 'code2_loss', 'activation_1_acc',
# 'label_acc', 'code1_acc', 'code2_acc']
# from discriminator.metrics_names
metrics = discriminator.train_on_batch(x, outputs)
fmt = "%d: [discriminator loss: %f, label_acc: %f]"
log = fmt % (i, metrics[0], metrics[6])
```

```
        # train the adversarial network for 1 batch
        # 1 batch of fake images with label=1.0 and
        # corresponding one-hot label or class + random codes
        # since the discriminator weights are frozen
        # in adversarial network only the generator is trained
        # generate fake images, labels and codes
        noise = np.random.uniform(-1.0,
                                  1.0,
                                  size=[batch_size, latent_size])
        fake_labels = np.eye(num_labels)[np.random.choice(num_labels,
                                                           batch_size)]
        fake_code1 = np.random.normal(scale=0.5,
                                      size=[batch_size, 1])
        fake_code2 = np.random.normal(scale=0.5,
                                      size=[batch_size, 1])
        # label fake images as real
        y = np.ones([batch_size, 1])

        # train the adversarial network
        # note that unlike in discriminator training,
        # we do not save the fake images in a variable
        # the fake images go to the discriminator
        # input of the adversarial for classification
        # log the loss and label accuracy
        inputs = [noise, fake_labels, fake_code1, fake_code2]
        outputs = [y, fake_labels, fake_code1, fake_code2]
        metrics  = adversarial.train_on_batch(inputs, outputs)
        fmt = "%s [adversarial loss: %f, label_acc: %f]"
        log = fmt % (log, metrics[0], metrics[6])

        print(log)
        if (i + 1) % save_interval == 0:
            # plot generator images on a periodic basis
            gan.plot_images(generator,
                            noise_input=noise_input,
                            noise_label=noise_label,
                            noise_codes=[noise_code1, noise_code2],
                            show=False,
                            step=(i + 1),
                            model_name=model_name)

    # save the model after training the generator
    # the trained generator can be reloaded for
    # future MNIST digit generation
    generator.save(model_name + ".h5")
```

Given the `tf.keras` implementation of InfoGAN, the next section presents the generator MNIST outputs with disentangled attributes.

Generator outputs of InfoGAN

Similar to all previous GANs that have been presented to us, we've trained our InfoGAN for 40,000 steps. After the training is completed, we're able to run the InfoGAN generator to generate new outputs using the model saved on the `infogan_mnist.h5` file. The following validations are conducted:

1. Generate digits 0 to 9 by varying the discrete labels from 0 to 9. Both continuous codes are set to zero. The results are shown in *Figure 6.1.5*. We can see that the InfoGAN discrete code can control the digits produced by the generator:

    ```
    python3 infogan-mnist-6.1.1.py --generator=infogan_mnist.h5
    --digit=0 --code1=0 --code2=0
    ```

    to

    ```
    python3 infogan-mnist-6.1.1.py --generator=infogan_mnist.h5
    --digit=9 --code1=0 --code2=0
    ```

    In *Figure 6.1.5* we can see the images generated by the InfoGAN:

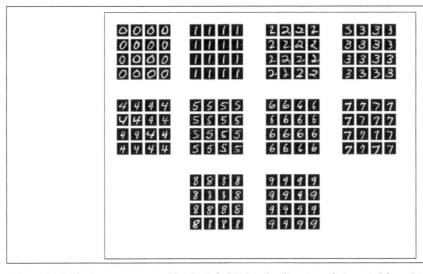

Figure 6.1.5: The images generated by the InfoGAN as the discrete code is varied from 0 to 9. Both continuous codes are set to zero

2. Examine the effect of the first continuous code to understand which attribute has been affected. We vary the first continuous code from -2.0 to 2.0 for digits 0 to 9. The second continuous code is set to 0.0. *Figure 6.1.6* shows that the first continuous code controls the thickness of the digit:

```
python3 infogan-mnist-6.1.1.py --generator=infogan_mnist.h5
--digit=0 --code1=0 --code2=0 --p1
```

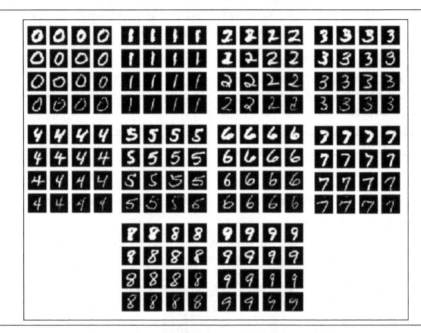

Figure 6.1.6: The images generated by InfoGAN as the first continuous code is varied from -2.0 to 2.0 for digits 0 to 9. The second continuous code is set to zero. The first continuous code controls the thickness of the digit

3. Similar to the previous step, but instead focusing more on the second continuous code. *Figure 6.1.7* shows that the second continuous code controls the rotation angle (tilt) of the writing style:

```
python3 infogan-mnist-6.1.1.py --generator=infogan_mnist.h5
--digit=0 --code1=0 --code2=0 --p2
```

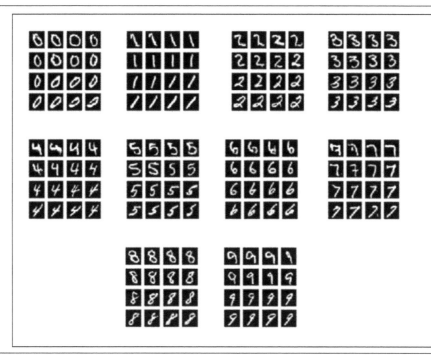

Figure 6.1.7: The images generated by InfoGAN as the second continuous code is varied from -2.0 to 2.0 for digits 0 to 9. The first continuous code is set to zero. The second continuous code controls the rotation angle (tilt) of the writing style

From these validation results, we can see that apart from the ability to generate MNIST-looking digits, InfoGAN expands the ability of conditional GANs such as CGAN and ACGAN. The network automatically learned two arbitrary codes that can control the specific attributes of the generator output. It would be interesting to see what additional attributes could be controlled if we increased the number of continuous codes beyond 2. This could be accomplished by augmenting the list of codes in the highlighted lines of *Listing 6.1.1* to *Listing 6.1.4*.

The results in this section demonstrated that the attributes of the generator outputs can be disentangled by maximizing the mutual information between the code and the data distribution. In the following section, a different approach on disentanglement is presented. The idea of StackedGAN is to inject the code at the feature level.

2. StackedGAN

In the same spirit as InfoGAN, StackedGAN proposes a method for disentangling latent representations for conditioning generator outputs. However, StackedGAN uses a different approach to the problem. Instead of learning how to condition the noise to produce the desired output, StackedGAN breaks down a GAN into a stack of GANs. Each GAN is trained independently in the usual discriminator-adversarial manner with its own latent code.

Figure 6.2.1 shows us how StackedGAN works in the context of hypothetical celebrity face generation, assuming that the *Encoder* network has been trained to classify celebrity faces:

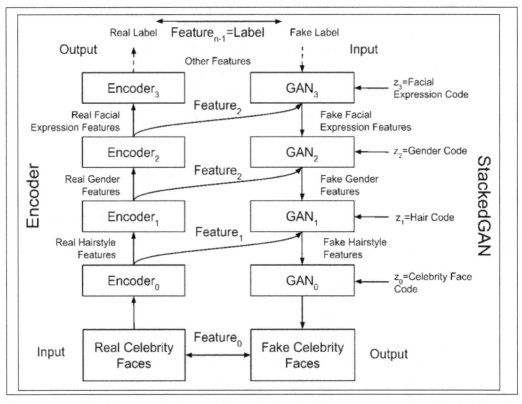

Figure 6.2.1: The basic idea of StackedGAN in the context of celebrity face generation. Assuming that there is a hypothetical deep encoder network that can perform classification on celebrity faces, a StackedGAN simply inverts the process of the encoder

The *Encoder* network is composed of a stack of simple encoders, *Encoder*$_i$ where $i = 0$ ... $n - 1$ corresponding to n features. Each encoder extracts certain facial features. For example, *Encoder*$_0$ may be the encoder for hairstyle features, *Features*$_1$. All the simple encoders contribute to making the overall *Encoder* perform correct predictions.

The idea behind StackedGAN is that if we would like to build a GAN that generates fake celebrity faces, we should simply invert the *Encoder*. StackedGAN consists of a stack of simpler GANs, GAN$_i$ *where* $i = 0$ ... $n - 1$ corresponding to n features. Each GAN$_i$ learns to invert the process of its corresponding encoder, *Encoder*$_i$. For example, GAN$_0$ generates fake celebrity faces from fake hairstyle features, which is the inverse of the *Encoder*$_0$ process.

Each GAN$_i$ uses a latent code, z_i, that conditions its generator output. For example, the latent code, z_0, can alter the hairstyle from curly to wavy. The stack of GANs can also act as one to synthesize fake celebrity faces, completing the inverse process of the whole *Encoder*. The latent code of each GAN$_i$, z_i, can be used to alter specific attributes of fake celebrity faces.

With the key idea of how the StackedGAN works, let's proceed to the next section and see how it is implemented in tf.keras.

Implementation of StackedGAN in Keras

The detailed network model of a StackedGAN can be seen in *Figure 6.2.2*. For conciseness, only two encoder-GANs per stack are shown. The figure may initially appear complex, but it is just a repetition of an encoder-GAN, meaning that if we understood how to train one encoder-GAN, the remainder utilize the same concept.

In this section, we assume that the StackedGAN is designed for MNIST digit generation.

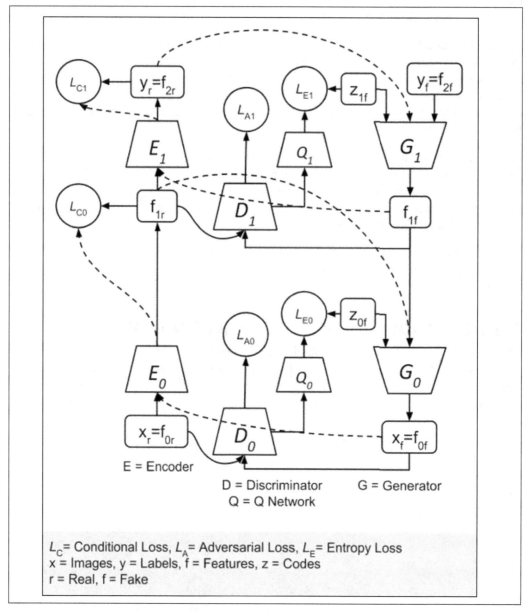

Figure 6.2.2: A StackedGAN comprises a stack of an encoder and a GAN. The encoder is pretrained to perform classification. *Generator$_1$, G_1,* learns to synthesize f_{1f} features conditioned on the fake label, y_f, and latent code, z_{1f}. *Generator$_0$, G_0,* produces fake images using both the fake features, f_{1f}, and latent code, z_{0f}.

StackedGAN starts with an *Encoder*. It could be a trained classifier that predicts the correct labels. The intermediate features vector, f_{1r}, is made available for GAN training. For MNIST, we can use a CNN-based classifier similar to what we discussed in *Chapter 1, Introducing Advanced Deep Learning with Keras*.

Figure 6.2.3 shows the *Encoder* and its network model implementation in `tf.keras`:

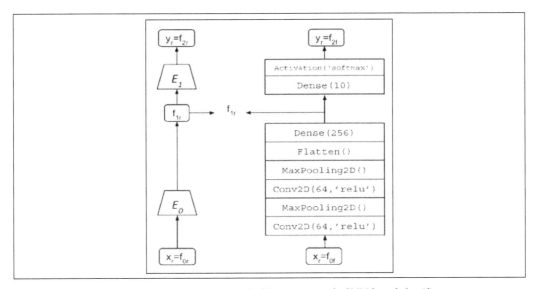

Figure 6.2.3: The encoder in StackedGAN is a simple CNN-based classifier

Listing 6.2.1 shows the `tf.keras` code for the preceding figure. It is similar to the CNN-based classifier in *Chapter 1, Introducing Advanced Deep Learning with Keras*, except that we use a `Dense` layer to extract the `256-dim` feature. There are two output models, *Encoder$_0$* and *Encoder$_1$*. Both will be used to train the StackedGAN.

Listing 6.2.1: `stackedgan-mnist-6.2.1.py`

```
def build_encoder(inputs, num_labels=10, feature1_dim=256):
    """ Build the Classifier (Encoder) Model sub networks

    Two sub networks:
    1) Encoder0: Image to feature1 (intermediate latent feature)
    2) Encoder1: feature1 to labels

    # Arguments
        inputs (Layers): x - images, feature1 -
            feature1 layer output
        num_labels (int): number of class labels
        feature1_dim (int): feature1 dimensionality
```

```
# Returns
    enc0, enc1 (Models): Description below
"""
kernel_size = 3
filters = 64

x, feature1 = inputs
# Encoder0 or enc0
y = Conv2D(filters=filters,
           kernel_size=kernel_size,
           padding='same',
           activation='relu')(x)
y = MaxPooling2D()(y)
y = Conv2D(filters=filters,
           kernel_size=kernel_size,
           padding='same',
           activation='relu')(y)
y = MaxPooling2D()(y)
y = Flatten()(y)
feature1_output = Dense(feature1_dim, activation='relu')(y)
# Encoder0 or enc0: image (x or feature0) to feature1
enc0 = Model(inputs=x, outputs=feature1_output, name="encoder0")

# Encoder1 or enc1
y = Dense(num_labels)(feature1)
labels = Activation('softmax')(y)
# Encoder1 or enc1: feature1 to class labels (feature2)
enc1 = Model(inputs=feature1, outputs=labels, name="encoder1")

# return both enc0 and enc1
return enc0, enc1
```

The $Encoder_0$ output, f_{1r}, is the 256-dim feature vector that we want $Generator_1$ to learn to synthesize. It is available as an auxiliary output of $Encoder_0$, E_0. The overall $Encoder$ is trained to classify MNIST digits, x_r. The correct labels, y_r, are predicted by $Encoder_1$, E_1. In the process, the intermediate set of features, f_{1r}, is learned and made available for $Generator_0$ training. Subscript r is used to emphasize and distinguish real data from fake data when the GAN is trained against this encoder.

Given that the *Encoder* inputs (x_r) intermediate features (f_{1r}) and labels (y_r), each GAN is trained in the usual discriminator–adversarial manner. The loss functions are given by *Equation 6.2.1* to *Equation 6.2.5* in *Table 6.2.1*. *Equation 6.2.1* and *Equation 6.2.2* are the usual loss functions of the generic GAN. StackedGAN has two additional loss functions, **Conditional** and **Entropy**.

Network	Loss Functions	Number
GAN	$\mathcal{L}^{(D)} = -\mathbb{E}_{x \sim p_{data}} \log \mathcal{D}(x) - \mathbb{E}_z \log\big(1 - \mathcal{D}(\mathcal{G}(z))\big)$	4.1.1
	$\mathcal{L}^{(G)} = -\mathbb{E}_z \log \mathcal{D}(\mathcal{G}(z))$	4.1.5
StackedGAN	$\mathcal{L}_i^{(D)} = -\mathbb{E}_{f_i \sim p_{data}} \log \mathcal{D}(f_i) - \mathbb{E}_{f_{i+1} \sim p_{data}, z_i} \log\Big(1 - \mathcal{D}(\mathcal{G}(f_{i+1}, z_i))\Big)$	6.2.1
	$\mathcal{L}_i^{(G)adv} = -\mathbb{E}_{f_{i+1} \sim p_{data}, z_i} \log \mathcal{D}(\mathcal{G}(f_{i+1}, z_i))$	6.2.2
	$\mathcal{L}_i^{(G)cond} = \big\| E_i(\mathcal{G}(f_{i+1}, z_i)), f_i \big\|_2$	6.2.3
	$\mathcal{L}_i^{(G)ent} = \| Q_i(\mathcal{G}(f_{i+1}, z_i)), z_i \|_2$	6.2.4
	$\mathcal{L}_i^{(G)} = \lambda_1 \mathcal{L}_i^{(G)adv} + \lambda_2 \mathcal{L}_i^{(G)cond} + \lambda_3 \mathcal{L}_i^{(G)ent}$	6.2.5
	where $\lambda_1, \lambda_2, and \lambda_3$ are weights and *i = Encoder and GAN id*	

Table 6.2.1: A comparison between the loss functions of GAN and StackedGAN. $\sim p_{data}$ means sampling from the corresponding encoder data (input, feature, or output)

The conditional loss function, $\mathcal{L}_i^{(G)cond}$ in *Equation 6.2.3*, ensures that the generator does not ignore the input, f_{i+1}, when synthesizing the output, f_i, from the input noise code, z_i. The encoder, $Encoder_i$, must be able to recover the generator input by inverting the process of the generator, $Generator_i$. The difference between the generator input and the recovered input using the encoder is measured by $L2$ or Euclidean distance (**mean squared error (MSE)**).

Figure 6.2.4 shows the network elements involved in the computation of $\mathcal{L}_0^{(G)cond}$:

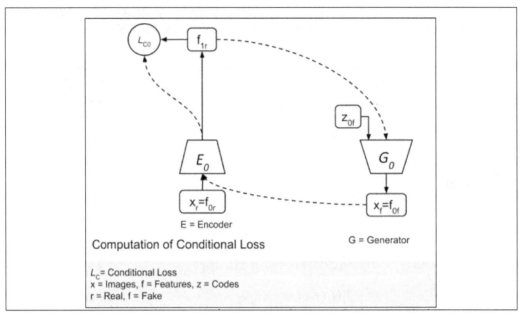

Figure 6.2.4: A simpler version of Figure 6.2.3 showing only the network elements involved in the computation of $\mathcal{L}_0^{(G)cond}$

The conditional loss function, however, introduces a new problem. The generator ignores the input noise code, z_i and simply relies on f_{i+1}. Entropy loss function, $\mathcal{L}_i^{(G)ent}$ in *Equation 6.2.4*, ensures that the generator does not ignore the noise code, z_i. The *Q network* recovers the noise code from the output of the generator. The difference between the recovered noise and the input noise is also measured by *L2* or Euclidean distance (MSE).

Figure 6.2.5 shows the network elements involved in the computation of $\mathcal{L}_0^{(G)ent}$:

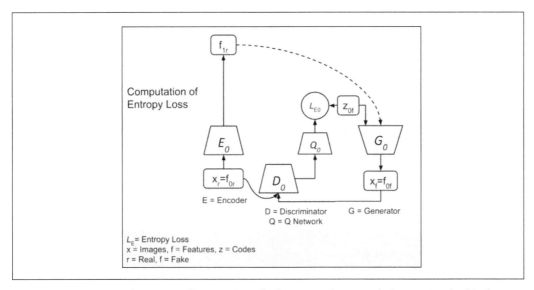

Figure 6.2.5: A simpler version of Figure 6.2.3 only showing us the network elements involved in the computation of $\mathcal{L}_0^{(G)ent}$

The last loss function is similar to the usual GAN loss. It comprises discriminator loss, $\mathcal{L}_i^{(D)}$, and generator (through adversarial) loss, $\mathcal{L}_i^{(G)adv}$. *Figure 6.2.6* shows the elements involved in the GAN loss.

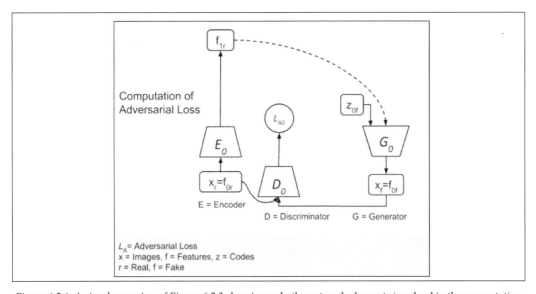

Figure 6.2.6: A simpler version of Figure 6.2.3 showing only the network elements involved in the computation of $\mathcal{L}_i^{(D)}$ and $\mathcal{L}_0^{(G)adv}$

In *Equation 6.2.5*, the weighted sum of the three generator loss functions is the final generator loss function. In the Keras code that we will present, all the weights are set to 1.0, except for the entropy loss, which is set to 10.0. In *Equation 6.2.1* to *Equation 6.2.5*, i refers to the encoder and GAN group ID or level. In the original paper, the network is first trained independently and then jointly. During independent training, the encoder is trained first. During joint training, both real and fake data are used.

The implementation of the StackedGAN generator and discriminator in `tf.keras` requires few changes to provide auxiliary points to access the intermediate features. *Figure 6.2.7* shows the generator `tf.keras` model.:

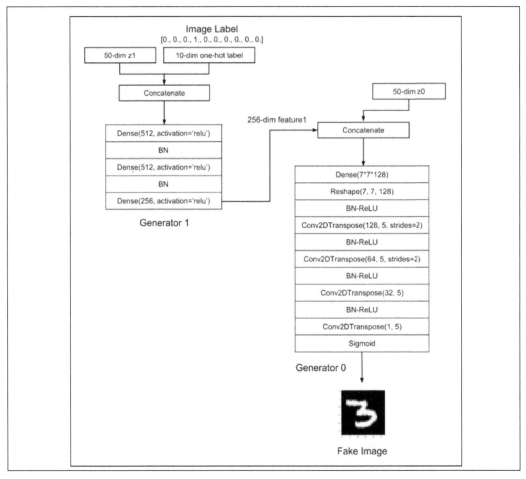

Figure 6.2.7: A StackedGAN generator model in Keras

Listing 6.2.2 illustrates the function that builds two generators (gen0 and gen1) corresponding to *Generator$_0$* and *Generator$_1$*. The gen1 generator is made of three Dense layers with labels and the noise code z_{1f} as inputs. The third layer generates the fake f_{1f} feature. The gen0 generator is similar to other GAN generators that we've presented and can be instantiated using the generator builder in gan.py:

```
# gen0: feature1 + z0 to feature0 (image)
gen0 = gan.generator(feature1, image_size, codes=z0)
```

The gen0 input is f_1 features and the noise code z_0. The output is the generated fake image, x_f:

Listing 6.2.2: stackedgan-mnist-6.2.1.py

```
def build_generator(latent_codes, image_size, feature1_dim=256):
    """Build Generator Model sub networks

    Two sub networks: 1) Class and noise to feature1
        (intermediate feature)
        2) feature1 to image

    # Arguments
        latent_codes (Layers): dicrete code (labels),
            noise and feature1 features
        image_size (int): Target size of one side
            (assuming square image)
        feature1_dim (int): feature1 dimensionality

    # Returns
        gen0, gen1 (Models): Description below
    """

    # Latent codes and network parameters
    labels, z0, z1, feature1 = latent_codes
    # image_resize = image_size // 4
    # kernel_size = 5
    # layer_filters = [128, 64, 32, 1]

    # gen1 inputs
    inputs = [labels, z1]        # 10 + 50 = 62-dim
    x = concatenate(inputs, axis=1)
    x = Dense(512, activation='relu')(x)
    x = BatchNormalization()(x)
    x = Dense(512, activation='relu')(x)
    x = BatchNormalization()(x)
```

```
fake_feature1 = Dense(feature1_dim, activation='relu')(x)
# gen1: classes and noise (feature2 + z1) to feature1
gen1 = Model(inputs, fake_feature1, name='gen1')

# gen0: feature1 + z0 to feature0 (image)
gen0 = gan.generator(feature1, image_size, codes=z0)

return gen0, gen1
```

Figure 6.2.8 shows the discriminator `tf.keras` model:

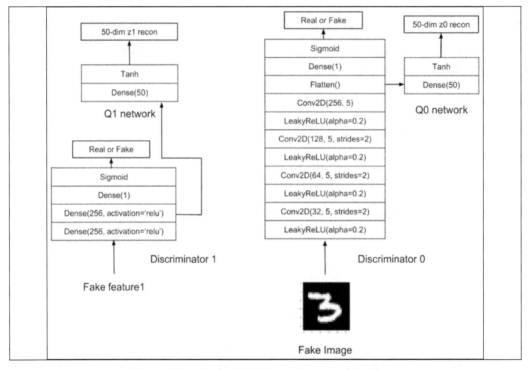

Figure 6.2.8: A StackedGAN discriminator model in Keras

We provide the functions to build *Discriminator$_0$* and *Discriminator$_1$* (`dis0` and `dis1`). The `dis0` discriminator is similar to a GAN discriminator, except for the feature vector input and the auxiliary network Q_0 that recovers z_0. The builder function in `gan.py` is used to create `dis0`:

```
dis0 = gan.discriminator(inputs, num_codes=z_dim)
```

The `dis1` discriminator is made of a three-layer MLP, as shown in *Listing 6.2.3*. The last layer discriminates between the real and fake f_1. Q_1 network shares the first two layers of `dis1`. Its third layer recovers z_1.

Listing 6.2.3: `stackedgan-mnist-6.2.1.py`

```python
def build_discriminator(inputs, z_dim=50):
    """Build Discriminator 1 Model

    Classifies feature1 (features) as real/fake image and recovers
    the input noise or latent code (by minimizing entropy loss)

    # Arguments
        inputs (Layer): feature1
        z_dim (int): noise dimensionality

    # Returns
        dis1 (Model): feature1 as real/fake and recovered latent code
    """

    # input is 256-dim feature1
    x = Dense(256, activation='relu')(inputs)
    x = Dense(256, activation='relu')(x)

    # first output is probability that feature1 is real
    f1_source = Dense(1)(x)
    f1_source = Activation('sigmoid',
                           name='feature1_source')(f1_source)

    # z1 reonstruction (Q1 network)
    z1_recon = Dense(z_dim)(x)
    z1_recon = Activation('tanh', name='z1')(z1_recon)

    discriminator_outputs = [f1_source, z1_recon]
    dis1 = Model(inputs, discriminator_outputs, name='dis1')
    return dis1
```

With all builder functions available, StackedGAN is assembled in *Listing 6.2.4*. Before training StackedGAN, the encoder is pretrained. Note that we already incorporated the three generator loss functions (adversarial, conditional, and entropy) in the adversarial model training. The Q network shares some common layers with the discriminator model. Therefore, its loss function is also incorporated in the discriminator model training.

Listing 6.2.4: `stackedgan-mnist-6.2.1.py`

```python
def build_and_train_models():
    """Load the dataset, build StackedGAN discriminator,
    generator, and adversarial models.
```

```
    Call the StackedGAN train routine.
    """

    # load MNIST dataset
    (x_train, y_train), (x_test, y_test) = mnist.load_data()

    # reshape and normalize images
    image_size = x_train.shape[1]
    x_train = np.reshape(x_train, [-1, image_size, image_size, 1])
    x_train = x_train.astype('float32') / 255

    x_test = np.reshape(x_test, [-1, image_size, image_size, 1])
    x_test = x_test.astype('float32') / 255

    # number of labels
    num_labels = len(np.unique(y_train))
    # to one-hot vector
    y_train = to_categorical(y_train)
    y_test = to_categorical(y_test)

    model_name = "stackedgan_mnist"
    # network parameters
    batch_size = 64
    train_steps = 10000
    lr = 2e-4
    decay = 6e-8
    input_shape = (image_size, image_size, 1)
    label_shape = (num_labels, )
    z_dim = 50
    z_shape = (z_dim, )
    feature1_dim = 256
    feature1_shape = (feature1_dim, )

    # build discriminator 0 and Q network 0 models
    inputs = Input(shape=input_shape, name='discriminator0_input')
    dis0 = gan.discriminator(inputs, num_codes=z_dim)
    # [1] uses Adam, but discriminator converges easily with RMSprop
    optimizer = RMSprop(lr=lr, decay=decay)
    # loss fuctions: 1) probability image is real (adversarial0 loss)
    # 2) MSE z0 recon loss (Q0 network loss or entropy0 loss)
    loss = ['binary_crossentropy', 'mse']
    loss_weights = [1.0, 10.0]
    dis0.compile(loss=loss,
                 loss_weights=loss_weights,
```

```
                     optimizer=optimizer,
                     metrics=['accuracy'])
dis0.summary() # image discriminator, z0 estimator

# build discriminator 1 and Q network 1 models
input_shape = (feature1_dim, )
inputs = Input(shape=input_shape, name='discriminator1_input')
dis1 = build_discriminator(inputs, z_dim=z_dim )
# loss fuctions: 1) probability feature1 is real
# (adversarial1 loss)
# 2) MSE z1 recon loss (Q1 network loss or entropy1 loss)
loss = ['binary_crossentropy', 'mse']
loss_weights = [1.0, 1.0]
dis1.compile(loss=loss,
                     loss_weights=loss_weights,
                     optimizer=optimizer,
                     metrics=['accuracy'])
dis1.summary() # feature1 discriminator, z1 estimator

# build generator models
feature1 = Input(shape=feature1_shape, name='feature1_input')
labels = Input(shape=label_shape, name='labels')
z1 = Input(shape=z_shape, name="z1_input")
z0 = Input(shape=z_shape, name="z0_input")
latent_codes = (labels, z0, z1, feature1)
gen0, gen1 = build_generator(latent_codes, image_size)
gen0.summary() # image generator
gen1.summary() # feature1 generator

# build encoder models
input_shape = (image_size, image_size, 1)
inputs = Input(shape=input_shape, name='encoder_input')
enc0, enc1 = build_encoder((inputs, feature1), num_labels)
enc0.summary() # image to feature1 encoder
enc1.summary() # feature1 to labels encoder (classifier)
encoder = Model(inputs, enc1(enc0(inputs)))
encoder.summary() # image to labels encoder (classifier)

data = (x_train, y_train), (x_test, y_test)
train_encoder(encoder, data, model_name=model_name)

# build adversarial0 model =
# generator0 + discriminator0 + encoder0
optimizer = RMSprop(lr=lr*0.5, decay=decay*0.5)
```

```
# encoder0 weights frozen
enc0.trainable = False
# discriminator0 weights frozen
dis0.trainable = False
gen0_inputs = [feature1, z0]
gen0_outputs = gen0(gen0_inputs)
adv0_outputs = dis0(gen0_outputs) + [enc0(gen0_outputs)]
# feature1 + z0 to prob feature1 is
# real + z0 recon + feature0/image recon
adv0 = Model(gen0_inputs, adv0_outputs, name="adv0")
# loss functions: 1) prob feature1 is real (adversarial0 loss)
# 2) Q network 0 loss (entropy0 loss)
# 3) conditional0 loss
loss = ['binary_crossentropy', 'mse', 'mse']
loss_weights = [1.0, 10.0, 1.0]
adv0.compile(loss=loss,
             loss_weights=loss_weights,
             optimizer=optimizer,
             metrics=['accuracy'])
adv0.summary()

# build adversarial1 model =
# generator1 + discriminator1 + encoder1
# encoder1 weights frozen
enc1.trainable = False
# discriminator1 weights frozen
dis1.trainable = False
gen1_inputs = [labels, z1]
gen1_outputs = gen1(gen1_inputs)
adv1_outputs = dis1(gen1_outputs) + [enc1(gen1_outputs)]
# labels + z1 to prob labels are real + z1 recon + feature1 recon
adv1 = Model(gen1_inputs, adv1_outputs, name="adv1")
# loss functions: 1) prob labels are real (adversarial1 loss)
# 2) Q network 1 loss (entropy1 loss)
# 3) conditional1 loss (classifier error)
loss_weights = [1.0, 1.0, 1.0]
loss = ['binary_crossentropy',
        'mse',
        'categorical_crossentropy']
adv1.compile(loss=loss,
             loss_weights=loss_weights,
             optimizer=optimizer,
             metrics=['accuracy'])
adv1.summary()
```

```
# train discriminator and adversarial networks
models = (enc0, enc1, gen0, gen1, dis0, dis1, adv0, adv1)
params = (batch_size, train_steps, num_labels, z_dim, model_name)
train(models, data, params)
```

Finally, the training function bears a resemblance to a typical GAN training, except that we only train one GAN at a time (that is, GAN_1 and then GAN_0). The code is shown in *Listing 6.2.5*. It's worth noting that the training sequence is:

1. *Discriminator*$_1$ and Q_1 networks by minimizing the discriminator and entropy losses

2. *Discriminator*$_0$ and Q_0 networks by minimizing the discriminator and entropy losses

3. *Adversarial*$_1$ network by minimizing the adversarial, entropy, and conditional losses

4. *Adversarial*$_0$ network by minimizing the adversarial, entropy, and conditional losses

Listing 6.2.5: `stackedgan-mnist-6.2.1.py`

```
def train(models, data, params):
    """Train the discriminator and adversarial Networks

    Alternately train discriminator and adversarial networks by batch.
    Discriminator is trained first with real and fake images,
    corresponding one-hot labels and latent codes.
    Adversarial is trained next with fake images pretending
    to be real, corresponding one-hot labels and latent codes.
    Generate sample images per save_interval.

    # Arguments
        models (Models): Encoder, Generator, Discriminator,
            Adversarial models
        data (tuple): x_train, y_train data
        params (tuple): Network parameters

    """
    # the StackedGAN and Encoder models
    enc0, enc1, gen0, gen1, dis0, dis1, adv0, adv1 = models
    # network parameters
    batch_size, train_steps, num_labels, z_dim, model_name = params
    # train dataset
```

```
(x_train, y_train), (_, _) = data
# the generator image is saved every 500 steps
save_interval = 500

# label and noise codes for generator testing
z0 = np.random.normal(scale=0.5, size=[16, z_dim])
z1 = np.random.normal(scale=0.5, size=[16, z_dim])
noise_class = np.eye(num_labels)[np.arange(0, 16) % num_labels]
noise_params = [noise_class, z0, z1]
# number of elements in train dataset
train_size = x_train.shape[0]
print(model_name,
      "Labels for generated images: ",
      np.argmax(noise_class, axis=1))

for i in range(train_steps):
    # train the discriminator1 for 1 batch
    # 1 batch of real (label=1.0) and fake feature1 (label=0.0)
    # randomly pick real images from dataset
    rand_indexes = np.random.randint(0,
                                     train_size,
                                     size=batch_size)
    real_images = x_train[rand_indexes]
    # real feature1 from encoder0 output
    real_feature1 = enc0.predict(real_images)
    # generate random 50-dim z1 latent code
    real_z1 = np.random.normal(scale=0.5,
                               size=[batch_size, z_dim])
    # real labels from dataset
    real_labels = y_train[rand_indexes]

    # generate fake feature1 using generator1 from
    # real labels and 50-dim z1 latent code
    fake_z1 = np.random.normal(scale=0.5,
                               size=[batch_size, z_dim])
    fake_feature1 = gen1.predict([real_labels, fake_z1])

    # real + fake data
    feature1 = np.concatenate((real_feature1, fake_feature1))
    z1 = np.concatenate((fake_z1, fake_z1))

    # label 1st half as real and 2nd half as fake
    y = np.ones([2 * batch_size, 1])
    y[batch_size:, :] = 0
```

```python
# train discriminator1 to classify feature1 as
# real/fake and recover
# latent code (z1). real = from encoder1,
# fake = from genenerator1
# joint training using discriminator part of
# advserial1 loss and entropy1 loss
metrics = dis1.train_on_batch(feature1, [y, z1])
# log the overall loss only
log = "%d: [dis1_loss: %f]" % (i, metrics[0])


# train the discriminator0 for 1 batch
# 1 batch of real (label=1.0) and fake images (label=0.0)
# generate random 50-dim z0 latent code
fake_z0 = np.random.normal(scale=0.5, size=[batch_size, z_
dim])
# generate fake images from real feature1 and fake z0
fake_images = gen0.predict([real_feature1, fake_z0])

# real + fake data
x = np.concatenate((real_images, fake_images))
z0 = np.concatenate((fake_z0, fake_z0))

# train discriminator0 to classify image
# as real/fake and recover latent code (z0)
# joint training using discriminator part of advserial0 loss
# and entropy0 loss
metrics = dis0.train_on_batch(x, [y, z0])
# log the overall loss only (use dis0.metrics_names)
log = "%s [dis0_loss: %f]" % (log, metrics[0])

# adversarial training
# generate fake z1, labels
fake_z1 = np.random.normal(scale=0.5,
                           size=[batch_size, z_dim])
# input to generator1 is sampling fr real labels and
# 50-dim z1 latent code
gen1_inputs = [real_labels, fake_z1]

# label fake feature1 as real
y = np.ones([batch_size, 1])

# train generator1 (thru adversarial) by fooling i
```

```
# the discriminator
# and approximating encoder1 feature1 generator
# joint training: adversarial1, entropy1, conditional1
metrics = adv1.train_on_batch(gen1_inputs,
                                [y, fake_z1, real_labels])
fmt = "%s [adv1_loss: %f, enc1_acc: %f]"
# log the overall loss and classification accuracy
log = fmt % (log, metrics[0], metrics[6])

# input to generator0 is real feature1 and
# 50-dim z0 latent code
fake_z0 = np.random.normal(scale=0.5,
                            size=[batch_size, z_dim])
gen0_inputs = [real_feature1, fake_z0]

# train generator0 (thru adversarial) by fooling
# the discriminator and approximating encoder1 imag
# source generator joint training:
# adversarial0, entropy0, conditional0
metrics = adv0.train_on_batch(gen0_inputs,
                                [y, fake_z0, real_feature1])
# log the overall loss only
log = "%s [adv0_loss: %f]" % (log, metrics[0])

print(log)
if (i + 1) % save_interval == 0:
    generators = (gen0, gen1)
    plot_images(generators,
                noise_params=noise_params,
                show=False,
                step=(i + 1),
                model_name=model_name)

# save the modelis after training generator0 & 1
# the trained generator can be reloaded for
# future MNIST digit generation
gen1.save(model_name + "-gen1.h5")
gen0.save(model_name + "-gen0.h5")
```

The code implementation of StackedGAN in `tf.keras` is now complete. After training, the generator outputs can be evaluated to examine whether certain attributes of synthesized MNIST digits can be controlled in a similar manner to what we did in InfoGAN.

Generator outputs of StackedGAN

After training the StackedGAN for 10,000 steps, the *Generator*$_0$ and *Generator*$_1$ models are saved on files. Stacked together, *Generator*$_0$ and *Generator*$_1$ can synthesize fake images conditioned on label and noise codes, z_0 and z_1.

The StackedGAN generator can be qualitatively validated by:

1. Varying the discrete labels from 0 to 9 with both noise codes, z_0 and z_1 sampled from a normal distribution with a mean of 0.5 and a standard deviation of 1.0. The results are shown in *Figure 6.2.9*. We're able to see that the StackedGAN discrete code can control the digits produced by the generator:

```
python3 stackedgan-mnist-6.2.1.py

--generator0=stackedgan_mnist-gen0.h5

--generator1=stackedgan_mnist-gen1.h5 --digit=0
```

to

```
python3 stackedgan-mnist-6.2.1.py

--generator0=stackedgan_mnist-gen0.h5

--generator1=stackedgan_mnist-gen1.h5 --digit=9
```

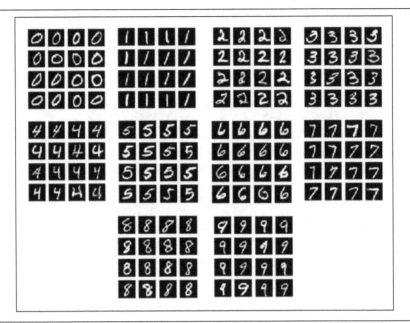

Figure 6.2.9: Images generated by StackedGAN as the discrete code is varied from 0 to 9. Both z_0 and z_1 have been sampled from a normal distribution with a mean of 0 and a standard deviation of 0.5

2. Varying the first noise code, z_0, as a constant vector from -4.0 to 4.0 for digits 0 to 9 is shown as follows. The second noise code, z_1, is set to a zero vector. *Figure 6.2.10* shows that the first noise code controls the thickness of the digit. For example, for digit 8:

```
python3 stackedgan-mnist-6.2.1.py
```

```
--generator0=stackedgan_mnist-gen0.h5
```

```
--generator1=stackedgan_mnist-gen1.h5 --z0=0 --z1=0 --p0
```

```
--digit=8
```

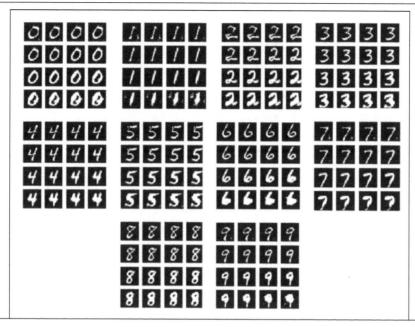

Figure 6.2.10: Images generated by using a StackedGAN as the first noise code, z_0, varies from a constant vector -4.0 to 4.0 for digits 0 to 9. z_0 appears to control the thickness of each digit

3. Varying the second noise code, z_1, as a constant vector from -1.0 to 1.0 for digits 0 to 9 is shown as follows. The first noise code, z_0, is set to a zero vector. *Figure 6.2.11* shows that the second noise code controls the rotation (tilt) and, to a certain extent, the thickness of the digit. For example, for digit 8:

```
python3 stackedgan-mnist-6.2.1.py
```

```
--generator0=stackedgan_mnist-gen0.h5
```

```
--generator1=stackedgan_mnist-gen1.h5 --z0=0 --z1=0 --p1
```

```
--digit=8
```

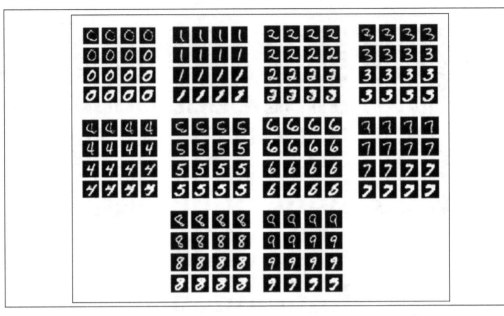

Figure 6.2.11: The images generated by StackedGAN as the second noise code, z_1, varies from a constant vector -1.0 to 1.0 for digits 0 to 9. z_1 appears to control the rotation (tilt) and the thickness of stroke of each digit

Figure 6.2.9 to *Figure 6.2.11* demonstrate that the StackedGAN has provided additional control in terms of the attributes of the generator outputs. The control and attributes are (label, which digit), (z_0, digit thickness), and (z_1, digit tilt). From this example, there are other possible experiments that we can control, such as:

- Increasing the number of elements in the stack from the current number of 2
- Decreasing the dimension of codes z_0 and z_1, like in InfoGAN

Figure 6.2.12 shows the differences between the latent codes of InfoGAN and StackedGAN:

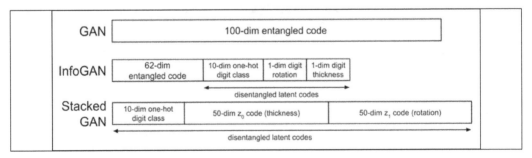

Figure 6.2.12: Latent representations for different GANs

The basic idea of disentangling codes is to put a constraint on the loss functions such that only specific attributes are affected by a code. Structure-wise, InfoGAN is easier to implement when compared to StackedGAN. InfoGAN is also faster to train.

4. Conclusion

In this chapter, we've discussed how to disentangle the latent representations of GANs. Earlier on in the chapter, we discussed how InfoGAN maximizes the mutual information in order to force the generator to learn disentangled latent vectors. In the MNIST dataset example, the InfoGAN uses three representations and a noise code as inputs. The noise represents the rest of the attributes in the form of an entangled representation. StackedGAN approaches the problem in a different way. It uses a stack of encoder-GANs to learn how to synthesize fake features and images. The encoder is first trained to provide a dataset of features. Then, the encoder-GANs are trained jointly to learn how to use the noise code to control attributes of the generator output.

In the next chapter, we will embark on a new type of GAN that is able to generate new data in another domain. For example, given an image of a horse, the GAN can perform an automatic transformation to an image of a zebra. The interesting feature of this type of GAN is that it can be trained without supervision and does not require paired sample data.

5. References

1. Xi Chen et al.: *InfoGAN: Interpretable Representation Learning by Information Maximizing Generative Adversarial Nets*. Advances in Neural Information Processing Systems, 2016 (http://papers.nips.cc/paper/6399-infogan-interpretable-representation-learning-by-information-maximizing-generative-adversarial-nets.pdf).

2. Xun Huang et al. *Stacked Generative Adversarial Networks*. IEEE Conference on Computer Vision and Pattern Recognition (CVPR). Vol. 2, 2017(http://openaccess.thecvf.com/content_cvpr_2017/papers/Huang_Stacked_Generative_Adversarial_CVPR_2017_paper.pdf).

7
Cross-Domain GANs

In computer vision, computer graphics, and image processing, a number of tasks involve translating an image from one form to another. The colorization of grayscale images, converting satellite images to maps, changing the artwork style of one artist to another, making night-time images into daytime, and summer photos to winter, are just a few examples. These tasks are referred to as **cross-domain transfer** and will be the focus of this chapter. An image in the source domain is transferred to a target domain, resulting in a new translated image.

A cross-domain transfer has a number of practical applications in the real world. As an example, in autonomous driving research, collecting road-scene driving data is both time-consuming and expensive. In order to cover as many scene variations as possible in that example, the roads would be traversed during different weather conditions, seasons, and times, giving us a large and varied amount of data. With the use of a cross-domain transfer, it's possible to generate new synthetic scenes that look real by translating existing images. For example, we may just need to collect road scenes in the summer from one area and gather road scenes in the winter from another place. Then, we can transform the summer images to winter and the winter images to summer. In this case, it reduces the number of tasks having to be done by half.

The generation of realistic synthesized images is an area that GANs excel at. Therefore, cross-domain translation is one of the applications of GANs. In this chapter, we're going to focus on a popular cross-domain GAN algorithm called *CycleGAN* [2]. Unlike other cross-domain transfer algorithms, such as a *pix2pix* [3], CycleGAN does not require aligned training images to work. In aligned images, the training data should be a pair of images made up of the source image and its corresponding target image; for example, a satellite image and the corresponding map derived from this image.

CycleGAN only requires the satellite data images and maps. The maps may be from other satellite data and not necessarily previously generated from the training data.

In this chapter, we will explore the following:

- The principles of CycleGAN, including its implementation in `tf.keras`
- Example applications of CycleGAN, including the colorization of grayscale images using the CIFAR10 dataset and style transfer as applied to MNIST digits and *Street View House Numbers (SVHN)* [1] datasets

Let's begin by talking about the principles behind CycleGAN.

1. Principles of CycleGAN

Translating an image from one domain to another is a common task in computer vision, computer graphics, and image processing. *Figure 7.1.1* shows edge detection, which is a common image translation task:

Figure 7.1.1: Example of an aligned image pair: left, original image, and right, transformed image using a Canny edge detector. The original photo was taken by the author.

In this example, we can consider the real photo (left) as an image in the source domain and the edge-detected photo (right) as a sample in the target domain. There are many other cross-domain translation procedures that have practical applications, such as:

- Satellite image to map
- Face image to emoji, caricature, or anime

- Body image to an avatar
- Colorization of grayscale photos
- Medical scan to a real photo
- Real photo to an artist's painting

There are many more examples of this in different fields. In computer vision and image processing, for example, we can perform the translation by inventing an algorithm that extracts features from the source image to translate it into the target image. The Canny edge operator is an example of such an algorithm. However, in many cases, the translation is very complex to hand-engineer, such that it is almost impossible to find a suitable algorithm. Both the source and target domain distributions are high-dimensional and complex.

A workaround on the image translation problem is to use deep learning techniques. If we have a sufficiently large dataset from both the source and target domains, we can train a neural network to model the translation. Since the images in the target domain must be automatically generated given a source image, they must look like real samples from the target domain. GANs are a suitable network for such cross-domain tasks. The *pix2pix* [3] algorithm is an example of a cross-domain algorithm.

The pix2pix algorithm bears a resemblance to **Conditional GAN (CGAN)** [4] that we discussed in *Chapter 4, Generative Adversarial Networks (GANs)*. We can recall that in CGAN, on top of the noise input, z, a condition such as of a `one-hot vector` constrains the generator's output. For example, in the MNIST digit, if we want the generator to output the digit 8, the condition is the `one-hot vector` [0, 0, 0, 0, 0, 0, 0, 0, 1, 0]. In pix2pix, the condition is the image to be translated. The generator's output is the translated image. The pix2pix algorithm is trained by optimizing the CGAN loss. To minimize blurring in the generated images, the *L1* loss is also included.

The main disadvantage of neural networks similar to pix2pix is that the training input and output images must be aligned. *Figure 7.1.1* is an example of an aligned image pair. The sample target image is generated from the source. In most occasions, aligned image pairs are not available or expensive to generate from the source images, or we have no idea on how to generate the target image from the given source image. What we have is sample data from the source and target domains. *Figure 7.1.2* is an example of data from the source domain (real photo) and the target domain (Van Gogh's art style) on the same sunflower subject. The source and target images are not necessarily aligned.

Unlike pix2pix, CycleGAN learns image translation as long as there is a sufficient amount of, and variation between, source and target data. No alignment is needed. CycleGAN learns the source and target distributions and how to translate from source to target distribution from given sample data. No supervision is needed. In the context of *Figure 7.1.2*, we just need thousands of photos of real sunflowers and thousands of photos of Van Gogh's paintings of sunflowers. After training the CycleGAN, we're able to translate a photo of sunflowers to a Van Gogh painting:

Figure 7.1.2: Example of an image pair that is not aligned: on the left, a photo of real sunflowers along University Avenue, University of the Philippines, and on the right, Sunflowers by Vincent Van Gogh at the National Gallery, London, UK. Original photos were taken by the author.

The next question is: how do we build a model that can learn from unpaired data? In the next section, we will build a CycleGAN that uses forward and backward cycle GANs and a cycle consistency check to eliminate the need for paired input data.

The CycleGAN model

Figure 7.1.3 shows the network model of the CycleGAN:

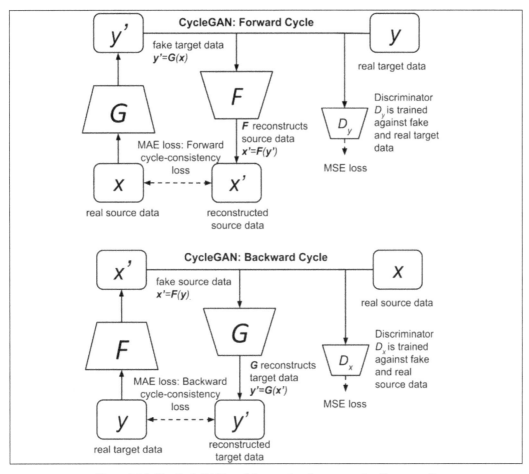

Figure 7.1.3: The CycleGAN model comprises four networks: Generator G,
Generator F, Discriminator D_y, and Discriminator D_x

Let's discuss *Figure 7.1.3* part by part. Let's first focus on the upper network, which is the Forward Cycle GAN. As shown in *Figure 7.1.4* below, the objective of the Forward Cycle CycleGAN is to learn the function:

$$y' = G(x) \qquad \text{(Equation 7.1.1)}$$

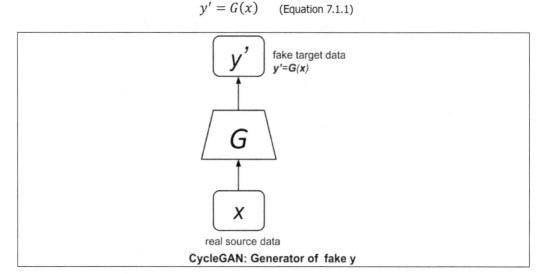

Figure 7.1.4: The CycleGAN Generator G of fake y

Equation 7.1.1 is simply the generator, G, of fake target data, y'. It converts data from the source domain, x, to the target domain, y.

To train the generator, we must build a GAN. This is the Forward Cycle GAN as shown in *Figure 7.1.5*. This figure shows that it is like a typical GAN in *Chapter 4, Generative Adversarial Networks (GANs)*, made of a generator G and a discriminator D_y that can be trained in the same adversarial manner. Learning is unsupervised by capitalizing only on the available real images, x, in the source domain and real images, y, in the target domain.

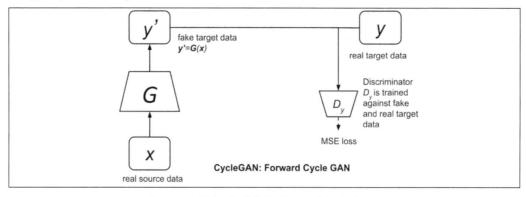

Figure 7.1.5: The CycleGAN Forward Cycle GAN

Unlike regular GANs, CycleGAN imposes the cycle-consistency constraint as shown in *Figure 7.1.6*. The forward cycle-consistency network ensures that the real source data can be reconstructed from the fake target data:

$$x' = F\big(G(x)\big) \quad \text{(Equation 7.1.2)}$$

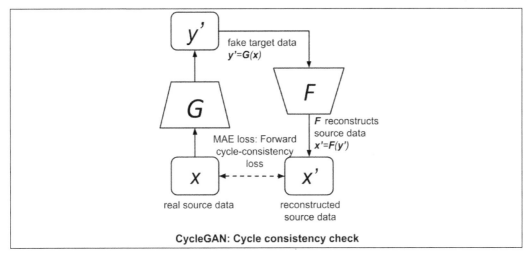

CycleGAN: Cycle consistency check

Figure 7.1.6: The CycleGAN cycle consistency check

This is done by minimizing the forward cycle-consistency *L1* loss:

$$\mathcal{L}_{forward-cyc} = \mathbb{E}_{x \sim p_{data}(x)} \Big[\big\| F\big(G(x)\big) - x \big\|_1 \Big] \quad \text{(Equation 7.1.3)}$$

The cycle-consistency loss uses *L1*, or **mean absolute error (MAE)**, since it generally results in less blurry image reconstruction compared to *L2*, or **mean squared error (MSE)**.

The cycle consistency check implies that although we have transformed source data *x* to domain *y*, the original features of *x* should remain intact in *y* and be recoverable. The network *F* is just another generator that we will borrow from the backward cycle GAN, as discussed next.

CycleGAN is symmetric. As shown in *Figure 7.1.7*, the Backward Cycle GAN is identical to the Forward Cycle GAN, but with the roles of source data *x* and target data *y* reversed. The source data is now *y* and the target data is now *x*. The roles of generators *G* and *F* are also reversed. *F* is now the generator, while *G* recovers the input. In the Forward Cycle GAN, the generator *F* was the network used to recover the source data, while *G* was the generator.

The objective of the Backward Cycle GAN generator is to synthesize:

$$x' = F(y) \quad \text{(Equation 7.1.2)}$$

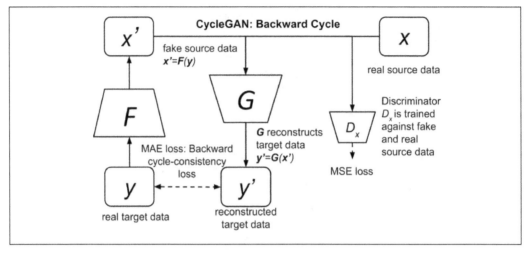

Figure 7.1.7: The CycleGAN Backward Cycle GAN

This is done by training the Backward Cycle GAN in an adversarial manner. The objective is for the generator F to learn how to fool the discriminator, $\mathcal{D}_x$.

Furthermore, there is also an analogous backward cycle consistency imposed to recover the original source, y:

$$y' = G\big(F(y)\big) \quad \text{(Equation 7.1.4)}$$

This is done by minimizing the backward cycle-consistency *L1* loss:

$$\mathcal{L}_{backward-cyc} = \mathbb{E}_{y \sim p_{data}(y)} \left[\big\| G\big(F(y)\big) - y \big\|_1 \right] \quad \text{(Equation 7.1.5)}$$

In summary, the ultimate objective of CycleGAN is for the generator G to learn how to synthesize fake target data, y', that can fool the discriminator, $\mathcal{D}_y$, in the forward cycle. Since the network is symmetric, CycleGAN also wants the generator F to learn how to synthesize fake source data, x', that can fool the discriminator, $\mathcal{D}_x$, in the backward cycle. With this in mind, we can now put together all the loss functions.

Let's start with the GAN part. Inspired by the better perceptual quality of *Least Squares GAN (LSGAN)* [5], as described in *Chapter 5, Improved GANs*, CycleGAN also uses MSE for the discriminator and generator losses. Recall that the difference between LSGAN and the original GAN entails use of the MSE loss instead of a binary cross-entropy loss.

CycleGAN expresses the generator-discriminator loss functions as:

$$\mathcal{L}_{forward-GAN}^{(D)} = \mathbb{E}_{y \sim p_{data}(y)}\left(\mathcal{D}_y(y) - 1\right)^2 + \mathbb{E}_{x \sim p_{data}(x)}\mathcal{D}_y(G(x))^2 \quad \text{(Equation 7.1.6)}$$

$$\mathcal{L}_{forward-GAN}^{(G)} = \mathbb{E}_{x \sim p_{data}(x)}\left(\mathcal{D}_y(G(x)) - 1\right)^2 \quad \text{(Equation 7.1.7)}$$

$$\mathcal{L}_{backward-GAN}^{(D)} = \mathbb{E}_{x \sim p_{data}(x)}\left(\mathcal{D}_x(x) - 1\right)^2 + \mathbb{E}_{y \sim p_{data}(y)}\mathcal{D}_x(F(y))^2 \quad \text{(Equation 7.1.8)}$$

$$\mathcal{L}_{backward-GAN}^{(G)} = \mathbb{E}_{y \sim p_{data}(y)}\left(\mathcal{D}_x(F(y)) - 1\right)^2 \quad \text{(Equation 7.1.9)}$$

$$\mathcal{L}_{GAN}^{(D)} = \mathcal{L}_{forward-GAN}^{(D)} + \mathcal{L}_{backward-GAN}^{(D)} \quad \text{(Equation 7.1.10)}$$

$$\mathcal{L}_{GAN}^{(G)} = \mathcal{L}_{forward-GAN}^{(G)} + \mathcal{L}_{backward-GAN}^{(G)} \quad \text{(Equation 7.1.11)}$$

The second set of loss functions are the cycle-consistency losses, which can be derived by summing up the contribution from the forward and backward GANs:

$$\mathcal{L}_{cyc} = \mathcal{L}_{forward-cyc} + \mathcal{L}_{backward-cyc}$$

$$\mathcal{L}_{cyc} = \mathbb{E}_{x \sim p_{data}(x)}\left[\left\|F(G(x)) - x\right\|_1\right] + \mathbb{E}_{y \sim p_{data}(y)}\left[\left\|G(F(y)) - y\right\|_1\right] \quad \text{(Equation 7.1.12)}$$

The total CycleGAN loss is:

$$\mathcal{L} = \lambda_1 \mathcal{L}_{GAN} + \lambda_2 \mathcal{L}_{cyc} \quad \text{(Equation 7.1.13)}$$

CycleGAN recommends the following weight values, $\lambda_1 = 1.0$ and $\lambda_2 = 10.0$, to give more importance to the cyclic consistency check.

The training strategy is similar to the vanilla GAN. *Algorithm 7.1.1* summarizes the CycleGAN training procedure.

Algorithm 7.1.1: CycleGAN Training

Repeat for n training steps:

1. Minimize $\mathcal{L}_{forward-GAN}^{(D)}$ by training the forward-cycle discriminator using real source and target data. A minibatch of real target data, y, is labeled 1.0. A minibatch of fake target data, $y' = G(x)$, is labeled 0.0.

2. Minimize $\mathcal{L}_{backward-GAN}^{(D)}$ by training the backward-cycle discriminator using real source and target data. A minibatch of real source data, x, is labeled 1.0. A minibatch of fake source data, $x' = F(y)$, is labeled 0.0.

3. Minimize $\mathcal{L}_{GAN}^{(G)}$ and $\mathcal{L}_{cyc}$ by training the forward-cycle and backward-cycle generators in the adversarial networks. A minibatch of fake target data, $y' = G(x)$, is labeled 1.0. A minibatch of fake source data, $x' = F(y)$, is labeled 1.0. The weights of the discriminators are frozen.

In neural-style transfer problems, the color composition may not be successfully transferred from the source image to the fake target image. This problem is shown in *Figure 7.1.8*:

| Source Domain: Real Sunflower | Target Domain: Van Gogh's Sunflower Style | Predicted Target Domain: Van Gogh's Sunflower Style w/o the right color composition |

Figure 7.1.8: During style transfer, the color composition may not be transferred successfully. To address this issue, the identity loss is added to the total loss function

To address this problem, CycleGAN proposes to include the forward and backward-cycle identity loss function:

$$\mathcal{L}_{identity} = \mathbb{E}_{x \sim p_{data}(x)}[\|F(x) - x\|_1] + \mathbb{E}_{y \sim p_{data}(y)}[\|G(y) - y\|_1] \quad \text{(Equation 7.1.14)}$$

The total CycleGAN loss becomes:

$$\mathcal{L} = \lambda_1 \mathcal{L}_{GAN} + \lambda_2 \mathcal{L}_{cyc} + \lambda_3 \mathcal{L}_{identity} \quad \text{(Equation 7.1.15)}$$

where $\lambda_3 = 0.5$. The identity loss is also optimized during adversarial training. *Figure 7.1.9* highlights the auxiliary network of CycleGAN implementing the identity regularizer:

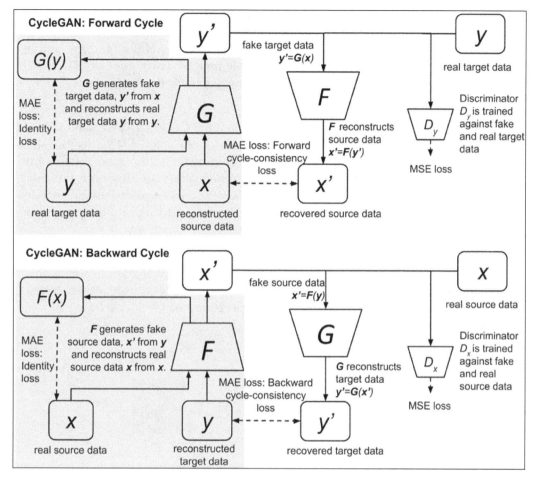

Figure 7.1.9: The CycleGAN model with the identity regularizing network
as highlighted on the left side of the image

In the next section, we will implement CycleGAN in `tf.keras`.

Implementing CycleGAN using Keras

Let's tackle a simple problem that CycleGAN can address. In *Chapter 3, Autoencoders*, we used an autoencoder to colorize grayscale images from the CIFAR10 dataset. We can recall that the CIFAR10 dataset comprises 50,000 trained items of data and 10,000 test data samples of 32 x 32 RGB images belonging to 10 categories. We can convert all color images into grayscale using rgb2gray (RGB), as discussed in *Chapter 3, Autoencoders*.

Following on from that, we can use the grayscale train images as source domain images and the original color images as the target domain images. It's worth noting that although the dataset is aligned, the input to our CycleGAN is a random sample of color images and a random sample of grayscale images. Thus, our CycleGAN will not see the training data as aligned. After training, we'll use the test grayscale images to observe the performance of the CycleGAN.

As discussed in the previous sections, to implement the CycleGAN, we need to build two generators and two discriminators. The generator of CycleGAN learns the latent representation of the source input distribution and translates this representation into target output distribution. This is exactly what autoencoders do. However, typical autoencoders similar to the ones discussed in *Chapter 3, Autoencoders*, use an encoder that downsamples the input until the bottleneck layer, at which point the process is reversed in the decoder.

This structure is not suitable in some image translation problems since many low-level features are shared between the encoder and decoder layers. For example, in colorization problems, the form, structure, and edges of the grayscale image are the same as in the color image. To circumvent this problem, the CycleGAN generators use a *U-Net* [7] structure, as shown in *Figure 7.1.10*:

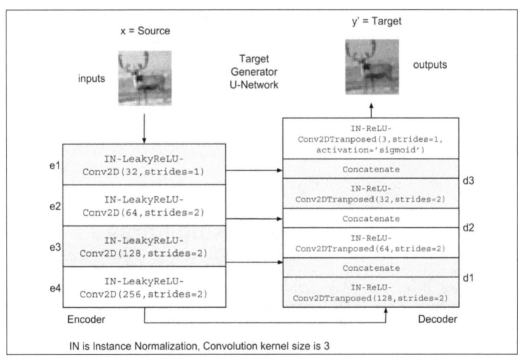

Figure 7.1.10: Implementation of the forward cycle generator G in Keras. The generator is a U-Network [7] comprising an encoder and decoder.

In a U-Net structure, the output of the encoder layer, e_{n-i}, is concatenated with the output of the decoder layer, d_i, where $n = 4$ is the number of encoder/decoder layers and $i = 1, 2,$ and 3 are layer numbers that share information.

We should note that although the example uses $n = 4$, problems with a higher input/ output dimensions may require a deeper encoder/decoder layer. The U-Net structure enables a free flow of feature-level information between the encoder and decoder.

An encoder layer is made of `Instance Normalization(IN)-LeakyReLU-Conv2D`, while the decoder layer is made of `IN-ReLU-Conv2D`. The encoder/decoder layer implementation is shown in *Listing 7.1.1*, while the generator implementation is shown in *Listing 7.1.2*.

The complete code is available on GitHub:

`https://github.com/PacktPublishing/Advanced-Deep-Learning-with-Keras`

Instance Normalization (IN) is **Batch Normalization (BN)** per sample of data (that is, IN is BN per image or per feature). In style transfer, it's important to normalize the contrast per sample, and not per batch. IN is equivalent to contrast normalization. Meanwhile, BN breaks contrast normalization.

Remember to install `tensorflow-addons` before using IN:

$ pip install tensorflow-addons

Listing 7.1.1: `cyclegan-7.1.1.py`

```
def encoder_layer(inputs,
                  filters=16,
                  kernel_size=3,
                  strides=2,
                  activation='relu',
                  instance_norm=True):
    """Builds a generic encoder layer made of Conv2D-IN-LeakyReLU
    IN is optional, LeakyReLU may be replaced by ReLU

    """

    conv = Conv2D(filters=filters,
```

```
                           kernel_size=kernel_size,
                           strides=strides,
                           padding='same')

    x = inputs
    if instance_norm:
        x = InstanceNormalization(axis=3)(x)
    if activation == 'relu':
        x = Activation('relu')(x)
    else:
        x = LeakyReLU(alpha=0.2)(x)
    x = conv(x)
    return x


def decoder_layer(inputs,
                  paired_inputs,
                  filters=16,
                  kernel_size=3,
                  strides=2,
                  activation='relu',
                  instance_norm=True):
    """Builds a generic decoder layer made of Conv2D-IN-LeakyReLU
    IN is optional, LeakyReLU may be replaced by ReLU
    Arguments: (partial)
    inputs (tensor): the decoder layer input
    paired_inputs (tensor): the encoder layer output
        provided by U-Net skip connection &
        concatenated to inputs.

    """

    conv = Conv2DTranspose(filters=filters,
                           kernel_size=kernel_size,
                           strides=strides,
                           padding='same')

    x = inputs
    if instance_norm:
        x = InstanceNormalization(axis=3)(x)
    if activation == 'relu':
        x = Activation('relu')(x)
    else:
        x = LeakyReLU(alpha=0.2)(x)
```

```
x = conv(x)
x = concatenate([x, paired_inputs])
return x
```

Moving on to the generator implementation:

Listing 7.1.2: `cyclegan-7.1.1.py`

Generator implementation in Keras:

```
def build_generator(input_shape,
                    output_shape=None,
                    kernel_size=3,
                    name=None):
    """The generator is a U-Network made of a 4-layer encoder
    and a 4-layer decoder. Layer n-i is connected to layer i.

    Arguments:
    input_shape (tuple): input shape
    output_shape (tuple): output shape
    kernel_size (int): kernel size of encoder & decoder layers
    name (string): name assigned to generator model

    Returns:
    generator (Model):

    """

    inputs = Input(shape=input_shape)
    channels = int(output_shape[-1])
    e1 = encoder_layer(inputs,
                       32,
                       kernel_size=kernel_size,
                       activation='leaky_relu',
                       strides=1)
    e2 = encoder_layer(e1,
                       64,
                       activation='leaky_relu',
                       kernel_size=kernel_size)
    e3 = encoder_layer(e2,
                       128,
                       activation='leaky_relu',
                       kernel_size=kernel_size)
    e4 = encoder_layer(e3,
                       256,
                       activation='leaky_relu',
                       kernel_size=kernel_size)


    d1 = decoder_layer(e4,
```

```
                        e3,
                        128,
                        kernel_size=kernel_size)
    d2 = decoder_layer(d1,
                        e2,
                        64,
                        kernel_size=kernel_size)
    d3 = decoder_layer(d2,
                        e1,
                        32,
                        kernel_size=kernel_size)
    outputs = Conv2DTranspose(channels,
                              kernel_size=kernel_size,
                              strides=1,
                              activation='sigmoid',
                              padding='same')(d3)

    generator = Model(inputs, outputs, name=name)

    return generator
```

The discriminator of CycleGAN is similar to a vanilla GAN discriminator. The input image is downsampled several times (in this example, three times). The final layer is a `Dense` (1) layer, which predicts the probability that the input is real. Each layer is similar to the encoder layer of the generator except that no IN is used. However, in large images, computing the image as real or fake with a single number turns out to be parameter-inefficient and results in poor image quality for the generator.

The solution is to use PatchGAN [6], which divides the image into a grid of patches and uses a grid of scalar values to predict the probability that the patches are real. The comparison between the vanilla GAN discriminator and a 2 x 2 PatchGAN discriminator is shown in *Figure 7.1.11*:

Figure 7.1.11: A comparison between GAN and PatchGAN discriminators

In this example, the patches do not overlap and meet at their boundaries. However, in general, patches may overlap.

We should note that PatchGAN is not introducing a new type of GAN in CycleGAN. To improve the generated image quality, instead of having one output to discriminate, we have four outputs to discriminate if we use a 2 x 2 PatchGAN. There are no changes in the loss functions. Intuitively, this makes sense since the whole image will look more real if every patch or section of the image looks real.

Figure 7.1.12 shows the discriminator network as implemented in `tf.keras`. The illustration shows the discriminator determining the likelihood of the input image or a patch being a color CIFAR10 image:

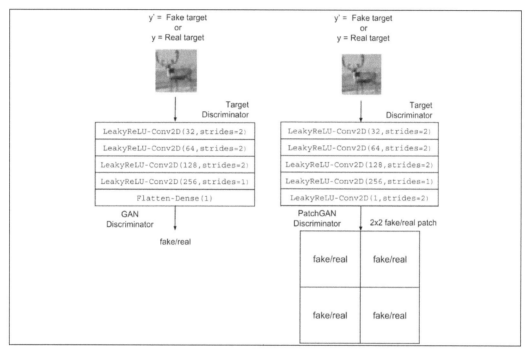

Figure 7.1.12: The target discriminator, D$_{y'}$ implementation in `tf.keras`.
The PatchGAN discriminator is shown on the right

Since the output image is small at only 32 x 32 RGB, a single scalar representing that the image is real is sufficient. However, we also evaluate the results when PatchGAN is used. *Listing 7.1.3* shows the function builder for the discriminator:

Listing 7.1.3: `cyclegan-7.1.1.py`

Discriminator implementation in `tf.keras`:

```
def build_discriminator(input_shape,
```

```
                      kernel_size=3,
                      patchgan=True,
                      name=None):
    """The discriminator is a 4-layer encoder that outputs either
a 1-dim or a n x n-dim patch of probability that input is real

Arguments:
input_shape (tuple): input shape
kernel_size (int): kernel size of decoder layers
patchgan (bool): whether the output is a patch
    or just a 1-dim
name (string): name assigned to discriminator model

Returns:
discriminator (Model):

    """

    inputs = Input(shape=input_shape)
    x = encoder_layer(inputs,
                      32,
                      kernel_size=kernel_size,
                      activation='leaky_relu',
                      instance_norm=False)
    x = encoder_layer(x,
                      64,
                      kernel_size=kernel_size,
                      activation='leaky_relu',
                      instance_norm=False)
    x = encoder_layer(x,
                      128,
                      kernel_size=kernel_size,
                      activation='leaky_relu',
                      instance_norm=False)
    x = encoder_layer(x,
                      256,
                      kernel_size=kernel_size,
                      strides=1,
                      activation='leaky_relu',
                      instance_norm=False)

    # if patchgan=True use nxn-dim output of probability
    # else use 1-dim output of probability
    if patchgan:
```

```
        x = LeakyReLU(alpha=0.2)(x)
        outputs = Conv2D(1,
                        kernel_size=kernel_size,
                        strides=2,
                        padding='same')(x)
    else:
        x = Flatten()(x)
        x = Dense(1)(x)
        outputs = Activation('linear')(x)


    discriminator = Model(inputs, outputs, name=name)

    return discriminator
```

Using the generator and discriminator builders, we are now able to build the CycleGAN. *Listing 7.1.4* shows the builder function. In line with our discussion in the previous section, two generators, g_source = F and g_target = G, and two discriminators, d_source = D_x and d_target = D_y, are instantiated. The forward cycle is $x' = F\big(G(x)\big)$ = reco_source = g_source(g_target(source_input)). The backward cycle is $y' = G\big(F(y)\big)$ = reco_target = g_target(g_source (target_input)).

The inputs to the adversarial model are the source and target data, while the outputs are the outputs of $\mathcal{D}_x$ and $\mathcal{D}_y$ and the reconstructed inputs, x' and y'. The identity network is not used in this example due to the difference between the number of channels in the grayscale image and the color image. We use the recommended loss weights of $\lambda_1 = 1.0$ and $\lambda_2 = 10.0$ for the GAN and cyclic consistency losses, respectively. Similar to GANs in the previous chapters, we use RMSprop with a learning rate of 2e-4 and a decay rate of 6e-8 for the optimizer of the discriminators. The learning and decay rate for the adversarial is half of that of the discriminator's.

Listing 7.1.4: cyclegan-7.1.1.py

CycleGAN builder in tf.keras:

```
def build_cyclegan(shapes,
                   source_name='source',
                   target_name='target',
                   kernel_size=3,
                   patchgan=False,
                   identity=False
                   ):
    """Build the CycleGAN
```

```
1) Build target and source discriminators
2) Build target and source generators
3) Build the adversarial network

Arguments:
shapes (tuple): source and target shapes
source_name (string): string to be appended on dis/gen models
target_name (string): string to be appended on dis/gen models
kernel_size (int): kernel size for the encoder/decoder
    or dis/gen models
patchgan (bool): whether to use patchgan on discriminator
identity (bool): whether to use identity loss

Returns:
(list): 2 generator, 2 discriminator,
    and 1 adversarial models

"""

source_shape, target_shape = shapes
lr = 2e-4
decay = 6e-8
gt_name = "gen_" + target_name
gs_name = "gen_" + source_name
dt_name = "dis_" + target_name
ds_name = "dis_" + source_name

# build target and source generators
g_target = build_generator(source_shape,
                           target_shape,
                           kernel_size=kernel_size,
                           name=gt_name)
g_source = build_generator(target_shape,
                           source_shape,
                           kernel_size=kernel_size,
                           name=gs_name)
print('---- TARGET GENERATOR ----')
g_target.summary()
print('---- SOURCE GENERATOR ----')
g_source.summary()

# build target and source discriminators
d_target = build_discriminator(target_shape,
                               patchgan=patchgan,
```

```
                                       kernel_size=kernel_size,
                                       name=dt_name)
      d_source = build_discriminator(source_shape,
                                     patchgan=patchgan,
                                     kernel_size=kernel_size,
                                     name=ds_name)
      print('---- TARGET DISCRIMINATOR ----')
      d_target.summary()
      print('---- SOURCE DISCRIMINATOR ----')
      d_source.summary()

      optimizer = RMSprop(lr=lr, decay=decay)
      d_target.compile(loss='mse',
                       optimizer=optimizer,
                       metrics=['accuracy'])
      d_source.compile(loss='mse',
                       optimizer=optimizer,
                       metrics=['accuracy'])

      d_target.trainable = False
      d_source.trainable = False

      # build the computational graph for the adversarial model
      # forward cycle network and target discriminator
      source_input = Input(shape=source_shape)
      fake_target = g_target(source_input)
      preal_target = d_target(fake_target)
      reco_source = g_source(fake_target)

      # backward cycle network and source discriminator
      target_input = Input(shape=target_shape)
      fake_source = g_source(target_input)
      preal_source = d_source(fake_source)
      reco_target = g_target(fake_source)

      # if we use identity loss, add 2 extra loss terms
      # and outputs
      if identity:
          iden_source = g_source(source_input)
          iden_target = g_target(target_input)
          loss = ['mse', 'mse', 'mae', 'mae', 'mae', 'mae']
          loss_weights = [1., 1., 10., 10., 0.5, 0.5]
          inputs = [source_input, target_input]
          outputs = [preal_source,
```

```
                    preal_target,
                    reco_source,
                    reco_target,
                    iden_source,
                    iden_target]
        else:
            loss = ['mse', 'mse', 'mae', 'mae']
            loss_weights = [1., 1., 10., 10.]
            inputs = [source_input, target_input]
            outputs = [preal_source,
                       preal_target,
                       reco_source,
                       reco_target]

        # build adversarial model
        adv = Model(inputs, outputs, name='adversarial')
        optimizer = RMSprop(lr=lr*0.5, decay=decay*0.5)
        adv.compile(loss=loss,
                    loss_weights=loss_weights,
                    optimizer=optimizer,
                    metrics=['accuracy'])
        print('---- ADVERSARIAL NETWORK ----')
        adv.summary()

        return g_source, g_target, d_source, d_target, adv
```

We follow the training procedure that we can recall from *Algorithm 7.1.1* in the previous section. *Listing 7.1.5* shows the CycleGAN training. The minor difference between this training and the vanilla GAN is that there are two discriminators to be optimized. However, there is only one adversarial model to optimize. For every 2,000 steps, the generators save the predicted source and target images. We'll use a batch size of 32. We also tried a batch size of 1, but the output quality is almost the same and takes a longer amount of time to train (43 ms/image for a batch size of 1 versus 3.6 ms/image for a batch size of 32 on an NVIDIA GTX 1060).

Listing 7.1.5: `cyclegan-7.1.1.py`

CycleGAN training routine in `tf.keras`:

```
    def train_cyclegan(models,
                       data,
                       params,
                       test_params,
                       test_generator):
        """ Trains the CycleGAN.
```

```
1) Train the target discriminator
2) Train the source discriminator
3) Train the forward and backward cyles of
   adversarial networks

Arguments:
models (Models): Source/Target Discriminator/Generator,
    Adversarial Model
data (tuple): source and target training data
params (tuple): network parameters
test_params (tuple): test parameters
test_generator (function): used for generating
    predicted target and source images
"""


# the models
g_source, g_target, d_source, d_target, adv = models
# network parameters
batch_size, train_steps, patch, model_name = params
# train dataset
source_data, target_data, test_source_data, test_target_data\
        = data

titles, dirs = test_params

# the generator image is saved every 2000 steps
save_interval = 2000
target_size = target_data.shape[0]
source_size = source_data.shape[0]

# whether to use patchgan or not
if patch > 1:
    d_patch = (patch, patch, 1)
    valid = np.ones((batch_size,) + d_patch)
    fake = np.zeros((batch_size,) + d_patch)
else:
    valid = np.ones([batch_size, 1])
    fake = np.zeros([batch_size, 1])

valid_fake = np.concatenate((valid, fake))
start_time = datetime.datetime.now()

for step in range(train_steps):
```

```python
# sample a batch of real target data
rand_indexes = np.random.randint(0,
                                 target_size,
                                 size=batch_size)
real_target = target_data[rand_indexes]

# sample a batch of real source data
rand_indexes = np.random.randint(0,
                                 source_size,
                                 size=batch_size)
real_source = source_data[rand_indexes]
# generate a batch of fake target data fr real source data
fake_target = g_target.predict(real_source)

# combine real and fake into one batch
x = np.concatenate((real_target, fake_target))
# train the target discriminator using fake/real data
metrics = d_target.train_on_batch(x, valid_fake)
log = "%d: [d_target loss: %f]" % (step, metrics[0])

# generate a batch of fake source data fr real target data
fake_source = g_source.predict(real_target)
x = np.concatenate((real_source, fake_source))
# train the source discriminator using fake/real data
metrics = d_source.train_on_batch(x, valid_fake)
log = "%s [d_source loss: %f]" % (log, metrics[0])

# train the adversarial network using forward and backward
# cycles. the generated fake source and target
# data attempts to trick the discriminators
x = [real_source, real_target]
y = [valid, valid, real_source, real_target]
metrics = adv.train_on_batch(x, y)
elapsed_time = datetime.datetime.now() - start_time
fmt = "%s [adv loss: %f] [time: %s]"
log = fmt % (log, metrics[0], elapsed_time)
print(log)
if (step + 1) % save_interval == 0:
    test_generator((g_source, g_target),
                   (test_source_data, test_target_data),
                   step=step+1,
                   titles=titles,
                   dirs=dirs,
                   show=False)
```

```
# save the models after training the generators
g_source.save(model_name + "-g_source.h5")
g_target.save(model_name + "-g_target.h5")
```

Finally, before we can use the CycleGAN to build and train functions, we have to perform some data preparation. The modules `cifar10_utils.py` and `other_utils.py` load the `CIFAR10` training and test data. Please refer to the source code for details of these two files. After loading, the train and test images are converted to grayscale to generate the source data and test source data.

Listing 7.1.6 shows how the CycleGAN is used to build and train a generator network (`g_target`) for colorization of grayscale images. Since CycleGAN is symmetric, we also build and train a second generator network (`g_source`) that converts from color to grayscale. Two CycleGAN colorization networks were trained. The first uses discriminators with a scalar output similar to vanilla GAN, while the second uses a 2 x 2 PatchGAN.

Listing 7.1.6: `cyclegan-7.1.1.py`

CycleGAN for colorization:

```
def graycifar10_cross_colorcifar10(g_models=None):
    """Build and train a CycleGAN that can do
       grayscale <--> color cifar10 images
    """

    model_name = 'cyclegan_cifar10'
    batch_size = 32
    train_steps = 100000
    patchgan = True
    kernel_size = 3
    postfix = ('%dp' % kernel_size) \
            if patchgan else ('%d' % kernel_size)

    data, shapes = cifar10_utils.load_data()
    source_data, _, test_source_data, test_target_data = data
    titles = ('CIFAR10 predicted source images.',
              'CIFAR10 predicted target images.',
              'CIFAR10 reconstructed source images.',
              'CIFAR10 reconstructed target images.')
    dirs = ('cifar10_source-%s' % postfix, \
            'cifar10_target-%s' % postfix)

    # generate predicted target(color) and source(gray) images
```

```
    if g_models is not None:
        g_source, g_target = g_models
        other_utils.test_generator((g_source, g_target),
                                    (test_source_data, \
                                            test_target_data),
                                step=0,
                                titles=titles,
                                dirs=dirs,
                                show=True)
    return


# build the cyclegan for cifar10 colorization
models = build_cyclegan(shapes,
                        "gray-%s" % postfix,
                        "color-%s" % postfix,
                        kernel_size=kernel_size,
                        patchgan=patchgan)
# patch size is divided by 2^n since we downscaled the input
# in the discriminator by 2^n (ie. we use strides=2 n times)
patch = int(source_data.shape[1] / 2**4) if patchgan else 1
params = (batch_size, train_steps, patch, model_name)
test_params = (titles, dirs)
# train the cyclegan
train_cyclegan(models,
                data,
                params,
                test_params,
                other_utils.test_generator)
```

In the next section, we will examine the generator outputs of CycleGAN for colorization.

Generator outputs of CycleGAN

Figure 7.1.13 shows the colorization results of CycleGAN. The source images are from the test dataset:

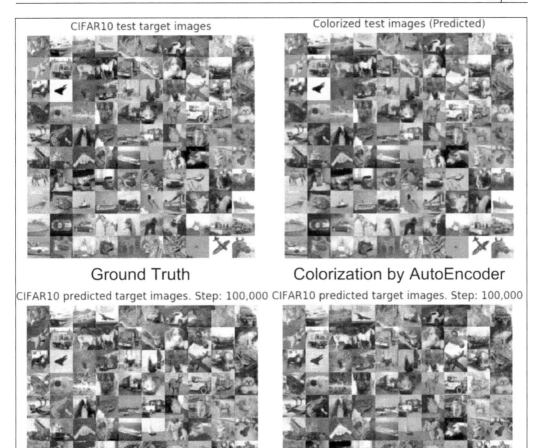

Figure 7.1.13: Colorization using different techniques. Shown are the ground truth, colorization using autoencoder (Chapter 3, Autoencoders,), colorization using CycleGAN with a vanilla GAN discriminator, and colorization using CycleGAN with a PatchGAN discriminator. Best viewed in color. The original color photos can be found on the book's GitHub repository at https://github.com/PacktPublishing/Advanced-Deep-Learning- with-Keras/blob/master/chapter7-cross-domain-gan/README.md

For comparison, we show the ground truth and the colorization results using a plain autoencoder described in *Chapter 3, Autoencoders*. Generally, all colorized images are perceptually acceptable. Overall, it seems that each colorization technique has both its own pros and cons. All colorization methods are not consistent with the right color of the sky and vehicle.

For example, the sky in the background of the plane (third row, second column) is white. The autoencoder got it right, but the CycleGAN thinks it is light brown or blue.

For the sixth row, sixth column, the boat on the dark sea had an overcast sky, but was colorized with blue sky and blue sea by the autoencoder and blue sea and white sky by CycleGAN without PatchGAN. Both predictions make sense in the real world. Meanwhile, the prediction of CycleGAN with PatchGAN is similar to the ground truth. On the second-to-last row and second column, no method was able to predict the red color of the car. On animals, both flavors of CycleGAN have colors close to the ground truth.

Since CycleGAN is symmetric, it also predicts the grayscale image given a color image. *Figure 7.1.14* shows the color to grayscale conversion performed by the two CycleGAN variations. The target images are from the test dataset. Except for minor differences in the grayscale shades of some images, the predictions are generally accurate.

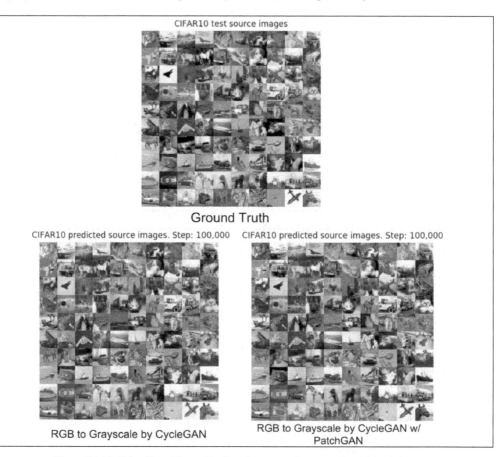

Figure 7.1.14: Color (from Figure 7.1.9) to the grayscale conversion of CycleGAN

To train the CycleGAN for colorization, the command is:

```
python3 cyclegan-7.1.1.py -c
```

The reader can run the image translation by using the pretrained models for CycleGAN with PatchGAN:

```
python3 cyclegan-7.1.1.py --cifar10_g_source=cyclegan_cifar10-g_source.h5
--cifar10_g_target=cyclegan_cifar10-g_target.h5
```

In this section, we demonstrated one practical application of CycleGAN on colorization. In the next section, we will train a CycleGAN on more challenging datasets. The source domain MNIST is drastically different from the target domain SVHN dataset [1].

CycleGAN on MNIST and SVHN datasets

We're now going to tackle a more challenging problem. Suppose we use MNIST digits in grayscale as our source data, and we want to borrow style from *SVHN* [1], which is our target data. The sample data in each domain is shown in *Figure 7.1.15*:

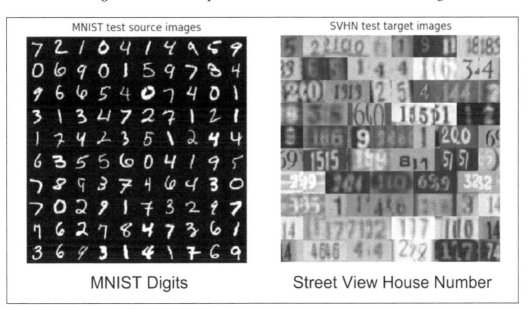

Figure 7.1.15: Two different domains with data that are not aligned. The original color photo can be found on the book's GitHub repository at https://github.com/PacktPublishing/Advanced-Deep-Learning-with-Keras/blob/master/chapter7-cross-domain-gan/README.md

We can reuse all the build and train functions for CycleGAN that were discussed in the previous section to perform style transfer. The only difference is that we have to add routines for loading MNIST and SVHN data. The SVHN dataset can be found at `http://ufldl.stanford.edu/housenumbers/`.

We introduce the `mnist_svhn_utils.py` module to help us with this task. *Listing 7.1.7* shows the initialization and training of the CycleGAN for cross-domain transfer.

The CycleGAN structure is the same as in the previous section, except that we use a kernel size of five since the two domains are drastically different.

Listing 7.1.7: `cyclegan-7.1.1.py`

CycleGAN for cross-domain style transfer between MNIST and SVHN:

```
def mnist_cross_svhn(g_models=None):
    """Build and train a CycleGAN that can do mnist <--> svhn
    """

    model_name = 'cyclegan_mnist_svhn'
    batch_size = 32
    train_steps = 100000
    patchgan = True
    kernel_size = 5
    postfix = ('%dp' % kernel_size) \
            if patchgan else ('%d' % kernel_size)

    data, shapes = mnist_svhn_utils.load_data()
    source_data, _, test_source_data, test_target_data = data
    titles = ('MNIST predicted source images.',
              'SVHN predicted target images.',
              'MNIST reconstructed source images.',
              'SVHN reconstructed target images.')
    dirs = ('mnist_source-%s' \
            % postfix, 'svhn_target-%s' % postfix)
```

```
# generate predicted target(svhn) and source(mnist) images
if g_models is not None:
    g_source, g_target = g_models
    other_utils.test_generator((g_source, g_target),
                                (test_source_data, \
                                        test_target_data),
                                step=0,
                                titles=titles,
                                dirs=dirs,
                                show=True)
    return


# build the cyclegan for mnist cross svhn
models = build_cyclegan(shapes,
                        "mnist-%s" % postfix,
                        "svhn-%s" % postfix,
                        kernel_size=kernel_size,
                        patchgan=patchgan)
# patch size is divided by 2^n since we downscaled the input
# in the discriminator by 2^n (ie. we use strides=2 n times)
patch = int(source_data.shape[1] / 2**4) if patchgan else 1
params = (batch_size, train_steps, patch, model_name)
test_params = (titles, dirs)
# train the cyclegan
train_cyclegan(models,
                data,
                params,
                test_params,
                other_utils.test_generator)
```

The results for transferring the MNIST from the test dataset to SVHN are shown in *Figure 7.1.16*. The generated images have the style of SVHN, but the digits are not completely transferred. For example, on the fourth row, digits 3, 1, and 3 are stylized by CycleGAN.

However, on the third row, digits 9, 6, and 6 are stylized as 0, 6, 01, 0, 65, and 68 for the CycleGAN without and with PatchGAN, respectively:

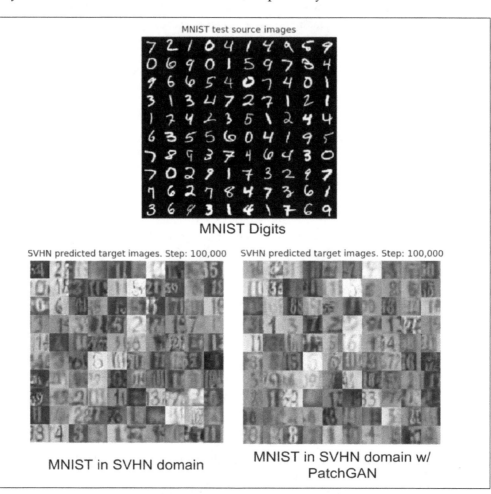

MNIST test source images

MNIST Digits

SVHN predicted target images. Step: 100,000   SVHN predicted target images. Step: 100,000

MNIST in SVHN domain

MNIST in SVHN domain w/ PatchGAN

Figure 7.1.16: Style transfer of test data from the MNIST domain to SVHN. The original color photos can be found on the book's GitHub repository at https://github.com/PacktPublishing/Advanced-Deep-Learning-with-Keras/ blob/master/chapter7-cross-domain-gan/README.md

The results of the backward cycle are shown in *Figure 7.1.17*. In this case, the target images are from the SVHN test dataset. The generated images have the style of MNIST, but the digits are not correctly translated. For example, on the first row, the digits 5, 2, and 210 are stylized as 7, 7, 8, 3, 3, and 1 for the CycleGAN without and with PatchGAN, respectively:

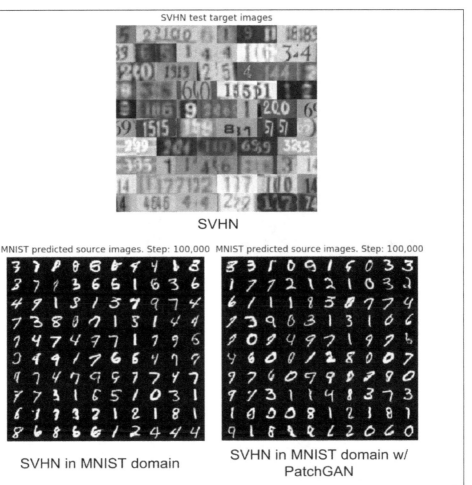

Figure 7.1.17: Style transfer of test data from the SVHN domain to MNIST. The original color photo can be found on the book's GitHub repository at https://github.com/PacktPublishing/Advanced-Deep-Learning-with-Keras/blob/master/chapter7-cross-domain-gan/README.md

In the case of PatchGAN, the output 1 is understandable given that the predicted MNIST digit is constrained to one digit. There are somehow correct predictions, such as in the second row, the last three columns of the SVHN digits, 6, 3, and 4 are converted to 6, 3, and 6 by CycleGAN without PatchGAN. However, the outputs on both flavors of CycleGAN are consistently single digit and recognizable.

The problem exhibited in the conversion from MNIST to SVHN, where a digit in the source domain is translated to another digit in the target domain, is called *label flipping* [8]. Although the predictions of CycleGAN are cycle-consistent, they are not necessarily semantic-consistent. The meaning of digits is lost during translation.

To address this problem, *Hoffman* [8] introduced an improved CycleGAN called **Cycle-Consistent Adversarial Domain Adaptation (CyCADA)**. The difference is that the additional semantic loss term ensures that the prediction is not only cycle-consistent, but also sematic-consistent.

Figure 7.1.18 shows CycleGAN reconstructing MNIST digits in the forward cycle. The reconstructed MNIST digits are almost identical to the source MNIST digits:

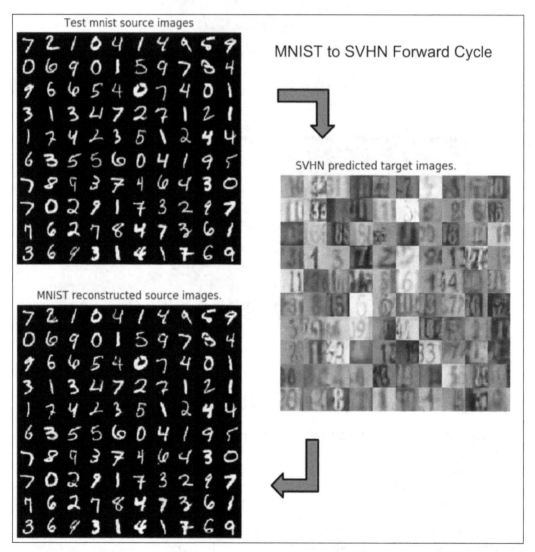

Figure 7.1.18: Forward cycle of CycleGAN with PatchGAN on MNIST (source) to SVHN (target). The reconstructed source is similar to the original source. The original color photo can be found on the book's GitHub repository at https://github.com/PacktPublishing/Advanced-Deep-Learning-with-Keras/blob/master/chapter7-cross-domain-gan/README.md

Figure 7.1.19 shows the CycleGAN reconstructing SVHN digits in the backward cycle:

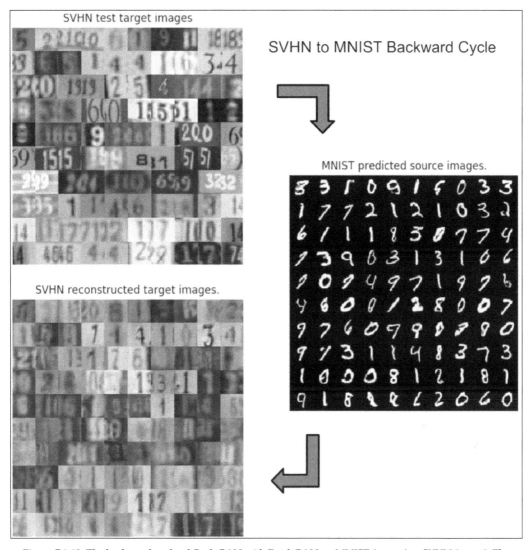

Figure 7.1.19: The backward cycle of CycleGAN with PatchGAN on MNIST (source) to SVHN (target). The reconstructed target is not entirely similar to the original target. The original color photos can be found on the book's GitHub repository at https://github.com/PacktPublishing/Advanced-Deep-Learning-with-Keras/blob/master/chapter7-cross-domain-gan/README.md

In *Figure 7.1.3*, CycleGAN is described to be cycle consistent. In other words, given source x, CycleGAN reconstructs the source in the forward cycle as x'. In addition, given target y, CycleGAN reconstructs the target in the backward cycle as y'.

Many target images are reconstructed. Some digits are clearly the same, such as the second row, in the last two columns (3 and 4), while some are the same but blurred, such as the first row, in the first two columns (5 and 2). Some digits are transformed to another digit, although the style remains like the second row, in the first two columns (from 33 and 6 to 1 and an unrecognizable digit).

To train the CycleGAN for MNIST to SVHN, the command is:

```
python3 cyclegan-7.1.1.py -m
```

The reader is encouraged to run the image translation by using the pretrained models of CycleGAN with PatchGAN:

```
python3 cyclegan-7.1.1.py --mnist_svhn_g_source=cyclegan_mnist_svhn-g_
source.h5 --mnist_svhn_g_target=cyclegan_mnist_svhn-g_target.h5
```

So far, we have only seen two practical applications of CycleGAN. Both are demonstrated on small datasets to emphasize the concept of reproducibility. As mentioned earlier in this chapter, there are many other practical applications of CycleGAN. The CycleGAN that we introduced here can serve as the foundation for translation of images with much bigger resolutions.

2. Conclusion

In this chapter, we've discussed CycleGAN as an algorithm that can be used for image translation. In CycleGAN, the source and target data are not necessarily aligned. We demonstrated two examples, *grayscale ↔ color*, and *MNIST ↔ SVHN*, although there are many other possible image translations that CycleGAN can perform.

In the next chapter, we'll embark on another type of generative model, **Variational AutoEncoders (VAEs)**. VAEs have a similar learning objective – how to generate new images (data). They focus on learning the latent vector modeled as a Gaussian distribution. We'll demonstrate other similarities in the problem being addressed by GANs in the form of conditional VAEs and the disentangling of latent representations in VAEs.

3. References

1. Yuval Netzer et al.: *Reading Digits in Natural Images with Unsupervised Feature Learning*. NIPS workshop on deep learning and unsupervised feature learning. Vol. 2011. No. 2. 2011 (https://www-cs.stanford.edu/~twangcat/papers/nips2011_housenumbers.pdf).

2. Zhu-Jun-Yan et al.: *Unpaired Image-to-Image Translation using Cycle-Consistent Adversarial Networks*. 2017 IEEE International Conference on Computer Vision (ICCV). IEEE, 2017 (`http://openaccess.thecvf.com/content_ICCV_2017/papers/Zhu_Unpaired_Image-To-Image_Translation_ICCV_2017_paper.pdf`).

3. Phillip Isola et al.: *Image-to-Image Translation with Conditional Adversarial Networks*. 2017 IEEE Conference on Computer Vision and Pattern Recognition (CVPR). IEEE, 2017 (`http://openaccess.thecvf.com/content_cvpr_2017/papers/Isola_Image-To-Image_Translation_With_CVPR_2017_paper.pdf`).

4. Mehdi Mirza and Simon Osindero. *Conditional Generative Adversarial Nets*. arXiv preprint arXiv:1411.1784, 2014 (`https://arxiv.org/pdf/1411.1784.pdf`).

5. Xudong Mao et al.: *Least Squares Generative Adversarial Networks*. 2017 IEEE International Conference on Computer Vision (ICCV). IEEE, 2017 (`http://openaccess.thecvf.com/content_ICCV_2017/papers/Mao_Least_Squares_Generative_ICCV_2017_paper.pdf`).

6. Chuan Li and Michael Wand. *Precomputed Real-Time Texture Synthesis with Markovian Generative Adversarial Networks*. European Conference on Computer Vision. Springer, Cham, 2016 (`https://arxiv.org/pdf/1604.04382.pdf`).

7. Olaf Ronneberger, Philipp Fischer, and Thomas Brox. *U-Net: Convolutional Networks for Biomedical Image Segmentation*. International Conference on Medical image computing and computer-assisted intervention. Springer, Cham, 2015 (`https://arxiv.org/pdf/1505.04597.pdf`).

8. Judy Hoffman et al.: *CyCADA: Cycle-Consistent Adversarial Domain Adaptation*. arXiv preprint arXiv:1711.03213, 2017 (`https://arxiv.org/pdf/1711.03213.pdf`).

8
Variational Autoencoders (VAEs)

Similar to **Generative Adversarial Networks** (**GANs**) that we've discussed in the previous chapters, **Variational Autoencoders** (**VAEs**) [1] belong to the family of generative models. The generator of VAEs is able to produce meaningful outputs while navigating its continuous latent space. The possible attributes of the decoder outputs are explored through the latent vector.

In GANs, the focus is on how to arrive at a model that approximates the input distribution. VAEs attempt to model the input distribution from a decodable continuous latent space. This is one of the possible underlying reasons why GANs are able to generate more realistic signals when compared to VAEs. For example, in image generation, GANs are able to produce more realistic-looking images, while VAEs, in comparison, generate images that are less sharp.

Within VAEs, the focus is on the variational inference of latent codes. Therefore, VAEs provide a suitable framework for both learning and efficient Bayesian inference with latent variables. For example, VAEs with disentangled representations enable latent code reuse for transfer learning.

In terms of structure, VAE bears a resemblance to an autoencoder. It is also made up of an encoder (also known as a recognition or inference model) and a decoder (also known as a generative model). Both VAEs and autoencoders attempt to reconstruct the input data while learning the latent vector.

However, unlike autoencoders, the latent space of VAE is continuous, and the decoder itself is used as a generative model.

In the same line of discussions on GANs that we discussed in the previous chapters, the VAE's decoder can also be conditioned. For example, in the MNIST dataset, we're able to specify the digit to produce given a one-hot vector. This class of conditional VAE is called CVAE [2]. VAE latent vectors can also be disentangled by including a regularizing hyperparameter on the loss function. This is called β-VAE [5]. For example, within MNIST, we're able to isolate the latent vector that determines the thickness or tilt angle of each digit. The goal of this chapter is to present:

- The principles of VAE
- An understanding of the reparameterization trick that facilitates the use of stochastic gradient descent on VAE optimization
- The principles of conditional VAE (CVAE) and β-VAE
- An understanding of how to implement VAE using `tf.keras`

We'll start off by talking about the underlying principles of VAE.

1. Principles of VAE

In a generative model, we're often interested in approximating the true distribution of our inputs using neural networks:

$$x \sim P_\theta(x) \quad \text{(Equation 8.1.1)}$$

In the preceding equation, θ represents the parameters determined during training. For example, in the context of the celebrity faces dataset, this is equivalent to finding a distribution that can draw faces. Similarly, in the MNIST dataset, this distribution can generate recognizable handwritten digits.

In machine learning, to perform a certain level of inference, we're interested in finding $P_\theta(x, z)$, a joint distribution between inputs, x, and latent variables, z. The latent variables are not part of the dataset but instead encode certain properties observable from inputs. In the context of celebrity faces, these might be facial expressions, hairstyles, hair color, gender, and so on. In the MNIST dataset, the latent variables may represent the digit and writing styles.

$P_\theta(x, z)$ is practically a distribution of input data points and their attributes. $P_\theta(x)$ can be computed from the marginal distribution:

$$P_\theta(x) = \int P_\theta(x, z)dz \quad \text{(Equation 8.1.2)}$$

In other words, considering all of the possible attributes, we end up with the distribution that describes the inputs. In celebrity faces, if we consider all the facial expressions, hairstyles, hair colors, and gender, the distribution describing the celebrity faces is recovered. In the MNIST dataset, if we consider all of the possible digits, writing styles, and so on, we end up with the distribution of handwritten digits.

The problem is that *Equation 8.1.2* is intractable. The equation does not have an analytic form or an efficient estimator. It cannot be differentiated with respect to its parameters. Therefore, optimization by a neural network is not feasible.

Using Bayes' theorem, we can find an alternative expression for *Equation 8.1.2*:

$$P_\theta(x) = \int P_\theta(x|z)P(z)dz \quad \text{(Equation 8.1.3)}$$

$P(z)$ is a prior distribution over z. It is not conditioned on any observations. If z is discrete and $P_\theta(x|z)$ is a Gaussian distribution, then $P_\theta(x)$ is a mixture of Gaussians. If z is continuous, $P_\theta(x)$ is an infinite mixture of Gaussians.

In practice, if we try to build a neural network to approximate $P_\theta(x|z)$ without a suitable loss function, it will just ignore z and arrive at a trivial solution, $P_\theta(x|z) = P_\theta(x)$. Therefore, *Equation 8.1.3* does not provide us with a good estimate of $P_\theta(x)$. Alternatively, *Equation 8.1.2* can also be expressed as:

$$P_\theta(x) = \int P_\theta(z|x)P(x)dz \quad \text{(Equation 8.1.4)}$$

However, $P_\theta(z|x)$ is also intractable. The goal of a VAE is to find a tractable distribution that closely estimates $P_\theta(z|x)$, an estimate of the conditional distribution of the latent attributes, z, given the input, x.

Variational inference

In order to make $P_\theta(z|x)$ tractable, VAE introduces the variational inference model (an encoder):

$$Q_\phi(z|x) \approx P_\theta(z|x) \quad \text{(Equation 8.1.5)}$$

$Q_\phi(z|x)$ provides a good estimate of $P_\theta(z|x)$. It is both parametric and tractable. $Q_\phi(z|x)$ can be approximated by deep neural networks by optimizing the parameter ϕ. Typically, $Q_\phi(z|x)$ is chosen to be a multivariate gaussian:

$$Q_\phi(z|x) = \mathcal{N}\big(z; \mu(x), diag(\sigma(x)^2)\big) \quad \text{(Equation 8.1.6)}$$

Both mean, $\mu(x)$, and standard, $\sigma(x)$, deviation are computed by the encoder neural network using the input data points. The diagonal matrix implies that the elements of z are independent.

In the next section, we will solve for the core equation of VAE. The core equation will lead us to an optimization algorithm that will help us determine the parameters of the inference model.

Core equation

The inference model, $Q_\phi(z|x)$, generates a latent vector, z, from input x. $Q_\phi(z|x)$ is like the encoder in an autoencoder model. On the other hand, $P_\theta(x|z)$ reconstructs the input from the latent code, z. $P_\theta(x|z)$ acts like the decoder in an autoencoder model. To estimate $P_\theta(x)$, we must identify its relationship with $Q_\phi(z|x)$ and $P_\theta(x|z)$.

If $Q_\phi(z|x)$ is an estimate of $P_\theta(z|x)$, the **Kullback–Leibler (KL)** divergence determines the distance between these two conditional densities:

$$D_{KL}\left(Q_\phi(z|x)\|P_\theta(z|x)\right) = \mathbb{E}_{z\sim Q}\left[\log Q_\phi(z|x) - \log P_\theta(z|x)\right] \quad \text{(Equation 8.1.7)}$$

Using Bayes' theorem:

$$P_\theta(z|x) = \frac{P_\theta(x|z)P_\theta(z)}{P_\theta(x)} \quad \text{(Equation 8.1.8)}$$

in *Equation 8.1.7*:

$$D_{KL}\left(Q_\phi(z|x)\|P_\theta(z|x)\right) = \mathbb{E}_{z\sim Q}\left[\log Q_\phi(z|x) - \log P_\theta(x|z) - \log P_\theta(z)\right] + \log P_\theta(x)$$
$$\text{(Equation 8.1.9)}$$

$\log P_\theta(x)$ can be taken out of the expectation since it is not dependent on $z\sim Q$. Rearranging *Equation 8.1.9* and recognizing that:

$\mathbb{E}_{z\sim Q}\left[\log Q_\phi(z|x) - \log P_\theta(z)\right] = D_{KL}\left(Q_\phi(z|x)\|P_\theta(z)\right)$, it follows that:

$$\log P_\theta(x) - D_{KL}\left(Q_\phi(z|x)\|P_\theta(z|x)\right) = \mathbb{E}_{z\sim Q}\left[\log P_\theta(x|z)\right] - D_{KL}\left(Q_\phi(z|x)\|P_\theta(z)\right)$$
$$\text{(Equation 8.1.10)}$$

Equation 8.1.10 is the core of VAEs. The left-hand side is the term $P_\theta(x)$, which we are maximizing less the error due to the distance of $Q_\phi(z|x)$ from the true $P_\theta(z|x)$. We can recall that the logarithm does not change the location of maxima (or minima). Given an inference model that provides a good estimate of $P_\theta(z|x)$, $D_{KL}\left(Q_\phi(z|x)\|P_\theta(z|x)\right)$ is approximately zero.

The first term, $P_\theta(x|z)$, on the right-hand side resembles a decoder that takes samples from the inference model to reconstruct the input.

The second term is another distance. This time it's between $Q_\phi(z|x)$ and the prior $P_\theta(z)$. The left side of *Equation 8.1.10* is also known as the **variational lower bound** or **evidence lower bound** (**ELBO**). Since the KL is always positive, ELBO is the lower bound of $\log P_\theta(x)$. Maximizing ELBO by optimizing the parameters ϕ and θ of the neural network means that:

- $D_{KL}\left(Q_\phi(z|x)\|P_\theta(z|x)\right) \to 0$ or the inference model is getting better in encoding the attributes x in z.

- $\log P_\theta(x|z)$ on the right-hand side of *Equation 8.1.10* is maximized or the decoder model is getting better in reconstructing x from the latent vector, z.

- In the next section, we will exploit the structure of *Equation 8.1.10* to determine the loss functions of the inference model (encoder) and decoder.

Optimization

The right-hand side of *Equation 8.1.10* has two important bits of information regarding the `loss` function of VAEs. The decoder term $\mathbb{E}_{z\sim Q}[\log P_\theta(x|z)]$ means that the generator takes z samples from the output of the inference model to reconstruct the inputs. Maximizing this term implies that we minimize the **Reconstruction Loss**, $\mathcal{L}_R$. If the image (data) distribution is assumed to be Gaussian, then MSE can be used.

If every pixel (data) is considered a Bernoulli distribution, then the loss function is a binary cross-entropy.

The second term, $-D_{KL}\left(Q_\phi(z|x)\|P_\theta(z)\right)$, turns out to be straightforward to evaluate. From *Equation 8.1.6*, Q_ϕ is a Gaussian distribution. Typically, $P_\theta(z) = P(z) = \mathcal{N}(0,I)$ is also a Gaussian with zero mean and standard deviation equal to 1.0. In *Equation 8.1.11*, we see that the KL term simplifies to:

$$-D_{KL}\left(Q_\phi(z|x)\|P_\theta(z)\right) = \frac{1}{2}\sum_{j=1}^{J}\left(1 + \log(\sigma_j)^2 - (\mu_j)^2 - (\sigma_j)^2\right) \quad \text{(Equation 8.1.11)}$$

where J is the dimensionality of z. Both μ_j and σ_j are functions of x computed through the inference model. To maximize: $-D_{KL}$, $\sigma_j \to 1$ and $\mu_j \to 0$. The choice of $P(z) = \mathcal{N}(0,I)$ stems from the property of the isotropic unit Gaussian, which can be morphed to an arbitrary distribution given a suitable function [6].

From *Equation 8.1.11*, the KL loss, $\mathcal{L}_{KL}$, is simply D_{KL}.

In summary, the VAE `loss` function is defined in *Equation 8.1.12* as:

$$\mathcal{L}_{VAE} = \mathcal{L}_R + \mathcal{L}_{KL} \quad \text{(Equation 8.1.12)}$$

Given the encoder and decoder models, there is one more problem to solve before we can build and train a VAE, the stochastic sampling block, which generates the latent attributes. In the next section, we will discuss this issue and how to resolve it using the reparameterization trick.

Reparameterization trick

The left-hand side of *Figure 8.1.1* below shows the VAE network. The encoder takes the input, x, and estimates the mean, μ, and the standard deviation, σ, of the multivariate Gaussian distribution of the latent vector, z. The decoder takes samples from the latent vector, z, to reconstruct the input as $\tilde{x}$. This seems straightforward until the gradient updates happen during backpropagation:

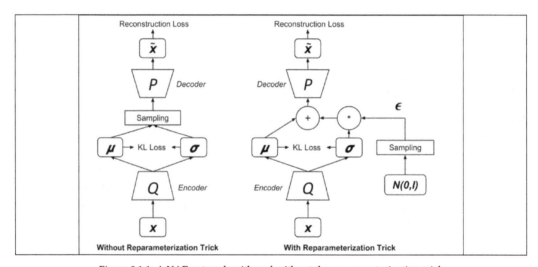

Figure 8.1.1: A VAE network with and without the reparameterization trick

Backpropagation gradients will not pass through the stochastic **Sampling** block. While it's fine to have stochastic inputs for neural networks, it's not possible for the gradients to go through a stochastic layer.

The solution to this problem is to push out the **Sampling** process as the input, as shown on the right side of *Figure 8.1.1*. Then, compute the sample as:

$$Sample = \mu + \epsilon\sigma \quad \text{(Equation 8.1.13)}$$

If ϵ and σ are expressed in vector format, then $\epsilon\sigma$ is element-wise multiplication. Using *Equation 8.1.13*, it appears as if sampling is directly coming from the latent space as originally intended. This technique is better known as the *Reparameterization trick*.

With *Sampling* now happening at the input, the VAE network can be trained using the familiar optimization algorithms, such as SGD, Adam, or RMSProp.

Before discussing how to implement VAE in `tf.keras`, let's first show how a trained decoder is tested.

Decoder testing

After training the VAE network, the inference model, including the addition and multiplication operator, can be discarded. To generate new meaningful outputs, samples are taken from the Gaussian distribution used in generating ϵ. *Figure 8.1.2* shows us the test setup of the decoder:

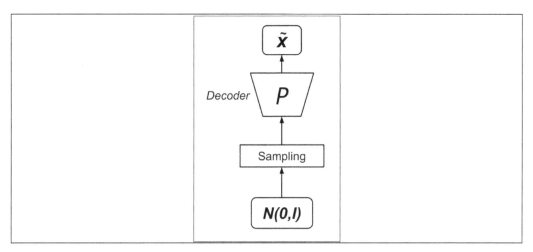

Figure 8.1.2: Decoder testing setup

With the reparameterization trick fixing the last issue on VAE, we are now ready to implement and train a variational autoencoder in `tf.keras`.

VAE in Keras

The structure of VAE bears a resemblance to a typical autoencoder. The difference is mainly on the sampling of the Gaussian random variables in the reparameterization trick. *Listing 8.1.1* shows the encoder, decoder, and VAE, which are implemented using MLP.

This code has also been contributed to the official Keras GitHub repository:

`https://github.com/keras-team/keras/blob/master/examples/variational_autoencoder.py`

For ease of visualization of the latent codes, the dimension of **z** is set to 2. The encoder is just a two-layer MLP, with the second layer generating the mean and log variance. The use of log variance is for simplicity in the computation of KL loss and the reparameterization trick. The third output of the encoder is the sampling of **z** using the reparameterization trick. We should note that in the sampling function, $e^{0.5\log \sigma^2} = \sqrt{\sigma^2} = \sigma$, since $\sigma > 0$ given that it is the standard deviation of the Gaussian distribution.

The decoder is also a two-layer MLP that takes samples of **z** to approximate the inputs. Both the encoder and the decoder use an intermediate dimension with a size of 512.

The VAE network is simply both the encoder and the decoder joined together. The `loss` function is the sum of both the *reconstruction loss* and *KL loss*. The VAE network has good results on the default Adam optimizer. The total number of parameters in the VAE network is 807,700.

The Keras code for the VAE MLP has pretrained weights. To test, we need to run:

`python3 vae-mlp-mnist-8.1.1.py --weights=vae_mlp_mnist.tf`

The complete code can be found at the following link: `https://github.com/PacktPublishing/Advanced-Deep-Learning-with-Keras`

Listing 8.1.1: `vae-mlp-mnist-8.1.1.py`

```
# reparameterization trick
# instead of sampling from Q(z|X), sample eps = N(0,I)
# z = z_mean + sqrt(var)*eps
def sampling(args):
    """Reparameterization trick by sampling
        fr an isotropic unit Gaussian.

    # Arguments:
        args (tensor): mean and log of variance of Q(z|X)

    # Returns:
        z (tensor): sampled latent vector
```

```
"""
    z_mean, z_log_var = args
    # K is the keras backend
    batch = K.shape(z_mean)[0]
    dim = K.int_shape(z_mean)[1]
    # by default, random_normal has mean=0 and std=1.0
    epsilon = K.random_normal(shape=(batch, dim))
    return z_mean + K.exp(0.5 * z_log_var) * epsilon


# MNIST dataset
(x_train, y_train), (x_test, y_test) = mnist.load_data()

image_size = x_train.shape[1]
original_dim = image_size * image_size
x_train = np.reshape(x_train, [-1, original_dim])
x_test = np.reshape(x_test, [-1, original_dim])
x_train = x_train.astype('float32') / 255
x_test = x_test.astype('float32') / 255

# network parameters
input_shape = (original_dim, )
intermediate_dim = 512
batch_size = 128
latent_dim = 2
epochs = 50

# VAE model = encoder + decoder
# build encoder model
inputs = Input(shape=input_shape, name='encoder_input')
x = Dense(intermediate_dim, activation='relu')(inputs)
z_mean = Dense(latent_dim, name='z_mean')(x)
z_log_var = Dense(latent_dim, name='z_log_var')(x)

# use reparameterization trick to push the sampling out as input
# note that "output_shape" isn't necessary
# with the TensorFlow backend
z = Lambda(sampling,
           output_shape=(latent_dim,),
           name='z')([z_mean, z_log_var])

# instantiate encoder model
encoder = Model(inputs, [z_mean, z_log_var, z], name='encoder')
```

```
# build decoder model
latent_inputs = Input(shape=(latent_dim,), name='z_sampling')
x = Dense(intermediate_dim, activation='relu')(latent_inputs)
outputs = Dense(original_dim, activation='sigmoid')(x)

# instantiate decoder model
decoder = Model(latent_inputs, outputs, name='decoder')

# instantiate VAE model
outputs = decoder(encoder(inputs)[2])
vae = Model(inputs, outputs, name='vae_mlp')

if __name__ == '__main__':
    parser = argparse.ArgumentParser()
    help_ = "Load tf model trained weights"
    parser.add_argument("-w", "--weights", help=help_)
    help_ = "Use binary cross entropy instead of mse (default)"
    parser.add_argument("--bce", help=help_, action='store_true')
    args = parser.parse_args()
    models = (encoder, decoder)
    data = (x_test, y_test)

    # VAE loss = mse_loss or xent_loss + kl_loss
    if args.bce:
        reconstruction_loss = binary_crossentropy(inputs,
                                                   outputs)
    else:
        reconstruction_loss = mse(inputs, outputs)

    reconstruction_loss *= original_dim
    kl_loss = 1 + z_log_var - K.square(z_mean) - K.exp(z_log_var)
    kl_loss = K.sum(kl_loss, axis=-1)
    kl_loss *= -0.5
    vae_loss = K.mean(reconstruction_loss + kl_loss)
    vae.add_loss(vae_loss)
    vae.compile(optimizer='adam')
```

Figures 8.1.3 shows the encoder model, which is an MLP with two outputs, the mean and variance of the latent vectors. The lambda function implements the reparameterization trick to push the sampling of the stochastic latent codes outside the VAE network:

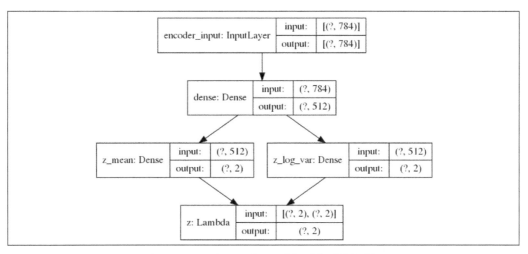

Figure 8.1.3: The encoder models of the VAE MLP

Figures 8.1.4 shows the decoder model. The 2-dim input comes from the lambda function. The output is the reconstructed MNIST digit:

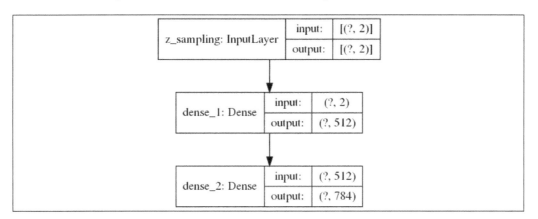

Figure 8.1.4: The decoder model of the VAE MLP

Figures 8.1.5 shows the complete VAE model. It is made by joining the encoder and decoder models together:

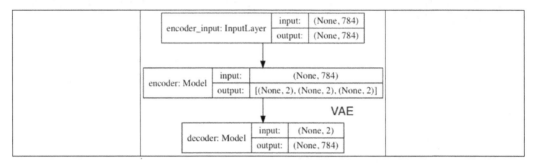

Figure 8.1.5: The VAE model using the MLP

Figure 8.1.6 shows the continuous space of the latent vector after 50 epochs using `plot_results()`. For simplicity, the function is not shown here but can be found in the rest of the code of `vae-mlp-mnist-8.1.1.py`. The function plots two images, the test dataset labels (*Figure 8.1.6*) and the sample generated digits (*Figure 8.1.7*), both as a function of **z**. Both plots demonstrate how the latent vector determines the attributes of the generated digits:

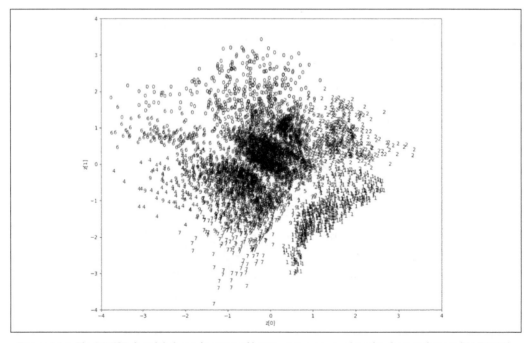

Figure 8.1.6: The MNIST digit label as a function of latent vector mean values for the test dataset (VAE MLP). The original image can be found on the book's GitHub repository at https://github.com/PacktPublishing/ Advanced-Deep-Learning-with-Keras/tree/master/chapter8-vae

Navigating through the continuous space will always result in an output that bears a resemblance to the MNIST digits. For example, the region of digit 9 is close to the region of digit 7. Moving from 9 near the center to the lower left morphs the digit to 7. Moving from the center up changes the generated digits from 3 to 5, and finally to 0. The morphing of the digits is more evident in *Figure 8.1.7* which is another way of interpreting *Figure 8.1.6*.

In *Figure 8.1.7*, the generator output is displayed. The distribution of digits in the latent space is shown. It can be observed that all the digits are represented. Since the distribution is dense near the center, the change is rapid in the middle and slow in regions that have high mean values. We need to remember that *Figure 8.1.7* is a reflection of *Figure 8.1.6*. For example, digit 0 is in the upper-left quadrant on both figures, while digit 1 is in the lower-right quadrant.

There are some unrecognizable digits in *Figure 8.1.7*, especially in the top-right quadrant. From *Figure 8.1.6*, it can be observed that this region is mostly empty and far away from the center:

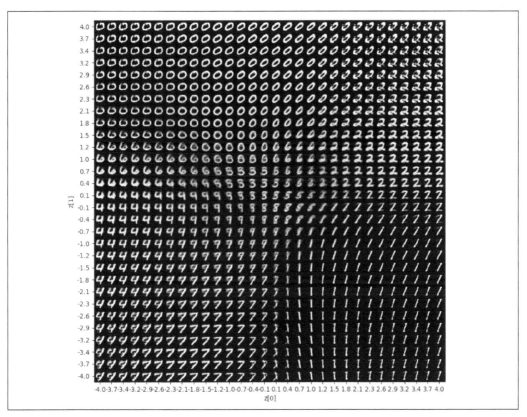

Figure 8.1.7: The digits generated as a function of latent vector mean values (VAE MLP). For ease of interpretation, the range of values for the mean is similar to Figure 8.1.6

In this section, we demonstrated how to implement VAE in the MLP. We also interpreted the results of navigating the latent space. In the next section, we will implement the same VAE using CNN.

Using CNN for AE

In the original paper, *Auto-encoding Variational Bayes* [1], the VAE network was implemented using MLP, which is similar to what we covered in the previous section. In this section, we'll demonstrate that using CNN will result in a significant improvement in the quality of the digits produced and a remarkable reduction in the number of parameters down to 134,165.

Listing 8.1.3 shows the encoder, decoder, and VAE network. This code was also contributed to the official Keras GitHub repository:

```
https://github.com/keras-team/keras/blob/master/examples/variational_
autoencoder_deconv.py
```

For conciseness, some lines of code that are similar to the MLP VAE are no longer shown. The encoder is made of two layers of CNN and two layers of MLP in order to generate the latent code. The encoder output structure is similar to the MLP implementation seen in the previous section. The decoder is made up of one layer of `Dense` and three layers of transposed CNN.

The Keras code for the VAE CNN has pretrained weights. To test, we need to run:

```
python3 vae-cnn-mnist-8.1.2.py --weights=vae_cnn_mnist.tf
```

Listing 8.1.3: `vae-cnn-mnist-8.1.2.py`

VAE in `tf.keras` using CNN layers:

```
# network parameters
input_shape = (image_size, image_size, 1)
batch_size = 128
kernel_size = 3
filters = 16
latent_dim = 2
epochs = 30

# VAE model = encoder + decoder
# build encoder model
inputs = Input(shape=input_shape, name='encoder_input')
x = inputs
for i in range(2):
    filters *= 2
```

```
    x = Conv2D(filters=filters,
               kernel_size=kernel_size,
               activation='relu',
               strides=2,
               padding='same')(x)

# shape info needed to build decoder model
shape = K.int_shape(x)

# generate latent vector Q(z|X)
x = Flatten()(x)
x = Dense(16, activation='relu')(x)
z_mean = Dense(latent_dim, name='z_mean')(x)
z_log_var = Dense(latent_dim, name='z_log_var')(x)

# use reparameterization trick to push the sampling out as input
# note that "output_shape" isn't necessary
# with the TensorFlow backend
z = Lambda(sampling,
           output_shape=(latent_dim,),
           name='z')([z_mean, z_log_var])


# instantiate encoder model
encoder = Model(inputs, [z_mean, z_log_var, z], name='encoder')

# build decoder model
latent_inputs = Input(shape=(latent_dim,), name='z_sampling')
x = Dense(shape[1] * shape[2] * shape[3],
          activation='relu')(latent_inputs)
x = Reshape((shape[1], shape[2], shape[3]))(x)

for i in range(2):
    x = Conv2DTranspose(filters=filters,
                        kernel_size=kernel_size,
                        activation='relu',
                        strides=2,
                        padding='same')(x)
    filters //= 2

outputs = Conv2DTranspose(filters=1,
                          kernel_size=kernel_size,
                          activation='sigmoid',
                          padding='same',
```

```
                    name='decoder_output')(x)

# instantiate decoder model
decoder = Model(latent_inputs, outputs, name='decoder')

# instantiate VAE model
outputs = decoder(encoder(inputs)[2])
vae = Model(inputs, outputs, name='vae')
```

Figure 8.1.8 shows the CNN encoder model's two outputs, the mean and variance of the latent vectors. The lambda function implements the reparameterization trick to push the sampling of the stochastic latent codes outside the VAE network:

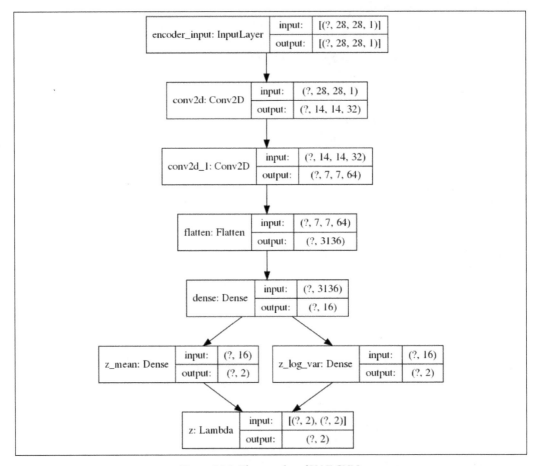

Figure 8.1.8: The encoder of VAE CNN

Figure 8.1.9 shows the CNN decoder model. The 2-dim input comes from the lambda function. The output is the reconstructed MNIST digit:

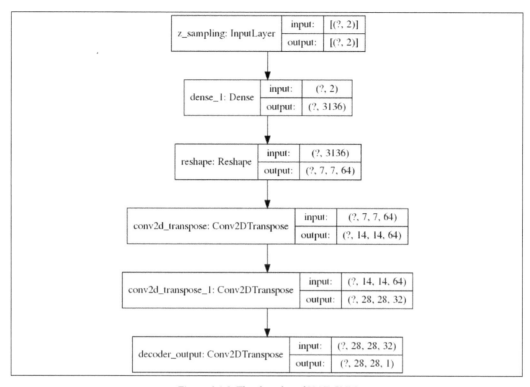

Figure 8.1.9: The decoder of VAE CNN

Figure 8.1.10 shows the complete CNN VAE model. It is made by joining the encoder and decoder models together:

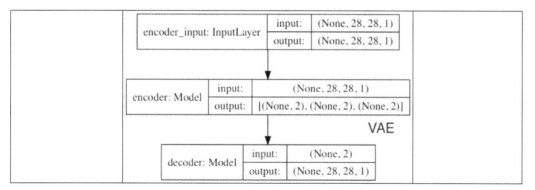

Figure 8.1.10: The VAE model using CNNs

The VAE was trained for 30 epochs. *Figure 8.1.11* shows the distribution of digits as we navigate the continuous latent space of a VAE. For example, from the center to the right, the digit changes from 2 to 0:

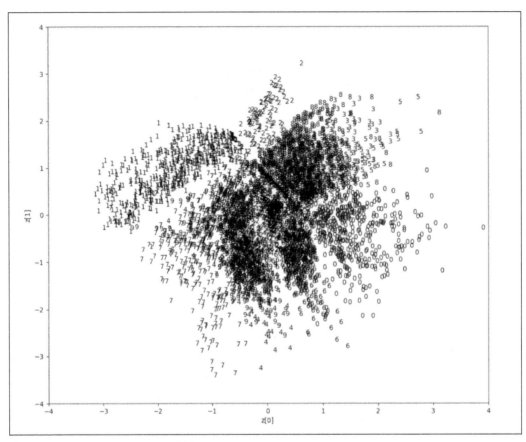

Figure 8.1.11: The MNIST digit label as a function of latent vector mean values for the test dataset (VAE CNN). The original image can be found on the book's GitHub repository at https://github.com/PacktPublishing/ Advanced-Deep-Learning-with-Keras/tree/master/chapter8-vae.

Figure 8.1.12 shows us the output of the generative model. Qualitatively, there are fewer digits that are ambiguous as compared to *Figure 8.1.7* with the MLP implementation:

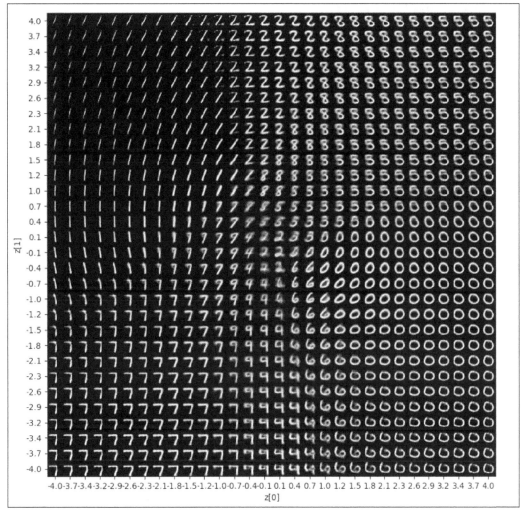

Figure 8.1.12: The digits generated as a function of latent vector mean values (VAE CNN). For ease of interpretation, the range of values for the mean is similar to Figure 8.1.11

The previous two sections discussed the implementation of VAE using MLP or CNN. We analyzed the results of both implementations and showed that the CNN results in a lower parameter count and better perceptive quality. In the next section, we will demonstrate how to implement conditioning in VAE so that we can control which digit to generate.

2. Conditional VAE (CVAE)

Conditional VAE [2] is similar to the idea of CGAN. In the context of the MNIST dataset, if the latent space is randomly sampled, VAE has no control over which digit will be generated. CVAE is able to address this problem by including a condition (a one-hot label) of the digit to produce. The condition is imposed on both the encoder and decoder inputs.

Formally, the core equation of VAE in *Equation 8.1.10* is modified to include the condition, c:

$$\log P_\theta(x|c) - D_{KL}\left(Q_\phi(z|x,c)\|P_\theta(z|x,c)\right)$$
$$= \mathbb{E}_{z\sim Q}[\log P_\theta(x|z,c)] - D_{KL}\left(Q_\phi(z|x,c)\|P_\theta(z|c)\right) \qquad \text{(Equation 8.2.1)}$$

Similar to VAEs, *Equation 8.2.1* means that if we want to maximize the output conditioned c, $P_\theta(x|c)$, then the two loss terms must be minimized:

- Reconstruction loss of the decoder given both the latent vector and the condition.

- KL loss between the encoder given both the latent vector and the condition and the prior distribution given the condition. Similar to a VAE, we typically choose $P_\theta(z|c) = P(z|c) = \mathcal{N}(0,I)$.

Implementing CVAE requires a few modifications in the code of the VAE. For the CVAE, the VAE CNN implementation is used since it results in a smaller network with perceptually better digits produced.

Listing 8.2.1 highlights the changes made to the original code of VAE for MNIST digits. The encoder input is now a concatenation of the original input image and its one-hot label. The decoder input is now a combination of the latent space sampling and the one-hot label of the image it should generate. The total number of parameters is 174,437. The codes related to β-VAE will be discussed in the next section of this chapter.

There are no changes in the loss function. However, the one-hot labels are supplied during training, testing, and the plotting of results.

Listing 8.2.1: `cvae-cnn-mnist-8.2.1.py`

CVAE in `tf.keras` using CNN layers. Highlighted are the changes made to support CVAE:

```
# compute the number of labels
num_labels = len(np.unique(y_train))
```

```
# network parameters
input_shape = (image_size, image_size, 1)
label_shape = (num_labels, )
batch_size = 128
kernel_size = 3
filters = 16
latent_dim = 2
epochs = 30

# VAE model = encoder + decoder
# build encoder model
inputs = Input(shape=input_shape, name='encoder_input')
y_labels = Input(shape=label_shape, name='class_labels')
x = Dense(image_size * image_size)(y_labels)
x = Reshape((image_size, image_size, 1))(x)
x = keras.layers.concatenate([inputs, x])
for i in range(2):
    filters *= 2
    x = Conv2D(filters=filters,
               kernel_size=kernel_size,
               activation='relu',
               strides=2,
               padding='same')(x)

# shape info needed to build decoder model
shape = K.int_shape(x)

# generate latent vector Q(z|X)
x = Flatten()(x)
x = Dense(16, activation='relu')(x)
z_mean = Dense(latent_dim, name='z_mean')(x)
z_log_var = Dense(latent_dim, name='z_log_var')(x)

# use reparameterization trick to push the sampling out as input
# note that "output_shape" isn't necessary
# with the TensorFlow backend
z = Lambda(sampling,
           output_shape=(latent_dim,),
           name='z')([z_mean, z_log_var])

# instantiate encoder model
encoder = Model([inputs, y_labels],
                [z_mean, z_log_var, z],
```

```
                        name='encoder')

    # build decoder model
    latent_inputs = Input(shape=(latent_dim,), name='z_sampling')
    x = concatenate([latent_inputs, y_labels])
    x = Dense(shape[1]*shape[2]*shape[3], activation='relu')(x)
    x = Reshape((shape[1], shape[2], shape[3]))(x)

    for i in range(2):
        x = Conv2DTranspose(filters=filters,
                            kernel_size=kernel_size,
                            activation='relu',
                            strides=2,
                            padding='same')(x)
        filters //= 2

    outputs = Conv2DTranspose(filters=1,
                              kernel_size=kernel_size,
                              activation='sigmoid',
                              padding='same',
                              name='decoder_output')(x)

    # instantiate decoder model
    decoder = Model([latent_inputs, y_labels],
                    outputs,
                    name='decoder')

    # instantiate vae model
    outputs = decoder([encoder([inputs, y_labels])[2], y_labels])
    cvae = Model([inputs, y_labels], outputs, name='cvae')
```

Figure 8.2.1 shows the encoder of the CVAE model. The additional input, the conditioning label in the form of a one-hot vector, class_labels, is indicated:

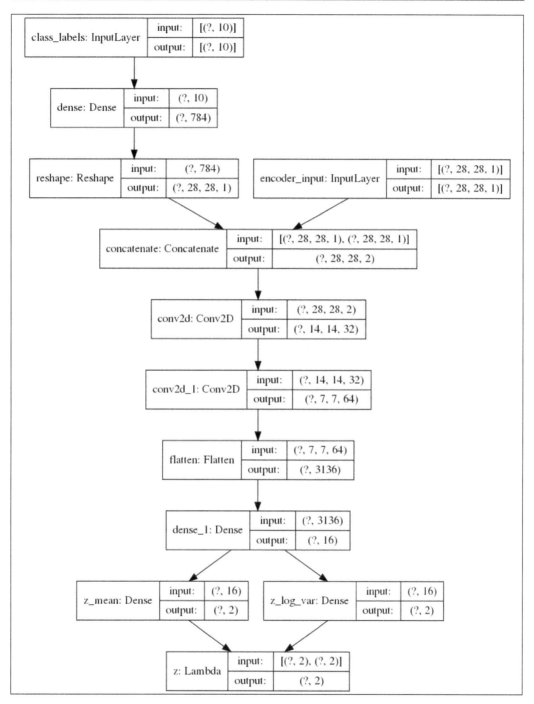

Figure 8.2.1: The encoder in CVAE CNN. The input now comprises the concatenation of the VAE input and a conditioning label

Figure 8.2.2 shows the decoder of the CVAE model. The additional input, the conditioning label in the form of a one-hot vector, `class_labels`, is indicated:

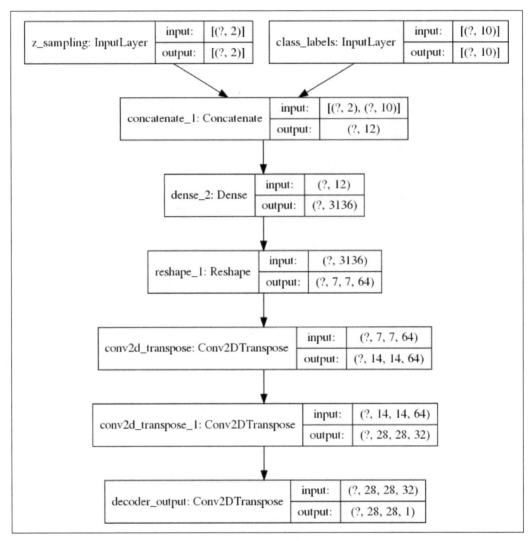

Figure 8.2.2: The decoder in CVAE CNN. The input now comprises
the concatenation of the z sampling and a conditioning label

Figure 8.2.3 shows the complete CVAE model, which is the encoder and decoder joined together. The additional input, the conditioning label in the form of a one-hot vector, `class_labels`, is indicated:

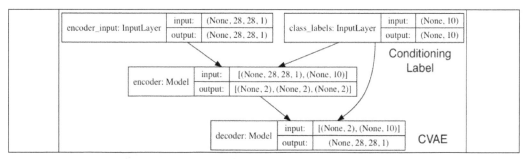

Figure 8.2.3: The CVAE model using a CNN. The input now comprises a VAE input and a conditioning label

In *Figure 8.2.4*, the distribution of the mean per label is shown after 30 epochs. Unlike in *Figure 8.1.6* and *Figure 8.1.11* in the previous sections, each label is not concentrated on a region but distributed across the plot. This is expected since every sampling in the latent space should generate a specific digit. Navigating the latent space changes the attribute of that specific digit. For example, if the digit specified is 0, then navigating the latent space will still produce a 0, but the attributes, such as tilt angle, thickness, and other writing style aspects, will be different.

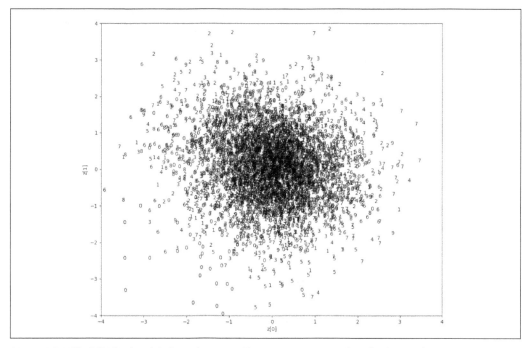

Figure 8.2.4: The MNIST digit label as a function of latent vector mean values for the test dataset (CVAE CNN). The original image can be found on the book's GitHub repository at https://github.com/PacktPublishing/ Advanced-Deep-Learning-with-Keras/tree/master/chapter8-vae

Figure 8.2.4 is more clearly shown in *Figure 8.2.5* for digits 0 to 5. Each frame has the same digit, with the attributes changing smoothly as we navigate the latent codes:

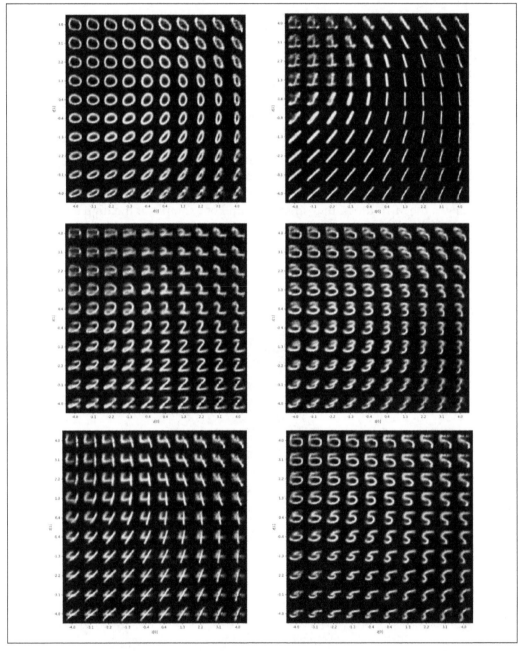

Figure 8.2.5: Digits 0 to 5 generated as a function of latent vector mean values and a one-hot label (CVAE CNN). For ease of interpretation, the range of values for the mean is similar to Figure 8.2.4

Figure 8.2.6 shows *Figure 8.2.4* for digits 6 to 9:

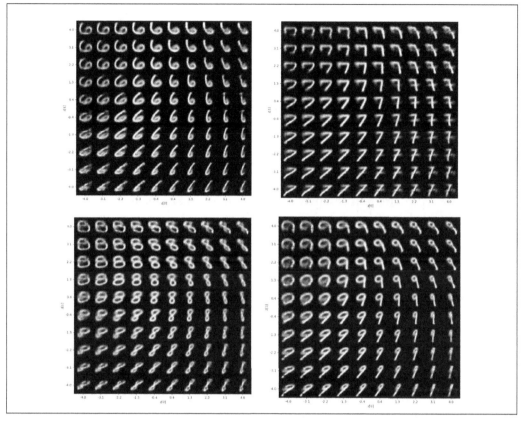

Figure 8.2.6: Digits 6 to 9 generated as a function of latent vector mean values and a one-hot label (CVAE CNN). For ease of interpretation, the range of values for the mean is similar to Figure 8.2.4

For ease of comparison, the range of values for the latent vector is the same as in *Figure 8.2.4*. Using the pretrained weights, a digit (for example, 0) can be generated by executing the command:

```
python3 cvae-cnn-mnist-8.2.1.py –bce --weights=cvae_cnn_mnist.tf
--digit=0
```

In *Figure 8.2.5* and *Figure 8.2.6*, it can be noticed that the width and roundness (if applicable) of each digit change as $z[0]$ is traced from left to right. Meanwhile, the tilt angle and roundness (if applicable) of each digit changes as $z[1]$ is navigated from top to bottom. As we move away from the center of the distribution, the image of the digit starts to degrade. This is expected since the latent space is a circle.

Other noticeable variations in attributes may be digit-specific. For example, the horizontal stroke (arm) for digit 1 becomes visible in the upper left quadrant. The horizontal stroke (crossbar) for digit 7 can be seen in the right quadrants only.

In the next section, we will discover that CVAE is actually just a special case of another type of VAE called β-VAE.

3. β-VAE – VAE with disentangled latent representations

In *Chapter 6, Disentangled Representation GANs*, the concept and importance of the disentangled representation of latent codes were discussed. We can recall that a disentangled representation is where single latent units are sensitive to changes in single generative factors while being relatively invariant to changes in other factors [3]. Varying a latent code results in changes in one attribute of the generated output, while the remainder of the properties remain the same.

In the same chapter, InfoGAN [4] demonstrated to us that for the MNIST dataset, it is possible to control which digit to generate and the tilt and thickness of the writing style. Observing the results in the previous section, it can be noticed that the VAE is intrinsically disentangling the latent vector dimensions to a certain extent. For example, looking at digit 8 in *Figure 8.2.6*, navigating $z[1]$ from top to bottom decreases the width and roundness while rotating the digit clockwise. Increasing $z[0]$ from left to right also decreases the width and roundness while rotating the digit counterclockwise. In other words, $z[1]$ controls the clockwise rotation, while $z[0]$ affects the counterclockwise rotation, and both of them alter the width and roundness.

In this section, we'll demonstrate that a simple modification in the loss function of VAE forces the latent codes to disentangle further. The modification is the positive constant weight, $\beta > 1$, acting as a regularizer on the KL loss:

$$\mathcal{L}_{\beta-VAE} = \mathcal{L}_R + \beta\mathcal{L}_{KL} \quad \text{(Equation 8.3.1)}$$

This variation of VAE is called β-VAE [5]. The implicit effect of β is tighter standard deviation. In other words, β forces the latent codes in the posterior distribution, $Q_\phi(\mathbf{z}|\mathbf{x})$, to be independent.

It is straightforward to implement β-VAE. For example, for the CVAE from the previous example, the required modification is the extra **beta** factor in `kl_loss`:

```
kl_loss = 1 + z_log_var - K.square(z_mean) - K.exp(z_log_var)
kl_loss = K.sum(kl_loss, axis=-1)
kl_loss *= -0.5 * beta
```

CVAE is a special case of β-VAE with $\beta = 1$. Everything else is the same. However, determining the value of β requires some trial and error. There must be a careful balance between the reconstruction error and regularization for latent code independence. The disentanglement is maximized at around $\beta = 9$. When the value of $\beta > 9$, β-VAE is forced to learn one disentangled representation only while muting the other latent dimension.

Figure 8.3.1 and *Figure 8.3.2* show the latent vector means for β-VAE with $\beta = 9$ and $\beta = 10$:

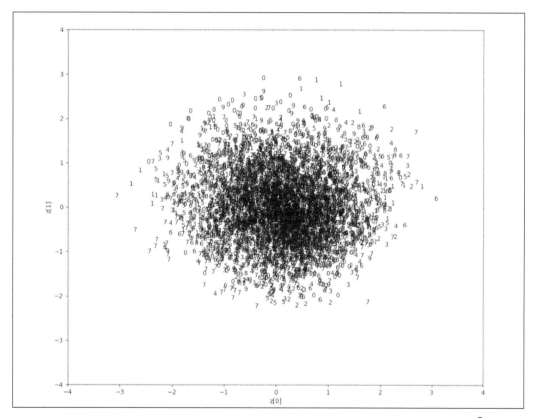

Figure 8.3.1: The MNIST digit label as a function of latent vector mean values for the test dataset (β-VAE with $\beta = 9$). The original image can be found on the book's GitHub repository at https://github.com/ PacktPublishing/ Advanced- Deep-Learning-with-Keras/tree/master/chapter8-vae

With $\beta = 9$, the distribution has smaller standard deviation compared to CVAE. With $\beta = 10$, there is only latent code that is learned. The distribution is practically shrunk to one dimension, with the first latent code $z[0]$ ignored by the encoder and decoder.

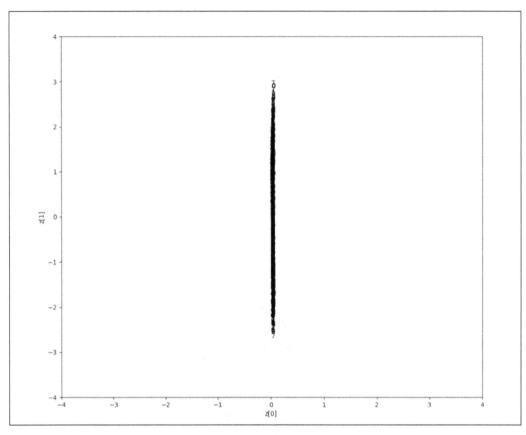

Figure 8.3.2: The MNIST digit label as a function of latent vector mean values for the test dataset (β-VAE with $\beta = 10$)

The original image can be found on the book's GitHub repository at `https://github.com/PacktPublishing/Advanced-Deep-Learning-with-Keras/tree/master/chapter8-vae`.

These observations are reflected in *Figure 8.3.3*. β-VAE with $\beta = 9$ has two latent codes that are practically independent. $z[0]$ determines the tilt of the writing style, while $z[1]$ specifies the width and roundness (if applicable) of the digits. For β-VAE with $\beta = 10$, $z[0]$ is muted. Increasing $z[0]$ does not alter the digit in a significant way. $z[1]$ determines the tilt angle and width of the writing style:

Figure 8.3.3: Digits 0 to 3 generated as a function of latent vector mean values and a one-hot label (β-VAE β =1, 9, and 10). For ease of interpretation, the range of values for the mean is similar to Figure 8.3.1

The `tf.keras` code for β-VAE has pretrained weights. To test β-VAE with $\beta = 9$ generating digit 0, we need to run the following command:

```
python3 cvae-cnn-mnist-8.2.1.py --beta=9 --bce --weights=beta-cvae_cnn_
mnist.tf --digit=0
```

In summary, we have demonstrated that disentangled representation learning is easier to implement on β-VAE compared to GANs. All we need is to tune a single hyperparameter.

4. Conclusion

In this chapter, we've covered the principles of VAEs. As we learned in the principles of VAEs, they bear a resemblance to GANs from the point of view of both attempts to create synthetic outputs from latent space. However, it can be noticed that the VAE networks are much simpler and easier to train compared to GANs. It's becoming clear how CVAE and β-VAE are similar in concept to conditional GANs and disentangled representation GANs, respectively.

VAEs have an intrinsic mechanism to disentangle the latent vectors. Therefore, building a β -VAE is straightforward. We should note, however, that interpretable and disentangled codes are important in building intelligent agents.

In the next chapter, we're going to focus on reinforcement learning. Without any prior data, an agent learns by interacting with the world around it. We'll discuss how the agent can be rewarded for correct actions, and punished for the wrong ones.

5. References

1. Diederik P. Kingma and Max Welling. *Auto-encoding Variational Bayes*. arXiv preprint arXiv:1312.6114, 2013 (`https://arxiv.org/pdf/1312.6114.pdf`).

2. Kihyuk Sohn, Honglak Lee, and Xinchen Yan. *Learning Structured Output Representation Using Deep Conditional Generative Models*. Advances in Neural Information Processing Systems, 2015 (`http://papers.nips.cc/paper/5775-learning-structured-output-representation-using-deep-conditional-generative-models.pdf`).

3. Yoshua Bengio, Aaron Courville, and Pascal Vincent. *Representation Learning*.

4. *A Review and New Perspectives*. IEEE transactions on Pattern Analysis and Machine Intelligence 35.8, 2013: 1798-1828 (`https://arxiv.org/pdf/1206.5538.pdf`).

5. Xi Chen et al.: *Infogan: Interpretable Representation Learning by Information Maximizing Generative Adversarial Nets*. Advances in Neural Information Processing Systems, 2016 (`http://papers.nips.cc/paper/6399-infogan-interpretable-representation-learning-by-information-maximizing-generative-adversarial-nets.pdf`).

6. I. Higgins, L. Matthey, A. Pal, C. Burgess, X. Glorot, M. Botvinick, S. Mohamed, and A. Lerchner. β-VAE: *Learning Basic Visual Concepts with a Constrained Variational Framework*. ICLR, 2017 (`https://openreview.net/pdf?id=Sy2fzU9gl`).

7. Carl Doersch. *Tutorial on variational autoencoders*. arXiv preprint arXiv:1606.05908, 2016 (`https://arxiv.org/pdf/1606.05908.pdf`).

9

Deep Reinforcement Learning

Reinforcement Learning (**RL**) is a framework that is used by an agent for decision making. The agent is not necessarily a software entity, such as you might see in video games. Instead, it could be embodied in hardware such as a robot or an autonomous car. An embodied agent is probably the best way to fully appreciate and utilize RL, since a physical entity interacts with the real world and receives responses.

The agent is situated within an **environment**. The environment has a **state** that can be partially or fully observable. The agent has a set of **actions** that it can use to interact with its environment. The result of an action transitions the environment to a new state. A corresponding scalar **reward** is received after executing an action.

The goal of the agent is to maximize the accumulated future reward by learning a **policy** that will decide which action to take given a state.

RL has a strong similarity to human psychology. Humans learn by experiencing the world. Wrong actions result in a certain form of penalty and should be avoided in the future, whilst actions that are correct are rewarded and should be encouraged. This strong similarity to human psychology has convinced many researchers to believe that RL can lead us toward true **Artificial Intelligence** (**AI**).

RL has been around for decades. However, beyond simple world models, RL has struggled to scale. This is where **Deep Learning** (**DL**) came into play. It solved this scalability problem, which opened up the era of **Deep Reinforcement Learning** (**DRL**). In this chapter, our focus is on DRL. One of the notable examples in DRL is the work of DeepMind on agents that were able to surpass the best human performance on different video games.

In this chapter, we discuss both RL and DRL.

In summary, the goal of this chapter is to present:

- The principles of RL
- The RL technique, Q-learning
- Advanced topics, including **Deep Q-Network (DQN)**, and **Double Q-Learning (DDQN)**
- Instructions on how to implement RL on Python and DRL using `tf.keras`

Let's start with the fundamentals, the principles behind RL.

1. Principles of Reinforcement Learning (RL)

Figure 9.1.1 shows the perception-action-learning loop that is used to describe RL. The environment is a soda can sitting on the floor. The agent is a mobile robot whose goal is to pick up the soda can. It observes the environment around it and tracks the location of the soda can through an onboard camera. The observation is summarized in a form of a state that the robot will use to decide which action to take. The actions it takes may pertain to low-level control, such as the rotation angle/speed of each wheel, the rotation angle/speed of each joint of the arm, and whether the gripper is open or closed.

Alternatively, the actions may be high-level control moves such as moving the robot forward/backward, steering with a certain angle, and grab/release. Any action that moves the gripper away from the soda receives a negative reward. Any action that closes the gap between the gripper location and the soda receives a positive reward. When the robot arm successfully picks up the soda can, it receives a big positive reward. The goal of RL is to learn the optimal policy that helps the robot to decide which action to take given a state to maximize the accumulated discounted reward:

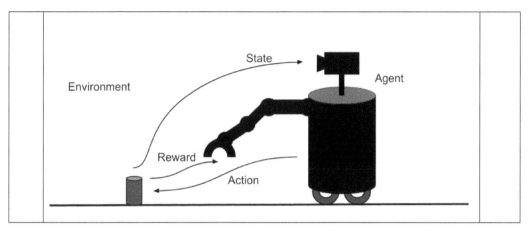

Figure 9.1.1: The perception-action-learning loop in RL

Formally, the RL problem can be described as a **Markov decision process (MDP)**.

For simplicity, we'll assume a *deterministic* environment where a certain action in a given state will consistently result in a known next state and reward. In a later section of this chapter, we'll look at how to consider stochasticity. At timestep t:

- The environment is in a state, s_t, from the state space, $\mathcal{S}$, which may be discrete or continuous. The starting state is s_0, while the terminal state is s_T.

- The agent takes an action, s_a from the action space, $\mathcal{A}$, by obeying the policy, $\pi(a_t|s_t)$. $\mathcal{A}$ may be discrete or continuous.

- The environment transitions to a new state, s_{t+1}, using the state transition dynamics $\mathcal{T}(s_{t+1}|s_t, a_t)$. The next state is only dependent on the current state and action. $\mathcal{T}$ is not known to the agent.

- The agent receives a scalar reward using a reward function, $r_{t+1} = R(s_t, a_t)$, with $r: \mathcal{A} \times \mathcal{S} \to \mathbb{R}$. The reward is only dependent on the current state and action. R is not known to the agent.

- Future rewards are discounted by γ^k, where $\gamma \in [0,1]$ and k is the future timestep.

- *Horizon*, H, is the number of timesteps, T, needed to complete one episode from s_0 to s_T.

The environment may be fully or partially observable. The latter is also known as a **partially observable MDP** or **POMDP**. Most of the time, it's unrealistic to fully observe the environment. To improve the observability, past observations are also taken into consideration with the current observation. The state comprises the sufficient observations about the environment for the policy to decide on which action to take. Recalling *Figure 9.1.1*, this could be the three dimensional position of the soda can with respect to the robot gripper as estimated by the robot camera.

Every time the environment transitions to a new state, the agent receives a scalar reward, r_{t+1}. In *Figure 9.1.1*, the reward could be +1 whenever the robot gets closer to the soda can, -1 whenever it gets farther away, and +100 when it closes the gripper and successfully picks up the soda can. The goal of the agent is to learn an optimal policy, π^*, that maximizes the return from all states:

$$\pi^* = argmax_\pi R_t \quad \text{(Equation 9.1.1)}$$

The return is defined as the discounted cumulative reward, $R_t = \sum_{k=0}^{T} \gamma^k r_{t+k}$. It can be observed from *Equation 9.1.1* that future rewards have lower weights compared to immediate rewards since generally, $\gamma^k < 1.0$, where $\gamma \in [0,1]$. At the extremes, when $\gamma = 0$, only the immediate reward matters. When $\gamma = 1$, future rewards have the same weight as the immediate reward.

Return can be interpreted as a measure of the value of a given state by following an arbitrary policy, π:

$$V^\pi(s_t) = R_t = \sum_{k=0}^{T} \gamma^k r_{t+k} \quad \text{(Equation 9.1.2)}$$

To put the RL problem in another way, the goal of the agent is to learn the optimal policy that maximizes V^π for all states s:

$$\pi^* = argmax_\pi V^\pi(s) \quad \text{(Equation 9.1.3)}$$

The value function of the optimal policy is simply V^*. In *Figure 9.1.1*, the optimal policy is the one that generates the shortest sequence of actions that brings the robot closer and closer to the soda can until it is fetched. The closer the state to the goal state, the higher its value. The sequence of events leading to the goal (or terminal state) can be modeled as the *trajectory* or *rollout* of the policy:

$$Trajectory = (s_0 a_0 r_1 s_1, s_1 a_1 r_2 s_2, \dots, s_{T-1} a_{T-1} r_T s_T) \quad \text{(Equation 9.1.4)}$$

If the MDP is *episodic*, when the agent reaches the terminal state, s_T, the state is reset to s_0. If T is finite, we have a finite horizon. Otherwise, the horizon is infinite. In *Figure 9.1.1*, if the MDP is *episodic*, after collecting the soda can, the robot may look for another soda can to pick up and the RL problem repeats.

A key objective of RL is therefore to find a policy that maximizes the value of each state. In the next section, we will present a learning algorithm for the policy that can be used to maximize the value function.

2. The Q value

If the RL problem is to find π^*, how does the agent learn by interacting with the environment? *Equation 9.1.3* does not explicitly indicate the action to try and the succeeding state to compute the return. In RL, it is easier to learn π^* by using the Q value:

$$\pi^* = argmax_a Q(s, a) \quad \text{(Equation 9.2.1)}$$

where:

$$V^*(s) = \max_a Q(s, a) \quad \text{(Equation 9.2.2)}$$

In other words, instead of finding the policy that maximizes the value for all states, *Equation 9.2.1* looks for the action that maximizes the quality (Q) value for all states. After finding the Q value function, V^*, and hence π^*, are determined by *Equation 9.2.2* and *Equation 9.1.3*, respectively.

If, for every action, the reward and the next state can be observed, we can formulate the following iterative or trial-and-error algorithm to learn the Q value:

$$Q(s, a) = r + \gamma \max_{a'} Q(s', a') \quad \text{(Equation 9.2.3)}$$

For notational simplicity, s' and a' are the next state and action, respectively. *Equation 9.2.3* is known as the Bellman equation, which is the core of the Q-learning algorithm. Q-learning attempts to approximate the first-order expansion of return or value (*Equation 9.1.2*) as a function of both current state and action. From zero knowledge of the dynamics of the environment, the agent tries an action a, observes what happens in the form of a reward, r, and next state, s'. $\max_{a'} Q(s', a')$ chooses the next logical action that will give the maximum Q value for the next state. With all terms in *Equation 9.2.3* known, the Q value for that current state-action pair is updated. Doing the update iteratively will eventually enable the agent to learn the Q value function.

Q-learning is an *off-policy* RL algorithm. It learns how to improve a policy by not directly sampling experiences from that policy. In other words, the Q values are learned independent of the underlying policy being used by the agent. When the Q value function has converged, only then is the optimal policy determined using *Equation 9.2.1*.

Before giving an example of how to use Q-learning, note that the agent must continually explore its environment while gradually taking advantage of what it has learned so far. This is one of the issues in RL – finding the right balance between *exploration* and *exploitation*. Generally, during the start of learning, the action is random (exploration). As the learning progresses, the agent takes advantage of the Q value (exploitation). For example, at the start, 90% of the action is random and 10% stems from the Q value function. At the end of each episode, this is gradually decreased. Eventually, the action is 10% random and 90% from the Q value function.

In the next section, we will give a concrete example as to how Q-learning is used in a simple deterministic environment.

3. Q-learning example

To illustrate the Q-learning algorithm, we need to consider a simple deterministic environment, as shown in *Figure 9.3.1*. The environment has six states.

The rewards for allowed transitions are shown. The reward is non-zero in two cases. Transition to the **Goal (G)** state has a +100 reward, while moving into the **Hole (H)** state has a -100 reward. These two states are terminal states and constitute the end of one episode from the **Start** state:

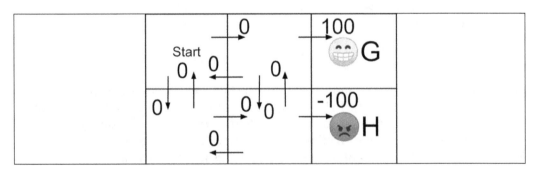

Figure 9.3.1: Rewards in a simple deterministic world

To formalize the identity of each state, we use a (*row, column*) identifier as shown in *Figure 9.3.2*. Since the agent has not learned anything yet about its environment, the Q-table also shown in *Figure 9.3.2* has zero initial values. In this example, the discount factor $\gamma = 0.9$. Recall that in the estimate of the current Q value, the discount factor determines the weight of future Q values as a function of the number of steps, γ^k. In *Equation 9.2.3*, we only consider the immediate future Q value, $k = 1$.

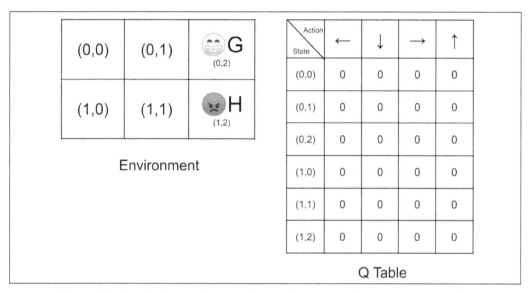

Figure 9.3.2: States in the simple deterministic environment and the agent's initial Q-table

Initially, the agent assumes a policy that selects a random action 90% of the time and exploits the Q-table 10% of the time. Suppose the first action is randomly chosen and indicates a move to the right. *Figure 9.3.3* illustrates the computation of the new Q value of state (0, 0) for a move to the right. The next state is (0, 1). The reward is 0, and the maximum of all the next state's Q values is zero. Therefore, the Q value of state (0, 0) for a move to the right remains 0.

To easily track the initial state and next state, we use different shades of gray on both the environment and the Q-table — lighter gray for the initial state, and darker gray for the next state.

In choosing the next action for the next state, the candidate actions are in the thicker border:

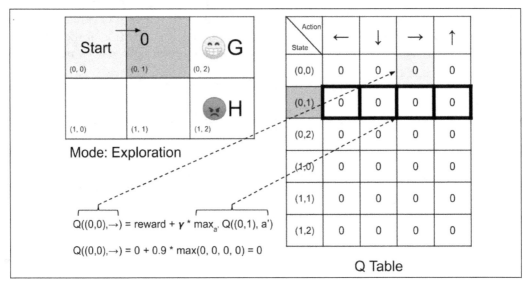

Figure 9.3.3: Assuming the action taken by the agent is a move to the right, an update to the Q value of state (0, 0) is shown

Let's suppose that the next randomly chosen action is a move in a downward direction. *Figure 9.3.4* shows no change in the Q value of state (0, 1) for the move in a downward direction:

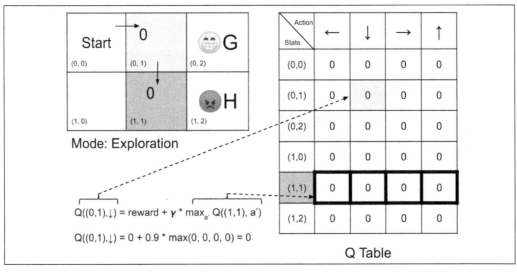

Figure 9.3.4: Assuming the action chosen by the agent is a move down, an update to the Q value of state (0, 1) is shown

In *Figure 9.3.5*, the agent's third random action is a move to the right;

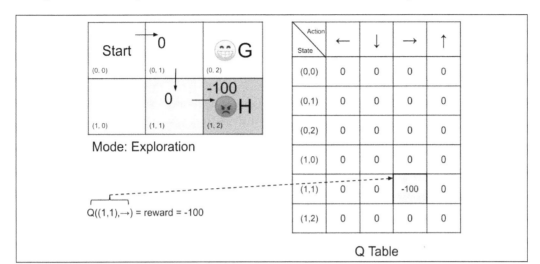

Figure 9.3.5: Assuming the action chosen by the agent is a move to the right,
an update to the Q value of state (1, 1) is shown

It encountered the **H** state and received a -100 reward. This time, the update is non-zero. The new Q value for the state (1, 1) is -100 for the move to the right. Note that since this is a terminal state, there are no next states. One episode has just finished, and the **agent** returns to the **Start** state.

Let's suppose the **agent** is still in exploration mode, as shown in *Figure 9.3.6*:

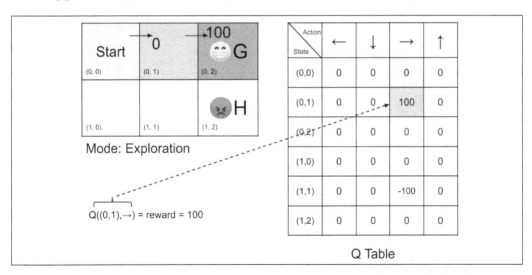

Figure 9.3.6: Assuming the actions chosen by the agent are two successive moves to the right,
an update to the Q value of state (0, 1) is shown

The first step it took for the second episode was a move to the right. As expected, the update is 0. However, the second random action it chose is also a move to the right. The agent reached the **G** state and received a big +100 reward. The Q value for the state (0, 1) moving to the right becomes 100. The second episode is done, and the **agent** goes back to the **Start** state.

At the beginning of the third episode, the random action taken by the agent is a move to the right. The Q value of state (0, 0) is now updated with a non-zero value because the next state's possible actions have 100 as the maximum Q value. *Figure 9.3.7* shows the computation involved. The Q value of the next state (0, 1) ripples back to the earlier state (0, 0). It is like giving credit to the earlier states that helped in finding the **G** state.

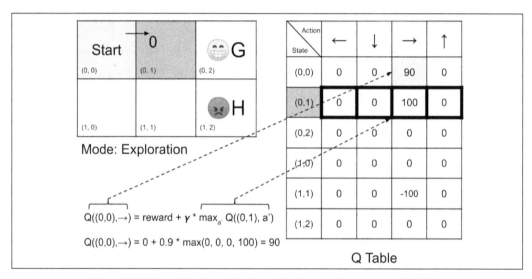

Figure 9.3.7: Assuming the action chosen by the agent is a move to the right,
an update to the Q value of state (0, 0) is shown

The progress in the Q-table has been substantial. In fact, in the next episode, if, for some reason, the policy decided to exploit the Q-table instead of randomly exploring the environment, the first action is to move to the right according to the computation in *Figure 9.3.8*. In the first row of the Q-table, the action that results in the maximum Q value is a move to the right. For the next state (0, 1), the second row of the Q-table suggests that the next action is still to move to the right. The **agent** has successfully reached its goal. The policy guided the agent on the right set of actions to achieve its goal:

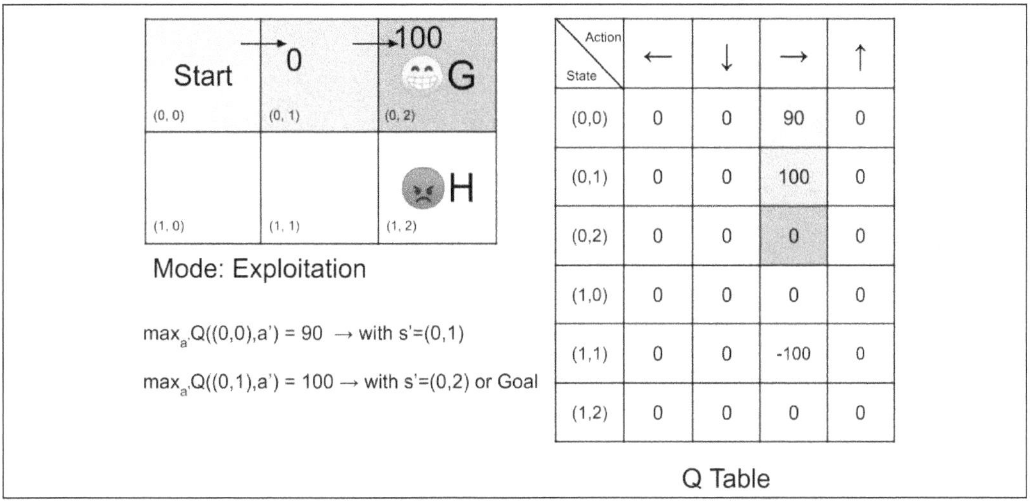

Action State	←	↓	→	↑
(0,0)	0	0	90	0
(0,1)	0	0	100	0
(0,2)	0	0	0	0
(1,0)	0	0	0	0
(1,1)	0	0	-100	0
(1,2)	0	0	0	0

Q Table

Figure 9.3.8: In this instance, the agent's policy decided to exploit the Q-table to
determine the action at states (0, 0) and (0, 1). The Q-table suggests moving to the right for both states

If the Q-learning algorithm continues to run indefinitely, the Q-table will converge. The assumptions for convergence are that the RL problem must be a deterministic MDP with bounded rewards, and all states are visited infinitely often.

In the next section, we will simulate the environment using Python. We will also show the code implementation of the Q-learning algorithm.

Q-Learning in Python

The environment and the Q-learning discussed in the previous section can be implemented in Python. Since the policy is just a simple table, at this point in time, there is no need to use the `tf.keras` library. *Listing 9.3.1* shows `q-learning-9.3.1.py`, the implementation of the simple deterministic world (environment, agent, action, and Q-table algorithms) using the `QWorld` class. For conciseness, the functions dealing with the user interface are not shown.

In this example, the environment dynamics is represented by `self.transition_table`. At every action, `self.transition_table` determines the next state. The reward for executing an action is stored in `self.reward_table`. The two tables are consulted every time an action is executed by the `step()` function. The Q-learning algorithm is implemented by the `update_q_table()` function. Every time the agent needs to decide which action to take, it calls the `act()` function. The action may be randomly drawn or decided by the policy using the Q-table. The percentage chance that the action chosen is random is stored in the `self.epsilon` variable, which is updated by the `update_epsilon()` function using a fixed `epsilon_decay`.

Before executing the code in *Listing 9.3.1*, we need to run:

```
sudo pip3 install termcolor
```

to install the `termcolor` package. This package helps in visualizing text outputs on the Terminal.

 The complete code can be found on GitHub at `https://github.com/PacktPublishing/Advanced-Deep-Learning-with-Keras`.

Listing 9.3.1: `q-learning-9.3.1.py`

A simple deterministic MDP with six states:

```python
from collections import deque
import numpy as np
import argparse
import os
import time
from termcolor import colored


class QWorld:
    def __init__(self):
        """Simulated deterministic world made of 6 states.
        Q-Learning by Bellman Equation.
        """
        # 4 actions
        # 0 - Left, 1 - Down, 2 - Right, 3 - Up
        self.col = 4

        # 6 states
        self.row = 6

        # setup the environment
        self.q_table = np.zeros([self.row, self.col])
        self.init_transition_table()
        self.init_reward_table()

        # discount factor
        self.gamma = 0.9

        # 90% exploration, 10% exploitation
```

```
        self.epsilon = 0.9
        # exploration decays by this factor every episode
        self.epsilon_decay = 0.9
        # in the long run, 10% exploration, 90% exploitation
        self.epsilon_min = 0.1

        # reset the environment
        self.reset()
        self.is_explore = True


    def reset(self):
        """start of episode"""
        self.state = 0
        return self.state

    def is_in_win_state(self):
        """agent wins when the goal is reached"""
        return self.state == 2

    def init_reward_table(self):
        """
        0 - Left, 1 - Down, 2 - Right, 3 - Up
        ----------------
        | 0 | 0 | 100  |
        ----------------
        | 0 | 0 | -100 |
        ----------------
        """
        self.reward_table = np.zeros([self.row, self.col])
        self.reward_table[1, 2] = 100.
        self.reward_table[4, 2] = -100.


    def init_transition_table(self):
        """
        0 - Left, 1 - Down, 2 - Right, 3 - Up
        ------------
        | 0 | 1 | 2 |
        ------------
        | 3 | 4 | 5 |
        ------------
        """
        self.transition_table = np.zeros([self.row, self.col],
```

```
                                               dtype=int)

        self.transition_table[0, 0] = 0
        self.transition_table[0, 1] = 3
        self.transition_table[0, 2] = 1
        self.transition_table[0, 3] = 0

        self.transition_table[1, 0] = 0
        self.transition_table[1, 1] = 4
        self.transition_table[1, 2] = 2
        self.transition_table[1, 3] = 1

        # terminal Goal state
        self.transition_table[2, 0] = 2
        self.transition_table[2, 1] = 2
        self.transition_table[2, 2] = 2
        self.transition_table[2, 3] = 2

        self.transition_table[3, 0] = 3
        self.transition_table[3, 1] = 3
        self.transition_table[3, 2] = 4
        self.transition_table[3, 3] = 0

        self.transition_table[4, 0] = 3
        self.transition_table[4, 1] = 4
        self.transition_table[4, 2] = 5
        self.transition_table[4, 3] = 1

        # terminal Hole state
        self.transition_table[5, 0] = 5
        self.transition_table[5, 1] = 5
        self.transition_table[5, 2] = 5
        self.transition_table[5, 3] = 5


    def step(self, action):
        """execute the action on the environment
        Argument:
            action (tensor): An action in Action space
        Returns:
            next_state (tensor): next env state
            reward (float): reward received by the agent
            done (Bool): whether the terminal state
                is reached
```

```
    """
    # determine the next_state given state and action
    next_state = self.transition_table[self.state, action]
    # done is True if next_state is Goal or Hole
    done = next_state == 2 or next_state == 5
    # reward given the state and action
    reward = self.reward_table[self.state, action]
    # the enviroment is now in new state
    self.state = next_state
    return next_state, reward, done


def act(self):
    """determine the next action
        either fr Q Table(exploitation) or
        random(exploration)
    Return:
        action (tensor): action that the agent
            must execute
    """
    # 0 - Left, 1 - Down, 2 - Right, 3 - Up
    # action is from exploration
    if np.random.rand() <= self.epsilon:
        # explore - do random action
        self.is_explore = True
        return np.random.choice(4,1)[0]

    # or action is from exploitation
    # exploit - choose action with max Q-value
    self.is_explore = False
    action = np.argmax(self.q_table[self.state])
    return action


def update_q_table(self, state, action, reward, next_state):
    """Q-Learning - update the Q Table using Q(s, a)
    Arguments:
        state (tensor) : agent state
        action (tensor): action executed by the agent
        reward (float): reward after executing action
            for a given state
        next_state (tensor): next state after executing
            action for a given state
    """
```

```
# Q(s, a) = reward + gamma * max_a' Q(s', a')
q_value = self.gamma * np.amax(self.q_table[next_state])
q_value += reward
self.q_table[state, action] = q_value



def update_epsilon(self):
    """update Exploration-Exploitation mix"""
    if self.epsilon > self.epsilon_min:
        self.epsilon *= self.epsilon_decay
```

The perception-action-learning loop is illustrated in *Listing 9.3.2*. At every episode, the environment resets to the **Start** state. The action to execute is chosen and applied to the environment. The **reward** and **next** state are observed and used to update the Q-table. The episode is completed (done = True) upon reaching the **Goal** or **Hole** state.

For this example, the Q-learning runs for 100 episodes or 10 wins, whichever comes first. Due to the decrease in the value of the self.epsilon variable at every episode, the agent starts to favor exploitation of the Q-table to determine the action to perform given a state. To see the Q-learning simulation, we simply need to run the following command:

python3 q-learning-9.3.1.py

Listing 9.3.2: q-learning-9.3.1.py

The main Q-learning loop:

```
# state, action, reward, next state iteration
for episode in range(episode_count):
    state = q_world.reset()
    done = False
    print_episode(episode, delay=delay)
    while not done:
        action = q_world.act()
        next_state, reward, done = q_world.step(action)
        q_world.update_q_table(state, action, reward, next_state)
        print_status(q_world, done, step, delay=delay)
        state = next_state
        # if episode is done, perform housekeeping
        if done:
            if q_world.is_in_win_state():
                wins += 1
                scores.append(step)
                if wins > maxwins:
```

```
                print(scores)
                exit(0)
            # Exploration-Exploitation is updated every episode
            q_world.update_epsilon()
            step = 1
        else:
            step += 1
```

Figure 9.3.9 shows the screenshot if `maxwins` = `2000` (2000x Goal state is reached) and `delay` = `0`. To see the final Q-table only, execute:

`python3 q-learning-9.3.1.py --train`

```
    Step 2 : Exploit (Right)
    -------------
    |   |   | G |
    -------------
    |   |   | H |
    -------------
    Q-Table (Epsilon: 0.25)
    [[   0.      72.9     90.      81.   ]
     [   0.      81.     100.      90.   ]
     [   0.       0.       0.       0.   ]
     [   0.      72.9     81.      81.   ]
     [  72.9    65.61  -100.      90.   ]
     [   0.       0.       0.       0.   ]]
    -------EPISODE DONE--------
    deque([45, 5, 2, 2, 2, 2, 3, 4, 2, 2], maxlen=10)
    rowels-mbp:chapter9-drl rowel$
```

Figure 9.3.9: A screenshot showing the Q-table after 2,000 wins on the part of the agent

The Q-table has converged and shows the logical action that the agent can take given a state. For example, in the first row or state (0, 0), the policy advises a move to the right. The same goes for the state (0, 1) on the second row. The second action reaches the **Goal** state. The `scores` variable dump shows that the minimum number of steps taken decreases as the agent gets correct actions from the policy.

From *Figure 9.3.9*, we can compute the value of each state from *Equation 9.2.2*, $V^*(s) = \max_a Q(s, a)$. For example, for state (0, 0), $V^*(s) = \max_a(0.0, 72.9, 90.0, 81.0) = 90$.

Figure 9.3.10 shows the value for each state.

	Start 90	100	☺ G 0	
	81	90	☹ H 0	

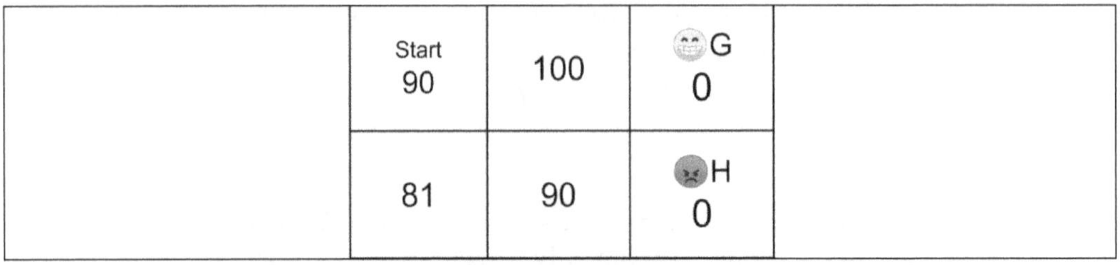

Figure 9.3.10: The value for each state from Figure 9.3.9 and Equation 9.2.2

This simple example illustrated all elements of Q-learning for an agent in a simple deterministic world. In the next section, we will present the slight modification needed to take stochasticity into account.

4. Nondeterministic environment

In the event that the environment is nondeterministic, both the reward and action are probabilistic. The new system is a stochastic MDP. To reflect the nondeterministic reward, the new value function is:

$$V^{\pi}(s_t) = \mathbb{E}[\![R_t]\!] = \mathbb{E}\left[\!\left[\sum_{k=0}^{T} \gamma^k \, r_{t+k}\right]\!\right] \quad \text{(Equation 9.4.1)}$$

The Bellman equation is modified as:

$$Q(s, a) = \mathbb{E}_{s'}\left[\!\left[r + \gamma \max_{a'} Q(s', a')\right]\!\right] \quad \text{(Equation 9.4.2)}$$

However, in this chapter, we will focus on deterministic environments. In the next section, we will present a more generalized Q-learning algorithm called **Temporal-Difference (TD)** learning.

5. Temporal-difference learning

Q-learning is a special case of a more generalized TD learning, $TD(\lambda)$. More specifically, it is a special case of one-step TD learning, $TD(0)$:

$$Q(s,a) = Q(s,a) + \alpha \left(r + \gamma \max_{a'} Q(s',a') - Q(s,a) \right)$$ (Equation 9.5.1)

Where α is the learning rate. Note that when $\alpha = 1$, *Equation 9.5.1* is similar to the Bellman equation. For simplicity, we also refer to *Equation 9.5.1* as Q-learning, or generalized Q-learning.

Previously, we referred to Q-learning as an off-policy RL algorithm since it learns the Q value function without directly using the policy that it is trying to optimize. An example of an *on-policy* one-step TD-learning algorithm is SARSA, which is similar to *Equation 9.5.1*:

$$Q(s,a) = Q(s,a) + \alpha \left(r + \gamma Q(s',a') - Q(s,a) \right)$$ (Equation 9.5.2)

The main difference is the use of the policy that is being optimized to determine a'. The terms s, a, r, s', and a' (thus the name SARSA) must be known to update the Q value function every iteration. Both Q-learning and SARSA use existing estimates in the Q value iteration, a process known as *bootstrapping*. In bootstrapping, we update the current Q value estimate from the reward and the subsequent Q value estimate(s).

Before presenting another example, there appears to be a need for a suitable RL simulation environment. Otherwise, we can only run RL simulations on very simple problems like in the previous example. Fortunately, OpenAI created Gym, `https://gym.openai.com`, which we'll cover in the following section.

Q-learning on OpenAI Gym

OpenAI Gym is a toolkit for developing and comparing RL algorithms. It works with most DL libraries, including `tf.keras`. The gym can be installed by running the following command:

```
sudo pip3 install gym
```

The gym has several environments where an RL algorithm can be tested against, such as toy text, classic control, algorithmic, Atari, and two-dimensional/three-dimensional robots. For example, `FrozenLake-v0` (*Figure 9.5.1*) is a toy text environment similar to the simple deterministic world used in the *Q-learning in Python* example:

```
        (Right)
    SFFF
    FHFH
    FFFH
    HFFG
```

Figure 9.5.1: The FrozenLake-v0 environment in OpenAI Gym

`FrozenLake-v0` has 12 states, the state marked **S** is the starting state, **F** is the frozen part of the lake, which is safe, **H** is the Hole state, which should be avoided, and **G** is the Goal state where the frisbee is located. The reward is +1 for transitioning to the Goal state. For all other states, the reward is **zero**.

In `FrozenLake-v0`, there are also four available actions (left, down, right, up) known as action space. However, unlike the simple deterministic world earlier, the actual movement direction is only partially dependent on the chosen action. There are two variations of the `FrozenLake-v0` environment; slippery and non-slippery. As expected, the slippery mode is more challenging.

An action applied to `FrozenLake-v0` returns the observation (equivalent to the next state), reward, done (whether the episode is finished), and a dictionary of debugging information. The observable attributes of the environment, known as observation space, are captured by the returned observation object.

Generalized Q-learning can be applied to the `FrozenLake-v0` environment. *Table 9.5.1* shows the improvement in performance of both slippery and non-slippery environments. A method of measuring the performance of the policy is the percentage of episodes executed that resulted in reaching the Goal state. The higher the percentage, the better. From the baseline of pure exploration (random action) of about 1.5%, the policy can achieve ~76% Goal state for the non-slippery environment and ~71% for the slippery environment. As expected, it is harder to control the slippery environment.

Mode	Run	Approx % Goal
Train non-slippery	`python3 q-frozenlake-9.5.1.py`	26
Test non-slippery	`python3 q-frozenlake-9.5.1.py -d`	76
Pure random action non-slippery	`python3 q-frozenlake-9.5.1.py -e`	1.5
Train slippery	`python3 q-frozenlake-9.5.1.py -s`	26
Test slippery	`python3 q-frozenlake-9.5.1.py -s -d`	71
Pure random slippery	`python3 q-frozenlake-9.5.1.py -s -e`	1.5

Table 9.5.1: Baseline and performance of generalized Q-learning on the
FrozenLake-v0 environment with a learning rate = 0.5

The code can still be implemented in Python and NumPy since it only requires a Q-table. *Listing 9.5.1* shows the implementation of the `QAgent` class. Apart from using the `FrozenLake-v0` environment from OpenAI Gym, the most important change is the implementation of the generalized Q-learning, as defined by *Equation 9.5.1* in the `update_q_table()` function.

Listing 9.5.1: `q-frozenlake-9.5.1.py`

Q-learning on the FrozenLake-v0 environment:

```
from collections import deque
import numpy as np
import argparse
import os
import time
import gym
from gym import wrappers, logger


class QAgent:
    def __init__(self,
                 observation_space,
                 action_space,
                 demo=False,
                 slippery=False,
                 episodes=40000):
        """Q-Learning agent on FrozenLake-v0 environment

        Arguments:
            observation_space (tensor): state space
            action_space (tensor): action space
            demo (Bool): whether for demo or training
            slippery (Bool): 2 versions of FLv0 env
```

```
        episodes (int): number of episodes to train
"""

self.action_space = action_space
# number of columns is equal to number of actions
col = action_space.n
# number of rows is equal to number of states
row = observation_space.n
# build Q Table with row x col dims
self.q_table = np.zeros([row, col])

# discount factor
self.gamma = 0.9

# initially 90% exploration, 10% exploitation
self.epsilon = 0.9
# iteratively applying decay til
# 10% exploration/90% exploitation
self.epsilon_min = 0.1
self.epsilon_decay = self.epsilon_min / self.epsilon
self.epsilon_decay = self.epsilon_decay ** \
                        (1. / float(episodes))

# learning rate of Q-Learning
self.learning_rate = 0.1

# file where Q Table is saved on/restored fr
if slippery:
    self.filename = 'q-frozenlake-slippery.npy'
else:
    self.filename = 'q-frozenlake.npy'

# demo or train mode
self.demo = demo
# if demo mode, no exploration
if demo:
    self.epsilon = 0


def act(self, state, is_explore=False):
    """determine the next action
        if random, choose from random action space
        else use the Q Table
    Arguments:
```

```
        state (tensor): agent's current state
        is_explore (Bool): exploration mode or not
    Return:
        action (tensor): action that the agent
            must execute
    """
    # 0 - left, 1 - Down, 2 - Right, 3 - Up
    if is_explore or np.random.rand() < self.epsilon:
        # explore - do random action
        return self.action_space.sample()

    # exploit - choose action with max Q-value
    action = np.argmax(self.q_table[state])
    return action


def update_q_table(self, state, action, reward, next_state):
    """TD(0) learning (generalized Q-Learning) with learning rate
    Arguments:
        state (tensor): environment state
        action (tensor): action executed by the agent for
            the given state
        reward (float): reward received by the agent for
            executing the action
        next_state (tensor): the environment next state
    """
    # Q(s, a) +=
    # alpha * (reward + gamma * max_a' Q(s', a') - Q(s, a))
    q_value = self.gamma * np.amax(self.q_table[next_state])
    q_value += reward
    q_value -= self.q_table[state, action]
    q_value *= self.learning_rate
    q_value += self.q_table[state, action]
    self.q_table[state, action] = q_value


def update_epsilon(self):
    """adjust epsilon"""
    if self.epsilon > self.epsilon_min:
        self.epsilon *= self.epsilon_decay
```

Listing 9.5.2 demonstrates the agent's perception-action-learning loop. At every episode, the environment resets by calling `env.reset()`. The action to execute is chosen by `agent.act()` and applied to the environment by `env.step(action)`. The reward and next state are observed and used to update the Q-table.

After every action, the TD learning is executed by `agent.update_q_table()`. Due to the decrease in the value of the `self.epsilon` variable at every episode's call to `agent.update_epsilon()`, the agent starts to favor exploitation of Q-table to determine the action to perform given a state. The episode is completed (`done = True`) upon reaching the Goal or Hole state. For this example, the TD learning runs for 4,000 episodes.

Listing 9.5.2: `q-frozenlake-9.5.1.py`.

Q-learning loop for the `FrozenLake-v0` environment:

```
# loop for the specified number of episode
for episode in range(episodes):
    state = env.reset()
    done = False
    while not done:
        # determine the agent's action given state
        action = agent.act(state, is_explore=args.explore)
        # get observable data
        next_state, reward, done, _ = env.step(action)
        # clear the screen before rendering the environment
        os.system('clear')
        # render the environment for human debugging
        env.render()
        # training of Q Table
        if done:
            # update exploration-exploitation ratio
            # reward > 0 only when Goal is reached
            # otherwise, it is a Hole
            if reward > 0:
                wins += 1

        if not args.demo:
            agent.update_q_table(state,
                                 action,
                                 reward,
                                 next_state)
            agent.update_epsilon()

        state = next_state
        percent_wins = 100.0 * wins / (episode + 1)
```

The `agent` object can operate in either slippery or non-slippery mode. After training, the agent can exploit the Q-table to choose the action to execute given any policy, as shown in the test mode of *Table 9.5.1*. There is a huge performance boost in using the learned policy as demonstrated in *Table 9.5.1*. With the use of the gym, many lines of code in constructing the environment are no longer needed. For example, unlike in the previous example, with the use of OpenAI Gym, we do not need to create the state transition table and the rewards table.

This will help us to focus on building a working RL algorithm. To run the code in slow motion or have a delay of 1 second per action:

```
python3 q-frozenlake-9.5.1.py -d -t=1
```

In this section, we demonstrated Q-learning on a more challenging environment. We also introduced the OpenAI Gym. However, our environment is still a toy environment. What if we have a huge number of states or actions? In that case, it is no longer feasible to use a Q-table. In the next section, we will use a deep neural network to learn the Q-table.

6. Deep Q-Network (DQN)

Using the Q-table to implement Q-learning is fine in small discrete environments. However, when the environment has numerous states or is continuous, as in most cases, a Q-table is not feasible or practical. For example, if we are observing a state made of four continuous variables, the size of the table is infinite. Even if we attempt to discretize the four variables into 1,000 values each, the total number of rows in the table is a staggering $1000^4 = 1e^{12}$. Even after training, the table is sparse – most of the cells in this table are zero.

A solution to this problem is called DQN [2], which uses a deep neural network to approximate the Q-table, as shown in *Figure 9.6.1*. There are two approaches to building the Q-network:

- The input is the state-action pair, and the prediction is the Q value
- The input is the state, and the prediction is the Q value for each action

The first option is not optimal since the network will be called a number of times equal to the number of actions. The second is the preferred method. The Q-network is called only once.

The most desirable action is simply the action with the biggest Q value.

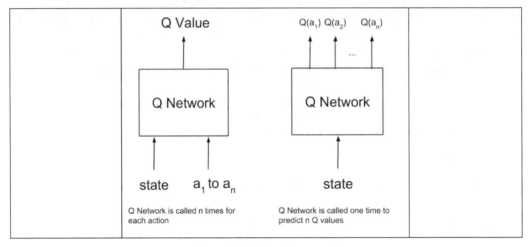

Figure 9.6.1: A deep Q-network

The data required to train the Q-network comes from the agent's experiences: $(s_0 a_0 r_1 s_1, s_1 a_1 r_2 s_2, \dots, s_{T-1} a_{T-1} r_T s_T)$. Each training sample is a unit of experience, $s_t a_t r_{t+1} s_{t+1}$. At a given state at timestep t, $s = s_t$, the action, $a = a_t$, is determined using the Q-learning algorithm similar to the previous section:

$$\pi(s) = \begin{cases} sample(a) & random < \varepsilon \\ \underset{a}{argmax}\, Q(s,a) & otherwise \end{cases} \quad \text{(Equation 9.6.1)}$$

For notational simplicity, we omit the subscript and the use of bold letters. Note that $Q(s, a)$ is the Q-network. Strictly speaking, it is $Q(a|s)$ since the action is moved to the prediction stage (in other words, output) as shown on the right of *Figure 9.6.1*. The action with the highest Q value is the action that is applied to the environment to get the reward, $r = r_{t+1}$, the next state, $s' = s_{t+1}$, and a Boolean done, indicating whether the next state is terminal. From *Equation 9.5.1* on generalized Q-learning, an MSE loss function can be determined by applying the chosen action:

$$\mathcal{L} = \left(r + \gamma \max_{a'} Q(s', a') - Q(s, a) \right)^2 \quad \text{(Equation 9.6.2)}$$

where all terms are familiar from the previous discussion on Q-learning and $Q(a|s) \rightarrow Q(s, a)$. The term $\max_{a'} Q(a'|s') \rightarrow \max_{a'} Q(s', a')$. In other words, using the Q-network, predict the Q value of each action given the next state and get the maximum from among them. Note that at the terminal state, s', $\max_{a'} Q(a'|s') = \max_{a'} Q(s', a') = 0$.

However, it turns out that training the Q-network is unstable. There are two problems causing the instability: 1) high correlation between samples; and 2) a non-stationary target. A high correlation is due to the sequential nature of sampling experiences. DQN addressed this issue by creating a buffer of experiences. The training data is randomly sampled from this buffer. This process is known as **experience replay**.

The issue of the non-stationary target is due to the target network $Q(s', a')$ that is modified after every mini batch of training. A small change in the target network can create a significant change in the policy, the data distribution, and the correlation between the current Q value and target Q value. This is resolved by freezing the weights of the target network for C training steps. In other words, two identical Q-networks are created. The target Q-network parameters are copied from the Q-network under training every C training steps.

The deep Q-network algorithm is summarized in *Algorithm 9.6.1*.

Algorithm 9.6.1: **DQN algorithm**

Require: Initialize replay memory D to capacity N

Require: Initialize action-value function Q with random weights θ

Require: Initialize target action-value function Q_{target} with weights $\theta^- = \theta$

Require: Exploration rate, ε, and discount factor, Υ

1. for *episode* = 1, ... , M, do:
2.   Given initial state s
3.   for *step* = 1, ... , T do:
4.   Choose action $a = \begin{cases} sample(a) & random < \varepsilon \\ \underset{a}{\mathrm{argmax}}\, Q(s, a; \theta) & otherwise \end{cases}$
5.   Execute action a, observe reward r, and Next state s'
6.   Store transition (s, a, r, s') in D
7.   Update the state, $s = s'$
8.   // experience replay
9.   Sample a mini batch of episode experiences $(s_j, a_j, r_{j+1}, s_{j+1})$ from D
10. $Q_{max} = \begin{cases} r_{j+1} & \textit{if episode terminates at } j + 1 \\ r_{j+1} + \gamma \underset{a_{j+1}}{\max} Q_{target}\left(s_{j+1}, a_{j+1}; \theta^-\right) & \textit{otherwise} \end{cases}$

11.   Perform gradient descent step on $\left(Q_{max} - Q(s_j, a_j; \theta)\right)^2$ w.r.t. parameters θ

12.   // periodic update of target network

13.   Every C steps, $Q_{target} = Q$, in other words, set $\theta^- = \theta$

14.   end

15. end

Algorithm 9.6.1 sums up all the techniques needed in order to implement Q-learning on environments with discrete action space and continuous state space. In the next section, we will demonstrate how DQN is used in a more challenging OpenAI Gym environment.

DQN on Keras

To illustrate DQN, the `CartPole-v0` environment of the OpenAI Gym is used. `CartPole-v0` is a pole balancing problem. The goal is to keep the pole from falling over. The environment is two dimensional. The action space is made of two discrete actions (left and right movements). However, the state space is continuous and comprises four variables:

- Linear position
- Linear velocity
- Angle of rotation
- Angular velocity

The `CartPole-v0` environment is shown in *Figure 9.6.1*:

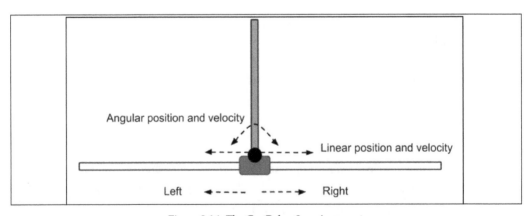

Figure 9.6.1: The CartPole-v0 environment

Initially, the pole is upright. A reward of +1 is provided for every timestep that the pole remains upright. The episode ends when the pole exceeds 15 degrees from the vertical, or 2.4 units from the center. The CartPole-v0 problem is considered solved if the average reward is 195.0 in 100 consecutive trials:

Listing 9.6.1 shows us the DQN implementation for CartPole-v0. The DQNAgent class represents the agent using DQN. Two Q-networks are created:

- A Q-network, or Q, in *Algorithm 9.6.1*
- A target Q-network, or Q_{target}, in *Algorithm 9.6.1*

Both networks are MLP with 3 hidden layers of 256 units each. Both networks are created by means of the build_model() method. The Q-network is trained during **experience replay**, *replay()*. At a regular interval of C = 10 training steps, the Q-network parameters are copied to the target Q-network by update_weights(). This implements line 13, Q_{target} = Q, in *Algorithm 9.6.1*. After every episode, the ratio of exploration-exploitation is decreased by update_epsilon() to take advantage of the learned policy.

Listing 9.6.1: dqn-cartpole-9.6.1.py

DQN in tf.keras:

```
class DQNAgent:
    def __init__(self,
                 state_space,
                 action_space,
                 episodes=500):
        """DQN Agent on CartPole-v0 environment

        Arguments:
            state_space (tensor): state space
            action_space (tensor): action space
            episodes (int): number of episodes to train
        """
        self.action_space = action_space

        # experience buffer
        self.memory = []

        # discount rate
        self.gamma = 0.9

        # initially 90% exploration, 10% exploitation
        self.epsilon = 1.0
```

```
            # iteratively applying decay til
            # 10% exploration/90% exploitation
            self.epsilon_min = 0.1
            self.epsilon_decay = self.epsilon_min / self.epsilon
            self.epsilon_decay = self.epsilon_decay ** \
                                 (1. / float(episodes))

            # Q Network weights filename
            self.weights_file = 'dqn_cartpole.h5'
            # Q Network for training
            n_inputs = state_space.shape[0]
            n_outputs = action_space.n
            self.q_model = self.build_model(n_inputs, n_outputs)
            self.q_model.compile(loss='mse', optimizer=Adam())
            # target Q Network
            self.target_q_model = self.build_model(n_inputs, n_outputs)
            # copy Q Network params to target Q Network
            self.update_weights()

            self.replay_counter = 0
            self.ddqn = True if args.ddqn else False


    def build_model(self, n_inputs, n_outputs):
        """Q Network is 256-256-256 MLP

        Arguments:
            n_inputs (int): input dim
            n_outputs (int): output dim

        Return:
            q_model (Model): DQN
        """
        inputs = Input(shape=(n_inputs, ), name='state')
        x = Dense(256, activation='relu')(inputs)
        x = Dense(256, activation='relu')(x)
        x = Dense(256, activation='relu')(x)
        x = Dense(n_outputs,
                    activation='linear',
                    name='action')(x)
        q_model = Model(inputs, x)
        q_model.summary()
        return q_model
```

```
def act(self, state):
    """eps-greedy policy
    Return:
        action (tensor): action to execute
    """
    if np.random.rand() < self.epsilon:
        # explore - do random action
        return self.action_space.sample()

    # exploit
    q_values = self.q_model.predict(state)
    # select the action with max Q-value
    action = np.argmax(q_values[0])
    return action


def remember(self, state, action, reward, next_state, done):
    """store experiences in the replay buffer
    Arguments:
        state (tensor): env state
        action (tensor): agent action
        reward (float): reward received after executing
            action on state
        next_state (tensor): next state
    """
    item = (state, action, reward, next_state, done)
    self.memory.append(item)

def get_target_q_value(self, next_state, reward):
    """compute Q_max
        Use of target Q Network solves the
        non-stationarity problem
    Arguments:
        reward (float): reward received after executing
            action on state
        next_state (tensor): next state
    Return:
        q_value (float): max Q-value computed by
            DQN or DDQN
    """
    # max Q value among next state's actions
    if self.ddqn:
        # DDQN
```

```
            # current Q Network selects the action
            # a'_max = argmax_a' Q(s', a')
            action = np.argmax(self.q_model.predict(next_state)[0])
            # target Q Network evaluates the action
            # Q_max = Q_target(s', a'_max)
            q_value = self.target_q_model.predict(\
                                        next_state)[0][action]
        else:
            # DQN chooses the max Q value among next actions
            # selection and evaluation of action is
            # on the target Q Network
            # Q_max = max_a' Q_target(s', a')
            q_value = np.amax(\
                    self.target_q_model.predict(next_state)[0])

        # Q_max = reward + gamma * Q_max
        q_value *= self.gamma
        q_value += reward
        return q_value


    def replay(self, batch_size):
        """experience replay addresses the correlation issue
            between samples
        Arguments:
            batch_size (int): replay buffer batch
                sample size
        """
        # sars = state, action, reward, state' (next_state)
        sars_batch = random.sample(self.memory, batch_size)
        state_batch, q_values_batch = [], []

        # fixme: for speedup, this could be done on the tensor level
        # but easier to understand using a loop
        for state, action, reward, next_state, done in sars_batch:
            # policy prediction for a given state
            q_values = self.q_model.predict(state)

            # get Q_max
            q_value = self.get_target_q_value(next_state, reward)

            # correction on the Q value for the action used
            q_values[0][action] = reward if done else q_value
```

```
            # collect batch state-q_value mapping
            state_batch.append(state[0])
            q_values_batch.append(q_values[0])

        # train the Q-network
        self.q_model.fit(np.array(state_batch),
                         np.array(q_values_batch),
                         batch_size=batch_size,
                         epochs=1,
                         verbose=0)

        # update exploration-exploitation probability
        self.update_epsilon()

        # copy new params on old target after
        # every 10 training updates
        if self.replay_counter % 10 == 0:
            self.update_weights()

        self.replay_counter += 1


    def update_epsilon(self):
        """decrease the exploration, increase exploitation"""
        if self.epsilon > self.epsilon_min:
            self.epsilon *= self.epsilon_decay
```

To implement line 10 in *Algorithm 9.6.1* during **experience replay** replay(), for each experience unit (s_j, a_j, r_{j+1}, and s_{j+1}) the Q value for the action a_j is set to Q_{max}. All other actions have their Q values unchanged.

This is implemented by the following lines in the DQNAgent replay() function:

```
# policy prediction for a given state q_values = self.q_model.
predict(state)

# get Q_max
q_value = self.get_target_q_value(next_state)

# correction on the Q value for the action used q_values[0][action] =
reward if done else q_value
```

Only the action a_j has a non-zero loss equal to $\left(Q_{max} - Q(s_j, a_j; \theta)\right)^2$, as shown by line 11 of *Algorithm 9.6.1*. Note that the experience replay is called by the perception-action-learning loop in *Listing 9.6.2* after the end of each episode, assuming that there is sufficient data in the buffer (in other words, the buffer size is greater than, or equal to, the batch size). During experience replay, one batch of experience units is randomly sampled and used to train the Q-network.

Similar to the Q-table, `act()` implements the ϵ-greedy policy, *Equation 9.6.1*.

Experiences are stored by `remember()` in the replay buffer. Q is computed by means of the `get_target_q_value()` function.

Listing 9.6.2 summarizes the agent's perception-action-learning loop. At every episode, the environment resets by calling `env.reset()`. The action to execute is chosen by `agent.act()` and applied to the environment by `env.step(action)`. The reward and next state are observed and stored in the replay buffer. After every action, the agent calls `replay()` to train the DQN and adjust the exploration-exploitation ratio.

The episode is completed (`done = True`) when the pole exceeds 15 degrees from the vertical, or 2.4 units from the center. For this example, Q-learning runs for a maximum of 3,000 episodes if the DQN agent cannot solve the problem. The `CartPole-v0` problem is considered solved if the `average mean_score` reward is 195.0 over 100 consecutive trials, `win_trials`.

Listing 9.6.2: `dqn-cartpole-9.6.1.py`

Training loop of DQN in `tf.keras`:

```
# Q-Learning sampling and fitting
for episode in range(episode_count):
    state = env.reset()
    state = np.reshape(state, [1, state_size])
    done = False
    total_reward = 0
    while not done:
        # in CartPole-v0, action=0 is left and action=1 is right
        action = agent.act(state)
        next_state, reward, done, _ = env.step(action)
        # in CartPole-v0:
        # state = [pos, vel, theta, angular speed]
        next_state = np.reshape(next_state, [1, state_size])
        # store every experience unit in replay buffer
        agent.remember(state, action, reward, next_state, done)
        state = next_state
```

```
        total_reward += reward


    # call experience relay
    if len(agent.memory) >= batch_size:
        agent.replay(batch_size)

    scores.append(total_reward)
    mean_score = np.mean(scores)
    if mean_score >= win_reward[args.env_id] \
            and episode >= win_trials:
        print("Solved in episode %d: \
                Mean survival = %0.2lf in %d episodes"
                % (episode, mean_score, win_trials))
        print("Epsilon: ", agent.epsilon)
        agent.save_weights()
        break
    if (episode + 1) % win_trials == 0:
        print("Episode %d: Mean survival = \
                %0.2lf in %d episodes" %
                ((episode + 1), mean_score, win_trials))
```

Across the average of 10 runs, CartPole-v0 is solved by DQN within 822 episodes. We need to take note that the results may vary every time the training runs.

Since the introduction of DQN, successive papers have proposed improvements to *Algorithm 9.6.1*. One good example is **Double DQN (DDQN)**, which is discussed next.

Double Q-learning (DDQN)

In DQN, the target Q-network selects and evaluates every action, resulting in an overestimation of the Q value. To resolve this issue, DDQN [3] proposes to use the Q-network to choose the action and use the target Q-network to evaluate the action.

In DQN, as summarized by *Algorithm 9.6.1*, the estimate of the Q value in line 10 is:

$$
Q_{max} = \begin{cases} r_{j+1} & \textit{if episode terminates at } j+1 \\ r_{j+1} + \gamma \max_{a_{j+1}} Q_{target}\left(s_{j+1}, a_{j+1}; \theta^-\right) & \textit{otherwise} \end{cases}
$$

- Q_{target} chooses and evaluates the action, a_{j+1}.

DDQN proposes to change line 10 to:

$$
Q_{max}
= \begin{cases}
r_{j+1} & \textit{if episode terminates at } j+1 \\
r_{j+1} + \gamma\, Q_{target}\left(s_{j+1}, \underset{a_{j+1}}{\arg\max}\, Q\left(s_{j+1}, a_{j+1}; \theta\right); \theta^{-}\right) & \textit{otherwise}
\end{cases}
$$

The term $\underset{a_{j+1}}{\arg\max}\, Q\left(s_{j+1}, a_{j+1}; \theta\right)$ lets the Q function to choose the action. Then, this action is evaluated by Q_{target}.

Listing 9.6.3 shows when we create a new DDQNAgent class, which inherits from the DQNAgent class. Only the get_target_q_value() method is overridden to implement the change in the computation of the maximum Q value.

Listing 9.6.3: dqn-cartpole-9.6.1.py:

```
class DDQNAgent(DQNAgent):
    def __init__(self,
                 state_space,
                 action_space,
                 episodes=500):
        super().__init__(state_space,
                         action_space,
                         episodes)
        """DDQN Agent on CartPole-v0 environment

        Arguments:
            state_space (tensor): state space
            action_space (tensor): action space
            episodes (int): number of episodes to train
        """

        # Q Network weights filename
        self.weights_file = 'ddqn_cartpole.h5'

    def get_target_q_value(self, next_state, reward):
        """compute Q_max
            Use of target Q Network solves the
            non-stationarity problem
        Arguments:
            reward (float): reward received after executing
                action on state
            next_state (tensor): next state
        Returns:
```

```
        q_value (float): max Q-value computed
    """
    # max Q value among next state's actions
    # DDQN
    # current Q Network selects the action
    # a'_max = argmax_a' Q(s', a')
    action = np.argmax(self.q_model.predict(next_state)[0])
    # target Q Network evaluates the action
    # Q_max = Q_target(s', a'_max)
    q_value = self.target_q_model.predict(\
                                    next_state)[0][action]

    # Q_max = reward + gamma * Q_max
    q_value *= self.gamma
    q_value += reward
    return q_value
```

For comparison, across the average of 10 runs, `CartPole-v0` is solved by DDQN within 971 episodes. To use DDQN, run the following command:

python3 dqn-cartpole-9.6.1.py -d

Both DQN and DDQN demonstrated that with DL, Q-learning was able to scale up and solve problems with continuous state space and discrete action space. In this chapter, we demonstrated DQN only on one of the simplest problems with continuous state space and discrete action space. In the original paper, DQN [2] demonstrated that it can achieve super-human levels of performance in many Atari games.

7. Conclusion

In this chapter, we've been introduced to DRL, a powerful technique believed by many researchers to be the most promising lead toward AI. We have gone over the principles of RL. RL is able to solve many toy problems, but the Q-table is unable to scale to more complex real-world problems. The solution is to learn the Q-table using a deep neural network. However, training deep neural networks on RL is highly unstable due to sample correlation and the non-stationarity of the target Q-network.

DQN proposed a solution to these problems using experience replay and separating the target network from the Q-network under training. DDQN suggested further improvement of the algorithm by separating the action selection from action evaluation to minimize the overestimation of the Q value. There are other improvements proposed for the DQN. Prioritized experience replay [6] argues that the experience buffer should not be sampled uniformly.

Instead, experiences that are more important based on TD errors should be sampled more frequently to accomplish more efficient training. [7] proposes a dueling network architecture to estimate the state value function and the advantage function. Both functions are used to estimate the Q value for faster learning.

The approach presented in this chapter is value iteration/fitting. The policy is learned indirectly by finding an optimal value function. In the next chapter, the approach will be to learn the optimal policy directly by using a family of algorithms called policy gradient methods. Learning the policy has many advantages. In particular, policy gradient methods can deal with both discrete and continuous action spaces.

8. References

1. Sutton and Barto: *Reinforcement Learning: An Introduction*, 2017 (`http://incompleteideas.net/book/bookdraft2017nov5.pdf`).

2. Volodymyr Mnih et al.: *Human-level Control through Deep Reinforcement Learning*. Nature 518.7540, 2015: 529 (`http://www.davidqiu.com:8888/research/nature14236.pdf`).

3. Hado Van Hasselt, Arthur Guez, and David Silver: *Deep Reinforcement Learning with Double Q-Learning*. AAAI. Vol. 16, 2016 (`http://www.aaai.org/ocs/index.php/AAAI/AAAI16/paper/download/12389/11847`).

4. Kai Arulkumaran et al.: *A Brief Survey of Deep Reinforcement Learning*. arXiv preprint arXiv:1708.05866, 2017 (`https://arxiv.org/pdf/1708.05866.pdf`).

5. David Silver: *Lecture Notes on Reinforcement Learning* (`http://www0.cs.ucl.ac.uk/staff/d.silver/web/Teaching.html`).

6. Tom Schaul et al.: *Prioritized experience replay*. arXiv preprint arXiv:1511.05952, 2015 (`https://arxiv.org/pdf/1511.05952.pdf`).

7. Ziyu Wang et al.: *Dueling Network Architectures for Deep Reinforcement Learning*. arXiv preprint arXiv:1511.06581, 2015 (`https://arxiv.org/pdf/1511.06581.pdf`).

10

Policy Gradient Methods

In this chapter, we're going to introduce algorithms that directly optimize the policy network in reinforcement learning. These algorithms are collectively referred to as *policy gradient methods*. Since the policy network is directly optimized during training, the policy gradient methods belong to the family of *on-policy* reinforcement learning algorithms. Like value-based methods, which we discussed in *Chapter 9, Deep Reinforcement Learning*, policy gradient methods can also be implemented as deep reinforcement learning algorithms.

A fundamental motivation in studying the policy gradient methods is addressing the limitations of Q-learning. We'll recall that Q-learning is about selecting the action that maximizes the value of the state. With the Q function, we're able to determine the policy that enables the agent to decide on which action to take for a given state. The chosen action is simply the one that gives the agent the maximum value. In this respect, Q-learning is limited to a finite number of discrete actions. It's not able to deal with continuous action space environments. Furthermore, Q-learning is not directly optimizing the policy. In the end, reinforcement learning is about finding that optimal policy that the agent will be able to use in order to decide upon which action it should take in order to maximize the return.

In contrast, policy gradient methods are applicable to environments with discrete or continuous action spaces. In addition, the four policy gradient methods that we will be presenting in this chapter are directly optimizing the performance measure of the policy network. This results in a trained policy network that the agent can use to act in its environment optimally.

In summary, the goal of this chapter is to present:

- The policy gradient theorem
- Four policy gradient methods: **REINFORCE, REINFORCE with baseline, Actor-Critic**, and **Advantage Actor-Critic (A2C)**
- A guide on how to implement the policy gradient methods in `tf.keras` in a continuous action space environment

Let's begin by getting into the theorem.

1. Policy gradient theorem

As discussed in *Chapter 9, Deep Reinforcement Learning*, the agent is situated in an environment that is in state s, an element of state space, $\mathcal{S}$. The state space $\mathcal{S}$ may be discrete or continuous. The agent takes an action a_t from the action space $\mathcal{A}$ by obeying the policy, $\pi(a_t|s_t)$. $\mathcal{A}$ may be discrete or continuous. As a result of executing the action a_t, the agent receives a reward r_{t+1} and the environment transitions to a new state, s_{t+1}. The new state is dependent only on the current state and action. The goal of the agent is to learn an optimal policy π^* that maximizes the return from all states:

$$\pi^* = argmax_\pi R_t \quad \text{(Equation 9.1.1)}$$

The return, R_t, is defined as the discounted cumulative reward from time t until the end of the episode or when the terminal state is reached:

$$V^\pi(s_t) = R_t = \sum_{k=0}^{T} \gamma^k r_{t+k} \quad \text{(Equation 9.1.2)}$$

From *Equation 9.1.2*, the return can also be interpreted as a value of a given state by following the policy π. It can be observed from *Equation 9.1.1* that future rewards have lower weights compared to immediate rewards since generally, $\gamma^k < 1.0$ where $\gamma \in [0,1]$.

So far, we have only considered learning the policy by optimizing a value-based function, $Q(s, a)$.

Our goal in this chapter is to directly learn the policy by parameterizing $\pi(a_t|s_t) \to \pi(a_t|s_t, \theta)$. By means of parameterization, we can use a neural network to learn the policy function.

Learning the policy means that we are going to maximize a certain objective function, $\mathcal{J}(\theta)$, which is a performance measure with respect to parameter θ. In episodic reinforcement learning, the performance measure is the value of the start state. In a continuous case, the objective function is the average reward rate.

Maximizing the objective function, $\mathcal{J}(\theta)$, is done by performing gradient ascent. In gradient ascent, the gradient update is in the direction of the derivative of the function being optimized. So far, all our loss functions are optimized by minimization or by performing gradient descent. Later, in the tf.keras implementation, we will see that gradient ascent can be performed by simply negating the objective function and performing gradient descent.

The advantage of learning the policy directly is that it can be applied to both discrete and continuous action spaces. For discrete action spaces:

$$\pi(a_i|s_t, \boldsymbol{\theta}) = softmax(a_i) \ for \ a_i \in \mathcal{A} \quad \text{(Equation 10.1.1)}$$

where a_i is the i-th action. a_i can be the prediction of a neural network or a linear function of state-action features:

$$a_i = \phi(s_t, a_i)^T \ \theta \quad \text{(Equation 10.1.2)}$$

$\phi(s_t, a_i)$ is any function, such as an encoder, that converts the state-action to features.

$\pi(a_i|s_t, \theta)$ determines the probability of each a_i . For example, in the cartpole balancing problem in the previous chapter, the goal is to keep the pole upright by moving the cart along the two-dimensional axis to the left or to the right. In this case, a_0 and a_1 are the probabilities of the left and right movements, respectively. In general, the agent takes the action with the highest probability, $a_t = \max_i \pi(a_i|s_t, \theta)$.

For continuous action spaces, $\pi(a_t|s_t, \theta)$ samples an action from a probability distribution given the state. For example, if the continuous action space is the range $a_t \in [-1.0, 1.0]$, then $\pi(a_t|s_t, \theta)$ is usually a Gaussian distribution whose mean and standard deviation are predicted by the policy network. The predicted action is a sample from this Gaussian distribution. To ensure that no invalid predictions are generated, the action is clipped between -1.0 and 1.0.

Formally, for continuous action spaces, the policy is a sample from a Gaussian distribution:

$$\pi(a_t|s_t, \theta) = a_t \sim \mathcal{N}\big(\mu(s_t), \sigma^2(s_t)\big) \quad \text{(Equation 10.1.3)}$$

The mean, μ, and standard deviation, σ, are both functions of the state features:

$$\mu(s_t) = \phi(s_t)^T \theta_\mu \quad \text{(Equation 10.1.4)}$$

$$\sigma(s_t) = \zeta(\phi(s_t)^T \theta_\sigma) \quad \text{(Equation 10.1.5)}$$

$\phi(s_t)$ is any function that converts the state to its features. $\zeta(x) = \log(1 + e^x)$ is the `softplus` function that ensures positive values of standard deviation. One way of implementing the state feature function, $\phi(s_t)$, is to use the encoder of an autoencoder network. At the end of this chapter, we will train an autoencoder and use the encoder part as the state feature function. Training a policy network is therefore a matter of optimizing the parameters $\theta = [\theta_\mu \quad \theta_\sigma]$.

Given a continuously differentiable policy function, $\pi(a_t|s_t, \theta)$, the policy gradient can be computed as:

$$\nabla J(\theta) = \mathbb{E}_\pi \left[\frac{\nabla_\theta \pi(a_t|s_t, \theta)}{\pi(a_t|s_t, \theta)} Q^\pi(s_t, a_t) \right] = \mathbb{E}_\pi [\nabla_\theta \ln \pi (a_t|s_t, \theta) Q^\pi(s_t, a_t)] \quad \text{(Equation 10.1.6)}$$

Equation 10.1.6 is also known as the *Policy Gradient Theorem*. It is applicable to both discrete and continuous action spaces. The gradient with respect to the parameter θ is computed from the natural logarithm of the policy action sampling scaled by the Q value. *Equation 10.1.6* takes advantage of the property of the natural logarithm, $\dfrac{\nabla x}{x} = \nabla \ln x$.

The policy gradient theorem is intuitive in the sense that the performance gradient is estimated from the target policy samples and is proportional to the policy gradient. The policy gradient is scaled by the Q value to encourage actions that positively contribute to the state value. The gradient is also inversely proportional to the action probability to penalize frequently occurring actions that do not contribute to improved performance.

For proof of the policy gradient theorem, please refer to [2] and lecture notes from David Silver on reinforcement learning:
`http://www0.cs.ucl.ac.uk/staff/d.silver/web/`
`Teaching_files/pg.pdf`

There are subtle advantages associated with policy gradient methods. For example, in some card-based games, value-based methods have no straightforward procedure in handling stochasticity, unlike policy-based methods. In policy-based methods, the action probability changes smoothly with the parameters.

Meanwhile, value-based actions may suffer from drastic changes with respect to small changes in parameters. Lastly, the dependence of policy-based methods on parameters leads us to different formulations on how to perform gradient ascent on the performance measure. These are the four policy gradient methods to be presented in the succeeding sections.

Policy-based methods have their own disadvantages as well. They are generally harder to train because of the tendency to converge on a local optimum instead of the global optimum. In the experiments to be presented at the end of this chapter, it is easy for an agent to become comfortable and to choose actions that do not necessarily give the highest value. The policy gradient is also characterized by high variance.

The gradient updates are frequently overestimated. Furthermore, training policy-based methods are time-consuming. Training requires thousands of episodes (that is, not sample-efficient). Each episode only provides a small number of samples. Typical training in the implementation provided at the end of the chapter would take about an hour for 1,000 episodes on a GTX 1060 GPU.

In the following sections, we discuss the four policy gradient methods. While the discussion focuses on continuous action spaces, the concept is generally applicable to discrete action spaces.

2. Monte Carlo policy gradient (REINFORCE) method

The simplest policy gradient method is REINFORCE [4], which is a Monte Carlo policy gradient method:

$$\nabla J(\theta) = \mathbb{E}_\pi [R_t \nabla_\theta \ln \pi (a_t|s_t, \theta)] \quad \text{(Equation 10.2.1)}$$

where R_t is the return as defined in *Equation 9.1.2*. R_t is an unbiased sample of $Q^\pi(s_t, a_t)$ in the policy gradient theorem.

Algorithm 10.2.1 summarizes the REINFORCE algorithm [2]. REINFORCE is a Monte Carlo algorithm. It does not require knowledge of the dynamics of the environment (in other words, model-free). Only experience samples, $(s_i a_i r_{i+1} s_{i+1})$, are needed to optimally tune the parameters of the policy network, $\pi(a_t|s_t, \theta)$. The discount factor, γ, takes into consideration the fact that rewards decrease in value as the number of steps increases. The gradient is discounted by γ^t. Gradients taken at later steps have smaller contributions. The learning rate, α, is a scaling factor of the gradient update.

The parameters are updated by performing gradient ascent using the discounted gradient and learning rate. As a Monte Carlo algorithm, REINFORCE requires that the agent completes an episode before processing the gradient updates. Also due to its Monte Carlo nature, the gradient update of REINFORCE is characterized by high variance.

Algorithm 10.2.1 REINFORCE

Require: A differentiable parameterized target policy network, $\pi(a_t|s_t, \theta)$.

Require: Discount factor, $\gamma \in [0,1]$ and learning rate α. For example, $\gamma = 0.99$ and $\alpha = 1e - 3$.

Require: θ_0, initial policy network parameters (for example, $\theta_0 \rightarrow 0$).

1. Repeat.
2. Generate an episode $\langle s_0 a_0 r_1 s_1, s_1 a_1 r_2 s_2, \dots, s_{T-1} a_{T-1} r_T s_T \rangle$ by following $\pi(a_t|s_t, \theta)$.
3. **for** steps $t = 0, \dots, T - 1$ **do**.
4. Compute the return, $R_t = \sum_{k=0}^{T} \gamma^k r_{t+k}$.
5. Compute the discounted performance gradient, $\nabla J(\theta) = \gamma^t R_t \nabla_\theta \ln \pi (a_t|s_t, \theta)$.
6. Perform gradient ascent, $\theta = \theta + \alpha \nabla J(\theta)$.

In REINFORCE, the parameterized policy can be modeled by a neural network as shown in *Figure 10.2.1*:

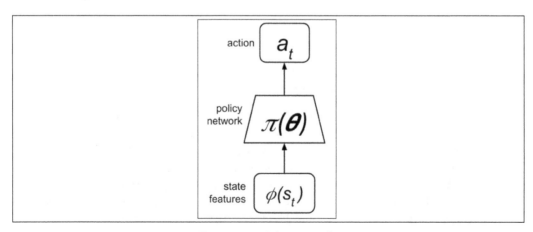

Figure 10.2.1: Policy network

As discussed in the previous section, in the case of continuous action spaces, the state input is converted into features. The state features are the inputs of the policy network. The Gaussian distribution representing the policy function has a mean and standard deviation that are both functions of the state features. The policy network, $\pi(\theta)$, could be an MLP, CNN, or an RNN depending on the nature of the state inputs. The predicted action is simply a sample from the policy function.

Listing 10.2.1 shows the `REINFORCEAgent` class, which implements *Algorithm 10.2.1* in `tf.keras.train_by_episode()`, is called after an episode is completed to compute the return per step. `train()` performs Lines 5 and 6 of *Algorithm 10.2.1* by optimizing the network for the objective function, `logp_model`. The parent class, `PolicyAgent`, implements the common lines in the algorithms of the four policy gradient methods that are covered in this chapter. `PolicyAgent` will be presented after discussing all the policy gradient methods.

Listing 10.2.1: `policygradient-car-10.1.1.py`

```
class REINFORCEAgent(PolicyAgent):
    def __init__(self, env):
        """Implements the models and training of
            REINFORCE policy gradient method
        Arguments:
            env (Object): OpenAI gym environment
        """
        super().__init__(env)


    def train_by_episode(self):
        """Train by episode
            Prepare the dataset before the step by step training
        """
        # only REINFORCE and REINFORCE with baseline
        # use the ff code
        # convert the rewards to returns
        rewards = []
        gamma = 0.99
        for item in self.memory:
            [_, _, _, reward, _] = item
            rewards.append(reward)


        # compute return per step
        # return is the sum of rewards from t til end of episode
        # return replaces reward in the list
        for i in range(len(rewards)):
            reward = rewards[i:]
```

```
        horizon = len(reward)
        discount =  [math.pow(gamma, t) for t in range(horizon)]
        return_ = np.dot(reward, discount)
        self.memory[i][3] = return_


    # train every step
    for item in self.memory:
        self.train(item, gamma=gamma)



def train(self, item, gamma=1.0):
    """Main routine for training
    Arguments:
        item (list) : one experience unit
        gamma (float) : discount factor [0,1]
    """
    [step, state, next_state, reward, done] = item

    # must save state for entropy computation
    self.state = state

    discount_factor = gamma**step
    delta = reward

    # apply the discount factor as shown in Algorithms
    # 10.2.1, 10.3.1 and 10.4.1
    discounted_delta = delta * discount_factor
    discounted_delta = np.reshape(discounted_delta, [-1, 1])
    verbose = 1 if done else 0

    # train the logp model (implies training of actor model
    # as well) since they share exactly the same set of
    # parameters
    self.logp_model.fit(np.array(state),
                        discounted_delta,
                        batch_size=1,
                        epochs=1,
                        verbose=verbose)
```

The following section proposes an improvement over the REINFORCE method.

3. REINFORCE with baseline method

The REINFORCE algorithm can be generalized by subtracting a baseline from the return, $\delta = R_t - B(s_t)$. The baseline function, $B(s_t)$, can be any function as long as it does not depend on a_t. The baseline does not alter the expectation of the performance gradient:

$$\nabla J(\theta) = \mathbb{E}_\pi\big[(R_t - B(s_t))\nabla_\theta \ln \pi\, (a_t|s_t, \theta)\big] = \mathbb{E}_\pi[R_t \nabla_\theta \ln \pi\, (a_t|s_t, \theta)] \quad \text{(Equation 10.3.1)}$$

Equation 10.3.1 implies that $\mathbb{E}_\pi[B(s_t)\nabla_\theta \ln \pi\, (a_t|s_t, \theta)] = 0$ since $B(s_t)$ is not a function of a_t. While the introduction of a baseline does not change the expectation, it reduces the variance of the gradient updates. The reduction in variance generally accelerates learning.

In most cases, we use the value function, $B(s_t) = V(s_t)$, as the baseline. If the return is overestimated, the scaling factor is proportionally reduced by the value function, resulting in a lower variance. The value function is also parameterized, $V(s_t) \to V(s_t, \theta_v)$, and is jointly trained with the policy network. In continuous action spaces, the state value can be a linear function of state features:

$$v_t = V(s_t, \theta_v) = \phi(s_t)^T \theta_v \quad \text{(Equation 10.3.2)}$$

Algorithm 10.3.1 summarizes the REINFORCE with baseline method [1]. This is similar to REINFORCE, except that the return is replaced by δ. The difference is we are now training two neural networks.

Algorithm 10.3.1 REINFORCE with baseline

Require: A differentiable parameterized target policy network, $\pi(a_t|s_t, \theta)$.

Require: A differentiable parameterized value network, $V(s_t, \theta_v)$.

Require: Discount factor, $\gamma \in [0,1]$, learning rate α for the performance gradient, and learning rate for the value gradient, α_v.

Require: θ_0, initial policy network parameters (for example, $\theta_0 \to 0$). θ_{v0}, initial value network parameters (for example, $\theta_{v0} \to 0$).

1. Repeat.
2. Generate an episode $\langle s_0 a_0 r_1 s_1, s_1 a_1 r_2 s_2, \dots, s_{T-1} a_{T-1} r_T s_T \rangle$ by following $\pi(a_t|s_t, \theta)$.
3. **for** steps $t = 0, \dots, T-1$ **do**.

4.   Compute the return, $R_t = \sum_{k=0}^{T} \gamma^k r_{t+k}$.

5.   Subtract the baseline, $\delta = R_t - V(s_t, \theta_v)$.

6.   Compute the discounted value gradient, $\nabla V(\theta_v) = \gamma^t \delta \nabla_{\theta_v} V(s_t, \theta_v)$.

7.   Perform gradient ascent, $\theta_v = \theta_v + \alpha_v \nabla V(\theta_v)$.

8.   Compute the discounted performance gradient,
      $\nabla J(\theta) = \gamma^t \delta \nabla_\theta \ln \pi(a_t|s_t, \theta)$.

9.   Perform gradient ascent, $\theta = \theta + \alpha \nabla J(\theta)$.

As shown in *Figure 10.3.1*, in addition to the policy network, $\pi(\theta)$, the value network, $V(\theta)$, is also trained at the same time. The policy network parameters are updated by the performance gradient, $\nabla J(\theta)$, while the value network parameters are adjusted by the value gradient, $\nabla V(\theta_v)$. Since REINFORCE is a Monte Carlo algorithm, it follows that the value function training is also a Monte Carlo algorithm.

The learning rates are not necessarily the same. Note that the value network is also performing gradient ascent.

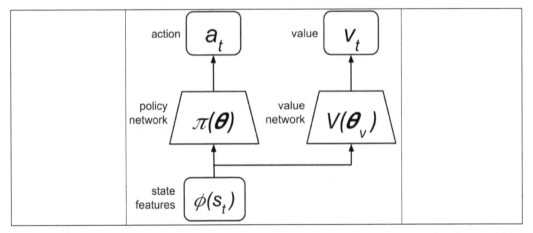

Figure 10.3.1: Policy and value networks. REINFORCE with baseline has a value network that computes the baseline

Listing 10.3.1 shows the `REINFORCEBaselineAgent` class, which implements *Algorithm 10.3.1* in `tf.keras`. It inherits from `REINFORCEAgent` since the two algorithms differ only in the `train()` method. Line 5 of *Algorithm 10.3.1* is computed by `delta = reward - self.value(state)[0]`. Then, the networks for the objective and value functions, `logp_model` and `value_model`, in lines 7 and 9 are optimized by calling the `fit()` method of their respective models.

Listing 10.3.1: `policygradient-car-10.1.1.py`

```python
class REINFORCEBaselineAgent(REINFORCEAgent):
    def __init__(self, env):
        """Implements the models and training of
            REINFORCE w/ baseline policy
            gradient method
        Arguments:
            env (Object): OpenAI gym environment
        """
        super().__init__(env)


    def train(self, item, gamma=1.0):
        """Main routine for training
        Arguments:
            item (list) : one experience unit
            gamma (float) : discount factor [0,1]
        """
        [step, state, next_state, reward, done] = item

        # must save state for entropy computation
        self.state = state

        discount_factor = gamma**step

        # reinforce-baseline: delta = return - value
        delta = reward - self.value(state)[0]

        # apply the discount factor as shown in Algorithms
        # 10.2.1, 10.3.1 and 10.4.1
        discounted_delta = delta * discount_factor
        discounted_delta = np.reshape(discounted_delta, [-1, 1])
        verbose = 1 if done else 0

        # train the logp model (implies training of actor model
        # as well) since they share exactly the same set of
        # parameters
        self.logp_model.fit(np.array(state),
                            discounted_delta,
                            batch_size=1,
                            epochs=1,
                            verbose=verbose)

        # train the value network (critic)
        self.value_model.fit(np.array(state),
                            discounted_delta,
```

```
                    batch_size=1,
                    epochs=1,
                    verbose=verbose)
```

In the next section, we will present an improvement over the REINFORCE with baseline method.

4. Actor-Critic method

In the REINFORCE with baseline method, the value is used as a baseline. It is not used to train the value function. In this section, we introduce a variation of REINFORCE with baseline, called the Actor-Critic method. The policy and value networks play the roles of actor and critic networks. The policy network is the actor deciding which action to take given the state. Meanwhile, the value network evaluates the decision made by the actor or policy network.

The value network acts as a critic that quantifies how good or bad the chosen action undertaken by the actor is. The value network evaluates the state value, $V(s, \theta_v)$, by comparing it with the sum of the reward received, r, and the discounted value of the observed next state, $\gamma V(s', \theta_v)$. The difference, δ, is expressed as:

$$\delta = r_{t+1} + \gamma V(s_{t+1}, \theta_v) - V(s_t, \theta_v) = r + \gamma V(s', \theta_v) - V(s, \theta_v) \quad \text{(Equation 10.4.1)}$$

where we dropped the subscripts of r and s for simplicity. *Equation 10.4.1* is similar to the temporal differencing in Q-learning discussed in *Chapter 9, Deep Reinforcement Learning*. The next state value is discounted by $\gamma \in [0.0, 1.0]$. Estimating distant future rewards is difficult. Therefore, our estimate is based only on the immediate future, $r + \gamma V(s', \theta_v)$. This is known as the *bootstrapping* technique.

The bootstrapping technique and the dependence on state representation in *Equation 10.4.1* often accelerates learning and reduces variance. From *Equation 10.4.1*, we notice that the value network evaluates the current state, $s = s_t$, which is due to the previous action, a_{t-1}, of the policy network. Meanwhile, the policy gradient is based on the current action, a_t. In a sense, the evaluation is delayed by one step.

Algorithm 10.4.1 summarizes the Actor-Critic method [1]. Apart from the evaluation of the state value, which is used to train both the policy and value networks, the training is done online. At every step, both networks are trained. This is unlike REINFORCE and REINFORCE with baseline, where the agent completes an episode before the training is performed. The value network is consulted twice, firstly, during the value estimate of the current state, and secondly, for the value of the next state. Both values are used in the computation of gradients.

Algorithm 10.4.1 Actor-Critic

Require: A differentiable parameterized target policy network, $\pi(a|s,\theta)$.

Require: A differentiable parameterized value network, $V(s,\theta_v)$.

Require: Discount factor, $\gamma \in [0,1]$, learning rate α for the performance gradient, and learning rate for the value gradient, α_v.

Require: θ_0, initial policy network parameters (for example, $\theta_0 \to 0$). θ_{v0}, initial value network parameters (for example, $\theta_{v0} \to 0$).

1. Repeat.
2.   **for** steps $t = 0, \dots, T-1$ **do**.
3.   Sample an action $a \sim \pi(a|s,\theta)$.
4.   Execute the action and observe the reward, r, and the next state, s'.
5.   Evaluate the state value estimate, $\delta = r + \gamma V(s',\theta_v) - V(s,\theta_v)$.
6.   Compute the discounted value gradient, $\nabla V(\theta_v) = \gamma^t \delta \nabla_{\theta_v} V(s,\theta_v)$.
7.   Perform gradient ascent, $\theta_v = \theta_v + \alpha_v \nabla V(\theta_v)$.
8.   Compute the discounted performance gradient, $\nabla J(\theta) = \gamma^t \delta \nabla_\theta \ln \pi (a|s,\theta)$.
9.   Perform gradient ascent, $\theta = \theta + \alpha \nabla J(\theta)$.
10. $s = s'$

Figure 10.4.1 shows the Actor-Critic network:

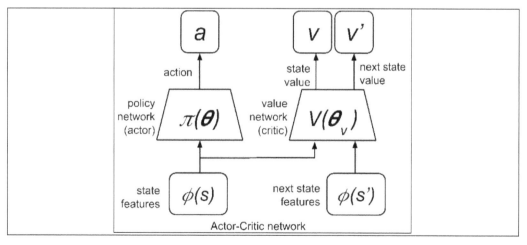

Figure 10.4.1: Actor-Critic network. Actor-Critic differs from REINFORCE with baseline by the second evaluation of value V', which is used to critique the policy

Listing 10.4.1 shows the `ActorCriticAgent` class, which implements *Algorithm 10.4.1* in `tf.keras`. Unlike the two REINFORCE methods, Actor-Critic does not wait for the episode to complete. Therefore, it does not implement `train_by_episode()`. At every experience unit, the networks for the objective and value functions, `logp_model` and `value_model`, in Lines 7 and 9 are optimized by calling the `fit()` method of their respective models. The delta variable stores the result of line 5.

Listing 10.4.1: `policygradient-car-10.1.1.py`

```
class ActorCriticAgent(PolicyAgent):
    def __init__(self, env):
        """Implements the models and training of
           Actor Critic policy gradient method
        Arguments:
            env (Object): OpenAI gym environment
        """
        super().__init__(env)


    def train(self, item, gamma=1.0):
        """Main routine for training
        Arguments:
            item (list) : one experience unit
            gamma (float) : discount factor [0,1]
        """
        [step, state, next_state, reward, done] = item

        # must save state for entropy computation
        self.state = state

        discount_factor = gamma**step

        # actor-critic: delta = reward - value
        #          + discounted_next_value
        delta = reward - self.value(state)[0]

        # since this function is called by Actor-Critic
        # directly, evaluate the value function here
        if not done:
            next_value = self.value(next_state)[0]
            # add  the discounted next value
            delta += gamma*next_value

        # apply the discount factor as shown in Algortihms
```

```
# 10.2.1, 10.3.1 and 10.4.1
discounted_delta = delta * discount_factor
discounted_delta = np.reshape(discounted_delta, [-1, 1])
verbose = 1 if done else 0

# train the logp model (implies training of actor model
# as well) since they share exactly the same set of
# parameters
self.logp_model.fit(np.array(state),
                    discounted_delta,
                    batch_size=1,
                    epochs=1,
                    verbose=verbose)
```

The final policy gradient method is A2C.

5. Advantage Actor-Critic (A2C) method

In the Actor-Critic method from the previous section, the objective is for the value function to evaluate the state value correctly. There are other techniques for training the value network. One obvious method is to use **mean square error** (**MSE**) in the value function optimization, similar to the algorithm in Q-learning. The new value gradient is equal to the partial derivative of the MSE between the return, R_t, and the state value:

$$\nabla V(\theta_v) = \frac{\partial \left(R_t - V(s, \theta_v)\right)^2}{\partial \theta_v} \quad \text{(Equation 10.5.1)}$$

As $\left(R_t - V(s, \theta_v)\right) \to 0$, the value network prediction gets more accurate in predicting the return for a given state. We refer to this variation of the Actor-Critic algorithm as Advantage Actor-Critic (A2C). A2C is a single-threaded or synchronous version of the Asynchronous Advantage Actor-Critic (A3C) by [3]. The quantity $\left(R_t - V(s, \theta_v)\right)$ is called the *Advantage*.

Algorithm 10.5.1 summarizes the A2C method. There are some differences between A2C and Actor-Critic. Actor-Critic is online or is trained on a per-experience sample. A2C is similar to the Monte Carlo algorithms, REINFORCE, and REINFORCE with baseline. It is trained after one episode has been completed. Actor-Critic is trained from the first state to the last state. A2C training starts from the last state and ends on the first state. In addition, the A2C policy and value gradients are no longer discounted by γ^t.

The corresponding network for A2C is similar to *Figure 10.4.1* since we only changed the method of gradient computation. To encourage agent exploration during training, the A3C algorithm [3] suggests that the gradient of the weighted entropy value of the policy function is added to the gradient function, $\beta \nabla_\theta H\big(\pi(a_t|s_t, \theta)\big)$. Recall that entropy is a measure of information or uncertainty of an event.

Algorithm 10.5.1 Advantage Actor-Critic (A2C)

Require: A differentiable parameterized target policy network, $\pi(a_t|s_t, \theta)$.

Require: A differentiable parameterized value network, $V(s_t, \theta_v)$.

Require: Discount factor, $\gamma \in [0,1]$, learning rate α for the performance gradient, learning rate for the value gradient, α_v and entropy weight, β.

Require: θ_0, initial policy network parameters (for example, $\theta_0 \to 0$). θ_{v0}, initial value network parameters (for example, $\theta_{v0} \to 0$).

1. Repeat.

2. Generate an episode $(s_0 a_0 r_1 s_1, s_1 a_1 r_2 s_2, \dots, s_{T-1} a_{T-1} r_T s_T)$ by following $\pi(a_t|s_t, \theta)$.

3. $R_t = \begin{cases} 0 & \text{if } s_T \text{ is terminal} \\ V(s_T, \theta_v) & \text{for non} - \text{terminal}, s_T, \text{bootstrap from last state} \end{cases}$

4. **for** steps $t = T - 1, \dots, 0$ **do**.

5. Compute the return, $R_t = r_t + \gamma R_t$.

6. Compute the value gradient, $\nabla V(\theta_v) = \dfrac{\partial\big(R_t - V(s, \theta_v)\big)^2}{\partial \theta_v}$.

7. Accumulate the gradient, $\theta_v = \theta_v + \alpha_v \nabla V(\theta_v)$.

8. Compute the performance gradient,
$\nabla J(\theta) = \nabla_\theta \ln \pi (a_t|s_t, \theta)\big(R_t - V(s, \theta_v)\big) + \beta \nabla_\theta H\big(\pi(a_t|s_t, \theta)\big).$

9. Perform gradient ascent, $\theta = \theta + \alpha \nabla J(\theta)$.

Listing 10.5.1 shows the A2CAgent class, which implements *Algorithm 10.5.1* in tf.keras. Unlike the two REINFORCE methods, the return is computed from the last experience unit or state to the first. At every experience unit, the networks for the objective and value functions, logp_model and value_model, in Lines 7 and 9 are optimized by calling the fit() method of their respective models. Note that during object instantiation, the beta or weight of the entropy loss is set to 0.9 to indicate that the entropy loss function will be used. Furthermore, value_model is trained using the MSE loss function.

Listing 10.5.1: `policygradient-car-10.1.1.py`

```python
class A2CAgent(PolicyAgent):
    def __init__(self, env):
        """Implements the models and training of
            A2C policy gradient method
        Arguments:
            env (Object): OpenAI gym environment
        """
        super().__init__(env)
        # beta of entropy used in A2C
        self.beta = 0.9
        # loss function of A2C value_model is mse
        self.loss = 'mse'


    def train_by_episode(self, last_value=0):
        """Train by episode
            Prepare the dataset before the step by step training
        Arguments:
            last_value (float): previous prediction of value net
        """
        # implements A2C training from the last state
        # to the first state
        # discount factor
        gamma = 0.95
        r = last_value
        # the memory is visited in reverse as shown
        # in Algorithm 10.5.1
        for item in self.memory[::-1]:
            [step, state, next_state, reward, done] = item
            # compute the return
            r = reward + gamma*r
            item = [step, state, next_state, r, done]
            # train per step
            # a2c reward has been discounted
            self.train(item)


    def train(self, item, gamma=1.0):
        """Main routine for training
        Arguments:
            item (list) : one experience unit
            gamma (float) : discount factor [0,1]
        """
        [step, state, next_state, reward, done] = item
```

```
# must save state for entropy computation
self.state = state

discount_factor = gamma**step

# a2c: delta = discounted_reward - value
delta = reward - self.value(state)[0]

verbose = 1 if done else 0

# train the logp model (implies training of actor model
# as well) since they share exactly the same set of
# parameters
self.logp_model.fit(np.array(state),
                    discounted_delta,
                    batch_size=1,
                    epochs=1,
                    verbose=verbose)

# in A2C, the target value is the return (reward
# replaced by return in the train_by_episode function)
discounted_delta = reward
discounted_delta = np.reshape(discounted_delta, [-1, 1])

# train the value network (critic)
self.value_model.fit(np.array(state),
                     discounted_delta,
                     batch_size=1,
                     epochs=1,
                     verbose=verbose)
```

In the four algorithms presented, they differ only in the objective function and value (if applicable) optimization. In the next section, we will present the unified code for the four algorithms.

6. Policy Gradient methods using Keras

The four policy gradient methods (*Algorithm 10.2.1* to *Algorithm 10.5.1*) discussed in the previous sections use identical policy and value network models. The policy and value networks in *Figure 10.2.1* to *Figure 10.4.1* have the same configurations. The four policy gradient methods differ only in:

- Performance and value gradient formulas
- Training strategy

In this section, we will discuss the implementation in `tf.keras` of the common routines of *Algorithm 10.2.1* to *Algorithm 10.5.1* in one code.

The complete code can be found at `https://github.com/PacktPublishing/Advanced-Deep-Learning-with-Keras`.

But before discussing the implementation, let's briefly explore the training environment.

Unlike Q-learning, policy gradient methods are applicable to both discrete and continuous action spaces. In our example, we'll demonstrate the four policy gradient methods on a continuous action space case example, `MountainCarContinuous-v0` of OpenAI gym, `https://gym.openai.com`. In case you are not familiar with OpenAI Gym, please refer to *Chapter 9, Deep Reinforcement Learning*.

A snapshot of the `MountainCarContinuous-v0` two-dimensional environment is shown in *Figure 10.6.1* In this two-dimensional environment, a car with a not too powerful engine is between two mountains:

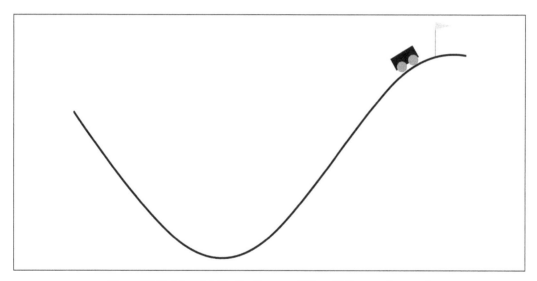

Figure 10.6.1: MountainCarContinuous-v0 OpenAI Gym environment

In order to reach the yellow flag on top of the mountain on the right, it must drive back and forth to gain enough momentum. The more energy (that is, the greater the absolute value of action) that is applied to the car, the smaller (or, the more negative) is the reward.

The reward is always negative, and it is only positive upon reaching the flag. In that case, the car receives a reward of +100. However, every action is penalized by the following code:

```
reward-= math.pow(action[0],2)*0.1
```

The continuous range of valid action values is [-1.0, 1.0]. Beyond the range, the action is clipped to its minimum or maximum value. Therefore, it makes no sense to apply an action value that is greater than 1.0 or less than -1.0.

The `MountainCarContinuous-v0` environment state has two elements:

- Car position
- Car velocity

The state is converted to state features by an encoder. Like action space, the state space is also continuous. The predicted action is the output of the policy model given the state. The output of the value function is the predicted value of the state.

As shown in *Figure 10.2.1* to *Figure 10.4.1*, before building the policy and value networks, we must first create a function that converts the state to features. This function is implemented by an encoder of an autoencoder similar to the ones implemented in *Chapter 3, Autoencoders*.

Figure 10.6.2 shows an autoencoder comprising an encoder and a decoder:

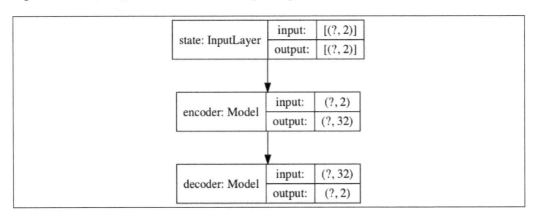

Figure 10.6.2: Autoencoder model

In *Figure 10.6.3*, the encoder is an MLP made of `Input(2)-Dense(256, activation='relu')-Dense(128, activation='relu')-Dense(32)`. Every state is converted into a 32-dim feature vector:

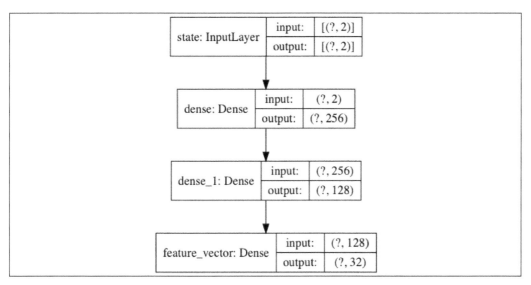

Figure 10.6.3: Encoder model

In *Figure 10.6.4*, the decoder is also an MLP but made of `Input(32)-Dense(128, activation='relu')-Dense(256, activation='relu')-Dense(2)`:

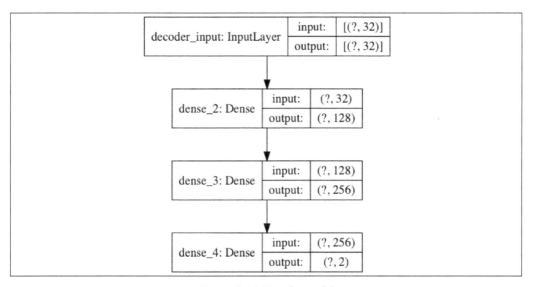

Figure 10.6.4: Decoder model

The autoencoder is trained for 10 epochs with an MSE, loss function, and `tf.keras` default Adam optimizer. We sampled 220,000 random states for the training and test dataset and applied a 200,000/20,000 train-test split. After training, the encoder weights are saved for future use in the policy and value networks' training. *Listing 10.6.1* shows the methods for building and training the autoencoder.

In the `tf.keras` implementation, all the routines that we will mention in this section are implemented as methods in the `PolicyAgent` class unless otherwise noted. The role of `PolicyAgent` is to represent policy gradient methods' common functionalities, including building and training the autoencoder network model and predicting the action, log probability, entropy, and state value. This is the super class of each policy gradient method agent class presented in *Listing 10.2.1* to *Listing 10.5.1*.

Listing 10.6.1: `policygradient-car-10.1.1.py`

Methods for building and training the feature autoencoder:

```
class PolicyAgent:
    def __init__(self, env):
        """Implements the models and training of
            Policy Gradient Methods
        Argument:
            env (Object): OpenAI gym environment
        """

        self.env = env
        # entropy loss weight
        self.beta = 0.0
        # value loss for all policy gradients except A2C
        self.loss = self.value_loss

        # s,a,r,s' are stored in memory
        self.memory = []

        # for computation of input size
        self.state = env.reset()
        self.state_dim = env.observation_space.shape[0]
        self.state = np.reshape(self.state, [1, self.state_dim])
        self.build_autoencoder()


    def build_autoencoder(self):
        """autoencoder to convert states into features
```

```
"""
# first build the encoder model
inputs = Input(shape=(self.state_dim, ), name='state')
feature_size = 32
x = Dense(256, activation='relu')(inputs)
x = Dense(128, activation='relu')(x)
feature = Dense(feature_size, name='feature_vector')(x)

# instantiate encoder model
self.encoder = Model(inputs, feature, name='encoder')
self.encoder.summary()
plot_model(self.encoder,
           to_file='encoder.png',
           show_shapes=True)

# build the decoder model
feature_inputs = Input(shape=(feature_size,),
                       name='decoder_input')
x = Dense(128, activation='relu')(feature_inputs)
x = Dense(256, activation='relu')(x)
outputs = Dense(self.state_dim, activation='linear')(x)

# instantiate decoder model
self.decoder = Model(feature_inputs,
                     outputs,
                     name='decoder')
self.decoder.summary()
plot_model(self.decoder,
           to_file='decoder.png',
           show_shapes=True)

# autoencoder = encoder + decoder
# instantiate autoencoder model
self.autoencoder = Model(inputs,
                         self.decoder(self.encoder(inputs)),
                         name='autoencoder')
self.autoencoder.summary()
plot_model(self.autoencoder,
           to_file='autoencoder.png',
           show_shapes=True)

# Mean Square Error (MSE) loss function, Adam optimizer
self.autoencoder.compile(loss='mse', optimizer='adam')
```

```
def train_autoencoder(self, x_train, x_test):
    """Training the autoencoder using randomly sampled
        states from the environment
    Arguments:
        x_train (tensor): autoencoder train dataset
        x_test (tensor): autoencoder test dataset
    """
    # train the autoencoder
    batch_size = 32
    self.autoencoder.fit(x_train,
                         x_train,
                         validation_data=(x_test, x_test),
                         epochs=10,
                         batch_size=batch_size)
```

Given the `MountainCarContinuous-v0` environment, the policy (or actor) model predicts the action that must be applied to the car. As discussed in the first section of this chapter on policy gradient methods, for continuous action spaces, the policy model samples an action from a Gaussian distribution, $\pi(a_t|s_t, \theta) = a_t \sim \mathcal{N}(\mu(s_t), \sigma^2(s_t))$. In `tf.keras`, this is implemented as:

```
import tensorflow_probability as tfp
    def action(self, args):
        """Given mean and stddev, sample an action, clip
            and return
            We assume Gaussian distribution of probability
            of selecting an action given a state
        Arguments:
            args (list) : mean, stddev list
        """
        mean, stddev = args
        dist = tfp.distributions.Normal(loc=mean, scale=stddev)
        action = dist.sample(1)
        action = K.clip(action,
                        self.env.action_space.low[0],
                        self.env.action_space.high[0])
        return action
```

The action is clipped between its minimum and maximum possible values. In this method, we use the `TensorFlow probability` package. It can be installed separately by:

```
pip3 install --upgrade tensorflow-probability
```

The role of the policy network is to predict the mean and standard deviation of the Gaussian distribution. *Figure 10.6.5* shows the policy network to model $\pi(a_t|s_t, \theta)$.

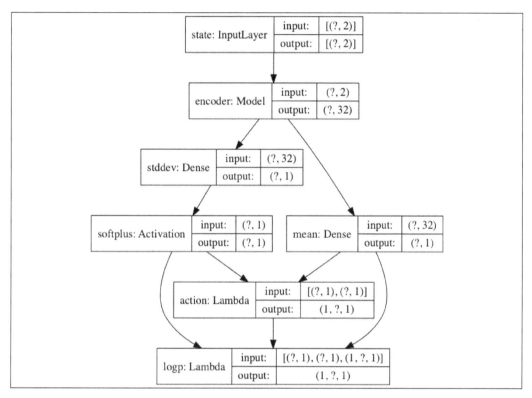

Figure 10.6.5: Policy model (actor model)

Note that the encoder model has pretrained weights that are frozen. Only the mean and standard deviation weights receive the performance gradient updates. The policy network is basically the implementation of *Equation 10.1.4* and *Equation 10.1.5*, which are repeated here for convenience:

$$\mu(s_t) = \phi(s_t)^T \theta_\mu \quad \text{(Equation 10.1.4)}$$

$$\sigma(s_t) = \zeta(\phi(s_t)^T \theta_\sigma) \quad \text{(Equation 10.1.5)}$$

where $\phi(s_t)$ is the encoder, θ_μ are the weights of the mean's Dense(1) layer, and θ_σ are the weights of the standard deviation's Dense(1) layer. We used a modified softplus function, $\zeta(\cdot)$, to avoid zero standard deviation:

```
def softplusk(x):
    """Some implementations use a modified softplus
        to ensure that the stddev is never zero
    Argument:
        x (tensor): activation input
    """
    return K.softplus(x) + 1e-10
```

The policy model builder is shown in *Listing 10.6.2*. Also included in this listing are the log probability, entropy, and value models, which we will discuss next.

Listing 10.6.2: `policygradient-car-10.1.1.py`

Method for building the policy (actor), logp, entropy, and value models from the encoded state features:

```
def build_actor_critic(self):
    """4 models are built but 3 models share the
        same parameters. hence training one, trains the rest.
        The 3 models that share the same parameters
            are action, logp, and entropy models.
        Entropy model is used by A2C only.
        Each model has the same MLP structure:
        Input(2)-Encoder-Output(1).
        The output activation depends on the nature
            of the output.
    """
    inputs = Input(shape=(self.state_dim, ), name='state')
    self.encoder.trainable = False
    x = self.encoder(inputs)
    mean = Dense(1,
                activation='linear',
                kernel_initializer='zero',
                name='mean')(x)
    stddev = Dense(1,
                kernel_initializer='zero',
                name='stddev')(x)
    # use of softplusk avoids stddev = 0
    stddev = Activation('softplusk', name='softplus')(stddev)
    action = Lambda(self.action,
                output_shape=(1,),
```

```
                           name='action')([mean, stddev])
self.actor_model = Model(inputs, action, name='action')
self.actor_model.summary()
plot_model(self.actor_model,
           to_file='actor_model.png',
           show_shapes=True)


logp = Lambda(self.logp,
              output_shape=(1,),
              name='logp')([mean, stddev, action])
self.logp_model = Model(inputs, logp, name='logp')
self.logp_model.summary()
plot_model(self.logp_model,
           to_file='logp_model.png',
           show_shapes=True)


entropy = Lambda(self.entropy,
                 output_shape=(1,),
                 name='entropy')([mean, stddev])
self.entropy_model = Model(inputs, entropy, name='entropy')
self.entropy_model.summary()
plot_model(self.entropy_model,
           to_file='entropy_model.png',
           show_shapes=True)


value = Dense(1,
              activation='linear',
              kernel_initializer='zero',
              name='value')(x)
self.value_model = Model(inputs, value, name='value')
self.value_model.summary()
plot_model(self.value_model,
           to_file='value_model.png',
           show_shapes=True)



# logp loss of policy network
loss = self.logp_loss(self.get_entropy(self.state),
                      beta=self.beta)
optimizer = RMSprop(lr=1e-3)
self.logp_model.compile(loss=loss, optimizer=optimizer)


optimizer = Adam(lr=1e-3)
self.value_model.compile(loss=self.loss, optimizer=optimizer)
```

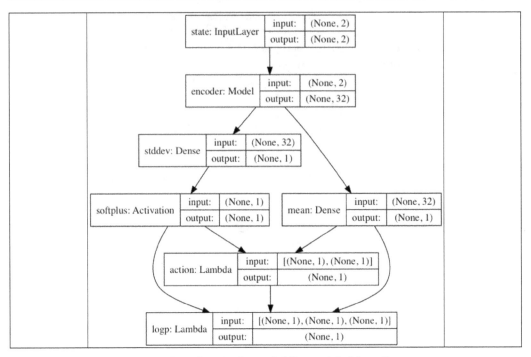

Figure 10.6.6: Gaussian log probability model of the policy

Apart from the policy network, $\pi(a_t|s_t,\theta)$, we must also have the action log probability (`logp`) network $ln\,\pi\,(a_t|s_t,\theta)$, since this is actually the one that calculates the gradient. As shown in *Figure 10.6.6*, the `logp` network is simply the policy network where an additional Lambda(1) layer computes the log probability of the Gaussian distribution given the action, mean, and standard deviation.

The `logp` network and actor (policy) model share the same set of parameters. The Lambda layer does not have any parameters. It is implemented by the following function:

```
def logp(self, args):
    """Given mean, stddev, and action compute
        the log probability of the Gaussian distribution
    Arguments:
        args (list) : mean, stddev action, list
    """
    mean, stddev, action = args
    dist = tfp.distributions.Normal(loc=mean, scale=stddev)
    logp = dist.log_prob(action)
    return logp
```

Training the `logp` network trains the actor model as well. In the training methods that are discussed in this section, only the `logp` network is trained.

As shown in *Figure 10.6.7*, the entropy model also shares parameters with the policy network:

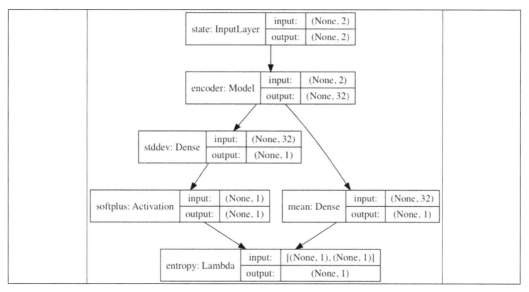

Figure 10.6.7: Entropy model

The output `Lambda(1)` layer computes the entropy of the Gaussian distribution given the mean and standard deviation using the following function:

```
def entropy(self, args):
    """Given the mean and stddev compute
        the Gaussian dist entropy
    Arguments:
        args (list) : mean, stddev list
    """
    mean, stddev = args
    dist = tfp.distributions.Normal(loc=mean, scale=stddev)
    entropy = dist.entropy()
    return entropy
```

The entropy model is only used by the A2C method.

Figure 10.6.8 shows the value model:

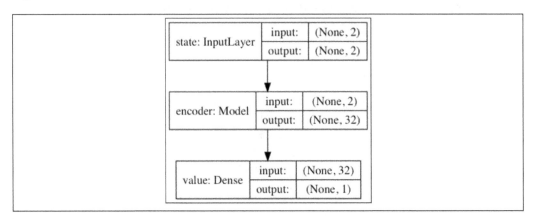

Figure 10.6.8: A value model

The model also uses the pretrained encoder with frozen weights to implement the following equation, *Equation 10.3.2*, which is repeated here for convenience:

$$v_t = V(s_t, \theta_v) = \phi(s_t)^T \theta_v \quad \text{(Equation 10.3.2)}$$

θ_v are the weights of the Dense(1) layer, the only layer that receives value gradient updates. *Figure 10.6.8* represents $V(s_t, \theta_v)$ in *Algorithm 10.3.1* to *Algorithm 10.5.1*. The value model can be built in a few lines:

```
inputs = Input(shape=(self.state_dim, ), name='state')
self.encoder.trainable = False
x = self.encoder(inputs)

value = Dense(1,
              activation='linear',
              kernel_initializer='zero',
              name='value')(x)
self.value_model = Model(inputs, value, name='value')
```

These lines are also implemented in the build_actor_critic() method, which is shown in *Listing 10.6.2*.

After building the network models, the next step is training. In *Algorithm 10.2.1* to *Algorithm 10.5.1*, we perform objective function maximization by gradient ascent. In tf.keras, we perform loss function minimization by gradient descent. The loss function is simply the negative of the objective function being maximized. The gradient descent is the negative of gradient ascent. *Listing 10.6.3* shows the logp and value loss functions.

We can take advantage of the common structure of the loss functions to unify the loss functions in *Algorithm 10.2.1* to *Algorithm 10.5.1*. The performance and value gradients differ only in their constant factors. All performance gradients have the common term, $\nabla_\theta \ln \pi (a_t|s_t, \theta)$. This is represented by y_pred in the policy log probability loss function, logp_loss(). The factor to the common term, $\nabla_\theta \ln \pi (a_t|s_t, \theta)$, depends on which algorithm and is implemented as y_true. *Table 10.6.1* shows the values of y_true. The remaining term is the weighted gradient of entropy, $\beta \nabla_\theta H\big(\pi(a_t|s_t, \theta)\big)$. This is implemented as the product of beta and entropy in the logp_loss() function. Only A2C uses this term, so, by default, self.beta=0.0. For A2C, self.beta=0.9.

Listing 10.6.3: policygradient-car-10.1.1.py

Loss functions of the logp and value networks:

```
def logp_loss(self, entropy, beta=0.0):
    """logp loss, the 3rd and 4th variables
        (entropy and beta) are needed by A2C
        so we have a different loss function structure
    Arguments:
        entropy (tensor): Entropy loss
        beta (float): Entropy loss weight
    """
    def loss(y_true, y_pred):
        return -K.mean((y_pred * y_true) \
                + (beta * entropy), axis=-1)

    return loss


def value_loss(self, y_true, y_pred):
    """Typical loss function structure that accepts
        2 arguments only
        this will be used by value loss of all methods
        except A2C
    Arguments:
        y_true (tensor): value ground truth
        y_pred (tensor): value prediction
    """
    return -K.mean(y_pred * y_true, axis=-1)
```

Algorithm	y_true of logp_loss	y_true of value_loss
10.2.1 REINFORCE	$\gamma^t R_t$	Not applicable
10.3.1 REINFORCE with baseline	$\gamma^t \delta$	$\gamma^t \delta$
10.4.1 Actor-Critic	$\gamma^t \delta$	$\gamma^t \delta$
10.5.1 A2C	$\left(R_t - V(s, \boldsymbol{\theta}_v)\right)$	R_t

Table 10.6.1: y_true value of `logp_loss` and value_loss

The code implementation for computing `y_true` in *Table 10.6.1* is shown in *Table 10.6.2*:

Algorithm	y_true formula	y_true in Keras
10.2.1 REINFORCE	$\gamma^t R_t$	`reward * discount_factor`
10.3.1 REINFORCE with baseline	$\gamma^t \delta$	`(reward - self.value(state)[0])* discount_factor`
10.4.1 Actor-Critic	$\gamma^t \delta$	`(reward - self.value(state)[0]` `+gamma*next_value)*discount_` `factor`
10.5.1 A2C	$\left(R_t - V(s, \theta_v)\right)$ and R_t	`(reward - self.value(state)[0])` and `reward`

Table 10.6.2: y_true value in Table 10.6.1

Similarly, the value loss functions of *Algorithm 10.3.1* and *Algorithm 10.4.1* have the same structure. The value loss functions are implemented in `tf.keras` as `value_loss()`, as shown in *Listing 10.6.3*. The common gradient factor $\nabla_{\theta_v} V(s_t, \theta_v)$ is represented by the tensor, `y_pred`. The remaining factor is represented by `y_true`. The `y_true` values are also shown in *Table 10.6.1*. REINFORCE does not use a value function. A2C uses the MSE loss function to learn the value function. In A2C, `y_true` represents the target value or ground truth.

With all the network models and loss functions in place, the last part is the training strategy, which is different for each algorithm. The training algorithm per policy gradient method has been discussed in *Listing 10.2.1* to *Listing 10.5.1*. *Algorithm 10.2.1*, *Algorithm 10.3.1*, and *Algorithm 10.5.1* wait for a complete episode to finish before training, so it runs both `train_by_episode()` and `train()`. The complete episode is saved in `self.memory`. Actor-Critic *Algorithm 10.4.1* trains per step and only runs `train()`.

Listing 10.6.4 shows how one episode unfolds when the agent executes and trains the policy and value models. The `for` loop is executed for 1,000 episodes. An episode terminates upon reaching 1,000 steps or when the car touches the flag. The agent executes the action predicted by the policy at every step. After each episode or step, the training routine is called.

Listing 10.6.4: `policygradient-car-10.1.1.py`

```
# sampling and fitting
for episode in range(episode_count):
    state = env.reset()
    # state is car [position, speed]
    state = np.reshape(state, [1, state_dim])
    # reset all variables and memory before the start of
    # every episode
    step = 0
    total_reward = 0
    done = False
    agent.reset_memory()
    while not done:
        # [min, max] action = [-1.0, 1.0]
        # for baseline, random choice of action will not move
        # the car pass the flag pole
        if args.random:
            action = env.action_space.sample()
        else:
            action = agent.act(state)
        env.render()
        # after executing the action, get s', r, done
        next_state, reward, done, _ = env.step(action)
        next_state = np.reshape(next_state, [1, state_dim])
        # save the experience unit in memory for training
        # Actor-Critic does not need this but we keep it anyway.
        item = [step, state, next_state, reward, done]
        agent.remember(item)

        if args.actor_critic and train:
            # only actor-critic performs online training
            # train at every step as it happens
            agent.train(item, gamma=0.99)
        elif not args.random and done and train:
            # for REINFORCE, REINFORCE with baseline, and A2C
            # we wait for the completion of the episode before
            # training the network(s)
```

```
                          # last value as used by A2C
                          if args.a2c:
                              v = 0 if reward > 0 else agent.value(next_state)
[0]
                              agent.train_by_episode(last_value=v)
                          else:
                              agent.train_by_episode()


                      # accumulate reward
                      total_reward += reward
                      # next state is the new state
                      state = next_state
                      step += 1
```

During training, we collected data to determine the performance of each policy gradient algorithm. In the next section, we summarize the results.

7. Performance evaluation of policy gradient methods

The 4 policy gradients methods were evaluated by training the agent for 1,000 episodes. We define 1 training session as 1,000 episodes of training. The first performance metric is measured by accumulating the number of times the car reached the flag in 1,000 episodes.

In this metric, A2C reached the flag the greatest number of times, followed by REINFORCE with baseline, Actor-Critic, and REINFORCE. The use of baseline or critic accelerates the learning. Note that these are training sessions, where the agent is continuously improving its performance. There were cases in the experiments where the agent's performance did not improve with time.

The second performance metric is based on the requirement that MountainCarContinuous-v0 is considered solved if the total reward per episode is at least 90.0. From the 5 training sessions per method, we selected 1 training session with the highest total reward for the last 100 episodes (episodes 900 to 999).

Figure 10.7.1 to *Figure 10.7.4* show the number of times the mountain car reached the flag during the execution of 1,000 episodes.

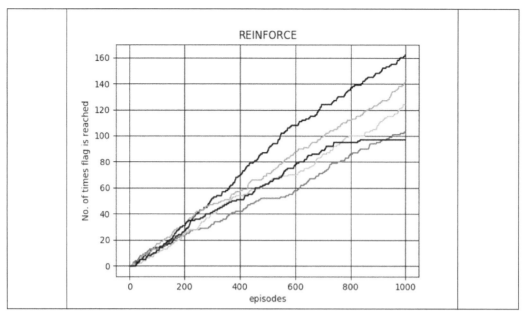

Figure 10.7.1: The number of times the mountain car reached the flag using the REINFORCE method

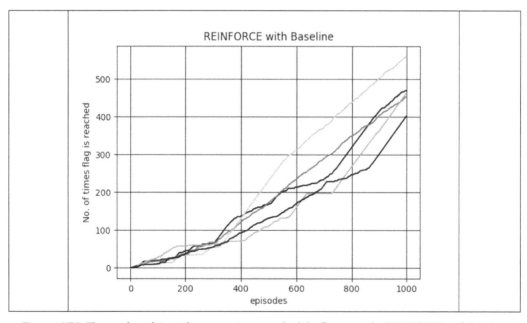

Figure 10.7.2: The number of times the mountain car reached the flag using the REINFORCE with baseline method

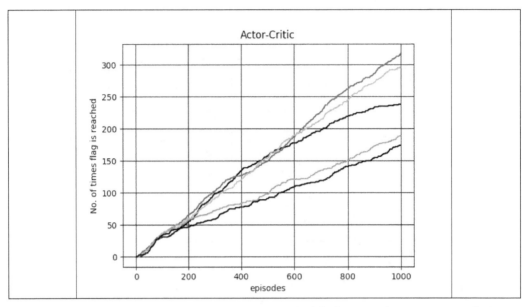

Figure 10.7.3: The number of times the mountain car reached the flag using the Actor-Critic method

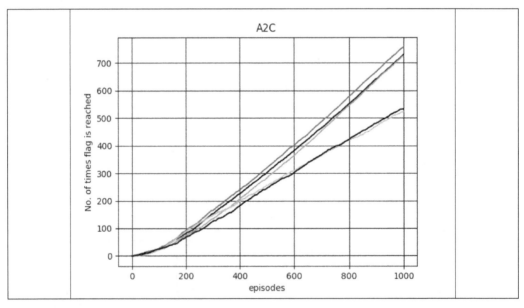

Figure 10.7.4: The number of times the mountain car reached the flag using the A2C method

Figure 10.7.5 to *Figure 10.7.8* show the total rewards for 1,000 episodes.

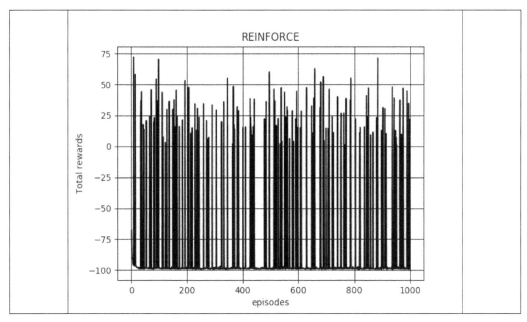

Figure 10.7.5: Total rewards received per episode using the REINFORCE method

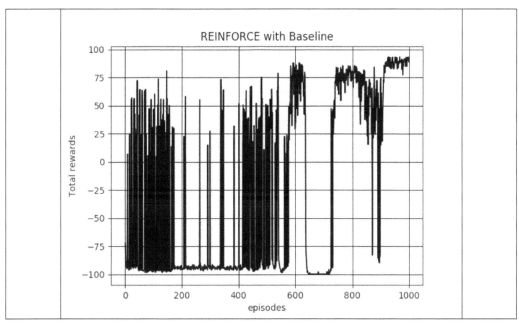

Figure 10.7.6: Total rewards received per episode using the REINFORCE with baseline method.

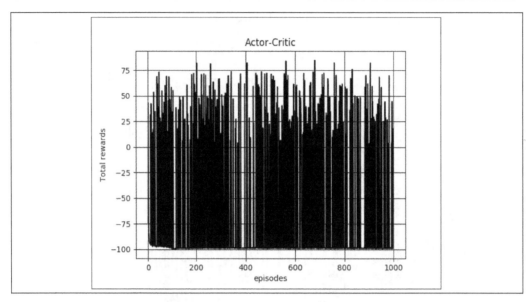

Figure 10.7.7: Total rewards received per episode using the Actor-Critic method

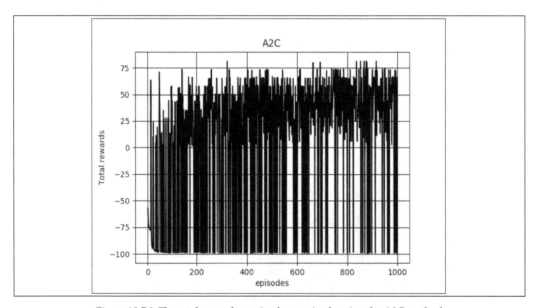

Figure 10.7.8: The total rewards received per episode using the A2C method

REINFORCE with baseline is the only method that was able to consistently achieve a total reward of about 90 within 1,000 episodes of training. A2C has the second-best performance, but could not consistently reach at least 90 for the total rewards.

In the experiments conducted, we used the same learning rate, 1e-3, for log probability and value network optimization. The discount factor is set to 0.99, except for A2C, which is easier to train at a discount factor of 0.95.

The reader is encouraged to run the trained network by executing:

```
python3 policygradient-car-10.1.1.py
--encoder_weights=encoder_weights.h5 --actor_weights=actor_weights.h5
```

Table 10.7.1 shows other modes of running `policygradient-car-10.1.1.py`. The weights file (that is, `*.h5`) can be replaced by your own pretrained weights file. Please consult the code to see the other potential options.

Purpose	Run
Train REINFORCE from scratch	`python3 policygradient-car-10.1.1.py`
Train REINFORCE with baseline from scratch	`python3 policygradient-car-10.1.1.py -b`
Train Actor-Critic from scratch	`python3 policygradient-car-10.1.1.py -a`
Train A2C from scratch	`python3 policygradient-car-10.1.1.py -c`

Train REINFORCE from previously saved weights	`python3 policygradient-car-10.1.1.py`
	`--encoder-weights=encoder_weights.h5`
	`--actor-weights=actor_weights.h5 --train`

Train REINFORCE with baseline from previously saved weights	`python3 policygradient-car-10.1.1.py`
	`--encoder-weights=encoder_weights.h5`
	`--actor-weights=actor_weights.h5`
	`--value-weights=value_weights.h5 -b --train`

Train Actor-Critic from previously saved weights	`python3 policygradient-car-10.1.1.py`
	`--encoder-weights=encoder_weights.h5`
	`--actor-weights=actor_weights.h5`
	`--value-weights=value_weights.h5 -a --train`

Train A2C from previously saved weights	`python3 policygradient-car-10.1.1.py`
	`--encoder-weights=encoder_weights.h5`
	`--actor-weights=actor_weights.h5`
	`--value-weights=value_weights.h5 -c --train`

Table 10.7.1: Different options in running policygradient-car-10.1.1.py

As a final note, our implementation of the policy gradient methods in `tf.keras` has some limitations. For example, training the actor model requires the action to be resampled. The action is first sampled and applied to the environment to observe the reward and next state. Then, another sample is taken to train the log probability model. The second sample is not necessarily the same as the first one, but the reward that is used for training comes from the first sampled action, which can introduce stochastic error in the computation of gradients.

8. Conclusion

In this chapter, we've covered the policy gradient methods. Starting with the policy gradient theorem, we formulated four methods to train the policy network. The four methods, REINFORCE, REINFORCE with baseline, Actor-Critic, and A2C algorithms, were discussed in detail. We explored how the four methods could be implemented in Keras. We then validated the algorithms by examining the number of times the agent successfully reached its goal and in terms of the total rewards received per episode.

Similar to the deep Q-network [2] that we discussed in the previous chapter, there are several improvements that can be done on the fundamental policy gradient algorithms. For example, the most prominent one is the A3C [3], which is a multithreaded version of A2C. This enables the agent to get exposed to different experiences simultaneously and to optimize the policy and value networks asynchronously. However, in the experiments conducted by OpenAI, `https://blog.openai.com/baselines-acktr-a2c/`, there is no strong advantage of A3C over A2C since the former could not take advantage of the strong GPUs available nowadays.

In the next two chapters, we will embark on a different area – object detection and semantic segmentation. Object detection enables an agent to identify and localize objects in a given image. Semantic segmentation identifies pixel regions in a given image based on object category.

9. References

1. Richard Sutton and Andrew Barto: *Reinforcement Learning: An Introduction*: `http://incompleteideas.net/book/bookdraft2017nov5.pdf` (2017)

2. Volodymyr Mnih et al.: *Human-level control through deep reinforcement learning*, Nature 518.7540 (2015): 529

3. Volodymyr Mnih et al.: *Asynchronous Methods for Deep Reinforcement Learning*, International conference on machine learning, 2016

4. Ronald Williams: *Simple statistical gradient-following algorithms for connectionist reinforcement learning*, Machine learning 8.3-4 (1992): 229-256

11
Object Detection

Object detection is one of the most important applications of computer vision. Object detection is the task of simultaneous localization and identification of an object that is present in an image. For autonomous vehicles to safely navigate the streets, the algorithm must detect the presence of pedestrians, roads, vehicles, traffic lights, signs, and unexpected obstacles. In security, the presence of an intruder can be used to trigger an alarm or inform the appropriate authorities.

Though important, object detection has been a long-standing problem in computer vision. Many algorithms have been proposed but are generally slow, with low precision and recall. Similar to what AlexNet [1] has achieved in the ImageNet large-scale image classification problem, deep learning has significantly advanced the area of object detection. State-of-the-art object detection methods can now run in real time and have a much higher precision and recall.

In this chapter, we focus on real-time object detection. In particular, we discuss the concept and implementation of **single-shot detection (SSD)**[2] in `tf.keras`. Compared to other deep learning detection algorithms, SSD achieves real-time detection speed on modern GPUs without significant degradation in performance. SSD is also easy to train end-to-end.

In summary, the goal of this chapter is to present:

- The concept of object detection
- The concept of multi-scale object detection

- SSD as a multi-scale object detection algorithm

- The implementation of SSD in `tf.keras`

We'll begin by introducing the concept of object detection.

1. Object detection

In object detection, the objective is to localize and identify an object in an image. *Figure 11.1.1* shows object detection where the target is a **Soda can**. Localization means that the bounding box of the object must be estimated. Using upper left corner pixel and lower right corner pixel coordinates is a common convention that is used to describe a bounding box. In *Figure 11.1.1*, the upper left corner pixel has coordinates. (x_{min}, y_{min}), while the lower right corner pixel has coordinates (x_{max}, y_{max}). The pixel coordinate system has the origin (0,0) at the upper left corner pixel of the entire image.

While performing localization, detection must also identify the object. Identification is the classic recognition or classification task in computer vision. At the minimum, object detection must identify if a bounding box belongs to a known object or to the background. An object detection network can be trained to detect one specific object only, like the **Soda can** in *Figure 11.1.1*. Everything else is considered background, and there is no need to show its bounding box. Multiple instances of the same object such as two or more **Soda cans** can also be detected by the same network, as shown in *Figure 11.1.2*.

Figure 11.1.1 Object detection is illustrated as the process of localizing and identifying an object in an image.

Figure 11.1.2 Multiple instances of the same object be detected by the same
network trained to detect one object instance.

If multiple objects in the scene are present, such as in *Figure 11.1.3*, the object
detection method can only identify one object it was trained on. The other two
objects will be classified as background and no bounding box will be assigned.

Figure 11.1.3 If the object detection is trained on detecting Soda cans only,
it will ignore the other two objects in the image.

However, if the network is retrained to detect the three objects: 1) **Soda can**, 2) **Juice can**, and 3) **Bottled water**, each will be localized and recognized simultaneously, as shown in *Figure 11.1.4*.

Figure 11.1.4 The object detection network can be retrained to detect all three objects even if the background is cluttered or the illumination is changed.

A good object detector must be robust in real-world environments. *Figure 11.1.4* shows a good object detection network can localize and identify known objects even if the background is cluttered or even in low-light conditions. Other factors that an object detector must be robust against are object transformation (rotation and/or translation), surface reflection, texture variation, and noise.

In summary, the objective of object detection is to simultaneously predict the following for each **recognizable** object in the image:

- y_{cls} or the category or class in the form of a one-hot vector
- $y_{box} = ((x_{min}, y_{min}), (x_{max}, y_{max}))$ or the bounding box coordinates in the form of pixel coordinates

With the basic concepts of object detection explained, we can begin to discuss some of the specific mechanics of object detection. We'll begin by introducing anchor boxes.

2. Anchor boxes

From the discussion in the previous section, we learned that object detection must predict both the bounding box region and the category of the object inside it. Suppose for the meantime our focus is on bounding box coordinates estimation.

How can a network predict the coordinates (x_{min}, y_{min}) and (x_{max}, y_{max})? A network can make an initial guess such as $(0,0)$ and (w, h) corresponding to the upper left corner pixel coordinates and the lower right corner pixel coordinates of the image. w is the image width, while h is the image height. Then, the network iteratively corrects the estimates by performing regression on the ground truth bounding box coordinates.

Estimating bounding box coordinates using raw pixels is not optimal due to high variance of possible pixel values. Instead of raw pixels, SSD minimizes pixel error values between the ground truth bounding box and predicted bounding box coordinates. For this example, the pixel error values are (x_{min}, y_{min}) and $(x_{max} - w, y_{max} - h)$. These values are called offsets.

To help the network figure out the correct bounding box coordinates, the image is divided into regions. Each region is called an **anchor box**. Then, the network estimates the **offsets** with respect to each anchor box. This results in a prediction that is closer to the ground truth.

For example, as shown in *Figure 11.2.1*, a common image size of 640 x 480 is divided into 2 x 1 regions resulting to two anchor boxes. Unlike the size of 2 x 2, a 2 x 1 division creates approximately square anchor boxes. In the first anchor box, the new offsets are (x_{min}, y_{min}) and $\left(x_{max} - {}^{w}/_{2}, y_{max} - h\right)$, which are smaller compared to the pixel error values with no anchor boxes. The offsets for the second anchor box are also smaller.

In *Figure 11.2.2*, the image is further divided. This time, the anchor boxes are 3 x 2. The second anchor box offsets are $\left(x_{min} - {}^{w}/_{3}, y_{min}\right)$ and $\left(x_{max} - {}^{2w}/_{3}, y_{max} - {}^{h}/_{2}\right)$, the smallest so far. However, if the image is further divided into 5 x 4, the offsets start to increase again. The main idea is that during the process of creating regions of various dimensions, an optimal anchor box size that is nearest to the ground truth bounding box will emerge. The use of multi-scale anchor boxes to effectively detect objects of different sizes underpins the concept of **multi-scale object detection** algorithms.

Finding an optimal anchor box is not zero cost. In particular, there are extraneous anchor boxes with offsets that are worse than using the entire image. In such cases, SSD proposes that these anchor boxes should not contribute to the overall optimization process and must be suppressed. In the following sections, the algorithm for excluding non-optimal anchor boxes will be discussed with more details.

So far, we already have three sets of anchor boxes.

The first one creates a 2 x 1 grid of anchor boxes each with dimensions $\left(^W/_2, h\right)$.

The second one creates a 3 x 2 grid of anchor boxes each with dimensions $\left(^W/_3, ^h/_2\right)$.

The third one creates a 5 x 4 grid of anchor boxes each with dimensions $\left(^W/_5, ^h/_4\right)$.

How many more sets anchor boxes do we need? It depends on the dimensions of the image and the dimensions of the smallest bounding box of the object. For the 640 x 480 image used in this example, other anchor boxes are:

10 x 8 grid of anchor boxes each with dimensions $\left(^W/_{10}, ^h/_8\right)$

20 x 15 grid of anchor boxes each with dimensions $\left(^W/_{20}, ^h/_{15}\right)$

40 x 30 grid of anchor boxes each with dimensions $\left(^W/_{40}, ^h/_{30}\right)$

For the 640 x 480 image with 40 x 30 grid of anchor boxes, the smallest anchor box covers a 16 x 16 pixels patch of the input image, also known as the **receptive field**. So far, the total number of bounding boxes is 1608. From the smallest, the **scaling factor** for all sizes can be summarized as:

$$s = \left[\left(\frac{1}{2}, 1\right), \left(\frac{1}{3}, \frac{1}{2}\right), \left(\frac{1}{5}, \frac{1}{4}\right), \left(\frac{1}{10}, \frac{1}{8}\right), \left(\frac{1}{20}, \frac{1}{15}\right), \left(\frac{1}{40}, \frac{1}{30}\right)\right] \quad \text{(Equation 11.2.1)}$$

How can the anchor boxes be further improved? The offsets may be reduced if we allow the anchor boxes to have different aspect ratios. The centroid of each resized anchor box is the same as the original anchor box. Other than the aspect ratio of 1, SSD [2] includes additional aspect ratios:

$$a = \left[1, 2, 3, \frac{1}{2}, \frac{1}{3}\right] \quad \text{(Equation 11.2.2)}$$

For each aspect ratio, a_i, the corresponding anchor box dimensions are:

$$(w_i, \ h_i) = \left(ws_{xj}\sqrt{a_i}, \ hs_{yj}\frac{1}{\sqrt{a_i}}\right) \quad \text{(Equation 11.2.3)}$$

(s_{xj}, s_{yj}) is the $j - th$ scaling factor from *Equation 11.2.1*.

Using five different aspect ratios per anchor box, the total number of anchor boxes increases to 1,608 x 5 = 8,040. *Figure 11.2.3* shows the anchor boxes for the case where $\left(s_{x4}, \ s_{y4}\right) = \left(\frac{1}{3}, \frac{1}{2}\right)$ and $a_{i\in\{0,1,3\}} = 1, 2, \frac{1}{2}$.

Note that to achieve a certain aspect ratio, we do not deform the anchor box. Instead, the anchor box width and height are adjusted.

For $a_0 = 1$, SSD recommends an additional anchor box with dimensions:

$$(w_5, \ h_5) = \left(w\sqrt{s_j s_{j+1}}, \ h\sqrt{s_j s_{j+1}}\right) \quad \text{(Equation 11.2.4)}$$

There are now six anchor boxes per region. Five are due to five aspect ratios and there's an additional one for an aspect ratio of 1. The new total number of anchor boxes increases to 9,648.

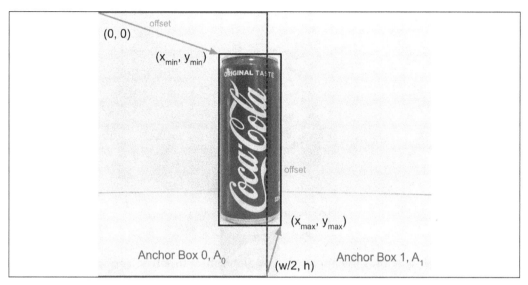

Figure 11.2.1 Dividing the image into regions, also known as anchor boxes, enables the network to have a prediction that is closer to the ground truth.

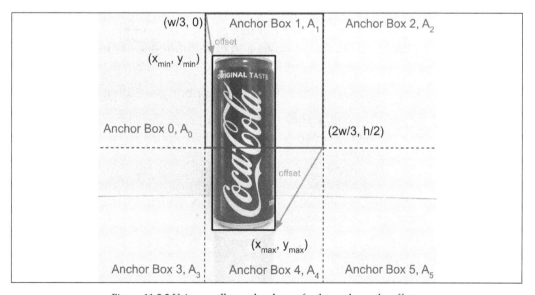

Figure 11.2.2 Using smaller anchor boxes further reduces the offsets.

Figure 11.2.3 Anchor boxes for one region with scaling factor $(s_{x4},\ s_{y4}) = \left(\frac{1}{3},\frac{1}{2}\right)$ and aspect ratios $a_{i\in\{0,1,3\}} = 1, 2, \frac{1}{2}$.

Listing 11.2.1 below shows the anchor boxes generation function `anchor_boxes()`. Given the input image shape (`image_shape`), aspect ratios (`aspect_ratios`), and scaling factors (`sizes`), the different anchor box sizes are computed and stored in a list named `width_height`. From the given feature map shape, (`feature_shape`) or (h_{fmap},w_{fmap}), and `width_height`, a tensor of anchor boxes is generated with dimensions $(h_{fmap},w_{fmap},n_{boxes},4)$. n_{boxes} or the number of anchor boxes per feature map point is computed based on the aspect ratios and one additional size for the aspect ratio equal to 1.

Listing 11.2.1: `layer_utils.py` function for the anchor box generation function:

```
def anchor_boxes(feature_shape,
                 image_shape,
                 index=0,
                 n_layers=4,
                 aspect_ratios=(1, 2, 0.5)):
    """ Compute the anchor boxes for a given feature map.
    Anchor boxes are in minmax format

    Arguments:
        feature_shape (list): Feature map shape
        image_shape (list): Image size shape
        index (int): Indicates which of ssd head layers
```

```
        are we referring to
    n_layers (int): Number of ssd head layers

Returns:
    boxes (tensor): Anchor boxes per feature map
"""

# anchor box sizes given an index of layer in ssd head
sizes = anchor_sizes(n_layers)[index]
# number of anchor boxes per feature map pt
n_boxes = len(aspect_ratios) + 1
# ignore number of channels (last)
image_height, image_width, _ = image_shape
# ignore number of feature maps (last)
feature_height, feature_width, _ = feature_shape

# normalized width and height
# sizes[0] is scale size, sizes[1] is sqrt(scale*(scale+1))
norm_height = image_height * sizes[0]
norm_width = image_width * sizes[0]

# list of anchor boxes (width, height)
width_height = []
# anchor box by aspect ratio on resized image dims
# Equation 11.2.3
for ar in aspect_ratios:
    box_width = norm_width * np.sqrt(ar)
    box_height = norm_height / np.sqrt(ar)
    width_height.append((box_width, box_height))
# multiply anchor box dim by size[1] for aspect_ratio = 1
# Equation 11.2.4
box_width = image_width * sizes[1]
box_height = image_height * sizes[1]
width_height.append((box_width, box_height))

# now an array of (width, height)
width_height = np.array(width_height)

# dimensions of each receptive field in pixels
grid_width = image_width / feature_width
grid_height = image_height / feature_height

# compute center of receptive field per feature pt
# (cx, cy) format
```

```python
    # starting at midpoint of 1st receptive field
    start = grid_width * 0.5
    # ending at midpoint of last receptive field
    end = (feature_width - 0.5) * grid_width
    cx = np.linspace(start, end, feature_width)

    start = grid_height * 0.5
    end = (feature_height - 0.5) * grid_height
    cy = np.linspace(start, end, feature_height)

    # grid of box centers
    cx_grid, cy_grid = np.meshgrid(cx, cy)

    # for np.tile()
    cx_grid = np.expand_dims(cx_grid, -1)
    cy_grid = np.expand_dims(cy_grid, -1)

    # tensor = (feature_map_height, feature_map_width, n_boxes, 4)
    # aligned with image tensor (height, width, channels)
    # last dimension = (cx, cy, w, h)
    boxes = np.zeros((feature_height, feature_width, n_boxes, 4))

    # (cx, cy)
    boxes[..., 0] = np.tile(cx_grid, (1, 1, n_boxes))
    boxes[..., 1] = np.tile(cy_grid, (1, 1, n_boxes))

    # (w, h)
    boxes[..., 2] = width_height[:, 0]
    boxes[..., 3] = width_height[:, 1]

    # convert (cx, cy, w, h) to (xmin, xmax, ymin, ymax)
    # prepend one dimension to boxes
    # to account for the batch size = 1
    boxes = centroid2minmax(boxes)
    boxes = np.expand_dims(boxes, axis=0)
    return boxes


def centroid2minmax(boxes):
    """Centroid to minmax format
    (cx, cy, w, h) to (xmin, xmax, ymin, ymax)
```

```
Arguments:
    boxes (tensor): Batch of boxes in centroid format

Returns:
    minmax (tensor): Batch of boxes in minmax format
"""
minmax= np.copy(boxes).astype(np.float)
minmax[..., 0] = boxes[..., 0] - (0.5 * boxes[..., 2])
minmax[..., 1] = boxes[..., 0] + (0.5 * boxes[..., 2])
minmax[..., 2] = boxes[..., 1] - (0.5 * boxes[..., 3])
minmax[..., 3] = boxes[..., 1] + (0.5 * boxes[..., 3])
return minmax
```

We've covered how anchor boxes assist object detections, and how they can be generated. In the next section, we'll look at a special kind of anchor box: the ground truth anchor box. Given an object in an image, it must be assigned to one of the many anchor boxes. This is called the ground truth anchor box.

3. Ground truth anchor boxes

From *Figure 11.2.3*, it appears that given an object bounding box, there are many ground truth anchor boxes that can be assigned to an object. In fact, just for the illustration in *Figure 11.2.3*, there are already 3 anchor boxes. If all anchor boxes per region are considered, there are 6 x 6 = 36 ground truth boxes just for $(s_{x4}, s_{y4}) = \left(\frac{1}{3}, \frac{1}{2}\right)$. Using all 9,648 anchor boxes is obviously excessive. Only one of all anchor boxes should be associated with the ground truth bounding box. All other anchor boxes are background anchor boxes. What is the criterion for choosing which one should be considered the ground truth anchor box for an object in the image?

The basis for choosing the anchor box is called **Intersection over Union (IoU)**. IoU is also known as *Jaccard index*. IoU is illustrated in *Figure 11.3.1*. Given 2 regions, an object bounding box, B_0 and an anchor box, A_1, IoU is equal to the area of overlap divided by the area of the combined regions:

$$IoU = \frac{A \cap B}{A \cup B} \quad \text{(Equation 11.3.1)}$$

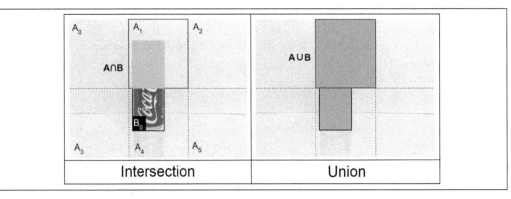

Figure 11.3.1 IoU is equal to Left) the area of intersection divided by Right)
the area of union between a candidate anchor box, A_i, and the object bounding box, B_0.

We removed the subscripts for generality of the equation. For a given object
bounding box, B_i, and for all anchor boxes, A_j, the ground truth anchor box, $A_{j(gt)}$,
is the one with the maximum IoU:

$$A_{j(gt)} = \max_j IoU\left(B_i, A_j\right) \quad \text{(Equation 11.3.2)}$$

Please note that for each object there is only one ground truth anchor box based on
Equation 11.3.2. Furthermore, the maximization must be done for all anchor boxes
in all scaling factors and sizes (aspect ratios and additional dimensions). In *Figure
11.3.1*, only one scaling factor-size is shown out of the 9,648 anchor boxes.

To illustrate *Equation 11.3.2*, suppose anchor boxes with an aspect ratio of 1 in
Figure 11.3.1 are considered. For each anchor box, the estimated IoU is shown in
Table 11.3.1. Since the maximum IoU of bounding box B_0 is 0.32 is with anchor box
A_1, A_1 is assigned the ground truth bounding box B_0. A_1 is also known as a **positive
anchor box**.

The category and offsets of a positive anchor box are determined with respect to its
ground truth bounding box. The category of a positive anchor box and its ground
truth bounding box are the same. Meanwhile, a positive anchor box offsets can be
computed as equal to the ground truth bounding box coordinates minus its own
bounding box coordinates.

What happens to the rest of anchor boxes, A_0, A_2, A_3, A_4, and A_5? We can give them
a second chance by finding which bounding box they have IoU greater than a certain
threshold.

For example, if the threshold is 0.5, then there is no ground truth bounding box that can be assigned to any of them. If the threshold is lowered to 0.25, then A_4 is also assigned the ground truth bounding box B_0 since its IoU is 0.30. A_4 is added to the list of positive anchor boxes. In this book, A_4 is called an extra positive anchor box. The remaining anchor boxes with no ground bounding boxes are called **negative anchor boxes**.

In the following section on loss functions, negative anchor boxes do not contribute to the offsets loss function.

	B_0
A_0	0
A_1	0.32
A_2	0
A_3	0
A_4	0.30
A_5	0

Table 11.3.1 IoU for each anchor box, $A_{j\in\{0..5\}}$, with object bounding box B_0 as shown in Figure 11.3.1.

If another image with 2 objects to be detected is loaded, we look for 2 positive anchor boxes with maximum IoU with bounding boxes B_0 and B_1. Then, we look for extra positive anchor boxes that satisfy the minimum IoU criterion with bounding boxes B_0 and B_1.

For simplicity of the discussion, we only consider one anchor box per region. In practice, all anchor boxes representing different scaling factor, sizes, and aspect ratios should be considered. In the next section, we discuss how to formulate the loss functions that will be optimized by the SSD network.

Listing 11.3.1 shows the implementation of `get_gt_data()` that computes the ground truth labels for anchor boxes.

Listing 11.3.1: `layer_utils.py`

```
def get_gt_data(iou,
                n_classes=4,
                anchors=None,
                labels=None,
                normalize=False,
                threshold=0.6):
    """Retrieve ground truth class, bbox offset, and mask
```

```
Arguments:
    iou (tensor): IoU of each bounding box wrt each anchor box
    n_classes (int): Number of object classes
    anchors (tensor): Anchor boxes per feature layer
    labels (list): Ground truth labels
    normalize (bool): If normalization should be applied
    threshold (float): If less than 1.0, anchor boxes>threshold
        are also part of positive anchor boxes

Returns:
    gt_class, gt_offset, gt_mask (tensor): Ground truth classes,
        offsets, and masks
"""
# each maxiou_per_get is index of anchor w/ max iou
# for the given ground truth bounding box
maxiou_per_gt = np.argmax(iou, axis=0)

# get extra anchor boxes based on IoU
if threshold < 1.0:
    iou_gt_thresh = np.argwhere(iou>threshold)
    if iou_gt_thresh.size > 0:
        extra_anchors = iou_gt_thresh[:,0]
        extra_classes = iou_gt_thresh[:,1]
        extra_labels = labels[extra_classes]
        indexes = [maxiou_per_gt, extra_anchors]
        maxiou_per_gt = np.concatenate(indexes,
                                       axis=0)
        labels = np.concatenate([labels, extra_labels],
                                axis=0)

# mask generation
gt_mask = np.zeros((iou.shape[0], 4))
# only indexes maxiou_per_gt are valid bounding boxes
gt_mask[maxiou_per_gt] = 1.0

# class generation
gt_class = np.zeros((iou.shape[0], n_classes))
# by default all are background (index 0)
gt_class[:, 0] = 1
# but those that belong to maxiou_per_gt are not
gt_class[maxiou_per_gt, 0] = 0
# we have to find those column indexes (classes)
maxiou_col = np.reshape(maxiou_per_gt,
                        (maxiou_per_gt.shape[0], 1))
```

```
        label_col = np.reshape(labels[:,4],
                                (labels.shape[0], 1)).astype(int)
        row_col = np.append(maxiou_col, label_col, axis=1)
        # the label of object in maxio_per_gt
        gt_class[row_col[:,0], row_col[:,1]]  = 1.0

        # offsets generation
        gt_offset = np.zeros((iou.shape[0], 4))

        #(cx, cy, w, h) format
        if normalize:
            anchors = minmax2centroid(anchors)
            labels = minmax2centroid(labels)
            # bbox = bounding box
            # ((bbox xcenter - anchor box xcenter)/anchor box width)/.1
            # ((bbox ycenter - anchor box ycenter)/anchor box height)/.1
            # Equation 11.4.8 Chapter 11
            offsets1 = labels[:, 0:2] - anchors[maxiou_per_gt, 0:2]
            offsets1 /= anchors[maxiou_per_gt, 2:4]
            offsets1 /= 0.1

            # log(bbox width / anchor box width) / 0.2
            # log(bbox height / anchor box height) / 0.2
            # Equation 11.4.8 Chapter 11
            offsets2 = np.log(labels[:, 2:4]/anchors[maxiou_per_gt, 2:4])
            offsets2 /= 0.2

            offsets = np.concatenate([offsets1, offsets2], axis=-1)

        # (xmin, xmax, ymin, ymax) format
        else:
            offsets = labels[:, 0:4] - anchors[maxiou_per_gt]

        gt_offset[maxiou_per_gt] = offsets

        return gt_class, gt_offset, gt_mask


def minmax2centroid(boxes):
    """Minmax to centroid format
    (xmin, xmax, ymin, ymax) to (cx, cy, w, h)

    Arguments:
        boxes (tensor): Batch of boxes in minmax format
```

```
Returns:
    centroid (tensor): Batch of boxes in centroid format
"""
centroid = np.copy(boxes).astype(np.float)
centroid[..., 0] = 0.5 * (boxes[..., 1] - boxes[..., 0])
centroid[..., 0] += boxes[..., 0]
centroid[..., 1] = 0.5 * (boxes[..., 3] - boxes[..., 2])
centroid[..., 1] += boxes[..., 2]
centroid[..., 2] = boxes[..., 1] - boxes[..., 0]
centroid[..., 3] = boxes[..., 3] - boxes[..., 2]
return centroid
```

`maxiou_per_gt = np.argmax(iou, axis=0)` implements *Equation 11.3.2*. Extra positive anchor boxes are determined based on a user-defined threshold implemented by: `iou_gt_thresh = np.argwhere(iou>threshold)`.

Finding extra positive anchor boxes happens only when the threshold is less than 1.0. The indexes of all anchor boxes with ground truth bounding boxes (that is combined positive anchor boxes and extra positive anchor boxes) become the basis of the ground truth mask:

`gt_mask[maxiou_per_gt] = 1.0`.

All other anchor boxes (negative anchor boxes) have mask of 0.0 and do not contribute in the offsets loss function optimization.

The class of each anchor box, `gt_class`, is assigned the class of its ground truth bounding box. Initially, all anchor boxes are assigned the background class:

```
# class generation
gt_class = np.zeros((iou.shape[0], n_classes))
# by default all are background (index 0)
gt_class[:, 0] = 1
```

Then, the class of each positive anchor box is assigned to its non-background object class:

```
# but those that belong to maxiou_per_gt are not
gt_class[maxiou_per_gt, 0] = 0
# we have to find those column indexes (classes)
maxiou_col = np.reshape(maxiou_per_gt,
                        (maxiou_per_gt.shape[0], 1))
label_col = np.reshape(labels[:,4],
                       (labels.shape[0], 1)).astype(int)
row_col = np.append(maxiou_col, label_col, axis=1)
```

```
# the label of object in maxio_per_gt
gt_class[row_col[:,0], row_col[:,1]]  = 1.0
```

`row_col[:,0]` are the indexes of positive anchor boxes, while `row_col[:,1]` are indexes of their non-background object class. Note that `gt_class` is an array of one-hot vectors. The values are all zero except at the index of the anchor box object. Index 0 is background, index 1 is the first non-background object, and so on. The last non-background object has an index equal to `n_classes-1`.

For example, if anchor box 0 is a negative anchor box and there are 4 object categories including the background, then:

```
gt_class[0] = [1.0, 0.0, 0.0, 0.0]
```

If anchor box 1 is a positive anchor box and its ground truth bounding box contains a **Soda can** with label 2, then:

```
gt_class[1] = [0.0, 0.0, 1.0, 0.0]
```

Lastly, the offsets are simply ground truth bounding box coordinates minus anchor box coordinates:

```
# (xmin, xmax, ymin, ymax) format
else:
    offsets = labels[:, 0:4] - anchors[maxiou_per_gt]
```

Note that we only compute the offsets of positive anchor boxes.

The offsets can be normalized if that option is chosen. Offsets normalization is discussed in the next section. We will see that:

```
#(cx, cy, w, h) format
if normalize:
    anchors = minmax2centroid(anchors)
    labels = minmax2centroid(labels)
    # bbox = bounding box
    # ((bbox xcenter - anchor box xcenter)/anchor box width)/.1
    # ((bbox ycenter - anchor box ycenter)/anchor box height)/.1
    # Equation 11.4.8
    offsets1 = labels[:, 0:2] - anchors[maxiou_per_gt, 0:2]
    offsets1 /= anchors[maxiou_per_gt, 2:4]
    offsets1 /= 0.1

    # log(bbox width / anchor box width) / 0.2
    # log(bbox height / anchor box height) / 0.2
    # Equation 11.4.8
    offsets2 = np.log(labels[:, 2:4]/anchors[maxiou_per_gt, 2:4])
```

```
offsets2 /= 0.2

offsets = np.concatenate([offsets1, offsets2], axis=-1)
```

is simply the implementation of *Equation 11.4.8* that is discussed in the next section and shown here for convenience:

$$y_{gt} = \left(\frac{\frac{c_{bx} - c_{ax}}{w_a}}{\sigma_x}, \frac{\frac{c_{by} - c_{ay}}{h_a}}{\sigma_y}, \frac{\log \frac{w_b}{w_a}}{\sigma_w}, \frac{\log \frac{h_b}{h_a}}{\sigma_h} \right) \quad \text{(Equation 11.4.8)}$$

Now that we've gained an understanding of the role of ground truth anchor boxes, we will move on to another key component in object detection: loss functions.

4. Loss functions

In SSD, there are thousands of anchor boxes. As discussed earlier in this chapter, the goal of object detection is to predict both the category and offsets of each anchor box. We can use the following loss functions for each prediction:

- $\mathcal{L}_{cls}$ - Categorical cross-entropy loss for y_{cls}
- $\mathcal{L}_{off}$ - L1 or L2 for y_{off}. Note that only positive anchor boxes contribute to $\mathcal{L}_{off}$ L1 is also known as **mean absolute error** (MAE) loss, while L2 is also known as **mean squared error** (MSE) loss.

The total loss function is:

$$\mathcal{L} = \mathcal{L}_{off} + \mathcal{L}_{cls} \quad \text{(Equation 11.4.1)}$$

For each anchor box, the network predicts the following:

- y_{cls} or the category or class in the form of a one-hot vector
- $y_{off} = ((x_{omin}, y_{omin}), (x_{omax}, y_{omax}))$ or the offsets in the form of pixel coordinates relative to anchor box.

For computational convenience, the offsets are better expressed in the form:

$$y_{off} = ((x_{omin}, y_{omin}), (x_{omax}, y_{omax})) \quad \text{(Equation 11.4.2)}$$

SSD is a supervised object detection algorithm. The following ground truth values are available:

- y_{label} or the class label of each object to detect
- $y_{gt} = (x_{gmin}, x_{gmax}, y_{gmin}, y_{gmax})$ or the ground truth offsets which are computed as:

$$y_{gt} = (x_{bmin} - x_{amin}, x_{bmax} - x_{amax}, y_{bmin} - y_{amin}, y_{bmax} - y_{amax}) \quad \text{(Equation 11.4.3)}$$

In other words, the ground truth offsets are computed as the ground truth offset of the object bounding box relative to anchor box. The minor tweak in the subscript of y_{box} is for clarity. As discussed in the previous section, the ground truth values are computed by `get_gt_data()` function.

However, SSD does not recommend to directly predict the raw pixel error values y_{off}. Instead, the normalized offset values are used. The ground truth bounding box and anchor box coordinates are first expressed in centroid-dimensions format:

$$y_{box} = ((x_{bmin}, y_{bmin}), (x_{bmax}, y_{bmax})) \rightarrow (c_{bx}, c_{by}, w_b, h_b)$$
$$y_{anchor} = ((x_{amin}, y_{amin}), (x_{amax}, y_{amax})) \rightarrow (c_{ax}, c_{ay}, w_a, h_a) \quad \text{(Equation 11.4.4)}$$

where:

$$(c_{bx}, c_{by}) = \left(x_{min} + \frac{x_{max} - x_{min}}{2}, y_{min} + \frac{y_{max} - y_{min}}{2}\right) \quad \text{(Equation 11.4.5)}$$

is the coordinate of the center of bounding box and:

$$(w_b, h_b) = (x_{max} - x_{min}, y_{max} - y_{min}) \quad \text{(Equation 11.4.6)}$$

corresponds to width and height respectively. The anchor box follows the same convention. The normalized ground truth offsets are expressed as:

$$y_{gt} = \left(\frac{c_{bx} - c_{ax}}{w_a}, \frac{c_{by} - c_{ay}}{h_a}, \log\frac{w_b}{w_a}, \log\frac{h_b}{h_a}\right) \quad \text{(Equation 11.4.7)}$$

Generally, the values of the elements of y_{gt} are small, $||y_{gt}|| << 1.0$. Small gradients can make it more difficult for the network training to converge.

To alleviate the problem, each element is divided by its estimated standard deviation. The resulting ground truth offsets:

$$y_{gt} = \left(\frac{\frac{c_{bx} - c_{ax}}{w_a}}{\sigma_x}, \frac{\frac{c_{by} - c_{ay}}{h_a}}{\sigma_y}, \frac{\log\frac{w_b}{w_a}}{\sigma_w}, \frac{\log\frac{h_b}{h_a}}{\sigma_h} \right) \quad \text{(Equation 11.4.8)}$$

The recommended values are: $\sigma_x = \sigma_y = 0.1$ and $\sigma_w = \sigma_h = 0.2$. In other words, the expected range of pixel error along x and y axes is $\pm10\%$, while for width and height it is $\pm20\%$. These values are purely arbitrary.

Listing 11.4.1: `loss.py` L1 and smooth L1 loss functions

```python
from tensorflow.keras.losses import Huber
def mask_offset(y_true, y_pred):
    """Pre-process ground truth and prediction data"""
    # 1st 4 are offsets
    offset = y_true[..., 0:4]
    # last 4 are mask
    mask = y_true[..., 4:8]
    # pred is actually duplicated for alignment
    # either we get the 1st or last 4 offset pred
    # and apply the mask
    pred = y_pred[..., 0:4]
    offset *= mask
    pred *= mask
    return offset, pred


def l1_loss(y_true, y_pred):
    """MAE or L1 loss
    """
    offset, pred = mask_offset(y_true, y_pred)
    # we can use L1
    return K.mean(K.abs(pred - offset), axis=-1)


def smooth_l1_loss(y_true, y_pred):
    """Smooth L1 loss using tensorflow Huber loss
    """
    offset, pred = mask_offset(y_true, y_pred)
    # Huber loss as approx of smooth L1
    return Huber()(offset, pred)
```

Furthermore, instead of L1 loss for y_{off}, SSD was inspired by Fast-RCNN [3] to use smooth L1:

$$\mathcal{L}_{off} = L1_{smooth}(u) = \begin{cases} \dfrac{(\sigma u)^2}{2} & if \ |u| < \dfrac{1}{\sigma^2} \\ |u| - \dfrac{1}{2\sigma^2} & otherwise \end{cases} \quad \text{(Equation 11.4.9)}$$

where u represents each element in the error between ground truth and prediction:

$$u = y_{gt} - y_{pred} \quad \text{(Equation 11.4.10)}$$

Smooth L1 is more robust compared to L1 and less sensitive to outliers. In SSD, $\sigma = 1$. As $\sigma \to \infty$, smooth L1 approaches L1. Both L1 and smooth L1 loss functions are shown in *Listing 11.4.1*. The mask_offset() method ensures that the offsets are computed on predictions with ground truth bounding boxes only. The smooth L1 function is the same as Huber loss when $\sigma = 1$ [8].

As a further improvement to the loss functions, RetinaNet [3] recommends that the categorical cross-entropy function for y_{cls}, CE, be replaced by focal loss, FL:

$$\mathcal{L}_{cls} = CE = -\sum_i y_i \log p_i \quad \text{(Equation 11.4.11)}$$

$$\mathcal{L}_{cls} = FL = -\alpha \sum_i y_i (1 - p_i)^\gamma \log p_i \quad \text{(Equation 11.4.12)}$$

The difference is the extra factor, $\alpha(1 - p_i)^\gamma$. In RetinaNet, object detection works best when $\gamma = 2$ and $\alpha = 0.25$. Focal loss is implemented in *Listing 11.4.2*.

Listing 11.4.2: loss.py Focal loss

```
def focal_loss_categorical(y_true, y_pred):
    """Categorical cross-entropy focal loss"""
    gamma = 2.0
    alpha = 0.25

    # scale to ensure sum of prob is 1.0
    y_pred /= K.sum(y_pred, axis=-1, keepdims=True)

    # clip the prediction value to prevent NaN and Inf
    epsilon = K.epsilon()
    y_pred = K.clip(y_pred, epsilon, 1. - epsilon)

    # calculate cross entropy
    cross_entropy = -y_true * K.log(y_pred)
```

```
# calculate focal loss
weight = alpha * K.pow(1 - y_pred, gamma)
cross_entropy *= weight

return K.sum(cross_entropy, axis=-1)
```

The motivation behind focal loss is that if we examine an image, the majority of the anchor boxes should be classified as background or negative anchor boxes. Only few positive anchor boxes are good candidates to represent the target object. The major contributors to cross-entropy loss are the negative anchor boxes. Thus, the contribution of positive anchor boxes during optimization is overpowered by the contribution of negative anchor boxes. This phenomenon is also known as **class imbalance**, where one or few classes dominate the rest. For additional details, Lin et al. [4] discuss class imbalance in the context of object detection.

With **focal loss**, we are confident early on during optimization that negative anchors boxes belong to background. Therefore, the term $(1 - p_i)^\gamma$ reduces the contribution of negative anchor boxes since $p_i \rightarrow 1.0$. For positive anchor boxes, the contribution is still significant since p_i is far from 1.0.

Now that we have discussed the concept of anchor boxes, ground truth anchor boxes, and loss functions, we are now ready to present SSD model architecture that implements the multi-scale object detection algorithm.

5. SSD model architecture

Figure 11.5.1 shows the model architecture of SSD that implements the conceptual framework of multi-scale single-shot object detection. The network accepts an RGB image and outputs several levels of prediction. A base or **backbone** network extracts features for the downstream task of classification and offset predictions. A good example of a backbone network is ResNet50 that is similar to what was discussed, implemented, and evaluated in *Chapter 2, Deep Neural Networks*. After the backbone network, the object detection task is performed by the rest of the network which we call **SSD head**.

The backbone network can be a pre-trained network with frozen weights (for example; previously trained for ImageNet classification) or jointly trained with object detection. If we used a pre-trained base network, we take advantage of reusing previously learned feature extraction filters from a large dataset. In addition, it accelerates learning as the backbone network parameters are frozen. Only the top layers in object detection are trained. In this book, the backbone network is jointly trained with object detection since we assume that we do not necessarily have access to a pre-trained backbone network.

The backbone network normally implements several rounds of downsampling either using strides = 2 or by max pooling. In the case of ResNet50, this is 4 times. The resulting dimensions of feature maps after the base network becomes $\left(\frac{w}{2^4}, \frac{h}{2^4}\right) = \left(\frac{w}{16}, \frac{h}{16}\right)$. The dimensions are exact if both image width and height are divisible by 16.

For example, for a 640 x 480 image, the resulting feature maps have dimensions 40 x 30 = 1,200. As discussed in the previous sections, this is the number of anchor boxes with aspect ratio equal to 1 after the base network. This figure is multiplied by the number of sizes per anchor box. In the previous sections, there are 6 different sizes due to aspect ratios and one additional size for aspect ratio of 1.

In this book, we will limit the aspect ratio to $a_{i \in \{0,1,3\}} = 1, 2, \frac{1}{2}$. Thus, there will only be 4 different sizes. For a 640 x 480 image, the total number of anchor boxes for the first set of anchor boxes is n_1 = 4,800.

In *Figure 11.5.1*, the dense grid is indicated to show that for the first set of predictions there is a big number of predictions (for example: 40 x 30 x 4) resulting in a huge number of patches. Although there are 4 sizes per anchor box, only the 16 x 16 anchor box that corresponds to aspect ratio of 1 is shown for clarity.

This anchor box is also the receptive field size of each element in 40 x 30 x $n_{filters}$ feature maps. $n_{filters}$ is the number of filters in the last convolutional layer of the backbone network. For each anchor box, both the class and offsets are predicted.

All in all, there are n_1 class and n_1 offsets predictions. The dimension of 1-hot class prediction is equal to number of categories of object to detect plus 1 for the background. The dimension of each offsets variable prediction is 4 corresponding to the (x, y) offsets to the 2 corners of the predicted bounding box.

The class predictor is made of a convolutional layer terminated by an activation layer that is using *softmax* for categorical cross-entropy loss. The offsets predictor is a separate convolutional layer with linear activation.

Additional feature extraction blocks can be applied after the base network. Each feature extractor block is in the form of `Conv2D(strides=2)-BN-ELU`. After the feature extraction block, the feature map size is halved, and the number of filters is doubled. For example, the first feature extractor block after the base network has 20 x 15 x 2 $n_{filters}$ feature maps. From this feature maps, n_2 class and n_2 offset predictions are made using convolutional layers. n_2 = 20 x 15 x 4 = 1,200

The process of adding feature extraction blocks with class and offsets predictors can continue. In the previous sections, for a 640 x 480 image, this could be up to $2 \times 1 \times 2^5$ $n_{filters}$ feature maps producing n_6 class and n_6 offsets predictions where $n_6 = 2 \times 1 \times 4 = 8$. This corresponds to 6 layers of feature extraction and prediction blocks. After the 6th block, the total number of anchor map predictions for a 640 x 480 image is 9,648.

In the previous sections, the scaling factor sizes of anchor boxes was arranged in decreasing order:

$$\left[\left(\frac{1}{2}, 1\right), \left(\frac{1}{3}, \frac{1}{2}\right), \left(\frac{1}{5}, \frac{1}{4}\right), \left(\frac{1}{10}, \frac{1}{8}\right), \left(\frac{1}{20}, \frac{1}{15}\right), \left(\frac{1}{40}, \frac{1}{30}\right) \right] \quad \text{Equation 11.5.1}$$

It was done for clarity of the discussion. In this section, it should be realized that the scaling factor size actually begins with the feature map size after the backbone network. In reality, the scaling factor should be in increasing order:

$$\left[\left(\frac{1}{40}, \frac{1}{30}\right), \left(\frac{1}{20}, \frac{1}{15}\right), \left(\frac{1}{10}, \frac{1}{8}\right), \left(\frac{1}{5}, \frac{1}{4}\right), \left(\frac{1}{3}, \frac{1}{2}\right), \left(\frac{1}{2}, 1\right) \right] \quad \text{(Equation 11.5.2)}$$

This means that if we reduced the number of feature extraction blocks to 4, the scaling factors are:

$$\left[\left(\frac{1}{40}, \frac{1}{30}\right), \left(\frac{1}{20}, \frac{1}{15}\right), \left(\frac{1}{10}, \frac{1}{8}\right), \left(\frac{1}{5}, \frac{1}{4}\right) \right] \quad \text{(Equation 11.5.3)}$$

In cases where the feature map width or height is not divisible by 2 (for example: 15), the ceiling function is applied (for example: $ceiling\left(\frac{15}{2}\right) = 8$). However, in the original SSD [2] implementation, the scaling factors used were simplified to a [0.2, 0.9] range scaled linearly by the number of scaling factors or the number of feature extraction blocks, n_layers:

```
s = np.linspace(0.2, 0.9, n_layers + 1)
```

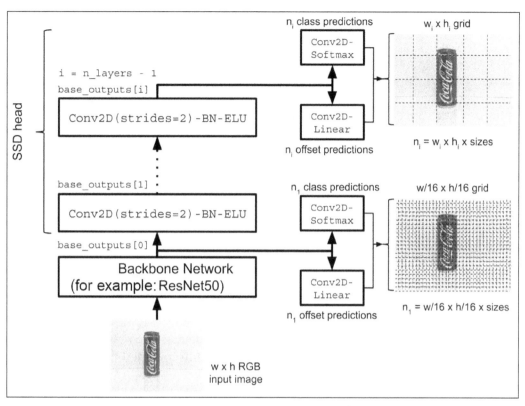

Figure 11.5.1 The SSD model architecture. Please note that for the $\frac{w}{16} \times \frac{h}{16}$ grid, the number of anchor boxes may not be exact. The grid shows how tightly packed the anchor boxes are.

Having discussed SSD model architecture, let's now look at how the SSD model architecture is implemented in Keras.

6. SSD model architecture in Keras

Unlike the code examples in the previous chapters, the `tf.keras` implementation of SSD is more involved. In comparison to other `tf.keras` implementations of SSD, the code example presented in this chapter focuses on explaining the key concepts of multi-scale object detection. Some parts of the code implementation can be further optimized such as caching of ground truth anchor boxes classes, offsets, and masks. In our example, the ground truth values are computed by a thread every time an image is loaded from the filesystem.

Figure 11.6.1 shows an overview of code blocks that comprise the `tf.keras` implementation of SSD. An SSD object in `ssd-11.6.1.py` builds, trains, and evaluates an SSD model. It sits on top of SSD model creator with the help of `model.py` and `resnet.py` and a multi-threaded data generator in `data_generator.py`. SSD model implements the SSD architecture as shown in *Figure 11.5.1*. The implementation of each major block will be discussed in detail in the succeeding sections.

The SSD model uses a ResNet as its backbone network. It calls the ResNet V1 or V2 model creator in `resnet.py`. Unlike the examples in previous chapters, the dataset used by SSD is made of thousands of high-resolution images. A multi-threaded data generator loads and queues these images from the filesystem. It also computes the ground truth labels of anchor boxes. Without a multi-threaded data generator, loading and queueing of images and computation of ground truth values during training will be very slow.

There are many small but important routines that work behind the scenes. These are collectively stored in the utilities block. These routines create anchor boxes, compute IoUs, establish ground truth labels, run non-maximum suppression, draw labels and boxes, show detected objects on video frames, provide loss functions, and so on.

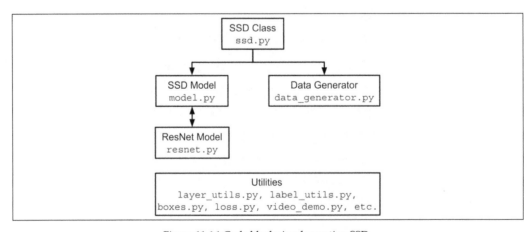

Figure 11.6.1 Code blocks implementing SSD.

7. SSD objects in Keras

Listing 11.7.1, displayed shortly, shows the SSD class. Two main routines are illustrated:

1. Creation of the SSD model using `build_model()`
2. Instantiating a data generator through `build_generator()`

`build_model` first creates a data dictionary from the train labels. The dictionary stores image filenames and ground truth bounding box coordinates and class for every object in each image. Afterward, the backbone and SSD network models are constructed. The most important product of model creation is `self.ssd` – the network model of SSD.

The labels are stored in a csv file. For the sample training images that is used in this book, the labels are saved in `dataset/drinks/labels_train.csv` with the format:

```
frame,xmin,xmax,ymin,ymax,class_id
0001000.jpg,310,445,104,443,1
0000999.jpg,194,354,96,478,1
0000998.jpg,105,383,134,244,1
0000997.jpg,157,493,89,194,1
0000996.jpg,51,435,207,347,1
0000995.jpg,183,536,156,283,1
0000994.jpg,156,392,178,266,2
0000993.jpg,207,449,119,213,2
0000992.jpg,47,348,213,346,2
...
```

Listing 11.7.1: `ssd-11.6.1.py`

```
class SSD:
    """Made of an ssd network model and a dataset generator.
    SSD defines functions to train and validate
    an ssd network model.

    Arguments:
        args: User-defined configurations

    Attributes:
        ssd (model): SSD network model
        train_generator: Multi-threaded data generator for training
    """
```

```
def __init__(self, args):
    """Copy user-defined configs.
    Build backbone and ssd network models.
    """
    self.args = args
    self.ssd = None
    self.train_generator = None
    self.build_model()


def build_model(self):
    """Build backbone and SSD models."""
    # store in a dictionary the list of image files and labels
    self.build_dictionary()

    # input shape is (480, 640, 3) by default
    self.input_shape = (self.args.height,
                        self.args.width,
                        self.args.channels)

    # build the backbone network (eg ResNet50)
    # the number of feature layers is equal to n_layers
    # feature layers are inputs to SSD network heads
    # for class and offsets predictions
    self.backbone = self.args.backbone(self.input_shape,
                                       n_layers=self.args.layers)


    # using the backbone, build ssd network
    # outputs of ssd are class and offsets predictions
    anchors, features, ssd = build_ssd(self.input_shape,
                                       self.backbone,
                                       n_layers=self.args.layers,
                                       n_classes=self.n_classes)
    # n_anchors = num of anchors per feature point (eg 4)
    self.n_anchors = anchors
    # feature_shapes is a list of feature map shapes
    # per output layer - used for computing anchor boxes sizes
    self.feature_shapes = features
    # ssd network model
    self.ssd = ssd

def build_dictionary(self):
    """Read input image filenames and obj detection labels
```

```
                from a csv file and store in a dictionary.
                """
                # train dataset path
                path = os.path.join(self.args.data_path,
                                    self.args.train_labels)

                # build dictionary:
                # key=image filaname, value=box coords + class label
                # self.classes is a list of class labels
                self.dictionary, self.classes = build_label_dictionary(path)
                self.n_classes = len(self.classes)
                self.keys = np.array(list(self.dictionary.keys()))

        def build_generator(self):
            """Build a multi-thread train data generator."""

            self.train_generator = \
                    DataGenerator(args=self.args,
                                  dictionary=self.dictionary,
                                  n_classes=self.n_classes,
                                  feature_shapes=self.feature_shapes,
                                  n_anchors=self.n_anchors,
                                  shuffle=True)
```

Listing 11.7.2 shows another important method in SSD object, `train()`. Indicated are the options to use default loss functions or improved loss functions as discussed in the previous sections. There is also an option to choose smooth L1 only.

`self.ssd.fit_generator()` is the most important call in this function. It starts the supervised training with the aid of the multi-threaded data generator. At every epoch, two callback functions are executed. First, the model weights are saved to a file. Then, a modified learning rate scheduler used in the same way as in *Chapter 2, Deep Neural Networks*, for ResNet models is called:

Listing 11.7.2: `ssd-11.6.1.py`

```
        def train(self):
            """Train an ssd network."""
            # build the train data generator
            if self.train_generator is None:
                self.build_generator()

            optimizer = Adam(lr=1e-3)
            # choice of loss functions via args
            if self.args.improved_loss:
```

```
                print_log("Focal loss and smooth L1", self.args.verbose)
                loss = [focal_loss_categorical, smooth_l1_loss]
            elif self.args.smooth_l1:
                print_log("Smooth L1", self.args.verbose)
                loss = ['categorical_crossentropy', smooth_l1_loss]
            else:
                print_log("Cross-entropy and L1", self.args.verbose)
                loss = ['categorical_crossentropy', l1_loss]

            self.ssd.compile(optimizer=optimizer, loss=loss)

    . . .

            # prepare callbacks for saving model weights
            # and learning rate scheduler
            # learning rate decreases by 50% every 20 epochs
            # after 60th epoch
            checkpoint = ModelCheckpoint(filepath=filepath,
                                         verbose=1,
                                         save_weights_only=True)
            scheduler = LearningRateScheduler(lr_scheduler)

            callbacks = [checkpoint, scheduler]
            # train the ssd network
            self.ssd.fit_generator(generator=self.train_generator,
                                   use_multiprocessing=True,
                                   callbacks=callbacks,
                                   epochs=self.args.epochs,
                                   workers=self.args.workers)
```

In the next sections, we will discuss additional details of the SSD architecture implementation in Keras. In particular, the implementation of SSD model and the multi-threaded data generator.

8. SSD model in Keras

Listing 11.8.1 shows the SSD model creation function `build_ssd()`. The model is illustrated in *Figure 11.5.1*. The function retrieves n_layers of output features from the backbone or base network by calling `base_outputs = backbone(inputs)`.

In this book, the `backbone()` is `build_resnet()`. The ResNet models that can be generated by `build_resnet()` are similar to the residual networks discussed in *Chapter 2, Deep Neural Networks*. The `build_resnet()` function can be replaced by any function name that builds the base network.

As shown in *Figure 11.5.1*, the return value `base_outputs` is a list of output features that will be the input to class and offset prediction layers. For example, the first output `base_outputs[0]`, is used to generate n_1 class predictions and n_1 offset predictions.

In the `for` loop of `build_ssd()` the class prediction is the `classes` variable, while the offsets prediction is the `offsets` variable. After the `for` loop iteration, the class predictions are concatenated and eventually merged into one `classes` variable with dimensions:

$$\left(n_{mini-batch}, n_{anchor-boxes}, n_{categories}\right)$$

The same procedure is done for `offsets` variable. The resulting dimensions are:

$$\left(n_{mini-batch}, n_{anchor-boxes}, 4\right)$$

where $n_{mini-batch}$ is the mini-batch size and $n_{anchor-boxes}$ is the number of anchor boxes. The number of `for` loop iterations is equal to `n_layers`. This number is also equal to the desired number of anchor boxes scaling factors or the number of feature extraction blocks of the SSD head.

The function `build_ssd()` returns the number of anchor boxes per feature point or region, the feature shape per before class, and offset prediction layers, and the SSD model itself.

Listing 11.8.1: `model.py`

```
def build_ssd(input_shape,
              backbone,
              n_layers=4,
              n_classes=4,
              aspect_ratios=(1, 2, 0.5)):
    """Build SSD model given a backbone

    Arguments:
        input_shape (list): input image shape
        backbone (model): Keras backbone model
        n_layers (int): Number of layers of ssd head
        n_classes (int): Number of obj classes
        aspect_ratios (list): annchor box aspect ratios

    Returns:
        n_anchors (int): Number of anchor boxes per feature pt
        feature_shape (tensor): SSD head feature maps
        model (Keras model): SSD model
```

```
    """
    # number of anchor boxes per feature map pt
    n_anchors = len(aspect_ratios) + 1

    inputs = Input(shape=input_shape)
    # no. of base_outputs depends on n_layers
    base_outputs = backbone(inputs)

    outputs = []
    feature_shapes = []
    out_cls = []
    out_off = []

    for i in range(n_layers):
        # each conv layer from backbone is used
        # as feature maps for class and offset predictions
        # also known as multi-scale predictions
        conv = base_outputs if n_layers==1 else base_outputs[i]
        name = "cls" + str(i+1)
        classes  = conv2d(conv,
                          n_anchors*n_classes,
                          kernel_size=3,
                          name=name)

        # offsets: (batch, height, width, n_anchors * 4)
        name = "off" + str(i+1)
        offsets  = conv2d(conv,
                          n_anchors*4,
                          kernel_size=3,
                          name=name)

        shape = np.array(K.int_shape(offsets))[1:]
        feature_shapes.append(shape)

        # reshape the class predictions, yielding 3D tensors of
        # shape (batch, height * width * n_anchors, n_classes)
        # last axis to perform softmax on them
        name = "cls_res" + str(i+1)
        classes = Reshape((-1, n_classes),
                          name=name)(classes)

        # reshape the offset predictions, yielding 3D tensors of
        # shape (batch, height * width * n_anchors, 4)
        # last axis to compute the (smooth) L1 or L2 loss
```

```
        name = "off_res" + str(i+1)
        offsets = Reshape((-1, 4),
                          name=name)(offsets)
        # concat for alignment with ground truth size
        # made of ground truth offsets and mask of same dim
        # needed during loss computation
        offsets = [offsets, offsets]
        name = "off_cat" + str(i+1)
        offsets = Concatenate(axis=-1,
                              name=name)(offsets)

        # collect offset prediction per scale
        out_off.append(offsets)

        name = "cls_out" + str(i+1)

        #activation = 'sigmoid' if n_classes==1 else 'softmax'
        #print("Activation:", activation)

        classes = Activation('softmax',
                             name=name)(classes)

        # collect class prediction per scale
        out_cls.append(classes)

    if n_layers > 1:
        # concat all class and offset from each scale
        name = "offsets"
        offsets = Concatenate(axis=1,
                              name=name)(out_off)
        name = "classes"
        classes = Concatenate(axis=1,
                              name=name)(out_cls)
    else:
        offsets = out_off[0]
        classes = out_cls[0]

    outputs = [classes, offsets]
    model = Model(inputs=inputs,
                  outputs=outputs,
                  name='ssd_head')

    return n_anchors, feature_shapes, model
```

As mentioned in the previous sections, unlike small datasets like MNIST and CIFAR-10, the images used in SSD are big. Hence, it is not possible to load the images in a tensor variable. In the next section, we introduce a multi-threaded data generator that will allow us to load images concurrently from the filesystem and avoid memory bottleneck.

9. Data generator model in Keras

SSD requires a lot of labeled high-resolution images for object detection. Unlike the previous chapters where the dataset used can be loaded into memory to train the model, SSD implements a multi-threaded data generator. The task of the multi-threaded generator is to load multiple mini-batches of images and their corresponding labels. Because of multi-threading, the GPU can be kept busy as one thread feeds it with data while the rest of CPU threads are in the queue ready to feed another batch data or loading a batch of images from the filesystem and computing the ground truth values. *Listing 11.9.1* shows the data generator model in Keras.

The DataGenerator class inherits from the Sequence class of Keras to ensure that it supports multi-processing. DataGenerator guarantees that the entire dataset is used in one epoch.

The length of the entire epoch given a batch size is returned by the __len__() method. Every request for a mini-batch of data is fulfilled by the __getitem__() method. After every epoch, the on_epoch_end() method is called to shuffle the entire batch if self.shuffle is True.

Listing 11.9.1: data_generator.py

```
class DataGenerator(Sequence):
    """Multi-threaded data generator.
    Each thread reads a batch of images and their object labels

    Arguments:
        args: User-defined configuration
        dictionary: Dictionary of image filenames and object labels
        n_classes (int): Number of object classes
        feature_shapes (tensor): Shapes of ssd head feature maps
        n_anchors (int): Number of anchor boxes per feature map pt
        shuffle (Bool): If dataset should be shuffled bef sampling
    """
    def __init__(self,
                 args,
                 dictionary,
                 n_classes,
```

```
                        feature_shapes=[],
                        n_anchors=4,
                        shuffle=True):
        self.args = args
        self.dictionary = dictionary
        self.n_classes = n_classes
        self.keys = np.array(list(self.dictionary.keys()))
        self.input_shape = (args.height,
                            args.width,
                            args.channels)
        self.feature_shapes = feature_shapes
        self.n_anchors = n_anchors
        self.shuffle = shuffle
        self.on_epoch_end()
        self.get_n_boxes()


    def __len__(self):
        """Number of batches per epoch"""
        blen = np.floor(len(self.dictionary) / self.args.batch_size)
        return int(blen)


    def __getitem__(self, index):
        """Get a batch of data"""
        start_index = index * self.args.batch_size
        end_index = (index+1) * self.args.batch_size
        keys = self.keys[start_index: end_index]
        x, y = self.__data_generation(keys)
        return x, y


    def on_epoch_end(self):
        """Shuffle after each epoch"""
        if self.shuffle == True:
            np.random.shuffle(self.keys)


    def get_n_boxes(self):
        """Total number of bounding boxes"""
        self.n_boxes = 0
        for shape in self.feature_shapes:
            self.n_boxes += np.prod(shape) // self.n_anchors
        return self.n_boxes
```

The bulk of the data generators work is done by the __data_generation() method as shown in *Listing 11.9.2*. Given a mini-batch, the method executes:

- imread() to read an image from the filesystem.

- labels = self.dictionary[key] to access the bounding box and class labels as stored in a dictionary. The first 4 items are the bounding box offsets. The last one is the class label.

- anchor_boxes() to generate anchor boxes.

- iou() to compute the IoU per anchor box with respect to the ground truth bounding box.

- get_gt_data() to assign the ground truth class and offsets per anchor box.

Sample data augmentation functions are also included but no longer discussed here such as addition of random noise, intensity rescaling, and exposure adjustment. __data_generation() returns the input *x* and output *y* pair where tensor *x* stores input images, while tensor *y* bundles the classes, offsets, and masks together.

Listing 11.9.2: data_generator.py

```
import layer_utils

from skimage.io import imread
    def __data_generation(self, keys):
        """Generate train data: images and
        object detection ground truth labels

        Arguments:
            keys (array): Randomly sampled keys
                (key is image filename)

        Returns:
            x (tensor): Batch images
            y (tensor): Batch classes, offsets, and masks
        """
        # train input data
        x = np.zeros((self.args.batch_size, *self.input_shape))
        dim = (self.args.batch_size, self.n_boxes, self.n_classes)
        # class ground truth
        gt_class = np.zeros(dim)
        dim = (self.args.batch_size, self.n_boxes, 4)
        # offsets ground truth
        gt_offset = np.zeros(dim)
        # masks of valid bounding boxes
        gt_mask = np.zeros(dim)
```

```
for i, key in enumerate(keys):
    # images are assumed to be stored in self.args.data_path
    # key is the image filename
    image_path = os.path.join(self.args.data_path, key)
    image = skimage.img_as_float(imread(image_path))
    # assign image to a batch index
    x[i] = image
    # a label entry is made of 4-dim bounding box coords
    # and 1-dim class label
    labels = self.dictionary[key]
    labels = np.array(labels)
    # 4 bounding box coords are 1st four items of labels
    # last item is object class label
    boxes = labels[:,0:-1]
    for index, feature_shape in enumerate(self.feature_
shapes):
        # generate anchor boxes
        anchors = anchor_boxes(feature_shape,
                               image.shape,
                               index=index,
                               n_layers=self.args.layers)
        # each feature layer has a row of anchor boxes
        anchors = np.reshape(anchors, [-1, 4])
        # compute IoU of each anchor box
        # with respect to each bounding boxes
        iou = layer_utils.iou(anchors, boxes)

        # generate ground truth class, offsets & mask
        gt = get_gt_data(iou,
                         n_classes=self.n_classes,
                         anchors=anchors,
                         labels=labels,
                         normalize=self.args.normalize,
                         threshold=self.args.threshold)
        gt_cls, gt_off, gt_msk = gt
        if index == 0:
            cls = np.array(gt_cls)
            off = np.array(gt_off)
            msk = np.array(gt_msk)
        else:
            cls = np.append(cls, gt_cls, axis=0)
            off = np.append(off, gt_off, axis=0)
            msk = np.append(msk, gt_msk, axis=0)
```

```
          gt_class[i] = cls
          gt_offset[i] = off
          gt_mask[i] = msk


     y = [gt_class, np.concatenate((gt_offset, gt_mask), axis=-1)]

     return x, y
```

Now that we have a multi-threaded generator, we can use it to load images from a filesystem. In the next section, we demonstrate how to build our custom dataset by taking images of target objects and labeling them.

10. Example dataset

A small dataset made of 1,000 640 X 480 RGB train images and 50 640 X 480 RGB test images was collected using an inexpensive USB camera (A4TECH PK-635G). The dataset images were labeled using **VGG Image Annotator (VIA)** [5] to detect the three objects: 1) **Soda can**, 2) **Juice can**, and 3) **Bottled water**. *Figure 11.10.1* shows a sample UI of the labeling process.

A utility script for collecting images can be found in utils/video_capture.py in the GitHub repository. The script can speed up the data collection process since it automatically captures an image every 5 seconds.

Figure 11.10.1 Dataset labeling process using VGG Image Annotator (VIA)

Data collection and labeling is a time-consuming activity. In the industry, this is typically outsourced to a third-party annotation company. The use of automatic data labeling software is another option to accelerate the data labeling task.

With this example dataset, we can now train our object detection network.

11. SSD model training

The train and test datasets including labels in csv format can be downloaded from this link:

```
https://bit.ly/adl2-ssd
```

In the top-level folder (that is, *Chapter 11, Object Detection*), create the dataset folder, copy the downloaded file there, and extract it by running:

```
mkdir dataset
cp drinks.tar.gz dataset
cd dataset
tar zxvf drinks.tar.gz
cd..
```

The SSD model is trained for 200 epochs by executing:

```
python3 ssd-11.6.1.py --train
```

The default batch size, `--batch-size=4`, can be adjusted depending on the GPU memory. On 1080Ti, the batch size is 2. On 32GB V100, this could be 4 or 8 per GPU. `--train` represents model training option.

To support normalization of bounding box offsets, the `--normalize` option is included. To use improved loss functions, the `--improved_loss` option is added. If only smooth L1 is desired (no focal loss), use `-smooth-l1`. To illustrate:

- L1, no normalization:
    - ○ `python3 ssd-11.1.1.py --train`

- Improved loss functions, no normalization:
    - ○ `python3 ssd-11.1.1.py --train --improved-loss`

- Improved loss functions, with normalization:
    - ○ `python3 ssd-11.1.1.py --train -improved-loss --normalize`

- Smooth L1, with normalization:
  - ○ `python3 ssd-11.1.1.py --train --smooth-l1 --normalize`

After training the SSD network, there is one more issue that we need to address. How do we deal with multiple predictions for a given object? Before we test our trained model, we will first discuss the **Non-Maximum Suppression (NMS)** algorithm.

12. Non-Maximum Suppression (NMS) algorithm

After the model training is completed, the network predicts bounding box offsets and corresponding categories. In some cases, two or more bounding boxes refer to the same object creating redundant predictions. The situation is shown in the case of a **Soda can** in *Figure 11.12.1*. To remove redundant predictions, a NMS algorithm is called. In this book, both classic NMS and soft NMS [6] are covered as shown in *Algorithm 11.12.1*. Both algorithms assume that bounding boxes and the corresponding confidence scores or probabilities are known.

Figure 11.12.1 The network predicted two overlapping bounding boxes for the Soda can object. Only one valid bounding box is chosen and that is the one with the higher score of 0.99.

In classic NMS, the final bounding boxes are selected based on probabilities and stored in list $\mathcal{D}$ and with corresponding scores $\mathcal{S}$. All bounding boxes and corresponding probabilities are stored in initial lists $\mathcal{B}$ and $\mathcal{P}$. In lines 3 and 4, the bounding box with the maximum score p_m is used as reference, b_m.

The reference bounding box is added to the list of final selected bounding boxes $\mathcal{D}$ and removed from the list $\mathcal{B}$ as shown in line 5. Its score is added to list $\mathcal{S}$ and removed from $\mathcal{P}$. For the remaining bounding boxes, if the *IoU* with b_m is greater than or equal to a set threshold N_t, it is removed from $\mathcal{B}$. Its corresponding score is also removed from $\mathcal{P}$.

The steps are shown in lines 6 and 9-11. The steps remove all redundant bounding boxes with smaller scores. After all the remaining bounding boxes have been examined, the process starting at line 3 is repeated. The process continues until the list of bounding boxes $\mathcal{B}$ has been emptied. The algorithm returns the selected bounding boxes $\mathcal{D}$ and corresponding scores $\mathcal{S}$.

The problem with classic NMS is a bounding box that contains another object but with significant *IoU* with b_m will be unceremoniously removed from the list. Soft NMS [6] proposes that instead of outright removal from the list, the score of the overlapping bounding box is decreased at a negative exponential rate in proportion to the square of its IoU with b_m as shown in line 8.

The overlapping bounding box is given a second chance. Bounding boxes with smaller IoUs will have higher chances of survival in future iterations. In the future selections, it may in fact prove that it contains a different object that is different from b_m. Soft NMS is an easy drop-in replacement to classic NMS as shown in *Algorithm 11.12.1*. There is no need to retrain the SSD network. Soft NMS exhibits higher average precision compared to classic NMS.

Listing 11.12.1 illustrates both classic and soft NMS. Other than the final bounding boxes and corresponding scores, the corresponding objects are also returned. The code implements an early termination of NMS when the maximum score of the remaining bounding boxes is less than a certain threshold (for example: 0.2).

Algorithm 11.12.1 **NMS and Soft NMS**

Require: Bounding box predictions: B = $\{b_1, b_2, ..., b_n\}$

Require: Bounding box class confidence or scores: B = $\{b_1, b_2, ..., b_n\}$

Require: NMS minimum *IoU* threshold: N_t

1. $\mathcal{D} \leftarrow \{\ \}; \mathcal{S} \leftarrow \{\ \}$
2. while $\mathcal{B} \neq empty$ do
3. $m \leftarrow argmax\ \mathcal{P}$
4. $\mathcal{M} \leftarrow b_m; \mathcal{N} \leftarrow p_m,$
5. $\mathcal{D} \leftarrow \mathcal{D} \cup \mathcal{M}; \mathcal{B} \leftarrow \mathcal{B} - \mathcal{M}; \mathcal{S} \leftarrow \mathcal{S} \cup \mathcal{N}; \mathcal{P} \leftarrow \mathcal{P} - \mathcal{N};$
6.   for steps b_i in $\mathcal{B}$ do

7.   if $soft\_NMS = True$ then

8. $p_i = p_i e^{-\frac{IoU(\mathcal{M}, b_i)^2}{\sigma}}$

9.   elif $IoU(\mathcal{M}, b_i) \geq N_t$ then

10. $\mathcal{B} = \mathcal{B} - b_i; \mathcal{P} = \mathcal{P} - p_i$

11.   end

12.   end

13. end

14. return $\mathcal{D}, \mathcal{S}$

Listing 11.12.1: `boxes.py`

```python
def nms(args, classes, offsets, anchors):
    """Perform NMS (Algorithm 11.12.1).

    Arguments:
        args: User-defined configurations
        classes (tensor): Predicted classes
        offsets (tensor): Predicted offsets

    Returns:
        objects (tensor): class predictions per anchor
        indexes (tensor): indexes of detected objects
            filtered by NMS
        scores (tensor): array of detected objects scores
            filtered by NMS
    """

    # get all non-zero (non-background) objects
    objects = np.argmax(classes, axis=1)
    # non-zero indexes are not background
    nonbg = np.nonzero(objects)[0]

    # D and S indexes in Line 1
    indexes = []
    while True:
        # list of zero probability values
        scores = np.zeros((classes.shape[0],))
        # set probability values of non-background
        scores[nonbg] = np.amax(classes[nonbg], axis=1)

        # max probability given the list
```

```
# Lines 3 and 4
score_idx = np.argmax(scores, axis=0)
score_max = scores[score_idx]

# get all non max probability & set it as new nonbg
# Line 5
nonbg = nonbg[nonbg != score_idx]

# if max obj probability is less than threshold (def 0.8)
if score_max < args.class_threshold:
    # we are done
    break


# Line 5
indexes.append(score_idx)
score_anc = anchors[score_idx]
score_off = offsets[score_idx][0:4]
score_box = score_anc + score_off
score_box = np.expand_dims(score_box, axis=0)
nonbg_copy = np.copy(nonbg)

# get all overlapping predictions (Line 6)
# perform Non-Max Suppression (NMS)
for idx in nonbg_copy:
    anchor = anchors[idx]
    offset = offsets[idx][0:4]
    box = anchor + offset
    box = np.expand_dims(box, axis=0)
    iou = layer_utils.iou(box, score_box)[0][0]
    # if soft NMS is chosen (Line 7)
    if args.soft_nms:
        # adjust score: Line 8
        iou = -2 * iou * iou
        classes[idx] *= math.exp(iou)
    # else NMS (Line 9), (iou threshold def 0.2)
    elif iou >= args.iou_threshold:
        # remove overlapping predictions with iou>threshold
        # Line 10
        nonbg = nonbg[nonbg != idx]

# Line 2, nothing else to process
if nonbg.size == 0:
    break
```

```
# get the array of object scores
scores = np.zeros((classes.shape[0],))
scores[indexes] = np.amax(classes[indexes], axis=1)

return objects, indexes, scores
```

Given that we have a trained SSD network and a method to suppress redundant predictions, the next section discusses the validation on our test dataset. Basically, we want to know if our SSD can perform object detection on never seen before images.

13. SSD model validation

After training the SSD model for 200 epochs, the performance can be validated. Three possible metrics for evaluation are used: 1) **IoU**, 2) **Precision**, and 3) **Recall.**

The first metric is **mean IoU (mIoU)**. Given the ground truth test dataset, the IoU between the ground truth bounding box and predicted bounding box is computed. This is done for all ground truth and predicted bounding boxes after performing NMS. The average of all IoUs is computed as mIoU:

$$mIoU = \frac{1}{n_{box}} \sum_{i \in \{1,2,..n_{box}\}} \max_{j \in \{1,2,..n_{pred}\}} IoU(b_i, d_j) \quad \text{(Equation 11.13.1)}$$

where n_{box} is the number of ground truth bounding boxes b_i and n_{pred} is the number of predicted bounding boxes d_j. Please note that this metric does not validate if the two overlapping bounding boxes belong to the same class. If this is required, then the code can be easily modified. *Listing 11.13.1* shows the code implementation.

The second metric is **precision** as shown in *Equation 11.3.2*. It is the number of object categories correctly predicted (true positive or TP) divided by the sum of the number of object categories correctly predicted (true positive or TP) plus the number of object categories wrongly predicted (false positive or FP). Precision is a measure of how good SSD is at correctly identifying objects in an image. The closer precision is to 1.0, the better.

$$precision = \frac{TP}{TP + FP} \quad \text{(Equation 11.3.2)}$$

The third metric is **recall**, as shown in *Equation 11.3.3*. It is the number of object categories correctly predicted (true positive or TP) divided by the sum of the number of object categories correctly predicted (true positive or TP) plus the number of objects missed (false negative or FN). Recall is a measure of how good SSD is at not misclassifying objects in an image. The closer recall is to 1.0, the better.

$$recall = \frac{TP}{TP + FN} \quad \text{(Equation 11.3.3)}$$

If we take the mean for all images in the test dataset, they are called average precision and average recall. In object detection, the precision and recall curves over different mIoUs are used to measure the performance. For the sake of simplicity, we only compute values of these metrics for a certain class threshold (default is 0.5). Interested readers are referred to the Pascal VOC [7] paper for more details on object detection metrics.

The results of the evaluation are shown in *Table 11.13.1*. The results can be obtained by running:

- No normalization:
  - ```
    python3 ssd-11.6.1.py --restore-weights=ResNet56v2-
    4layer-extra_anchors-drinks-200.h5 --evaluate
    ```

- No normalization, smooth L1:
  - ```
    python3 ssd-11.6.1.py --restore-weights=ResNet56v2-
    4layer-smooth_l1-extra_anchors-drinks-200.h5 --evaluate
    ```

- With normalization:
  - ```
    python3 ssd-11.6.1.py --restore-weights=ResNet56v2-
    4layer-norm-extra_anchors-drinks-200.h5 --evaluate
    --normalize
    ```

- With normalization, smooth L1:
  - ```
    python3 ssd-11.6.1.py --restore-weights=ResNet56v2-
    4layer-norm-smooth_l1-extra_anchors-drinks-200.h5
    --evaluate --normalize
    ```

- With normalization, smooth L1, focal loss:
  - ```
    python3 ssd-11.6.1.py --restore-weights=ResNet56v2-
    4layer-norm-improved_loss-extra_anchors-drinks-200.h5
    --evaluate --normalize
    ```

The weights are available on GitHub.
    ```

On mIoU, the best performance is the unnormalized offsets option, while the normalized offsets setting has the highest average precision and recall. It is expected that the performance is not state of the art considering there are only 1,000 images in the training dataset. There is also no data augmentation applied.

From the results, the performance suffers when the improvements on loss functions are used. This happens either when using smooth L1 or focal loss function or both. *Figure 11.13.1* to *Figure 11.13.5* show sample predictions. Object detections on an image can be obtained by executing:

```
python3 ssd-11.6.1.py --restore-weights=<weights_file>
--image-file=<target_image_file> --evaluate
```

For example, to run object detection on dataset/drinks/0010050.jpg:

```
python3 ssd-11.6.1.py --restore-weights=ResNet56v2-4layer-extra_
anchors-drinks-200.h5 --image-file=dataset/drinks/0010050.jpg
--evaluate
```

If the model weights filename has the word norm in it, please append the --normalize option.

Listing 11.13.1: ssd-11.6.1.py

```python
def evaluate_test(self):
    # test labels csv path
    path = os.path.join(self.args.data_path,
                        self.args.test_labels)
    # test dictionary
    dictionary, _ = build_label_dictionary(path)
    keys = np.array(list(dictionary.keys()))
    # sum of precision
    s_precision = 0
    # sum of recall
    s_recall = 0
    # sum of IoUs
    s_iou = 0
    # evaluate per image
    for key in keys:
        # ground truth labels
        labels = np.array(dictionary[key])
        # 4 boxes coords are 1st four items of labels
        gt_boxes = labels[:, 0:-1]
        # last one is class
        gt_class_ids = labels[:, -1]
        # load image id by key
        image_file = os.path.join(self.args.data_path, key)
```

```
        image = skimage.img_as_float(imread(image_file))
        image, classes, offsets = self.detect_objects(image)
        # perform nms
        _, _, class_ids, boxes = show_boxes(args,
                                            image,
                                            classes,
                                            offsets,
                                            self.feature_shapes,
                                            show=False)

        boxes = np.reshape(np.array(boxes), (-1,4))
        # compute IoUs
        iou = layer_utils.iou(gt_boxes, boxes)
        # skip empty IoUs
        if iou.size ==0:
            continue
        # the class of predicted box w/ max iou
        maxiou_class = np.argmax(iou, axis=1)

        # true positive
        tp = 0
        # false positiove
        fp = 0
        # sum of objects iou per image
        s_image_iou = []
        for n in range(iou.shape[0]):
            # ground truth bbox has a label
            if iou[n, maxiou_class[n]] > 0:
                s_image_iou.append(iou[n, maxiou_class[n]])
                # true positive has the same class and gt
                if gt_class_ids[n] == class_ids[maxiou_class[n]]:
                    tp += 1
                else:
                    fp += 1

        # objects that we missed (false negative)
        fn = abs(len(gt_class_ids) - tp)
        s_iou += (np.sum(s_image_iou) / iou.shape[0])
        s_precision += (tp/(tp + fp))
        s_recall += (tp/(tp + fn))

n_test = len(keys)
print_log("mIoU: %f" % (s_iou/n_test),
          self.args.verbose)
```

```
print_log("Precision: %f" % (s_precision/n_test),
          self.args.verbose)
print_log("Recall: %f" % (s_recall/n_test),
          self.args.verbose)
```

The results are as follows, in *Table 11.13.1*:

	Un-normalized offsets	Un-normalized offsets, smooth L1	Normalized offsets	Normalized offsets, smooth L1	Normalized offsets, smooth L1, focal loss
mIoU	0.64	0.61	0.53	0.50	0.51
Average precision	0.87	0.86	0.90	0.85	0.85
Average recall	0.87	0.85	0.87	0.83	0.83

Table 11.13.1 Performance benchmark of SSD on the test dataset.

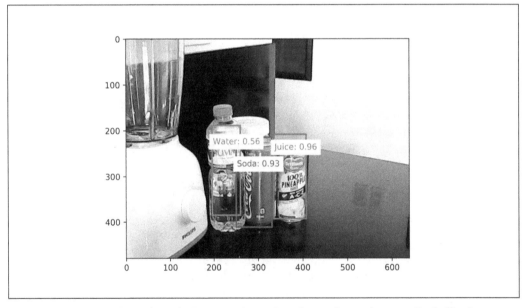

Figure 11.13.1 Example predictions on an image from the test dataset (unnormalized offsets).

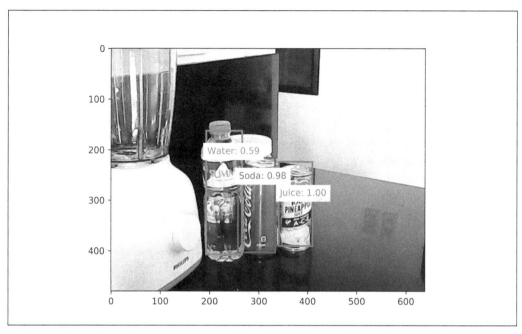

Figure 11.13.2 Example predictions on an image from the test dataset (unnormalized offsets, smooth L1).

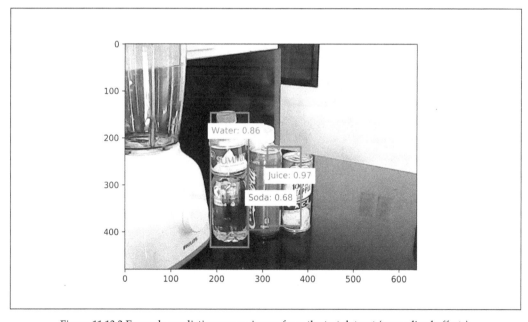

Figure 11.13.3 Example predictions on an image from the test dataset (normalized offsets).

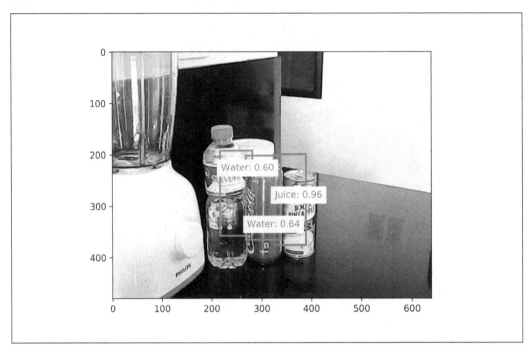

Figure 11.13.4 Example predictions on an image from the test dataset (normalized offsets, smooth L1).

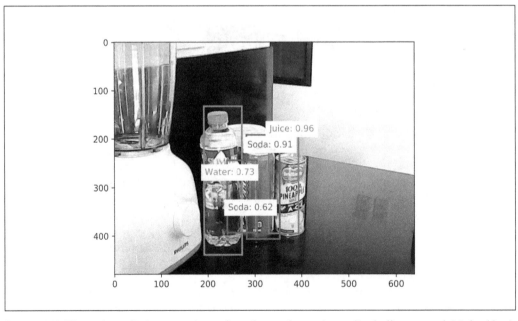

Figure 11.13.5 Example predictions on an image from the test dataset (normalized offsets, smooth L1, focal loss).

The results in this section validate our SSD model. An important lesson to learn is that as long as we understand the problem, no matter how complex it is we can incrementally build a working solution. SSD is by far the most complex model that we have covered in this book. It requires many utilities, modules, and a lot of data preparation and management to work.

14. Conclusion

In this chapter, the concept of multi-scale single shot object detection was discussed. Using anchor boxes that are centered on the centroid of the receptive field patches, the ground truth bounding box offsets are computed. Instead of raw pixel error, normalized pixel error encourages a bounded range that is more suitable for optimization.

The ground truth class label is assigned per anchor box. If an anchor box does not overlap an object, it is assigned the background class and its offset is not included in the offset loss computation. Focal loss has been proposed to improve the category loss function. The default L1 offset loss function can be replaced by a smooth L1 loss function.

Evaluation on the test dataset shows that normalized offset using default loss functions results in the best performance for average precision and recall while mIoU is improved when offsets normalization is removed. The performance can be improved by increasing the number and variation of train images.

In *Chapter 12*, *Semantic Segmentation*, builds upon the concepts developed in this chapter. In particular, we reuse the ResNet backbone network to build the segmentation network and the IoU metric for validation.

15. References

1. Krizhevsky Alex, Ilya Sutskever, and Geoffrey E. Hinton. *"Imagenet classification with deep convolutional neural networks."* Advances in neural information processing systems. 2012.

2. Liu Wei, et al. *"SSD: Single Shot MultiBox Detector."* European conference on computer vision. Springer, Cham, 2016.

3. Girshick Ross. *"Fast R-CNN."* Proceedings of the IEEE international conference on computer vision. 2015.

4. Lin Tsung-Yi, et al. *"Focal loss for Dense Object Detection.* "Proceedings of the IEEE international conference on computer vision. 2017.

5. Dutta, et al. *VGG Image Annotator* `http://www.robots.ox.ac.uk/~vgg/software/via/`

6. Bodla Navaneeth, et al. "*Soft-NMS--Improving Object Detection With One Line of Code.*" Proceedings of the IEEE international conference on computer vision. 2017.

7. Everingham Mark, et al. "*The Pascal Visual Object Classes (VOC) challenge.*" International journal of computer vision 88.2 (2010): 303-338.

8. "*Huber Loss.*" `https://en.wikipedia.org/wiki/Huber_loss`

12

Semantic Segmentation

In *Chapter 11, Object Detection*, we discussed object detection as an important computer vision algorithm with diverse practical applications. In this chapter, we will discuss another related algorithm called Semantic Segmentation. If the goal of object detection is to perform simultaneous localization and identification of each object in the image, in semantic segmentation, the aim is to classify each pixel according to its object class.

Extending the analogy further, in object detection, we use bounding boxes to show results. In semantic segmentation, all pixels for the same object belong to the same category. Visually, all pixels of the same object will have the same color. For example, all pixels belonging to the **soda can** category will be blue in color. Pixels for non-soda can objects will have a different color.

Similar to object detection, semantic segmentation has many practical applications. In medical imaging, it can be used to separate and measure regions of normal from abnormal cells. In satellite imaging, semantic segmentation can be used to measure forest cover or the extent of flooding during disasters. In general, semantic segmentation can be used to identify pixels belonging to the same class of object. Identifying the individual instances of each object is not important.

Curious readers may wonder what is the difference between different segmentation algorithms in general, and the semantic segmentation algorithm in particular? In the following section, we will qualify the different segmentation algorithms.

In summary, the goal of this chapter is to present:

- Different types of segmentation algorithms

- **Fully Convolutional Networks (FCNs)** as an implementation of the semantic segmentation algorithm

- Implementation and evaluation of FCN in `tf.keras`

We'll begin by discussing the different segmentation algorithms.

1. Segmentation

Segmentation algorithms partition an image into sets of pixels or regions. The purpose of partitioning is to understand better what the image represents. The sets of pixels may represent objects in the image that are of interest for a specific application. The manner in which we partition distinguishes the different segmentation algorithms.

In some applications, we are interested in specific countable objects in a given image. For example, in autonomous navigation, we are interested in instances of vehicles, traffic signs, pedestrians, and other objects on the roads. Collectively, these countable objects are called **things**. All other pixels are lumped together as background. This type of segmentation is called **instance segmentation**.

In other applications, we are not interested in countable objects but in amorphous uncountable regions, such as the sky, forests, vegetation, roads, grass, buildings, and bodies of water. These objects are collectively called **stuff**. This type of segmentation is called **semantic segmentation**.

Roughly, **things** and **stuff** together compose the entire image. If an algorithm can identify both things and stuff pixels, it is called **panoptic segmentation**, as defined by Kirilov et al. (2019) [1].

However, the distinction between things and stuff is not rigid. An application may consider countable objects collectively as stuff. For example, in a department store, it is impossible to identify instances of clothing on racks. They can be collectively lumped together as cloth stuff.

Figure 12.1.1 shows the distinction between different types of segmentation. The input image shows two soda cans and two juice cans on top of a table. The background is cluttered. Assuming that we are only interested in soda and juice cans, in instance segmentation, we assign a unique color to each object instance to distinguish the four objects individually. For semantic segmentation, we assume that we lump together all soda cans as stuff, juice cans as another stuff, and background as the last stuff. Basically, we have a unique color assigned to each stuff. Finally, in panoptic segmentation, we assume that only the background is stuff and we are only interested in instances of soda and juice cans.

For this book, we only explore semantic segmentation. Following the example in *Figure 12.1.1*, we will assign unique stuff categories to the objects that we used in *Chapter 11, Object Detection*: 1) **Water bottle**, 2) **Soda can**, and 3) **Juice can**. The fourth and last category is background.

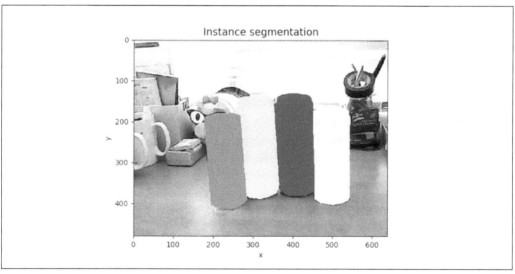

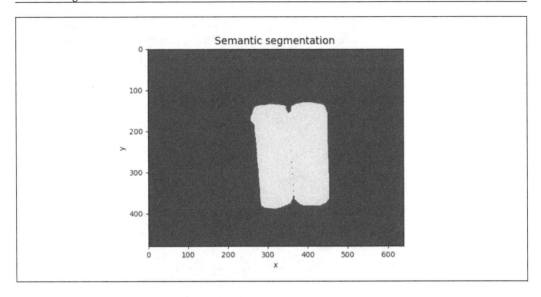

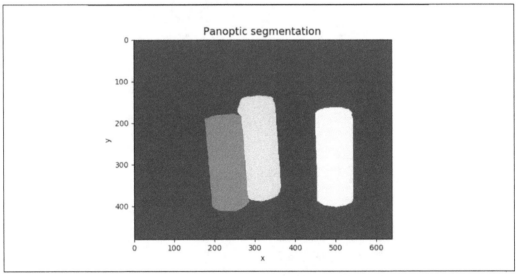

Figure 12.1.1: Four images showing the different segmentation algorithms. Best viewed in color. The original images can be found at https://github.com/PacktPublishing/Advanced-Deep-Learning-with-Keras/tree/master/chapter12-segmentation

2. Semantic segmentation network

From the previous section, we learned that the semantic segmentation network is a pixel-wise classifier. The network block diagram is shown in *Figure 12.2.1*. However, unlike a simple classifier (for example, the MNIST classifier in *Chapter 1, Introducing Advanced Deep Learning with Keras* and *Chapter 2, Deep Neural Networks*), where there is only one classifier generating a one-hot vector as output, in semantic segmentation, we have parallel classifiers running simultaneously. Each one is generating its own one-hot vector prediction. The number of classifiers is equal to the number of pixels in the input image or the product of image width and height. The dimension of each one-hot vector prediction is equal to the number of stuff object categories of interest.

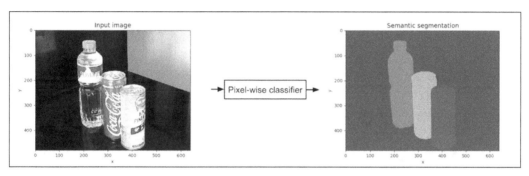

Figure 12.2.1: The semantic segmentation network can be viewed as a pixel-wise classifier. Best viewed in color. The original images can be found at https://github.com/PacktPublishing/Advanced-Deep-Learning-with-Keras/tree/master/chapter12-segmentation

For example, assuming we are interested in four of the categories: 0) **Background**, 1) **Water bottle**, 2) **Soda can**, and 3) **Juice can**, we can see in *Figure 12.2.2* that there are four pixels from each object category.

Each pixel is classified accordingly using a 4-dim `one-hot vector`. We use color shading to indicate the class category of the pixel. Using this knowledge, we can imagine that a semantic segmentation network predicts `image_width` x `image_height` 4-dim one-hot vectors as output, and one 4-dim one-hot vector per pixel:

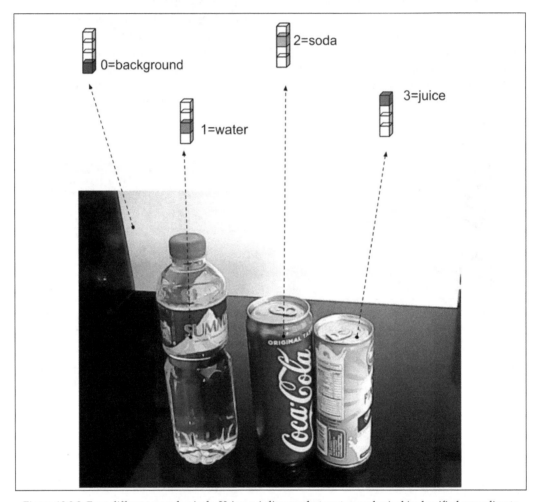

Figure 12.2.2: Four different sample pixels. Using a 4-dim one-hot vector, each pixel is classified according to its category. Best viewed in color. The original images can be found at https://github.com/PacktPublishing/Advanced-Deep-Learning-with-Keras/tree/master/chapter12-segmentation

Having understood the concept of semantic segmentation, we can now introduce a neural network pixel-wise classifier. Our semantic segmentation network architecture is inspired by *Fully Convolutional Network (FCN) by Long et al. (2015)* [2]. The key idea of FCN is to use multiple scales of feature maps in generating the final prediction.

Our semantic segmentation network is shown in *Figure 12.2.3*. Its input is an RGB image (for example, 640 x 480 x 3) and it outputs a tensor with similar dimensions except that the last dimension is the number of stuff categories (for example, 640 x 480 x 4 for a 4-stuff category). For visualization purposes, we map the output into RGB by assigning a color to each category:

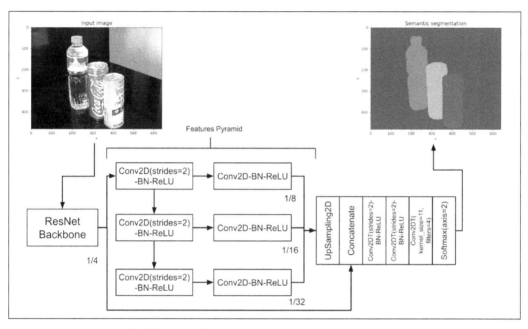

Figure 12.2.3: Network architecture of semantic segmentation. Kernel size is 3 unless indicated. Strides is 1 unless indicated. Best viewed in color. The original images can be found at https://github.com/ PacktPublishing/Advanced-Deep-Learning-with-Keras/tree/master/chapter12-segmentation

Similar to SSD that was discussed in *Chapter 11, Object Detection*, we employ a backbone network as a feature extractor. We use a similar ResNetv2 network in SSD. The ResNet backbone performs max pooling twice to arrive at the first set of feature maps with the dimensions being $\frac{1}{4}$ of the input image. The additional sets of feature maps are generated by using successive Conv2D(strides=2)-BN-ReLU layers, resulting in feature maps with dimensions $\left(\frac{1}{8}, \frac{1}{16}, \frac{1}{32}\right)$ of the input image.

Our semantic segmentation network architecture is further enhanced by the improvements made by *Pyramid Scene Parsing Network (PSPNet) by Zhao et al. (2017)* [3]. In PSPNet, each feature map is further processed by another convolutional layer. Furthermore, the first set of feature maps is also used.

Both FCN and PSPNet upsample the features pyramid to arrive at the same size as the first set of feature maps. Afterward, all upsampled features are fused together using a `Concatenate` layer. The concatenated layers are then processed twice by a transposed convolution with strides equal to 2 to put the original image width and height back. Lastly, a transposed convolution with a kernel size of 1 and filters equal to 4 (in other words, the number of categories) and a `Softmax` layer are used to generate the pixel-wise categorical prediction.

In the next section, we will discuss the `tf.keras` implementation of our segmentation network. We can reuse some network blocks in SSD from *Chapter 11, Object Detection*, to speed up our implementation.

3. Semantic segmentation network in Keras

As shown in *Figure 12.2.3*, we already have some of the key building blocks of our semantic segmentation network. We can reuse the ResNet model presented in *Chapter 2, Deep Neural Networks*. We just need to build the features' pyramid and the upsampling and prediction layers.

Borrowing the ResNet model that we developed in *Chapter 2, Deep Neural Networks*, and which was reused in *Chapter 11, Object Detection*, we extract a features' pyramid with four levels. *Listing 12.3.1* shows features' pyramid extraction from ResNet. `conv_layer()` is just a helper function to create a `Conv2D(strides=2)-BN-ReLU` layer.

Listing 12.3.1: `resnet.py`:

Features' pyramid function:

```
def features_pyramid(x, n_layers):
    """Generate features pyramid from the output of the
    last layer of a backbone network (e.g. ResNetv1 or v2)

    Arguments:
        x (tensor): Output feature maps of a backbone network
        n_layers (int): Number of additional pyramid layers

    Return:
        outputs (list): Features pyramid
    """
    outputs = [x]
    conv = AveragePooling2D(pool_size=2, name='pool1')(x)
```

```
        outputs.append(conv)
        prev_conv = conv
        n_filters = 512

        # additional feature map layers
        for i in range(n_layers - 1):
            postfix = "_layer" + str(i+2)
            conv = conv_layer(prev_conv,
                              n_filters,
                              kernel_size=3,
                              strides=2,
                              use_maxpool=False,
                              postfix=postfix)
            outputs.append(conv)
            prev_conv = conv

    return outputs
```

Listing 12.3.1 is just half of the features' pyramid. The remaining half is the convolution after each set of features. The other half is shown in *Listing 12.3.2*, together with the upsampling of each level of the pyramid. For example, features with dimensions of $1/8$ of the image size are upsampled by 2 to match their dimensions with the first set of features, which are $1/4$ of the image size. In the same listing, we also build the entire segmentation model, from the backbone network to the features' pyramid, to concatenating upsampled features' pyramids, and finally to further feature extractions, upsampling, and prediction. We use the n-dim (for example, 4-dim) Softmax layer at the output layer to perform pixel-wise classification.

Listing 12.3.2: model.py:

Building the semantic segmentation network:

```
    def build_fcn(input_shape,
                  backbone,
                  n_classes=4):
        """Helper function to build an FCN model.

        Arguments:
            backbone (Model): A backbone network
                such as ResNetv2 or v1
            n_classes (int): Number of object classes
                including background.
        """
```

```
inputs = Input(shape=input_shape)
features = backbone(inputs)

main_feature = features[0]
features = features[1:]
out_features = [main_feature]
feature_size = 8
size = 2
# other half of the features pyramid
# including upsampling to restore the
# feature maps to the dimensions
# equal to 1/4 the image size
for feature in features:
    postfix = "fcn_" + str(feature_size)
    feature = conv_layer(feature,
                         filters=256,
                         use_maxpool=False,
                         postfix=postfix)
    postfix = postfix + "_up2d"
    feature = UpSampling2D(size=size,
                           interpolation='bilinear',
                           name=postfix)(feature)
    size = size * 2
    feature_size = feature_size * 2
    out_features.append(feature)

# concatenate all upsampled features
x = Concatenate()(out_features)
# perform 2 additional feature extraction
# and upsampling
x = tconv_layer(x, 256, postfix="up_x2")
x = tconv_layer(x, 256, postfix="up_x4")
# generate the pixel-wise classifier
x = Conv2DTranspose(filters=n_classes,
                    kernel_size=1,
                    strides=1,
                    padding='same',
                    kernel_initializer='he_normal',
                    name="pre_activation")(x)
x = Softmax(name="segmentation")(x)

model = Model(inputs, x, name="fcn")

return model
```

Given the segmentation network model, we use the Adam optimizer with a learning rate of 1e-3 and a categorical cross-entropy loss function to train the network. *Listing 12.3.3* shows the model building and train function calls. The learning rate is halved every 20 epochs after 40 epochs. We monitor the network performance using the `AccuracyCallback`, similar to the SSD network in *Chapter 11, Object Detection*. The callback computes the performance using **mean IoU (mIoU)** metrics similar to the mean IoU for object detection. The weights of the best performing mean IoU are saved on a file. The network is trained for 100 epochs by calling `fit_generator()`.

Listing 12.3.3: `fcn-12.3.1.py`:

Initialization and training of a semantic segmentation network:

```
def build_model(self):
    """Build a backbone network and use it to
        create a semantic segmentation
        network based on FCN.
    """

    # input shape is (480, 640, 3) by default
    self.input_shape = (self.args.height,
                        self.args.width,
                        self.args.channels)

    # build the backbone network (eg ResNet50)
    # the backbone is used for 1st set of features
    # of the features pyramid
    self.backbone = self.args.backbone(self.input_shape,
                                       n_layers=self.args.layers)

    # using the backbone, build fcn network
    # output layer is a pixel-wise classifier
    self.n_classes =  self.train_generator.n_classes
    self.fcn = build_fcn(self.input_shape,
                         self.backbone,
                         self.n_classes)


def train(self):
    """Train an FCN"""
    optimizer = Adam(lr=1e-3)
    loss = 'categorical_crossentropy'
    self.fcn.compile(optimizer=optimizer, loss=loss)

    log = "# of classes %d" % self.n_classes
```

```
print_log(log, self.args.verbose)
log = "Batch size: %d" % self.args.batch_size
print_log(log, self.args.verbose)

# prepare callbacks for saving model weights
# and learning rate scheduler
# model weights are saved when test iou is highest
# learning rate decreases by 50% every 20 epochs
# after 40th epoch
accuracy = AccuracyCallback(self)
scheduler = LearningRateScheduler(lr_scheduler)

callbacks = [accuracy, scheduler]
# train the fcn network
self.fcn.fit_generator(generator=self.train_generator,
                       use_multiprocessing=True,
                       callbacks=callbacks,
                       epochs=self.args.epochs,
                       workers=self.args.workers)
```

The multithreaded data generator class, `DataGenerator`, is similar to what was used in *Chapter 11, Object Detection*. As shown in *Listing 12.3.4*, the `__data_generation (self, keys)` signature method was modified to generate a pair of image tensors and its corresponding pixel-wise ground truth labels or segmentation mask. In the next section, we will discuss how to generate ground truth labels.

Listing 12.3.4: `data_generator.py`:

Data generation method of the `DataGenerator` class for semantic segmentation:

```
def __data_generation(self, keys):
    """Generate train data: images and
    segmentation ground truth labels

    Arguments:
        keys (array): Randomly sampled keys
            (key is image filename)

    Returns:
        x (tensor): Batch of images
```

```
        y (tensor): Batch of pixel-wise categories
    """
    # a batch of images
    x = []
    # and their corresponding segmentation masks
    y = []

    for i, key in enumerate(keys):
        # images are assumed to be stored
        # in self.args.data_path
        # key is the image filename
        image_path = os.path.join(self.args.data_path, key)
        image = skimage.img_as_float(imread(image_path))
        # append image to the list
        x.append(image)
        # and its corresponding label (segmentation mask)
        labels = self.dictionary[key]
        y.append(labels)

    return np.array(x), np.array(y)
```

The semantic segmentation network is now complete. Using `tf.keras`, we have discussed its architecture implementation, initialization, and training.

Before we can run the training procedure, we need the training and test datasets with ground truth labels. In the next section, we will discuss the semantic segmentation dataset that we will use in this chapter.

4. Example dataset

We can use the dataset that we used in *Chapter 11, Object Detection*. Recall that we used a small dataset comprising 1,000 640 x 480 RGB train images and 50 640 x 480 RGB test images collected using an inexpensive USB camera (A4TECH PK-635G). However, instead of labeling using bounding boxes and categories, we traced the edges of each object category using a polygon shape. We used the same dataset annotator called **VGG Image Annotator (VIA)** [4] to manually trace the edges and assign the following labels: 1) **Water bottle**, 2) **Soda can**, and 3) **Juice can**.

Figure 12.4.1 shows a sample UI of the labeling process.

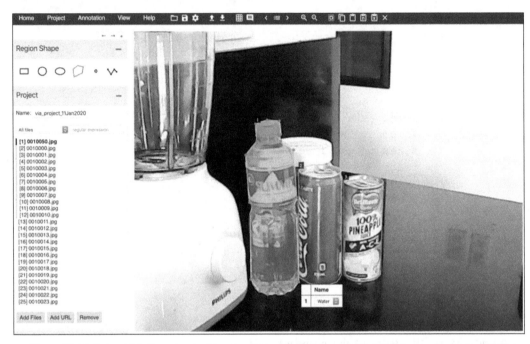

Figure 12.4.1: Dataset labeling process for semantic segmentation using the VGG Image Annotator (VIA)

The VIA labeling software saves the annotation on a JSON file. For the training and test datasets, these are:

```
segmentation_train.json
segmentation_test.json
```

The polygon region stored on the JSON files could not be used as it is. Each region has to be converted into a segmentation mask, which is a tensor with the dimensions $image_{width}$ x $image_{height}$ x $pixel - wise\_category$. In this dataset, the dimensions of the segmentation mask are 640 x 480 x 4. The category 0 is for background, and the rest are 1) for **Water bottle**, 2) for **Soda can**, and 3) for **Juice can**. In the `utils` folder, we created a tool, `generate_gt_segmentation.py`, to convert the JSON file into segmentation masks. For convenience, the ground truth data for training and testing is stored inside the compressed dataset, which we downloaded from `https://bit.ly/adl2-ssd` in the previous chapter:

```
segmentation_train.npy
segmentation_test.npy
```

Each file contains a dictionary of ground truth data in the format `image filename:` `segmentation mask`, which is loaded during training and validation. *Figure 12.4.2* shows an example of the segmentation mask of the image in *Figure 12.4.1*, visualized using colored pixels.

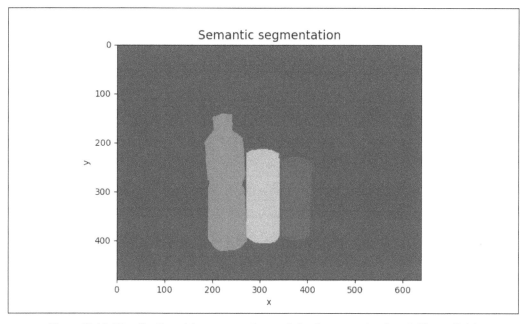

Figure 12.4.2: Visualization of the segmentation mask for the annotation done in Figure 12.4.1

We are now ready to train and validate the semantic segmentation network. In the next section, we will show the results of the semantic segmentation on the dataset that we annotated in this section.

5. Semantic segmentation validation

To train the semantic segmentation network, run the following command:

```
python3 fcn-12.3.1.py --train
```

At every epoch, the validation is also executed to determine the best performing parameters. For semantic segmentation, two metrics can be used. The first is mean IoU. This is similar to the mean IoU in object detection in the previous chapter. The difference is that the IoU is computed between the ground truth segmentation mask and the predicted segmentation mask for each stuff category. This includes the background. The mean IoU is simply the average of all IoUs for the test dataset.

Figure 12.5.1 shows the performance of our semantic segmentation network using mIoU at every epoch. The maximum mIoU is 0.91. This is relatively high. However, our dataset only has four object categories:

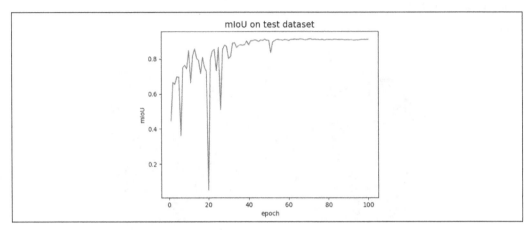

Figure 12.5.1: Semantic segmentation performance during training using mIoU for the test dataset

The second metric is average pixel accuracy. This is similar to how the accuracy is computed on a classifier prediction. The difference is that, instead of having one prediction, the segmentation network has a number of predictions equal to the number of pixels in the image. For each test input image, an average pixel accuracy is computed. Then, the mean for all the test images is computed.

Figure 12.5.2 shows the performance of our semantic segmentation network using average pixel accuracy at every epoch. The maximum average pixel accuracy is 97.9%. We can see the correlation between average pixel accuracy and mIoU:

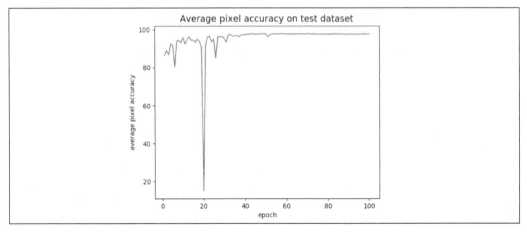

Figure 12.5.2: Semantic segmentation performance during training using average pixel accuracy for the test dataset

Figure 12.5.3 shows a sample of the input image, the ground truth semantic segmentation mask, and the predicted semantic segmentation mask:

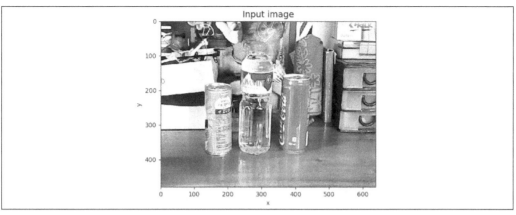

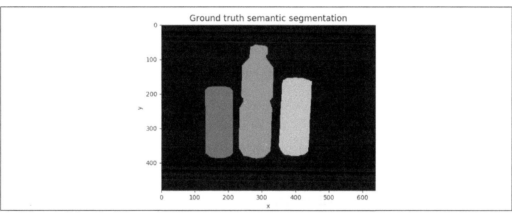

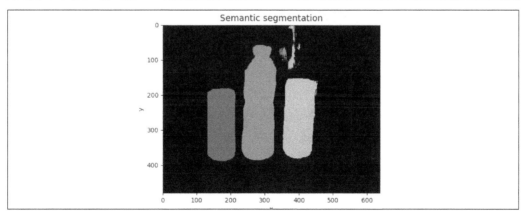

Figure 12.5.3: Sample input, ground truth, and prediction for semantic segmentation.
We assigned the color black for the background class instead of purple, as was used earlier

Overall, our semantic segmentation network that is based on FCN and improved by ideas from PSPNet is performing relatively well. Our semantic segmentation network is by no means optimized. The number of filters in the features' pyramid can be reduced to minimize the number of parameters, which is about 11.1 million. It is also interesting to explore increasing the number of levels in the features' pyramid. The reader may run validation by executing:

```
python3 fcn-12.3.1.py --evaluate
--restore-weights=ResNet56v2-3layer-drinks-best-iou.h5
```

In the next chapter, we will introduce unsupervised learning algorithms. There has been a strong motivation to develop unsupervised learning techniques considering the costly and time-consuming labeling needed in supervised learning. For example, in the semantic segmentation dataset in this chapter, it took one person about 4 days of manual labeling. Deep learning will not advance if it requires human labeling all the time.

6. Conclusion

In this chapter, the concept of segmentation was discussed. We learned that there are different categories of segmentation. Each has its own target application. This chapter focused on the network design, implementation, and validation of semantic segmentation.

Our semantic segmentation network was inspired by FCN, which has been the basis of many modern-day, state-of-the-art segmentation algorithms, such as Mask-R-CNN [5]. Our network was further enhanced by ideas from PSPNet, which won first place in the ImageNet 2016 parsing challenge.

Using the VIA labeling tool, a new dataset label for semantic segmentation was generated using the same set of images employed in *Chapter 11, Object Detection*. The segmentation mask labels all pixels belonging to the same object class.

Our semantic segmentation network was trained and validated using mean IoU and average pixel accuracy metrics. The performance on the test dataset shows that it can effectively classify pixels in our test images.

As mentioned in the last section of this chapter, the field of deep learning is realizing the limits of supervised learning due to the costs and time involved. The next chapter focuses on unsupervised learning. It takes advantage of the concept of mutual information that is used in information theory in the field of communications.

7. References

1. Kirillov, Alexander, et al.: *Panoptic Segmentation*. Proceedings of the IEEE conference on computer vision and pattern recognition. 2019.

2. Long, Jonathan, Evan Shelhamer, and Trevor Darrell: *Fully Convolutional Networks for Semantic Segmentation*. Proceedings of the IEEE conference on computer vision and pattern recognition. 2015.

3. Zhao, Hengshuang, et al.: *Pyramid Scene Parsing Network*. Proceedings of the IEEE conference on computer vision and pattern recognition. 2017.

4. Dutta, et al.: *VGG Image Annotator* `http://www.robots.ox.ac.uk/~vgg/software/via/`

5. He Kaiming, et al.: *Mask R-CNN*. Proceedings of the IEEE international conference on computer vision. 2017.

13

Unsupervised Learning Using Mutual Information

Many machine learning tasks such as classification, detection, and segmentation are dependent on labeled data. The performance of a network on these tasks is directly affected by the quality of labeling and the amount of data. The problem is that producing a sufficient amount of good-quality annotated data is costly and time-consuming.

To continue the progress of development in machine learning, new algorithms should be less dependent on human labelers. Ideally, a network should learn from unlabeled data, which is abundant due to the growth of the internet and the popularity of sensing devices such as smartphones and the **Internet of Things** (**IoT**). Learning from unlabeled data is a field of unsupervised learning. In some cases, unsupervised learning is also called self-supervised learning to emphasize the use of pure unlabeled data for training and the absence of human supervision. In this text, we will use the term unsupervised learning.

There are approaches that learn from unlabeled data in machine learning. The performance of these approaches can be improved using deep neural networks and new ideas in unsupervised learning. This is especially true when dealing with highly unstructured data such as text, image, audio, and video.

One of the successful approaches in unsupervised learning is maximizing mutual information between two random variables in a given neural network. In the field of information theory, **Mutual Information** (**MI**) is a measure of dependency between two random variables.

MI has recently been successful in extracting useful information from unlabeled data that could aid in learning downstream tasks. For example, MI is able to cluster latent code vectors such that a classification task becomes a simple linear separation problem.

In summary, the goal of this chapter is to present:

- The concept of Mutual Information
- Estimating MI using neural networks
- The maximization of MI on discrete and continuous random variables for downstream tasks
- The implementation of MI estimation networks in Keras

We will begin by introducing the concept of Mutual Information.

1. Mutual Information

Mutual Information is a measure of dependency between two random variables, X and Y. Sometimes, MI is also defined as the amount of information about X through observing Y. MI is also known as information gain or reduction in the uncertainty of X upon observing Y.

In contrast with correlation, MI can measure non-linear statistical dependence between X and Y. In deep learning, MI is a suitable method since most real-world data is unstructured and the dependency between input and output is generally non-linear. In deep learning, the end goal is to perform specific tasks such as classification, translation, regression, or detection on input data and a pre-trained model. These tasks are also known as downstream tasks.

Since MI can uncover important aspects of dependencies in inputs, intermediate features, representation, and outputs, which are random variables themselves, shared information generally improves the performance of models in downstream tasks.

Mathematically, the MI between two random variables X and Y can be defined as:

$$I(X;Y) = D_{KL}\big(P(X,Y) \parallel P(X)P(Y)\big) \quad \text{(Equation 13.1.1)}$$

where:

- $P(X, Y)$ is the joint distribution of X and Y on sample space X x Y.
- $P(X) P(Y)$ is the product of marginal distributions $P(X)$ and $P(Y)$ on sample spaces X and Y respectively.

In other words, MI is the **Kullback-Leibler (KL)** divergence between the joint distribution and the product of marginal distributions. Recall from *Chapter 5, Improved GANs*, KL is a measure of distance between two distributions. In the context of MI, the higher the KL distance, the higher the MI between two random variables, X and Y. By extension, the higher the MI, the higher the dependency of X on Y.

Since MI is equal to the KL divergence between the joint and product of marginal distributions, it implies that it is greater or equal to zero: $I(X;Y) \geq 0$. MI is exactly equal to zero when X and Y are independent random variables. When X and Y are independent, observing one random variable (for example, Y) does not give any information about the other random variable (for example, X). Therefore, MI is a measure of how far X and Y are from being independent.

If X and Y are **discrete random variables**, by expanding the KL divergence MI can be computed as:

$$I(X;Y) = \mathbb{E}_{(X,Y) \sim P(X,Y)} \, log \frac{P(X,Y)}{P(X)P(Y)} = \sum_{X \in \mathcal{X}} \sum_{Y \in \mathcal{Y}} P(X,Y) \, log \frac{P(X,Y)}{P(X)P(Y)} \quad \text{(Equation 13.1.2)}$$

where:

- $P(X, Y)$ is the joint **probability mass function (PMF)**.
- $P(X)$ and $P(Y)$ are marginal PMFs.

If the joint and marginal distributions are known, MI has an exact computation.

If X and Y are **continuous random variables**, by expanding the KL divergence, MI can be expressed as:

$$I(X;Y) = \int_X \int_Y p(x,y) \, log \frac{p(x,y)}{p(x)p(y)} \, dx \, dy \quad \text{(Equation 13.1.3)}$$

where:

- $p(x, y)$ is the joint **probability distribution function (PDF)**.
- $p(x)$ and $p(y)$ are marginal PDFs.

MI for continuous random variables is generally intractable and estimated by variational methods. In this chapter, we will discuss techniques for estimating MI between two continuous random variables.

Before discussing techniques for computing Mutual Information, let's first explain the relationship between MI and entropy. Entropy was informally introduced in *Chapter 6, Disentangled Representation GANs*, with applications in InfoGAN.

2. Mutual Information and Entropy

MI can also be interpreted in terms of entropy. Recall from *Chapter 6, Disentangled Representation GANs*, that entropy, $H(X)$, is a measure of the expected amount of information of a random variable X:

$$H(X) = -\mathbb{E}_{x \sim P(x)}[log\, P(x)] \quad \text{(Equation 13.2.1)}$$

Equation 13.2.1 implies that entropy is also a measure of uncertainty. The occurrence of uncertain events gives us a higher amount of surprise, or information. For example, news about an employee's unexpected promotion has a high amount of information, or entropy.

Using *Equation 13.2.1*, MI can be expressed as:

$$I(X;Y) = D_{KL}\big(P(X,Y) \,\|\, P(X)P(Y)\big) = \mathbb{E}\left[log\,\frac{P(X,Y)}{P(X)P(Y)}\right]$$

$$I(X;Y) = \mathbb{E}[log\, P(X,Y)] - \mathbb{E}[log\, P(X)] - \mathbb{E}[log\, P(Y)]$$

$$I(X;Y) = H\big(P(X)\big) + H\big(P(Y)\big) - H\big(P(X,Y)\big)$$

$$I(X;Y) = H(X) + H(Y) - H(X,Y) \quad \text{(Equation 13.2.2)}$$

Equation 13.2.2 implies that MI increases with marginal entropy but decreases with joint entropy. A more common expression for MI in terms of entropy is as follows:

$$I(X;Y) = \mathbb{E}\left[log\,\frac{P(X,Y)}{P(X)P(Y)}\right] = \mathbb{E}\left[log\,\frac{P(X|Y)}{P(X)}\right]$$

$$I(X;Y) = \mathbb{E}[log\, P(X|Y)] - \mathbb{E}[log\, P(X)]$$

$$I(X;Y) = H\big(P(X)\big) - H\big(P(X|Y)\big) = H(X) - H(X|Y) \quad \text{(Equation 13.2.3)}$$

Equation 13.2.3 tells us that MI increases with the entropy of a random variable but decreases with the conditional entropy on another random variable. Alternatively, MI is how much decrease in information or uncertainty in X, had we known Y.

Equivalently,

$$I(X;Y) = \mathbb{E}\left[log\,\frac{P(X,Y)}{P(X)P(Y)}\right] = \mathbb{E}\left[log\,\frac{P(Y|X)}{P(Y)}\right]$$

$$I(X;Y) = H\big(P(Y)\big) - H\big(P(Y|X)\big) = H(Y) - H(Y|X) \quad \text{(Equation 13.2.4)}$$

Equation 13.2.4 implies that MI is symmetric:

$$I(Y;X) = I(X;Y) \quad \text{(Equation 13.2.5)}$$

MI can also be expressed in terms of the conditional entropy of X and Y:

$$I(X;Y) = \mathbb{E}\left[log\,\frac{P(X,Y)}{P(X)P(Y)}\right] = \mathbb{E}[log\,P(X,Y)] - \mathbb{E}[log\,P(X)] - \mathbb{E}[log\,P(Y)] \quad \text{(Equation 13.2.6)}$$

Using Bayes' theorem:

$$I(X;Y) = \mathbb{E}[log\,P(X,Y)] - \mathbb{E}\left[log\,\frac{P(X,Y)}{P(Y|X)}\right] - \mathbb{E}\left[log\,\frac{P(X,Y)}{P(X|Y)}\right]$$

$$I(X;Y) = -\mathbb{E}[log\,P(X,Y)] + \mathbb{E}[log\,P(Y|X)] + \mathbb{E}[log\,P(X|Y)]$$

$$I(X;Y) = H\big(P(X,Y)\big) - H\big(P(Y|X)\big) - H\big(P(X|Y)\big)$$

$$I(X;Y) = H(X,Y) - H(Y|X) - H(X|Y) \quad \text{(Equation 13.2.7)}$$

Figure 13.2.1 summarizes all the relationships between MI and conditional and marginal entropies that we have discussed so far:

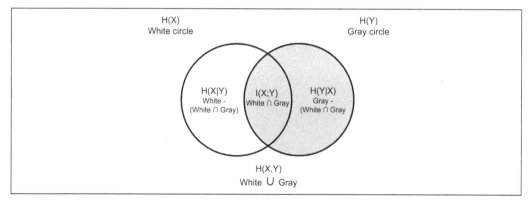

Figure 13.2.1 Venn diagram showing the relationships between MI and conditional and marginal entropies

Another interesting interpretation of MI is from *Equation 13.2.3*, which can be rewritten as:

$$H(X|Y) = H(X) - I(X;Y) \quad \text{(Equation 13.2.8)}$$

Since $H(X| Y)$ is the uncertainty of X upon observing Y, *Equation 13.2.8* tells us that we are more certain about X given Y if we can maximize MI. In *Figure 13.2.1*, the area of crescent shape $H(X| Y)$ decreases as the intersection between the circles representing MI increases.

As a more concrete example, suppose X is a random variable representing the event of observing a number between 0 and 255 inclusive in a given random byte. Assuming a uniform distribution, this translates to a probability of $P(X) = \dfrac{1}{256}$. The entropy of X in base 2 is:

$$H(X) = - \sum_{X \sim P(X)} P(X) \, log_2 \, P(X) = - \sum_{X \sim P(X)} \frac{1}{256} log_2 \frac{1}{256} = 256 \times \frac{8}{256} = 8$$

Suppose the random variable Y represents the 4 most significant bits of a random byte. If we observed that the 4 most significant bits are all zeros, then numbers 0 to 15 inclusive have $P(X) = \dfrac{1}{16}$, while the rest have $P(X) = 0$. The conditional entropy in base 2 is:

$$H(X|Y) = - \sum_{X \sim P(X|Y)} P(X|Y) \, log_2 \, P(X|Y) = - \sum_{X \sim P(X|Y)} \frac{1}{16} log_2 \frac{1}{16} = 16 \times \frac{4}{16} = 4$$

This gives us MI of $I(X;Y) = 8 - 4 = 4$. Note that the uncertainty or the amount of expected information in random variable X decreased upon knowing Y. The mutual information shared by X and Y is 4, which is also equal to the number of bits shared by the two random variables. *Figure 13.2.2* illustrates two cases where all bits are random and the four most significant bits are all 0.

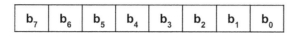

A) If all bits are unknown, the entropy of observing a number between 0 and 255 for a given random byte is 8.

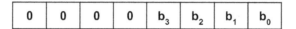

B) If bits b_4 to b_7 are all 0, the entropy of observing a number between 0 and 255 for a given random byte is 4. Only numbers 0 to 15 have non zero probability of 1/16. The rest have 0 probability.

Figure 13.2.2 Entropy when all bits are unknown versus when some bits are known

Given that we already have a good understanding of MI and entropy, we can now exploit this concept as a method for unsupervised learning.

3. Unsupervised learning by maximizing the Mutual Information of discrete random variables

A classic problem in deep learning is supervised classification. In *Chapter 1*, *Introducing Advanced Deep Learning with Keras*, and *Chapter 2*, *Deep Neural Networks*, we learned that in supervised classification, we need labeled input images. We performed classification on both the MNIST and CIFAR10 datasets. For MNIST, a 3-layer CNN and a Dense layer can achieve as much as 99.3% accuracy. For CIFAR10, using ResNet or DenseNet, we can achieve about 93% to 94% accuracy. Both MNIST and CIFAR10 are labeled datasets.

Unlike supervised learning, our objective in this chapter is to perform unsupervised learning. Our focus is on classification without labels. The idea is if we learn how to cluster latent code vectors of all training data, then a linear separation algorithm can classify each test input data latent vector.

To learn the clustering of latent code vectors without labels, our training objective is to maximize MI between the input image X and its latent code Y. Both X and Y are random variables. The idea is that *similar* looking images will have latent vectors that cluster into the same regions. Regions that are far from each other can be easily separated by a linear assignment problem. Thus, the problem of classification can be done in an unsupervised manner. Mathematically, the objective is to maximize:

$$I(X;Y) = H(X) - H(X|Y) \quad \text{(Equation 13.2.3)}$$

Intuitively, once we have observed Y, we are confident about X. The problem with *Equation 13.2.3* is we do not have a good estimate of the density $P(X|Y)$ to measure $H(X|Y)$.

Invariant Information Clustering (IIC) by Ji et al. [1] proposed to measure $I(X;Y)$ directly from joint and marginal distributions. The objective is to use *Equation 13.1.2* to measure the MI between two latent code random variables that refer to the same input. Let's assume that the input X is encoded as Z:

$$Z = \mathcal{E}(X)$$

The same input X is transformed as $\bar{X} = \mathcal{G}(X)$ such that $\bar{X}$ remains clearly classifiable with the same category as X. In image processing, $\mathcal{G}$ can be a common operation such as small rotation, random cropping, and shearing. Sometimes, operations such as contrast and brightness adjustment, edge detection, the addition of small amounts of noise, and normalization are also acceptable as long as the meaning of the resulting image remains the same. For example, if X is an image of a dog, after $\mathcal{G}$, $\bar{X}$ is still obviously a dog.

The latent code vector using the same encoder network is:

$$\bar{Z} = \mathcal{E}(\bar{X})$$

Therefore, we can rewrite *Equation 13.1.2* in terms of the two random variables Z and $\bar{Z}$ as:

$$I(Z;\bar{Z}) = \sum_{z \in Z} \sum_{\bar{z} \in \bar{Z}} P(Z,\bar{Z}) \log \frac{P(Z,\bar{Z})}{P(Z)P(\bar{Z})} \quad \text{(Equation 13.3.1)}$$

Where $P(Z)$ and $P(\bar{Z})$ can be interpreted as the marginal distributions of Z and $\bar{Z}$. For discrete random variables, Z and $\bar{Z}$ both $P(Z)$ and $P(\bar{Z})$ are categorical distributions. We can imagine that the encoder output is a *softmax* with dimensionality equal to the number of classes, N, in the train and test data distributions. For example, for MNIST, the encoder output is a 10-dimensional one-hot vector corresponding to the 10 digits in both the train and test datasets.

To determine each term in *Equation 13.3.1*, we start by estimating $P(Z,\bar{Z})$. IIC assumes Z and $\bar{Z}$ are independent such that the joint distribution can be estimated as:

$$P(Z,\bar{Z}) = P(Z)P(\bar{Z})^T \quad \text{(Equation 13.3.2)}$$

This creates an $N \times N$ matrix $P(Z,\bar{Z})$ where each element Z_{ij} corresponds to the probability of simultaneously observing two random variables $(Z_i, \bar{Z}_j)$. If this estimation is done for a large batch size, the mean of the large sample size estimates the joint probability.

Since we will use MI to estimate the density functions, IIC constraints the sampling to $(Z_i, \bar{Z}_i)$. Essentially, for every sample X_i, we compute its latent code, $P(Z_i) = \mathcal{E}(X_i)$. Then, we transform X_i and compute its latent code, $P(\bar{Z}_i) = \varepsilon(\bar{X}_i)$. The joint distribution is computed as:

$$P(Z,\bar{Z}) = \frac{1}{M} \sum_{i=1}^{M} P(Z_i)P(\bar{Z}_i)^T \quad \text{(Equation 13.3.3)}$$

Where M is the batch size. Since we use the same encoder $\mathcal{E}$ for both X_i and $\bar{X}_i$, the resulting joint distribution should be symmetrical. We enforce symmetry by executing:

$$P(Z,\bar{Z}) = \frac{P(Z,\bar{Z}) + P(Z,\bar{Z})^T}{2} \quad \text{(Equation 13.3.4)}$$

Given $P(Z, \bar{Z})$, the marginal distributions can be computed as:

$$P(Z) = \sum_{j=1}^{N} P(Z_i, \bar{Z}_j) \quad \text{(Equation 13.3.5)}$$

We sum all entries of the matrix row-wise. Similarly:

$$P(\bar{Z}) = \sum_{i=1}^{N} P(Z_i, \bar{Z}_j) \quad \text{(Equation 13.3.6)}$$

We sum all entries of the matrix column-wise.

Given all the terms in *Equation 13.3.1* we can train a neural network encoder $\mathcal{E}$ that maximizes MI or minimizes the negative MI using the loss function:

$$\mathcal{L}(Z, \bar{Z}) = -I(Z; \bar{Z}) = \sum_{Z \in Z} \sum_{\bar{Z} \in \bar{Z}} P(Z, \bar{Z})(\log P(Z) + \log P(\bar{Z}) - \log P(Z, \bar{Z})) \quad \text{(Equation 13.3.7)}$$

Before we implement unsupervised clustering, let us reflect again on the objective – maximize $I(Z; \bar{Z})$. Since X and $\bar{X} = \mathcal{G}(X)$ and their corresponding latent code vectors Z and $\bar{Z}$ share the same information, then the neural network encoder $\mathcal{E}$ should learn to map X and $\bar{X}$ into latent vectors Z and $\bar{Z}$ that have almost the same value in order to maximize their MI. In the context of MNIST, similar-looking digits will have latent code vectors that cluster in the same region in space.

If the latent code vector is the output of *softmax*, then it implies that we are performing unsupervised clustering, which can be converted to a classifier using a linear assignment algorithm. In this chapter, we will present two possible linear assignment algorithms that can be used to convert unsupervised clustering into unsupervised classification.

In the next section, we will discuss the encoder network model that can be used to implement unsupervised clustering. In particular, we will introduce the encoder network that can be used to estimate both $P(Z)$ and $P(\bar{Z})$.

4. Encoder network for unsupervised clustering

The encoder network implementation for unsupervised clustering is shown in *Figure 13.4.1*. It is an encoder with a VGG-like [2] backbone and a Dense layer with a *softmax* output. The simplest VGG-11 has a backbone, as shown in *Figure 13.4.2*.

For MNIST, using the simplest VGG-11 backbone decimates the feature map size to zero from 5 times the `MaxPooling2D` operations. Therefore, a scaled-down version of the VGG-11 backbone is used, as shown in *Figure 13.4.3*, when implemented in Keras. The same set of filters is used.

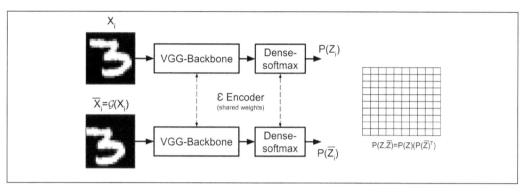

Figure 13.4.1 Network implementation of IIC encoder network $\mathcal{E}$. The input MNIST image is center cropped to 24 x 24 pixels. In this example, $\bar{X} = \mathcal{G}(X)$ is a random 24 x 24-pixel cropping operation.

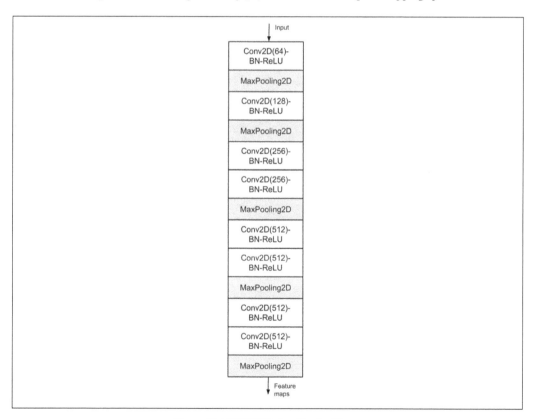

Figure 13.4.2 VGG-11 classifier backbone

In *Figure 13.4.3*, there are 4 `Conv2D-BN-ReLU Activation-MaxPooling2D` layers with filter sizes (64,128,256,512). The last `Conv2D` layer does not use `MaxPooling2D`. Therefore, the last `Conv2D` layer outputs a (3,3,512) feature map for a 24 x 24 x 1 cropped MNIST input.

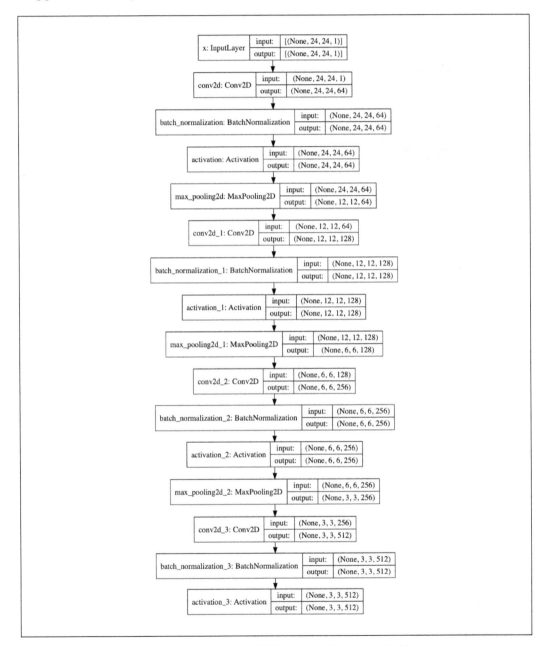

Figure 13.4.3 A scaled-down VGG is used as the encoder backbone

Figure 13.4.4 shows the Keras model diagram of *Figure 13.4.1*. To improve its performance, IIC performs overclustering. Two or more encoders are used to generate two or more marginal distributions $P(Z)$ and $P(\bar{Z})$. The corresponding joint distributions $P(Z, \bar{Z})$ are generated. In terms of the network model, this is implemented by an encoder with two or more heads.

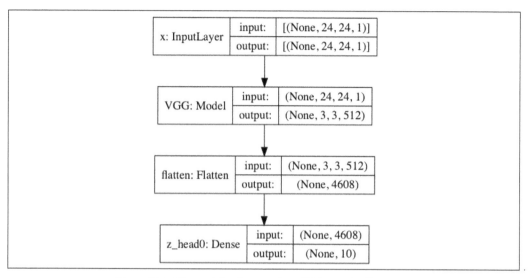

Figure 13.4.4 Network implementation of IIC encoder $\mathcal{E}$ in Keras

Figure 13.4.4 is a single-headed encoder, while *Figure 13.4.5* is a two-headed encoder. Notice that the two heads share the same VGG backbone.

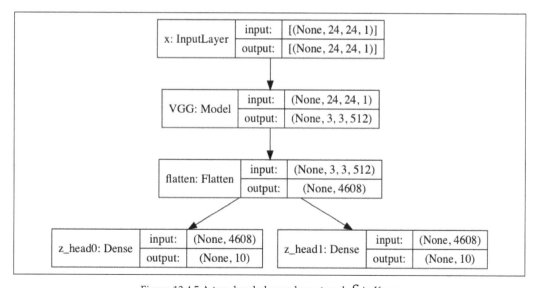

Figure 13.4.5 A two-headed encoder network $\mathcal{E}$ in Keras

In the following two sections, we will look into how the IIC network model is implemented, trained, and evaluated. We will also look into the linear assignment problem as a tool for designating a label for each cluster.

5. Unsupervised clustering implementation in Keras

The network model implementation in Keras for unsupervised clustering is shown in *Listing 13.5.1*. Only the initialization is shown. The network hyperparameters are stored in `args`. The VGG backbone object is supplied during initializations. Given a backbone, the model is actually just a `Dense` layer with a *softmax* activation, as shown in the `build_model()` method. There is an option to create multiple heads.

Similar to *Chapter 11, Object Detection*, we implemented a `DataGenerator` class to efficiently serve input data in a multithreaded fashion. A `DataGenerator` object generates the required paired train input data (that is, a Siamese input image) made of the input image X and its transformed image $\bar{X}$. The most critical method, `__data_generation()`, of the `DataGenerator` class is shown in *Listing 13.5.2*. The input image X is center cropped from the original input image. In the case of MNIST, this is 24 x 24-pixel center cropping. The transformed input image $\bar{X}$ is either randomly rotated by an angle in the range of ±20 or randomly cropped 16 x 16, 18 x 18, or 20 x 20 pixels from any part of the image and is resized back to 24 x 24 pixels. Crop sizes are stored in the `crop_sizes` list.

Note that only the input and transformed images are important in the data generated by the `DataGenerator` object. Also, the paired data that is needed by the loss function is concatenated along the batch axis. This will allow us to compute the loss function in a single batch of paired data.

Listing 13.5.1: `iic-13.5.1.py`. The IIC class showing initialization and model creation: class IIC:

```
def __init__(self,
            args,
            backbone):
    """Contains the encoder model, the loss function,
        loading of datasets, train and evaluation routines
        to implement IIC unsupervised clustering via mutual
        information maximization

    Arguments:
        args : Command line arguments to indicate choice
            of batch size, number of heads, folder to save
```

```
            weights file, weights file name, etc
         backbone (Model): IIC Encoder backbone (eg VGG)
      """
      self.args = args
      self.backbone = backbone
      self._model = None
      self.train_gen = DataGenerator(args, siamese=True)
      self.n_labels = self.train_gen.n_labels
      self.build_model()
      self.load_eval_dataset()
      self.accuracy = 0


  def build_model(self):
      """Build the n_heads of the IIC model
      """
      inputs = Input(shape=self.train_gen.input_shape, name='x')
      x = self.backbone(inputs)
      x = Flatten()(x)
      # number of output heads
      outputs = []
      for i in range(self.args.heads):
          name = "z_head%d" % i
          outputs.append(Dense(self.n_labels,
                               activation='softmax',
                               name=name)(x))
      self._model = Model(inputs, outputs, name='encoder')
      optimizer = Adam(lr=1e-3)
      self._model.compile(optimizer=optimizer, loss=self.mi_loss)
```

Listing 13.5.2: `data_generator.py`. The `DataGenerator` class method for generating paired input data to train the IIC encoder:

```
  def __data_generation(self, start_index, end_index):
      """Data generation algorithm. The method generates
          a batch of pair of images (original image X and
          transformed imaged Xbar). The batch of Siamese
          images is used to trained MI-based algorithms:
          1) IIC and 2) MINE (Section 7)

      Arguments:
          start_index (int): Given an array of images,
              this is the start index to retrieve a batch
          end_index (int): Given an array of images,
              this is the end index to retrieve a batch
```

```
    """

    d = self.crop_size // 2
    crop_sizes = [self.crop_size*2 + i for i in range(0,5,2)]
    image_size = self.data.shape[1] - self.crop_size
    x = self.data[self.indexes[start_index : end_index]]
    y1 = self.label[self.indexes[start_index : end_index]]

    target_shape = (x.shape[0], *self.input_shape)
    x1 = np.zeros(target_shape)
    if self.siamese:
        y2 = y1
        x2 = np.zeros(target_shape)

    for i in range(x1.shape[0]):
        image = x[i]
        x1[i] = image[d: image_size + d, d: image_size + d]
        if self.siamese:
            rotate = np.random.randint(0, 2)
            # 50-50% chance of crop or rotate
            if rotate == 1:
                shape = target_shape[1:]
                x2[i] = self.random_rotate(image,
                                           target_shape=shape)
            else:
                x2[i] = self.random_crop(image,
                                         target_shape[1:],
                                         crop_sizes)

    # for IIC, we are mostly interested in paired images
    # X and Xbar = G(X)
    if self.siamese:
        # If MINE Algorithm is chosen, use this to generate
        # the training data (see Section 9)
        if self.mine:
            y = np.concatenate([y1, y2], axis=0)
            m1 = np.copy(x1)
            m2 = np.copy(x2)
            np.random.shuffle(m2)

            x1 = np.concatenate((x1, m1), axis=0)
            x2 = np.concatenate((x2, m2), axis=0)
            x = (x1, x2)
            return x, y
```

```
        x_train = np.concatenate([x1, x2], axis=0)
        y_train = np.concatenate([y1, y2], axis=0)
        y = []
        for i in range(self.args.heads):
            y.append(y_train)
        return x_train, y


    return x1, y1
```

To implement the VGG backbone, the VGG class is implemented in Keras, as shown in *Listing 13.5.3*. The VGG class is flexible in that it can be configured in different ways (or different flavors of VGG). Option 'F' for IIC VGG backbone configuration cfg is shown. We use a helper function to generate Conv2D-BN-ReLU-MaxPooling2D layers.

Listing 13.5.3: vgg.py.

The VGG backbone class method in Keras:

```
cfg = {
    'F': [64, 'M', 128, 'M', 256, 'M', 512],
}

class VGG:
    def __init__(self, cfg, input_shape=(24, 24, 1)):
        """VGG network model creator to be used as backbone
            feature extractor

        Arguments:
            cfg (dict): Summarizes the network configuration
            input_shape (list): Input image dims
        """
        self.cfg = cfg
        self.input_shape = input_shape
        self._model = None
        self.build_model()

    def build_model(self):
        """Model builder uses a helper function
            make_layers to read the config dict and
            create a VGG network model
        """
        inputs = Input(shape=self.input_shape, name='x')
        x = VGG.make_layers(self.cfg, inputs)
        self._model = Model(inputs, x, name='VGG')

    @property
```

```
    def model(self):
        return self._model

    @staticmethod
    def make_layers(cfg,
                    inputs,
                    batch_norm=True,
                    in_channels=1):
        """Helper function to ease the creation of VGG
            network model

        Arguments:
            cfg (dict): Summarizes the network layer
                configuration
            inputs (tensor): Input from previous layer
            batch_norm (Bool): Whether to use batch norm
                between Conv2D and ReLU
            in_channel (int): Number of input channels
        """
        x = inputs
        for layer in cfg:
            if layer == 'M':
                x = MaxPooling2D()(x)
            elif layer == 'A':
                x = AveragePooling2D(pool_size=3)(x)
            else:
                x = Conv2D(layer,
                           kernel_size=3,
                           padding='same',
                           kernel_initializer='he_normal'
                           )(x)
                if batch_norm:
                    x = BatchNormalization()(x)
                x = Activation('relu')(x)

        return x
```

Going back to the IIC class, the key algorithm of IIC is the loss function that minimizes the negative MI. This method is shown in *Listing 13.5.4*. To evaluate the loss in a single batch, we look into y_pred and break it into two halves, lower and upper, corresponding to the encoder output for the input image X and its transformed image $\bar{X}$. Recall that the paired data is made by concatenating a batch of image X and a batch of its transformed image $\bar{X}$.

The lower half of `y_pred` is Z while the upper half is $\bar{Z}$. Following *Equation 10.3.2* to *Equation 10.3.7*, the joint distribution $P(Z, \bar{Z})$ and marginal distributions are computed. Finally, the negative MI is returned. Note that each head contributes equally to the total loss function. Hence the loss is scaled by the number of heads.

Listing 13.5.4: `iic-13.5.1.py`.

The `IIC` class loss function in Keras. The loss function minimizes the negative MI (that is, it maximizes the MI):

```
def mi_loss(self, y_true, y_pred):
    """Mutual information loss computed from the joint
        distribution matrix and the marginals

    Arguments:
        y_true (tensor): Not used since this is
            unsupervised learning
        y_pred (tensor): stack of softmax predictions for
            the Siamese latent vectors (Z and Zbar)
    """
    size = self.args.batch_size
    n_labels = y_pred.shape[-1]
    # lower half is Z
    Z = y_pred[0: size, :]
    Z = K.expand_dims(Z, axis=2)
    # upper half is Zbar
    Zbar = y_pred[size: y_pred.shape[0], :]
    Zbar = K.expand_dims(Zbar, axis=1)
    # compute joint distribution (Eq 10.3.2 & .3)
    P = K.batch_dot(Z, Zbar)
    P = K.sum(P, axis=0)
    # enforce symmetric joint distribution (Eq 10.3.4)
    P = (P + K.transpose(P)) / 2.0
    # normalization of total probability to 1.0
    P = P / K.sum(P)
    # marginal distributions (Eq 10.3.5 & .6)
    Pi = K.expand_dims(K.sum(P, axis=1), axis=1)
    Pj = K.expand_dims(K.sum(P, axis=0), axis=0)
    Pi = K.repeat_elements(Pi, rep=n_labels, axis=1)
    Pj = K.repeat_elements(Pj, rep=n_labels, axis=0)
    P = K.clip(P, K.epsilon(), np.finfo(float).max)
    Pi = K.clip(Pi, K.epsilon(), np.finfo(float).max)
    Pj = K.clip(Pj, K.epsilon(), np.finfo(float).max)
    # negative MI loss (Eq 10.3.7)
    neg_mi = K.sum((P * (K.log(Pi) + K.log(Pj) - K.log(P))))
    # each head contribute 1/n_heads to the total loss
    return neg_mi/self.args.heads
```

The IIC network training method is shown in *Listing 13.5.5*. Since we are using a `DataGenerator` object derived from the `Sequence` class, we can use the Keras `fit_generator()` method to train the model.

We use a learning rate scheduler that decreases the learning rate by 80% every 400 epochs. `AccuracyCallback` calls the `eval()` method, so we can record the performance of the network after every epoch.

The weights of the best performing model are optionally saved. In the `eval()` method, we use a linear classifier to assign a label to each cluster. The linear classifier `unsupervised_labels()` is a Hungarian algorithm that assigns a label to a cluster with the minimum cost.

This last step converts the unsupervised clustering into unsupervised classification. The `unsupervised_labels()` function is shown in *Listing 13.5.6*.

Listing 13.5.5: `iic-13.5.1.py`.

The IIC network training and evaluation:

```
def train(self):
    """Train function uses the data generator,
        accuracy computation, and learning rate
        scheduler callbacks
    """
    accuracy = AccuracyCallback(self)
    lr_scheduler = LearningRateScheduler(lr_schedule,
                                        verbose=1)
    callbacks = [accuracy, lr_scheduler]
    self._model.fit_generator(generator=self.train_gen,
                            use_multiprocessing=True,
                            epochs=self.args.epochs,
                            callbacks=callbacks,
                            workers=4,
                            shuffle=True)

def eval(self):
    """Evaluate the accuracy of the current model weights
    """
    y_pred = self._model.predict(self.x_test)
    print("")
    # accuracy per head
    for head in range(self.args.heads):
        if self.args.heads == 1:
            y_head = y_pred
        else:
```

```
              y_head = y_pred[head]
          y_head = np.argmax(y_head, axis=1)

          accuracy = unsupervised_labels(list(self.y_test),
                                          list(y_head),
                                          self.n_labels,
                                          self.n_labels)
          info = "Head %d accuracy: %0.2f%%"
          if self.accuracy > 0:
              info += ", Old best accuracy: %0.2f%%"
              data = (head, accuracy, self.accuracy)
          else:
              data = (head, accuracy)
          print(info % data)
          # if accuracy improves during training,
          # save the model weights on a file
          if accuracy > self.accuracy \
                  and self.args.save_weights is not None:
              self.accuracy = accuracy
              folder = self.args.save_dir
              os.makedirs(folder, exist_ok=True)
              path = os.path.join(folder, self.args.save_weights)
              print("Saving weights... ", path)
              self._model.save_weights(path)
```

Listing 13.5.6: `utils.py`.

The Hungarian algorithm assigns a label to a cluster with the minimum cost:

```
from scipy.optimize import linear_sum_assignment
def unsupervised_labels(y, yp, n_classes, n_clusters):
    """Linear assignment algorithm

    Arguments:
        y (tensor): Ground truth labels
        yp (tensor): Predicted clusters
        n_classes (int): Number of classes
        n_clusters (int): Number of clusters
    """
    assert n_classes == n_clusters

    # initialize count matrix
    C = np.zeros([n_clusters, n_classes])

    # populate count matrix
```

```
for i in range(len(y)):
    C[int(yp[i]), int(y[i])] += 1

# optimal permutation using Hungarian Algo
# the higher the count, the lower the cost
# so we use -C for linear assignment
row, col = linear_sum_assignment(-C)

# compute accuracy
accuracy = C[row, col].sum() / C.sum()

return accuracy * 100
```

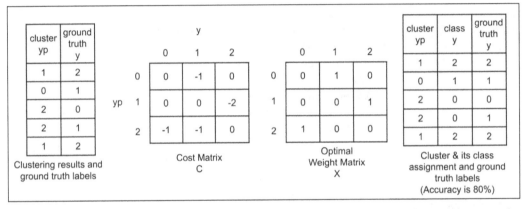

Figure 13.5.1 The linear assignment algorithm explained in a simple scenario of three clusters to be assigned optimally to three classes

As shown in *Figure 13.5.1*, the linear assignment problem is best explained using a simplified scenario of three clusters to be assigned to three classes. The linear assignment problem finds the one-to-one assignment of clusters to classes that result in the minimum total cost. On the left of *Figure 13.5.1*, the clustering results and the ground truth labels are shown.

The linear assignment problem finds the class or category for each cluster or how to assign labels to each cluster. The cost matrix C is also shown. For every cluster-ground truth pair, a cost matrix cell is decremented by 1. The row-column index of the cell is the cluster number-ground truth label index. Using the cost matrix, the job of the linear assignment problem is to find the optimal matrix X that results in the minimum total cost:

$$cost = min \sum_{i,j} c_{ij}x_{ij} \quad \text{(Equation 13.5.1)}$$

Where c_{ij} and x_{ij} are the elements of matrices C and X respectively. i and j are the indexes. The elements of X are subject to the following constraints:

$$x_{ij} \in \{0,1\}$$

$$\sum_{j} x_{ij} = 1 \quad \text{for } i = 1, 2, \dots, N$$

$$\sum_{i} x_{ij} = 1 \quad \text{for } j = 1, 2, \dots, N$$

X is a binary matrix. Each row is assigned to only one column. The linear assignment problem is therefore a combinatorial problem. The details of the optimal solution are beyond the scope of this book and are not discussed here.

The optimal weight matrix X is shown in *Figure 13.5.1*. Cluster 0 is assigned label 1. Cluster 1 is assigned to label 2. Cluster 2 is assigned to label 0. This can be intuitively verified from the cost matrix since this results in a minimum cost of -4 while ensuring each row is assigned to only one column.

Using this matrix, the cluster class assignment is shown in the right most table. With the cluster class assignment, there is only one error on the fourth row. The resulting accuracy is four-fifths, or 80%.

We can extend the linear assignment problem to the problem of assigning labels to our 10 MNIST clusters. We use the `linear_sum_assignment()` function in the `scipy` package. The function is based on the Hungarian algorithm. *Listing 13.5.6* shows the implementation of the cluster labeling process. For more details on the `linear_sum_assignment()` function see https://docs.scipy.org/doc/scipy-0.18.1/reference/generated/scipy.optimize.linear_sum_assignment.html.

To train the IIC model for the case of 1 head, execute:

```
python3 iic-13.5.1.py  --heads=1 --train --save-weights=head1.h5
```

For other numbers of heads, the options `--heads` and `--save-weights` should be modified accordingly. In the next section, we will examine the performance of IIC as an MNIST classifier.

6. Validation using MNIST

In this section, we'll look at the results following the validation of IIC using the MNIST test dataset. After running the cluster prediction on the test dataset, the linear assignment problem assigns a label to each cluster, essentially converting the clustering into classification. We computed the classification accuracy, as shown in *Table 13.6.1*. The IIC accuracy is higher than the 99.3% reported in the paper. However, it should be noted that not every training results in a high-accuracy classification.

Sometimes, we have to run the training multiple times since it appears that the optimization is stuck in a local minimum. Furthermore, we do not obtain the same level of performance for all heads in multi-head IIC models. *Table 13.6.1* reports the best performing head.

Number of heads	1	2	3	4	5
Accuracy, %	99.49	99.47	99.54	99.52	99.53

Table 13.6.1 Accuracy of IIC for different numbers of heads

The weights are available on GitHub. For example, to run validation on one-head IIC:

```
python3 iic-13.5.1.py --heads=1 --eval --restore-weights=head1-best.h5
```

In conclusion, we can see that it is possible to perform unsupervised classification. The results are in fact better than the supervised classification that we examined in *Chapter 2, Deep Neural Networks*. In the following sections, we will turn our attention to unsupervised learning for continuous random variables.

7. Unsupervised learning by maximizing the Mutual Information of continuous random variables

In previous sections, we learned that we can arrive at a good estimator of the MI of discrete random variables. We also demonstrated that with the help of a linear assignment algorithm, a network that performs clustering by maximizing MI leads to an accurate classifier.

If IIC is a good estimator of the MI of discrete random variables, what about continuous random variables? In this section, we discuss the **Mutual Information Network Estimator (MINE)** by Belghazi et al. [3] as an estimator of the MI of continuous random variables.

MINE proposes an alternative expression of KL-divergence in *Equation 13.1.1* to implement an MI estimator using a neural network. In MINE, the **Donsker-Varadhan (DV)** representation of KL-divergence is used:

$$D_{KL}(P(X,Y) \| P(X)P(Y)) = \sup_{T:\Omega \to \mathbb{R}} \mathbb{E}_{x,y \sim P(X,Y)}[T(x,y)] - log \, \mathbb{E}_{x \sim P(X), y \sim P(Y)}\left[e^{T(x,y)}\right]$$

(Equation 13.7.1)

Where the supremum is taken all over the space of function T. T is an arbitrary function that maps from the input space (such as an image) to a real number. Recall that supremum is roughly interpreted as a maximum. For T, we can choose from a family of functions $T_\theta = X \times Y \to \mathbb{R}$ that is parameterized by $\theta \in \Theta$. Therefore, we can represent T_θ, hence T, with a deep neural network that estimates the KL-divergence.

Given the exact (but intractable) representation of the MI, $I(X;Y)$, and its parameterized estimate $I_\theta(X;Y)$ as a tractable lower bound, we can safely state:

$$I(X;Y) \geq I_\theta(X;Y) \quad \text{(Equation 13.7.2)}$$

where the parameterized MI estimate is:

$$I_\theta(X;Y) = \sup_{\theta \in \Theta} \mathbb{E}_{x,y \sim P(X,Y)}[T_\theta(x,y)] - log \, \mathbb{E}_{x \sim P(X), y \sim P(Y)}\left[e^{T_\theta(x,y)}\right] \quad \text{(Equation 13.7.3)}$$

$I_\theta(X;Y)$ is also called the neural information measure. In the first expectation, the samples $(x,y) \sim P(X,Y)$ are taken from the joint distribution $P(X, Y)$. In the second expectation, the samples $x \sim P(X), y \sim P(Y)$ are taken from marginal distributions $P(X)$ and $P(Y)$.

Algorithm 13.7.1: MINE.

$\theta \leftarrow$ initialize all network parameters

While θ has not converged **do**:

1. Draw a mini batch, b, of samples from the joint distribution
$$\{(x^{(1)}, y^{(1)}), (x^{(2)}, y^{(2)}), ..., (x^{(b)}, y^{(b)})\} \sim P(X, Y)$$

2. Draw a mini batch, b, of samples from the marginal distributions
$$\{(\bar{x}^{(1)}), (\bar{x}^{(2)}), ..., (\bar{x}^{(b)})\} \sim P(X) \text{ and } \{(\bar{y}^{(1)}), (\bar{y}^{(2)}), ..., (\bar{y}^{(b)})\} \sim P(Y).$$

3. Evaluate the lower-bound: $\mathcal{V}(\theta) = \dfrac{1}{b} \displaystyle\sum_{i=1}^{b} T_\theta(x^{(i)}, y^{(i)}) - log \dfrac{1}{b} \displaystyle\sum_{i=1}^{b} e^{T_\theta(\bar{x}^{(i)}, \bar{y}^{(i)})}$

4. Evaluate the bias-corrected gradients: $\hat{G}(\theta) = \widehat{\nabla}_\theta \mathcal{V}(\theta)$

5. Update the network parameters: $\theta \leftarrow \theta - \epsilon \hat{G}(\theta)$, where ϵ is the learning rate.

Algorithm 13.7.1 summarizes the MINE algorithm. The samples from the marginal distribution are samples from the joint distribution with the other variable dropped. For example, samples x are simply samples (x, y) with the variable y dropped. After dropping values for variable y, samples x are shuffled. The same sampling method is done for y. For clarity, we use symbols $\bar{x}$ and $\bar{y}$ to identify samples from marginal distributions.

In the next section, we will use the MINE algorithm to estimate the MI in the case of a bivariate Gaussian distribution. We will show both the estimation of MI using an analytic method and the approximation of MI using MINE.

8. Estimating the Mutual Information of a bivariate Gaussian

In this section, we validate MINE on a bivariate Gaussian distribution. *Figure 13.8.1* shows a bivariate Gaussian distribution with mean and covariance:

$$\boldsymbol{\mu} = \begin{bmatrix} 0 & 0 \end{bmatrix} \quad \text{(Equation 13.8.1)}$$

$$\sigma = \begin{bmatrix} 1 & 0.5 \\ 0.5 & 1 \end{bmatrix} \quad \text{(Equation 13.8.2)}$$

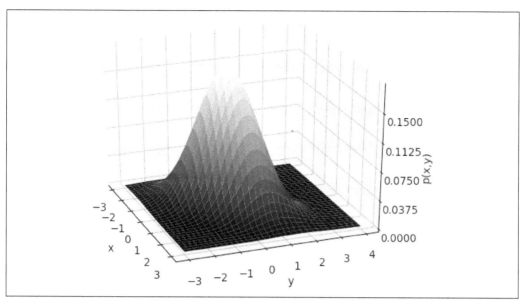

Figure 13.8.1 A two dimensional Gaussian distribution with mean and covariance as shown in Equation 13.8.1 and Equation 13.8.2

Our goal is to estimate MI by approximating *Equation 13.1.3*. The approximation can be done by obtaining a huge number of samples (such as 1 million) and creating a histogram with a large number of bins (such as 100 bins). *Listing 13.8.1* shows the manual computation of the MI of a bivariate Gaussian distribution using binning.

Listing 13.8.1: `mine-13.8.1.py`:

```
def sample(joint=True,
           mean=[0, 0],
           cov=[[1, 0.5], [0.5, 1]],
           n_data=1000000):
    """Helper function to obtain samples
        fr a bivariate Gaussian distribution

    Arguments:
        joint (Bool): If joint distribution is desired
        mean (list): The mean values of the 2D Gaussian
        cov (list): The covariance matrix of the 2D Gaussian
        n_data (int): Number of samples fr 2D Gaussian
    """
    xy = np.random.multivariate_normal(mean=mean,
                                        cov=cov,
                                        size=n_data)
    # samples fr joint distribution
```

```
        if joint:
            return xy
        y = np.random.multivariate_normal(mean=mean,
                                          cov=cov,
                                          size=n_data)

        # samples fr marginal distribution
        x = xy[:,0].reshape(-1,1)
        y = y[:,1].reshape(-1,1)

        xy = np.concatenate([x, y], axis=1)
        return xy


def compute_mi(cov_xy=0.5, n_bins=100):
    """Analytic computation of MI using binned
        2D Gaussian

    Arguments:
        cov_xy (list): Off-diagonal elements of covariance
            matrix
        n_bins (int): Number of bins to "quantize" the
            continuous 2D Gaussian
    """
    cov=[[1, cov_xy], [cov_xy, 1]]
    data = sample(cov=cov)
    # get joint distribution samples
    # perform histogram binning
    joint, edge = np.histogramdd(data, bins=n_bins)
    joint /= joint.sum()
    eps = np.finfo(float).eps
    joint[joint<eps] = eps
    # compute marginal distributions
    x, y = margins(joint)

    xy = x*y
    xy[xy<eps] = eps
    # MI is P(X,Y)*log(P(X,Y)/P(X)*P(Y))
    mi = joint*np.log(joint/xy)
    mi = mi.sum()
    return mi
```

The result of running:

```
python3 mine-13.8.1.py --gaussian
```

indicates the manually computed MI:

```
Computed MI: 0.145158
```

The covariance can be changed using the `--cov_xy` option. For example:

```
python3 mine-13.8.1.py  --gaussian --cov_xy=0.8
```

indicates the manually computed MI:

```
Computed MI: 0.510342
```

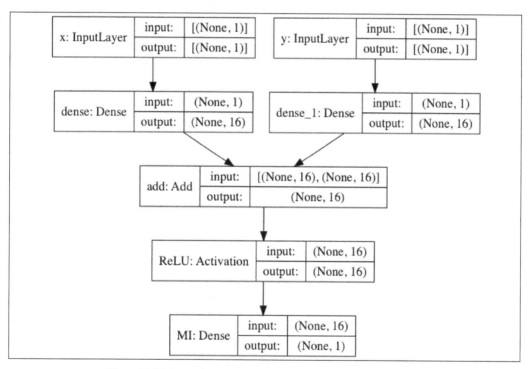

Figure 13.8.2 A simple MINE model for estimating the MI of random
variables *X* and *Y* of a bivariate Gaussian distribution

Listing 13.8.2: `mine-13.8.1.py`.

A simple MINE model to estimate the MI of random variables of a bivariate
Gaussian distribution:

```
class SimpleMINE:
    def __init__(self,
                 args,
                 input_dim=1,
                 hidden_units=16,
                 output_dim=1):
        """Learn to compute MI using MINE (Algorithm 13.7.1)

        Arguments:
            args : User-defined arguments such as off-diagonal
                elements of covariance matrix, batch size,
                epochs, etc
            input_dim (int): Input size dimension
            hidden_units (int): Number of hidden units of the
                MINE MLP network
            output_dim (int): Output size dimension
        """
        self.args = args
        self._model = None
        self.build_model(input_dim,
                         hidden_units,
                         output_dim)


    def build_model(self,
                    input_dim,
                    hidden_units,
                    output_dim):
        """Build a simple MINE model

        Arguments:
            See class arguments.
        """
        inputs1 = Input(shape=(input_dim), name="x")
        inputs2 = Input(shape=(input_dim), name="y")
        x1 = Dense(hidden_units)(inputs1)
        x2 = Dense(hidden_units)(inputs2)
        x = Add()([x1, x2])
        x = Activation('relu', name="ReLU")(x)
        outputs = Dense(output_dim, name="MI")(x)
```

```
        inputs = [inputs1, inputs2]
        self._model = Model(inputs,
                            outputs,
                            name='MINE')
        self._model.summary()

    def mi_loss(self, y_true, y_pred):
        """ MINE loss function

        Arguments:
            y_true (tensor): Not used since this is
                unsupervised learning
            y_pred (tensor): stack of predictions for
                joint T(x,y) and marginal T(x,y)
        """
        size = self.args.batch_size
        # lower half is pred for joint dist
        pred_xy = y_pred[0: size, :]

        # upper half is pred for marginal dist
        pred_x_y = y_pred[size : y_pred.shape[0], :]
        # implentation of MINE loss (Eq 13.7.3)
        loss = K.mean(pred_xy) \
               - K.log(K.mean(K.exp(pred_x_y)))
        return -loss


    def train(self):
        """Train MINE to estimate MI between
            X and Y of a 2D Gaussian
        """
        optimizer = Adam(lr=0.01)
        self._model.compile(optimizer=optimizer,
                            loss=self.mi_loss)
        plot_loss = []
        cov=[[1, self.args.cov_xy], [self.args.cov_xy, 1]]
        loss = 0.
        for epoch in range(self.args.epochs):
            # joint dist samples
            xy = sample(n_data=self.args.batch_size,
                        cov=cov)
            x1 = xy[:,0].reshape(-1,1)
            y1 = xy[:,1].reshape(-1,1)
            # marginal dist samples
```

```
xy = sample(joint=False,
            n_data=self.args.batch_size,
            cov=cov)
x2 = xy[:,0].reshape(-1,1)
y2 = xy[:,1].reshape(-1,1)

# train on batch of joint & marginal samples
x =   np.concatenate((x1, x2))
y =   np.concatenate((y1, y2))
loss_item = self._model.train_on_batch([x, y],
                                       np.zeros(x.shape))

loss += loss_item
plot_loss.append(-loss_item)
if (epoch + 1) % 100 == 0:
    fmt = "Epoch %d MINE MI: %0.6f"
    print(fmt % ((epoch+1), -loss/100))
    loss = 0.
```

Let's now use MINE to estimate the MI of this bivariate Gaussian distribution. *Figure 13.8.2* shows a simple 2-layer MLP as a model of T_θ. The input layers receive one batch of (x, y) from the joint distribution and one batch of $(\bar{x}, \bar{y})$ from the marginal distribution. The network is implemented in *Listing 13.8.2* in `build_model()`. Also shown in the same listing is the training routine for this simple MINE model.

The loss function implementing *Equation 13.7.3* is also shown in *Listing 13.8.2*. Note that the loss function does not use the ground truth values. It simply minimizes the negative MI estimate (and thus maximizes the MI). For this simple MINE model, the moving average loss is not implemented. We use the same function, `sample()`, in *Listing 13.8.1* to obtain both joint and marginal samples.

We can now estimate the MI of a bivariate Gaussian distribution using the same command:

```
python3 mine-13.8.1.py --gaussian
```

Figure 13.8.3 shows the MI estimate (negative of loss) as a function of the number of epochs. Below are the quantitative results on specific epochs at intervals of 100. The results for both manual and MINE computations are close. This validates MINE as a good estimator of the MI of continuous random variables.

```
Epoch 100 MINE MI: 0.112297

Epoch 200 MINE MI: 0.141723

Epoch 300 MINE MI: 0.142567

Epoch 400 MINE MI: 0.142087
```

```
Epoch 500 MINE MI: 0.142083
Epoch 600 MINE MI: 0.144755
Epoch 700 MINE MI: 0.141434
Epoch 800 MINE MI: 0.142480
Epoch 900 MINE MI: 0.143059
Epoch 1000 MINE MI: 0.142186
Computed MI: 0.147247
```

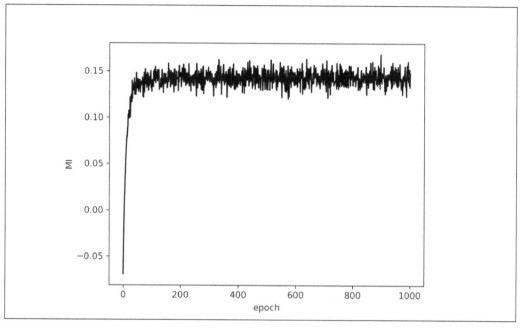

Figure 13.8.3 MI estimate as a function epoch for the simple MINE model.

So far, we have demonstrated MINE for the case of a bivariate Gaussian distribution. In the next section, we will use MINE on the same problem of unsupervised clustering of MNIST as we did with IIC.

9. Unsupervised clustering using continuous random variables in Keras

In the unsupervised classification of MNIST digits, we used IIC since the MI can be computed using discrete joint and marginal distributions. We obtained good accuracy with a linear assignment algorithm.

In this section, we will attempt to use MINE to perform clustering. We'll use the same key ideas from IIC: from a pair of images and their transformed versions $(X, \bar{X})$, maximize the MI of the corresponding encoded latent vectors $(Z, \bar{Z})$. By maximizing the MI, we perform clustering of the encoded latent vectors. The difference with MINE is that the encoded latent vectors are continuous and not in one-hot vector format, as used in IIC. Since the output of clustering is not in one-hot vector format, we will use a linear classifier. A linear classifier is an MLP without a non-linear activation layer such as ReLU. A linear classifier is used as an alternative to the linear assignment algorithm in the case of outputs that are not in one-hot vector format.

Figure 13.9.1 shows the network model of MINE. For the case of MNIST, variable x is sampled from the MNIST train dataset. Similar to IIC, the other input called variable y is just a transformed version of image x. During testing, the input image x is from the MNIST test dataset. Essentially, the data generation is the same as in IIC, as shown in *Listing 13.5.2*.

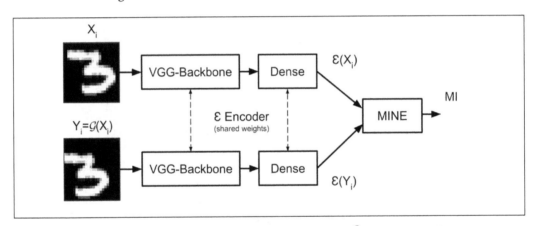

Figure 13.9.1 Network implementation of MINE using encoder network $\mathcal{E}$. The input MNIST image is center cropped to 24 x 24 pixels. In this example, $\bar{X} = Y = \mathcal{G}(X)$ is a random 24 x 24-pixel cropping operation.

The encoder network of *Figure 13.9.1* is shown in *Figure 13.9.2* when implemented in Keras. We left out the number of dimensions in the Dense output so that we can try out different dimensions (such as 10, 16, and 32).

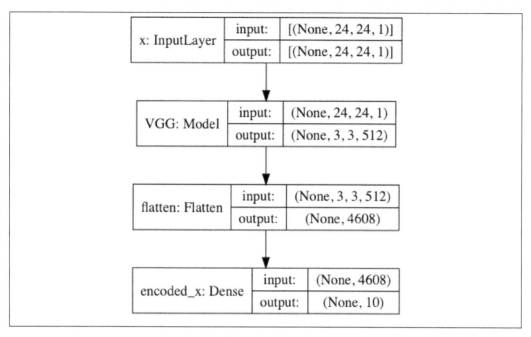

Figure 13.9.2 Encoder network $\mathcal{E}$ is a VGG network similar to the one used in IIC

The MINE network model is shown in *Figure 13.9.3,* and the code is shown in *Listing 13.9.1*. It is similar in architecture to the simple MINE implemented in the previous section except that we used 1,024 hidden units in the MLP instead of 16.

Listing 13.9.1: `mine-13.8.1.py`.

MINE network model for unsupervised clustering:

```
class MINE:
    def __init__(self,
                 args,
                 backbone):
        """Contains the encoder, SimpleMINE, and linear
            classifier models, the loss function,
            loading of datasets, train and evaluation routines
            to implement MINE unsupervised clustering via mutual
            information maximization

        Arguments:
            args : Command line arguments to indicate choice
                of batch size, folder to save
                weights file, weights file name, etc
            backbone (Model): MINE Encoder backbone (eg VGG)
```

```
        """
        self.args = args
        self.latent_dim = args.latent_dim
        self.backbone = backbone
        self._model = None
        self._encoder = None
        self.train_gen = DataGenerator(args,
                                       siamese=True,
                                       mine=True)
        self.n_labels = self.train_gen.n_labels
        self.build_model()
        self.accuracy = 0


def build_model(self):
    """Build the MINE model unsupervised classifier
    """
    inputs = Input(shape=self.train_gen.input_shape,
                   name="x")
    x = self.backbone(inputs)
    x = Flatten()(x)
    y = Dense(self.latent_dim,
              activation='linear',
              name="encoded_x")(x)
    # encoder is based on backbone (eg VGG)
    # feature extractor
    self._encoder = Model(inputs, y, name="encoder")
    # the SimpleMINE in bivariate Gaussian is used
    # as T(x,y) function in MINE (Algorithm 13.7.1)
    self._mine = SimpleMINE(self.args,
                            input_dim=self.latent_dim,
                            hidden_units=1024,
                            output_dim=1)
    inputs1 = Input(shape=self.train_gen.input_shape,
                    name="x")
    inputs2 = Input(shape=self.train_gen.input_shape,
                    name="y")
    x1 = self._encoder(inputs1)
    x2 = self._encoder(inputs2)
    outputs = self._mine.model([x1, x2])
    # the model computes the MI between
    # inputs1 and 2 (x and y)
    self._model = Model([inputs1, inputs2],
                        outputs,
```

```
                            name='encoder')
        optimizer = Adam(lr=1e-3)
        self._model.compile(optimizer=optimizer,
                            loss=self.mi_loss)
        self._model.summary()
        self.load_eval_dataset()
        self._classifier = LinearClassifier(\
                            latent_dim=self.latent_dim)
```

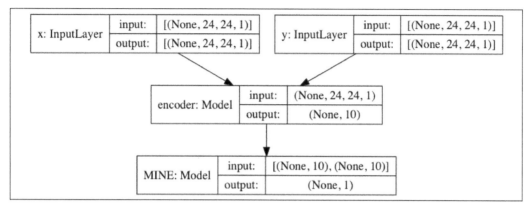

Figure 13.9.3 The MINE network model

As shown in *Listing 13.9.2*, the training routine is similar to the one in IIC. The difference is in the evaluation that is performed after every epoch. In this case, we train a linear classifier for a few epochs and use it to evaluate the clustered latent code vectors. When the accuracy improves, the model weights are optionally saved. The loss function and optimizer are similar in `SimpleMINE` as shown in *Listing 13.8.2* and are not repeated here.

Listing 13.9.2: `mine-13.8.1.py`.

MINE training and evaluation functions:

```
    def train(self):
        """Train MINE to estimate MI between
            X and Y (eg MNIST image and its transformed
            version)
        """
        accuracy = AccuracyCallback(self)
        lr_scheduler = LearningRateScheduler(lr_schedule,
                                            verbose=1)
        callbacks = [accuracy, lr_scheduler]
        self._model.fit_generator(generator=self.train_gen,
                            use_multiprocessing=True,
                            epochs=self.args.epochs,
                            callbacks=callbacks,
```

```
                                workers=4,
                                shuffle=True)
    def eval(self):
        """Evaluate the accuracy of the current model weights
        """
        # generate clustering predictions fr test data
        y_pred = self._encoder.predict(self.x_test)
        # train a linear classifier
        # input: clustered data
        # output: ground truth labels
        self._classifier.train(y_pred, self.y_test)
        accuracy = self._classifier.eval(y_pred, self.y_test)

        info = "Accuracy: %0.2f%%"
        if self.accuracy > 0:
            info += ", Old best accuracy: %0.2f%%"
            data = (accuracy, self.accuracy)
        else:
            data = (accuracy)
        print(info % data)
        # if accuracy improves during training,
        # save the model weights on a file
        if accuracy > self.accuracy \
            and self.args.save_weights is not None:
            folder = self.args.save_dir
            os.makedirs(folder, exist_ok=True)
            args = (self.latent_dim, self.args.save_weights)
            filename = "%d-dim-%s" % args
            path = os.path.join(folder, filename)
            print("Saving weights... ", path)
            self._model.save_weights(path)

        if accuracy > self.accuracy:
            self.accuracy = accuracy
```

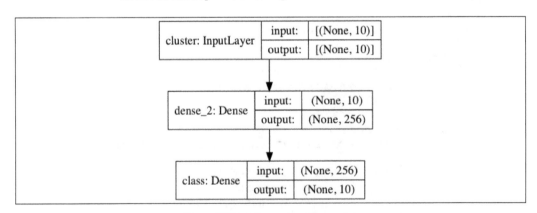

Figure 13.9.4 A linear classifier model

The linear classifier model is shown in *Figure 19.3.4*. It is an MLP with one hidden layer with 256 units. Since this model does not use a non-linear activation such as ReLU, it can be used as an approximation of the linear assignment algorithm to classify the output of the VGG-Dense encoder $\mathcal{E}$. *Listing 13.9.3* shows the linear classifier network model builder as implemented in Keras.

Listing 13.9.3: `mine-13.8.1.py`.

Linear classifier network:

```
class LinearClassifier:
    def __init__(self,
                 latent_dim=10,
                 n_classes=10):
        """A simple MLP-based linear classifier.
           A linear classifier is an MLP network
           without non-linear activations like ReLU.
           This can be used as a substitute to linear
           assignment algorithm.

        Arguments:
            latent_dim (int): Latent vector dimensionality
            n_classes (int): Number of classes the latent
                dim will be converted to.
        """
        self.build_model(latent_dim, n_classes)


    def build_model(self, latent_dim, n_classes):
        """Linear classifier model builder.

        Arguments: (see class arguments)
        """
        inputs = Input(shape=(latent_dim,), name="cluster")
        x = Dense(256)(inputs)
        outputs = Dense(n_classes,
                        activation='softmax',
                        name="class")(x)
        name = "classifier"
        self._model = Model(inputs, outputs, name=name)
        self._model.compile(loss='categorical_crossentropy',
                            optimizer='adam',
                            metrics=['accuracy'])
        self._model.summary()
```

The MINE unsupervised classifier can be trained by executing:

```
python3 mine-13.8.1.py  --train --batch-size=1024 --epochs=200
```

The batch size could be adjusted depending on the GPU memory available. To use a different latent dimension size (such as 64), use the `--latent-dim` option:

```
python3 mine-13.8.1.py  --train --batch-size=1024 --latent-dim=64
--epochs=200
```

In 200 epochs, the MINE network has the accuracy shown in *Figure 13.9.5*:

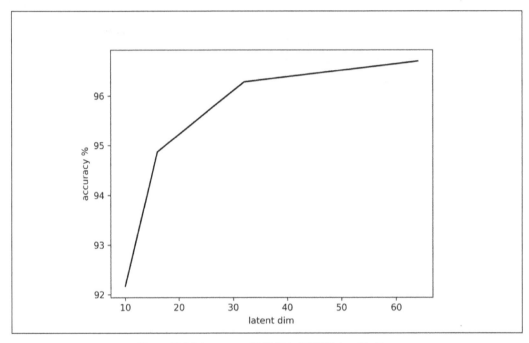

Figure 13.9.5 Accuracy of MINE in MNIST classification

As shown in *Figure 13.9.5*, at the default latent dim of 10, which is similar to IIC, MINE with a linear classifier achieves 93.86% accuracy. The accuracy increases with the value of the latent dimension. Since MINE is an approximation of the true MI, it is expected that its accuracy is less than IIC.

This concludes the chapter and the book. The area of unsupervised learning is nascent. This is a huge research opportunity given that one of the current barriers to the progress of AI is human labeling, which is costly and time-consuming. We expect breakthroughs in unsupervised learning in the next few years.

10. Conclusion

In this chapter, we discussed MI and the ways in which it can be useful in solving unsupervised tasks. Various online resources provide additional background about MI [4]. When used in clustering, maximizing MI forces the latent code vectors to cluster in regions that are suitable for easy labeling, either using linear assignment or a linear classifier.

We presented two measures of MI: IIC and MINE. We can closely approximate MI that leads to a classifier that performs with high accuracy by using IIC on discrete random variables. IIC is suitable for discrete probability distributions. For continuous random variables, MINE uses the Donsker-Varadhan form of KL-divergence to model a deep neural network that estimates MI. We demonstrated that MINE can closely approximate the MI of a bivariate Gaussian distribution. As an unsupervised method, MINE shows acceptable performance on classifying MNIST digits.

11. References

1. Ji, Xu, João F. Henriques, and Andrea Vedaldi. *Invariant Information Clustering for Unsupervised Image Classification and Segmentation.* International Conference on Computer Vision, 2019.

2. Simonyan, Karen, and Andrew Zisserman. *Very deep convolutional networks for large-scale image recognition.* arXiv preprint arXiv:1409.1556 (2014).

3. Belghazi, Mohamed Ishmael, et al. *Mutual Information Neural Estimation.* International Conference on Machine Learning. 2018.

4. https://en.wikipedia.org/wiki/Mutual_information

Other Books You May Enjoy

If you enjoyed this book, you may be interested in these other books by Packt:

Deep Learning with TensorFlow 2 and Keras - Second Edition

Antonio Gulli, Amita Kapoor, Sujit Pal

ISBN: 978-1-83882-341-2

- Build machine learning and deep learning systems with TensorFlow 2 and the Keras API
- Use Regression analysis, the most popular approach to machine learning
- Understand ConvNets (convolutional neural networks) and how they are essential for deep learning systems such as image classifiers
- Use GANs (generative adversarial networks) to create new data that fits with existing patterns
- Discover RNNs (recurrent neural networks) that can process sequences of input intelligently, using one part of a sequence to correctly interpret another

- Apply deep learning to natural human language and interpret natural language texts to produce an appropriate response

- Train your models on the cloud and put TF to work in real environments

- Explore how Google tools can automate simple ML workflows without the need for complex modelling

Python Machine Learning - Third Edition

Sebastian Raschka, Vahid Mirjalili

ISBN: 978-1-78995-575-0

- Master the frameworks, models, and techniques that enable machines to 'learn' from data

- Use scikit-learn for machine learning and TensorFlow for deep learning

- Apply machine learning to image classification, sentiment analysis, intelligent web applications, and more

- Build and train neural networks, GANs, and other models

- Discover best practices for evaluating and tuning models

- Predict continuous target outcomes using regression analysis

- Dig deeper into textual and social media data using sentiment analysis

Leave a review - let other readers know what you think

Please share your thoughts on this book with others by leaving a review on the site that you bought it from. If you purchased the book from Amazon, please leave us an honest review on this book's Amazon page. This is vital so that other potential readers can see and use your unbiased opinion to make purchasing decisions, we can understand what our customers think about our products, and our authors can see your feedback on the title that they have worked with Packt to create. It will only take a few minutes of your time, but is valuable to other potential customers, our authors, and Packt. Thank you!

Index

Symbols

100-layer DenseNet-BC for CIFAR10
  building 69-73
β -VAE 282

A

accuracy 19
Actor-Critic method 338-341
Adaptive Moments (Adam) 20
Advantage Actor-Critic (A2C)
       method 341-344
Anaconda
  URL 4
anchor box 372-379
Artificial Intelligence (AI) 289
autoencoder
  building, with Keras 81-90
  CNN, using 268-273
  decoder 78
  encoder 78
  principles 78-80
automatic colorization autoencoder 96-103
auxiliary classifier
       GAN (ACGAN) 133-168, 171

B

backbone network 390
backpropagation 23
Batch Normalization (BN) 112, 229
bootstrapping 307
Bottleneck 43

C

callbacks 62
class imbalance 390
CNN MNIST digit classifier
  summary 32
conditional GAN (CGAN)
  about 121, 171, 219
  generator outputs 242-245
  implementing, with Keras 227-242
  network model 221-227
  on MNIST dataset 245-252
  on SVHN dataset 245-252
Conditional VAE (CVAE) 274-282
continuous random variables
  about 443
  used, for unsupervised clustering in
      Keras 474-480
Conv2D-Batch Normalization(BN)-ReLU 55
convolution 30, 31
Convolutional Neural Network (CNN)
  about 5, 28, 30
  model summary 32, 34
  performance evaluation 32, 34
  used, for AE 268-273
  versus Multilayer Perceptron (MLP) 5, 6
  versus Recurrent Neural Network (RNN) 5, 7
core equation 258, 259
critic 106
cross-domain transfer 217
Cycle-Consistent Adversarial Domain
      Adaptation (CyCADA) 249
CycleGAN
  principles 218-220

K

Keras
    data generator model, using 402-406
    DCGAN, implementing 112-121
    Deep Q-Network (DQN), using 316-323
    InfoGAN, implementing 178-189
    installing 3-5
    reference link 53
    Semantic Segmentation Network 428-433
    SSD model architecture, using 394
    SSD model, using 398-402
    SSD objects, using 395-398
    StackedGAN, implementing 193-211
    unsupervised clustering,
        implementing 454-463
    unsupervised clustering, with continuous
        random variables 474-480
    URL 5
    used, as deep learning library 2, 3
    used, for building autoencoder 81-90
    used, for building model 13-15
    used, for implementing Conditional GAN
        (CGAN) 227-242
    used, for implementing WGAN 144-150
    used, in policy gradient method 344-360
    Variational Autoencoders (VAEs),
        using 261-268
Kullback-Leibler (KL) 135, 258, 443

L

label 7
Leaky ReLU 113
Least Squares GAN (LSGAN) 133, 151-155
linear_sum_assignment() function
    reference link 463
logistic sigmoid 17
Long Short-Term Memory (LSTM)
    about 39
    reference link 40
loss function
    about 6, 16-19, 386-390
    in Keras 18
lr_reducer() function 62

M

Markov decision process (MDP) 291
mean absolute error (MAE) 223, 386
mean IoU (mIoU) 412
mean squared error
    (MSE) 18, 79, 197, 223, 386
MLP MNIST digit classifier model
    summary 25-27
MNIST
    Invariant Information Clustering (IIC),
        validating 464
MNIST dataset 7, 8
MNIST Digit Classifier model 9, 12
model
    building, with Keras 13-15
    building, with MLP 13-15
model.fit() method 62
Monte-Carlo policy gradient method 331-334
Multilayer Perceptron (MLP)
    about 5, 6
    used, for building model 13-15
    versus Convolutional Neural Network
        (CNN) 5, 6
    versus Recurrent Neural Network (RNN) 5, 6
multi-scale object detection 373
Mutual Information (MI) 441-447
Mutual Information (MI), of bivariate Gaussian
    estimating 466-473
Mutual Information (MI), of continuous
    random variables
    maximizing, with unsupervised
        learning 464-466
Mutual Information (MI), of discrete random
    variables
    maximizing, with unsupervised
        learning 447-450
Mutual Information Network Estimator
    (MINE) 465

N

natural language processing (NLP) 35
negative anchor box 381
nondeterministic environment 306
Non-Maximum Suppression (NMS)
    algorithm 408-412

O

object detection 370-372
objective 6
offsets 373
OpenAI gym
  Q-learning, using 307-313
  reference link 307, 345
optimization 19-23, 259, 260
optimizer 6
output activation 16-19

P

panoptic segmentation 422
partially observable MDP (POMDP) 292
performance
  evaluating 23-25
policy gradient method
  Keras, using 344-360
  performance evaluation 360-366
  potential options 365
policy gradient theorem 328-331
pooling operations 31, 32
positive anchor box 380-386
precision 412
probability distribution function (PDF) 443
probability mass function (PMF) 443

Q

Q-learning
  example 294-306
  used, on OpenAI gym 307-313
Q value 293, 294

R

recall 413
receptive field 374
recognizable object 372
Reconstruction Loss 259
Rectified Linear Unit (ReLU) 113
Recurrent Neural Network (RNN)
  about 5, 35-41
  versus Convolutional Neural Network
    (CNN) 5, 6
  versus Multilayer Perceptron (MLP) 5, 6

regularization 15, 16
regularizer 6
reinforce algorithm
  about 332-334
  with baseline method 335-338
Reinforcement Learning (RL)
  about 289
  principles 290-292
  reference link 330
reparameterization trick 260, 261
ResNet 43, 62
ResNet v1 62
ResNet v2 62-66
ResNeXt 43
RNN MNIST digit classifier
  summary 38
Root Mean Squared Propagation
    (RMSprop) 20

S

Sampling 261
Sampling block 260
Sampling process 260
scaling factor 374
segmentation 422
semantic segmentation 421, 422
semantic segmentation network
  about 425-428
  in Keras 428-433
semantic segmentation validation 435-438
Sequential model API 3
SSD head 390
SSD model architecture
  about 390-393
  in Keras 394, 398-402
SSD model training 407
SSD model validation 412-419
SSD objects
  in Keras 395-398
StackedGAN
  about 192, 193
  generator outputs 211-215
  implementing, in Keras 193-211
stochastic gradient descent (SGD) 20
structural similarity index (SSIM) 79
SVHN dataset
  reference link 246

T

target 7
Temporal-Difference (TD) learning 306, 307
TensorFlow
  installing 3-5
test dataset 19
Transition layers 43
Transposed CNN 84

U

unsupervised clustering
  implementing, in Keras 454-463
  with continuous random variables, in
      Keras 473-480
  with encoder network 450-454
unsupervised learning
  about 77
  by maximizing Mutual Information
      (MI), of continuous random
      variables 464-466
  by maximizing Mutual Information (MI),
      of discrete random variables 447-450

V

Variational Autoencoders (VAEs)
  about 77
  CNN, used for AE 268-273
  core equation 258, 259
  decoder testing 261
  in Keras 261-268
  optimization 259, 260
  principles 256, 257
  reparameterization trick 260, 261
  used, with disentangled latent
      representation 282-285
  variational inference 257, 258
variational inference 257, 258
variational lower bound or evidence lower
      bound (ELBO) 259
Visual Geometry Group (VGG) 55
VGG Image Annotator (VIA) 406, 433

W

Wasserstein 1 133
Wasserstein GAN (WGAN)
  about 133, 134
  distance function 134-139
  implementing, with Keras 144-150
  Wasserstein loss, using 139-144
WideResNet 43

CPSIA information can be obtained
at www.ICGtesting.com
Printed in the USA
LVHW061231250722
724346LV00004B/18